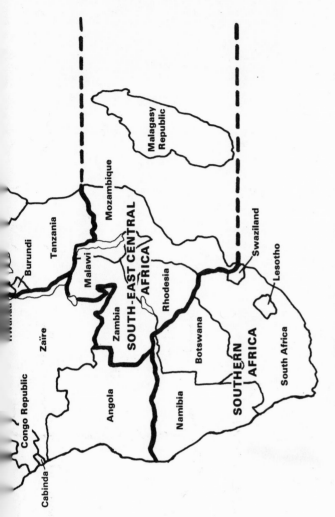

AFRICA: Political divisions, and regions used in this bibliography

Bibliography of New Religious Movements in Primal Societies,

Volume I: Black Africa

Harold W. Turner

G. K. HALL & CO., 70 LINCOLN STREET, BOSTON, MASS.

BL
80
A1
T8
v. 1

COPYRIGHT © 1977 BY HAROLD W. TURNER

Library of Congress Cataloging in Publication Data

Turner, Harold W
   Bibliography of new religious movements in primal societies.

   Includes index.
   CONTENTS: v. 1. Black Africa.
   1. Religion--Bibliography. 2. Religion,
Primitive--Bibliography. I. Title.
Z7833.T87 [BL80] 016.2   77-4732
ISBN 0-8161-7927-1

ISBN (U. K.)   0-86043-096-0

This publication is printed on permanent/durable acid-free paper
MANUFACTURED IN THE UNITED STATES OF AMERICA

Contents

CONTENTS

Introduction

This is the first of a bibliographic series of four volumes on new religious movements in primal societies; this volume covers sub-Saharan or Black Africa and will be followed by others devoted to North America, Latin America with the Caribbean, and Asia with Oceania. The religious movements with which this bibliographic series is concerned are defined as those which arise in the interaction of a primal society with another society where there is great disparity of power or sophistication. The subject has been treated at length in the article, "Tribal religions, new", in Encyclopaedia Britannica 1974 edition, Macropaedia vol. 18, 697-705; this should be read in conjunction with my earlier article, "A new field in the history of religions", Religion: Journal of Religion and Religions 1 (1), Spring 1971, 15-23.

These four volumes draw upon the extensive bibliographic and documentary resources of the Project for the Study of New Religious Movements in Primal Societies; this study centre was first announced in connection with the University of Lancaster in England, but in the event was established in the Department of Religious Studies in the University of Aberdeen, Scotland, in 1973.

The present volume on Black Africa is designed to correct, cumulate and update three earlier publications on this area -- A comprehensive bibliography of modern African religious movements edited jointly with Robert C. Mitchell (Northwestern University Press 1966), and the two supplements which appeared in the Journal of Religion in Africa 1 (3), 1968, 173-211, and 3 (3), 1970, 161-208. The promise of further supplements for the period after 1970 has now been fulfilled in this rather different manner.

The present edition adds material from the period 1970 to mid-1976; it also endeavours to include the increasing number of dissertations, both doctoral and masters', in this field, except where most of the material has been subsequently published; likewise senior

Introduction

undergraduate research papers are now included since these often contain valuable material, especially at the descriptive level, and are preserved in the relevant departments of universities or colleges. While naturally incomplete the items included will indicate the kind of work that is going on and where to look for it. Certain Islamic movements have also now been included even though there is some continuing uncertainty as to how far they represent religious and cultural interaction.

On the other hand this edition differs from the earlier publications in being selective rather than comprehensive. At the earlier stage it was more important and more feasible to include all published references; now it is neither possible nor necessary to do so. Therefore minor references, especially in secondary sources, repetitive material without new information or viewpoint, and lesser treatments of the same theme by the same author have been excluded. In two areas more drastic selection has become possible through the appearance of specialist bibliographies on Mau Mau (see item 1246), and on Kimbanguism and prophetism (see item 1105).

Other deletions from the earlier bibliographies have occurred through a more precise definition of the subject. Thus we have looked more closely at spirit possession cults, witchcraft eradication movements, and so-called "prophet" movements, and have deleted those which do not appear to have been shaped by the interaction of disparate cultures or to have revealed significantly new forms. Considerable uncertainty, however, remains in many cases, and some of these have been included. At the other end of the spectrum of movements there is similar doubt as to the relevance of conversion or revival movements of African origin which have speedily been absorbed in missions or the older churches; some of these have been omitted, as belonging rather to the history of the missions and churches concerned. Many of the independent churches included here as "new movements" are now joining Christian Councils and it is possible that before long it will be more relevant to consider these in the context of the general Christian history of their area. Bibliographies such as this series will, however, continue to present borderline problems which cannot be neatly resolved.

As in earlier editions material in newspapers or journals appearing more often than weekly is normally excluded. Likewise it is not possible to specify extensive and important materials not formally published but which could be available under certain circumstances; as an example there are the many reports presented to the Mennonite Board of Missions, Elkhart, Indiana, and covering some six or seven African countries since 1959.

The material has been grouped as before in terms of theory, Africa in general, regions and individual countries. The section on theory cannot pretend to be definitive in a subject that concerns so many disciplines and interests, and that is open to such diverse viewpoints. It will, however, serve as an introduction, and link the African field to the other areas of the world to which many of its items also apply. The general section includes material on Black Africa as a whole, or that which spans more than one of the five regions - as in item 255 which compares Kikuyu and Zulu movements. Individual countries have been designated in the light of the situation at the time of going to press, and have been re-grouped into somewhat different regions - a necessary if at times rather arbitrary procedure.

Annotations are not provided where titles are sufficiently indicative of contents, or where an item has been inaccessible and further information has not been secured. Although normally avoiding evaluative comment, we have made exceptions where items seem especially important or particularly perverse or erroneous. Occasionally the location of a rare or unusual item has been indicated.

A bibliography such as this has inevitable limitations. For instance, the number of items for the different countries does not necessarily correspond to the extent of the phenomenon in that area. Thus Mozambique, even as compared with Angola, is very poorly represented, for although it is known to have many movements there appears to have been little written about them. Other areas however, such as the Kimbanguist movements and the Nigerian aladuras, have received abundant attention. Similarly the movements themselves vary considerably in the production of their own published materials, and Ghana and Nigeria have been especially prolific in this respect. Comments on these and similar matters will be found in my article, "The study of new religious movements in Africa, 1968-1975", Religion: Journal of Religion and Religions 6 (1), Spring 1976, 88-98.

Further limitations derive from the sheer impossibility of searching all sources where material might occur, of being fully up-to-date in the contemporary aspects of the subject, or of inspecting all items known to exist and therefore completing all bibliographical details. Continuing but undue expense of time and money could reduce these limitations, but never eliminate them. Even incomplete information, however, can be useful, and in all cases will prove sufficient to identify the item concerned. We have drawn heavily on the bibliographies and references of others, in the knowledge that we may not have rectified their occasional errors. On the other hand, we hope that the users of this bibliography will not suffer overmuch from our own errors, but will be kind enough to inform us of them. Since the bibliographer in this field who demanded perfection would never publish he must humbly accept his own limitations and those inherent in the task.

Whatever accuracy and usefulness have been achieved owe much to a large number of people across the world who have volunteered otherwise unknown information or materials, as well as to those who were named in the previous introductions. For this edition special thanks

INTRODUCTION

must be given, firstly, to the staff of the inter-library loan section of the Aberdeen University Library at King's College who have
laboured over endless difficult items; and finally to Dr. Jocelyn
Murray, Spalding Research Fellow for the Project on New Religious
Movements, whose special knowledge of eastern Africa, bibliographical
skills, and meticulous handling of the entries have been of immeasur-
able assistance at every point in the preparation of this volume.

Bibliography of New Religious Movements in Primal Societies

Volume I: Black Africa

Theory

1   ABERLE, DAVID F[RIEND]. The Peyote religion among the Navaho
    (Viking Fund Publications in Anthropology, 42). Chicago:
    Aldine Publishing Company 1966, xxvi + 454 p.
       [Ch. 19, a classification of social movements. The
    constant and the variable characteristics of "transforma-
    tive" and "redemptive" movements, in relation to the
    "relative deprivation" of the situations in which they
    occur.]

2   AMES, MICHAEL M. Reaction to stress: a comparative study of
    nativism. Davidson Journal of Anthropology (Seattle) 3
    (1), 1957, 17-30. Mimeo.
       [A theoretical article which draws from non-African ex-
    amples to illustrate a conceptual framework.]

3   ARCHIVES DE SOCIOLOGIE DES RELIGIONS (Paris). No. 5=3
    (jan.-juin), 1958.
       [Special issue on messianism and millennialism; see
    especially Balandier, 91-95. See also articles in no. 4=2
    (juillet-déc.), 1957, and 6=3 (juillet-déc.), 1958.]

4   BANTON, MICHAEL [PARKER]. L'Afrique coloniale: du réflexe
    religieux. Sociologie des relations sociales. Paris:
    Payot 1971, 211-228.
       [Kimbanguism and other movements; their causes (not
    primarily as social protest); the role of prophets.]

5   BASTIDE, ROGER. Les métamorphoses du sacré dans les sociétés
    en transition. Civilisations 9 (4), 1959, 432-443.

6   BASTIDE, ROGER. Messianisme et développement économique et
    sociale. Cahiers Internationaux de Sociologie n.s.,
    no. 31=8 (juillet-déc.), 1961, 3-14. Reprinted in his Le
    prochain et le lointain. Paris: Cujas 1970, 275-286.
    Eng. trans., Messianism and social and economic develop-
    ment, in I. Wallerstein (ed.), Social change. The colonial
    situation. New York: J. Wiley 1966, 467-477.
       [An important theoretical article on the role of messianic
    movements in modernization, with examples from Zäire.]

Bibliography of New Religious Movements in Primal Societies

Theory

7   BECKMANN, DAVID M.   Trance: from Africa to Pentecostalism.
    Concordia Theological Monthly 45 (1), 1974, 11–26.
        [Trance which originated in African religions was given
    Christian legitimation in the Second Great Awakening in
    U.S.A. (early 19th c.) and later in the Azuza Street, Los
    Angeles, revival; it was carried back to Africa by
    missionaries.]

8   BESKOW, PER.   Crossing the frontiers in the second century, in
    P. Beyerhaus and C. F. Hallencreutz (eds.), The church
    crossing frontiers... Essays in honour of Bengt Sundkler
    (Studia Missionalia Upsaliensia XI).   Lund: Gleerup 1969,
    27–35.
        [Pp. 33–35, the similarity between Montanism and modern
    prophet movements.]

9   BEYERHAUS, PETER.   Begegnung mit messianischen Bewegungen –
    zur Kennzeichnung der Missionswissenschaft als theologische
    Disziplin.   Zeitschrift für Theologie und Kirche 64 (4),
    1967, 496–518.

10 BEYERHAUS, PETER.   Kann es eine Zusammenarbeit zwischen den
    christlichen Kirchen und den prophetischmessianischen
    Bewegungen Afrikas geben?   Evangelisches Missions Magazin
    (Basel) 111 (1), 1967, 12–28; idem, 111 (2), 1967, 78–87.

11 BEYERHAUS, PETER.   The encounter with messianic movements in
    Africa.   Aberdeen: Departments of Church History and
    Systematic Theology, University of Aberdeen 1968, 12 p.
    Mimeo.
        [Interpreted as a new post-Christian religion, nativistic
    and revitalizing, distinguished from independent churches,
    and sharing in both traditional and the new biblically-
    derived outlooks.]

12 BUDD, SUSAN.   Sociologists and religion.   London: Collier-
    Macmillan 1973, viii + 196 p.
        [Pp. 68–73, millenarianism and syncretism.]

13 CHENU, MARIE-DOMINIQUE.   Libération politique et messianisme
    religieuse.   Parole et Mission (Paris) 19, Oct. 1962,
    529–542.
        [The religious transformations involved in modernization,
    with special reference to Lanternari's survey.]

14 CLEMHOUT, SIMONE.   Typology of nativistic movements.   Man, 64
    (art. 7), Jan.-Feb. 1964. 6–7.

[Continues the anthropologists' discussion begun by
Linton, item 52, Wallace, items 78 and 84, Smith, items 65
and 84, and Voget, item 84, and incorporates categories
from several of these earlier attempts.]

15 CLEMHOUT, SIMONE. The psycho-sociological nature of nativistic
movements and the emergence of cultural growth. Anthropos
61 (1-2), 1966, 33-48.
    [Classification system; mainly China and Japan referred
to. The common factor in most movements is "a situation of
contrast between cultures in contact".]

16 COLPE, CARSTEN. Das Phänomen der nachchristlichen Religion in
Mythos und Messianismus, in C. H. Ratschow (ed.), Der
christliche Glaube und die Religionen. Hauptvorträge des
Evangelischen Theologenkongresses Wien 26-30 September 1966.
Berlin: Topelmann 1967, 42-87.
    [A systematic theological approach.]

17 DESROCHE, HENRI [CHARLES]. Les messianismes et la catégorie
de l'échec. Cahiers internationaux de sociologie, n.s.
35, juillet-déc. 1963, 161-184.
    [An historical and theoretical survey.]

18 DESROCHE, HENRI [CHARLES]. Sociologie de l'espérance (Archives
de sciences sociales). Paris: Calmann-Levy 1973, 253 p.
    [Pp. 94-101, Messianism--Oceania, sub-Saharan Africa,
North America, etc.]

19 DOUGLAS, [MARGARET] MARY. Natural symbols: explorations in
cosmology. London: Barrie and Rockliff 1970, 177 p.
    [Pp. 12-14, Peyote among the Navaho, based on Aberle,
1966; pp. 136-139, cargo cults as millennial; ch. 8,
witchcraft, and pp. 121-122, on witch-cleansing movements
as not truly millennial; passim, a typology of social
structures and their relation to millennialism, esp.
pp. 103-106, 150-155.]

20 DOUTRELOUX, A[LBERT]. Prophétisme et culture, in Fortes and
Dieterlen (eds.), item 203, 224-239.

21 DOZON, JEAN-PIERRE. Les mouvements politico-religieux
(syncrétismes, messianismes, néo-traditionalismes), in
M. Augé (ed.), La construction du monde. Religion/
représentations/idéologie. Paris: F. Maspero 1974,
75-111, annot. bibl.
    [Survey of research (mainly French) on African movements
with discussion of terminology and typology; Kimbanguism

Theory

and Kitawala analysed as religious ideologies with contrary effects.]

22 DU TOIT, B[RIAN] M[URRAY]. Beperkte Lidmaatskap: n'Anthropologies-Wetenskaplike Studie van Geheime organisasies. Cape Town: John Malherb Ltd. 1965, 193 p.
[Includes similarities between Afrikaner Broederbond and "revitalization movements" as two examples of "restricted membership" societies.]

23 ELIADE, MIRCEA. Dimensions religieuses du renouvellement cosmique. Eranos Jahrbuch (Zurich) 28, 1959, 241-275.
[An evaluation of millennial movements in primitive societies; all have the general character of renewal, and should be classed with New Year festivals and initiations.]

24 EMMET, DOROTHY [MARY]. Prophets and their societies. Journal of the Royal Anthropological Institute 86 (1), 1956, 13-23.
[Examines Weber's charismatic theory of the prophet type; describes the social role of prophets, and offers a typology.]

25 FABIAN, JOHANNES. Ideology and content. Sociologus N.S. 16, 1965, 1-18 (German summary).
[The importance of cultural, historical or meaning aspects of ideologies, and of theories of social change; as preparations for explaining "prophetic-messianic" movements (pp. 16-17).]

26 FABIAN, JOHANNES. Religion and change, in J. Paden and E. Soja (eds.), The African experience. Evanston: Northwestern University Press 1970, 381-399.

27 FABIAN, JOHANNES. Language, history and anthropology. Journal for the Philosophy of the Social Sciences, 1, 1971, 19-47.
[On methodology, with special reference to his study of the Jamaa movement.]

28 FABIAN, JOHANNES. Genres in an emerging tradition, in A. Eister (ed.), Changing perspectives in the scientific study of religion. New York and London: John Wiley & Sons 1974, 249-272.

29 FABIAN, JOHANNES. Taxonomy and ideology: on the boundaries of concept classification, in D. Kinkade (ed.), Linguistics and anthropology: in honour of C. F. Voegelin. Lissie, Netherlands: Peter de Ridder Press 1975.
[Jamaa used to illustrate his theory of cultural knowledge as ideology.]

6

30   FERNANDEZ, JAMES W[ILLIAM]. African religious movements –
       types and dynamics. Journal of Modern African Studies
       (London) 2 (4), 1964, 531-549. Also in R. Robertson (ed.),
       Sociology of Religion. Harmondsworth: Penguin Books 1969,
       384-404.
       [A single typology defined by the four quadrants of a
       biaxial co-ordinate system (traditional/acculturative and
       instrumental/expressive) giving separatist, syncretist,
       nativist and messianic types.]

31   FERNANDEZ, JAMES W[ILLIAM]. Politics and prophecy: African
       religious movements. Practical Anthropology (Tarrytown,
       N. Y.) 12 (2), Mar.-Apr. 1965, 71-75.
       [Functions and causes of African religious movements
       with four-fold typology: separatist, reformative, mes-
       sianic and nativist.]

32   FERNANDEZ, JAMES W[ILLIAM]. Preying among priests and prophets:
       oral data in the study of African religion. Folklore
       Institute Journal (The Hague) 6 (2-3), 1969, 200-217.
       [Pp. 208-209 on the special values of oral data from new
       religious movements.]

33   FLUSSER, DAVID. Salvation, present and future. Numen (Leiden)
       16 (2), 1969, 139-155.
       [Chiliastic movements within Semitic religions, especially
       Black Muslims, Seventh Day Adventism and Jehovah's Wit-
       nesses; inverse relation between strength of Christology
       and millennial emphasis; effects of nonfullment of
       hopes – as parallels to movements in primal societies.]

34   FRIESEN, J. STANLEY. The significance of indigenous movements
       for the study of church growth, in W. R. Shenk (ed.), The
       challenge of church growth. A symposium (Missionary
       Studies 1). Elkhart, Indiana: Institute of Mennonite
       Studies 1973, 79-106.
       [Tests "church growth" theory of D. M. McGavran against
       four examples of growth in independent African movements,
       and concludes that the theory needs modification to embrace
       these.]

35   GENSICHEN, HANS-WERNER. Der Syncretismus als Frage an die
       Christenheit heute. Evangelische Missions Zeitschrift
       (Stuttgart) N.F., 23 (2), Apr. 1966, 58-69.
       [Pp. 61 ff. discusses African separatist groups along
       with the "new religions" of Japan.]

Theory

36 HINCHLIFF, PETER BINGHAM. African separatists: heresy,
    schism or protest movements? in Derek Baker (ed.), Schism,
    heresy and religious protest (Studies in Church History 9).
    Cambridge: Cambridge University Press 1972, 391-404.

37 HODGKIN, THOMAS [LIONEL]. Mahdisme, messianisme et Marxisme
    dans le contexte africain. Présence africain, n.s. 74,
    1970, 128-153.

38 HOFSTRA, S. De Betekenis van Enkele Nieuwere Groepsverschijn-
    selen voor de Sociale Integratie van Veranderend Afrika.
    Mededelingen der Koninklijke Nederlandse Akademie van
    Wetenschappen (afd. Letterkunde). Nieuwe Reeks [new
    series] 18 (14), 1955.
        [Divides into four classes: mission-origin churches;
    so-called African churches; looser, smaller groups of a
    syncretistic character; irregularly organized movements
    of a messianic or prophetic kind. Also Islamic and ances-
    tral cults.]

39 KÖBBEN, A[NDRÉ] J. F. Prophetic movements as an expression of
    social protest. International Archives of Ethnography
    (Amsterdam) 14 (1), 1960, 117-164, bibl. Also, revised
    and updated, as: Profetische bewegingen als uiting van
    sociaal protest, in his Van primitieven tot wereld-burgers.
    Assen: Van Gorcum 1964, chapter 6 (pp. 94-154).
        [Discusses typology in terms of variations of content
    and form; criticism of Linton's and Wallace's classifica-
    tions; extensive bibliography.]

40 KOPPERS, WILHELM. Prophetism and messianic beliefs as a
    problem of ethnology and world history, in Proceedings of
    the XIth International Congress for the History of Reli-
    gions, Tokyo and Kyoto, 1958. Tokyo: Maruzen 1960, 39-50.
    German trans., Prophetismus und Messianismus als
    völkerkundliches und universalgeschichtliches Problem.
    Saekulum (Freiburg) 10 (1), 1959, 38-47.
        [Includes brief survey of each culture area based on
    Guariglia (1959), item 220, with some general theory.]

41 KOPYTOFF, IGOR. Classification of religious movements: ana-
    lytical and synthetic, in M. E. Spiro (chairman), Symposium
    on new approaches to the study of religion. Proceedings,
    American Ethnological Society, 1964, 77-90.
        [An analytical profile approach, illustrated by the Suku
    Holy Water movement in Zaïre.]

42 LA BARRE, WESTON. Materials for a history of studies of crisis cults:
    a bibliographic essay. Current Anthropology 12 (1), 1971, 3-44.
    ["World survey of crisis cults and theories about their
    causes", together with fifteen comments by scholars in
    various disciplines.]

43 LANTERNARI, VITTORIO. Movimenti profetico-salvifici a livello
    etnologico. Studi e materiali di storia della religioni
    32 (2), 1961, 284-308.
    [Review article on G. Guariglia, Prophetismus und
    Heilser-wartungs-Bewegungen... (1959).]

44 LANTERNARI, VITTORIO. Ancora sui movimenti profetici. Una
    replica necessaria. Studi e Materiali di Storia della
    Religioni 33 (1), 1962, 108-128.

45 LANTERNARI, VITTORIO. Messianism: its historical origin and mor-
    phology. History of Religions (Chicago) 2 (1), 1962, 52-72.
    [The "crisis theory".]

46 LANTERNARI, VITTORIO. L' acculturazione dei popoli excoloniali.
    Sapere (Milan), Aprile 1964, 201-207.

47 LANTERNARI, VITTORIO. Dinamica culturale e nuove religioni dei
    popoli arretrati. Atti, I Congresso di Scienza antropol-
    ogiche etnologiche e di folklore. Turin 1964, 289-293.

48 LANTERNARI, VITTORIO. I movimenti millenaristi e il compara-
    tivismo storico-religioso. Rivista Storica Italiana
    (Naples) 76 (3), 1964, 760-773.
    [Review article on S. Thrupp (ed.), item 69.]

48a LANTERNARI, VITTORIO. Desintegration culturelle et processus
    d'acculturation. Cahiers Internationaux de Sociologie
    juillet-déc. 1966, 117-132.

49 LANTERNARI, VITTORIO. Explanation of the new cults among
    primitive peoples and the problem of a conciliation between
    two different approaches, in Proceedings of the XIth Inter-
    national Association for the History of Religions ... 1965.
    Vol. 3. Leiden: E. J. Brill 1968, 48-56.
    [The anthropological and historical methods.]

50 LANTERNARI, VITTORIO. Nativistic and socio-religious move-
    ments: a reconsideration. Comparative Studies in Society
    and History 16 (4), 1974, 483-503, bibl.

51 LEWIS, I[OAN] M[YRDDIN]. Spirit possession and deprivation
    cults (Malinowski Memorial Lecture 1966). Man N.S. 1
    (3), 1966, 307-329.

Theory

> [P. 323, brief reference to new prophet movements stres-
> sing notions of "rewards in heaven", sustaining the moral
> order; final assimilation of such movements into ordinary
> social life.]

52 LINTON, RALPH. Nativistic movements. <u>American Anthropologist</u>
45 (2), 1943, 230-240.
> [An influential discussion with an anthropological
> typology in terms of revivalist or perpetuative, and
> magical or rational features.]

53 LJUNDAHL, AXEL. <u>Profetrörelser, deras orsaker, innebörd och
förutsattninger</u> (Stockholm Studies in Comparative Religion,
10). Stockholm: Almqvist and Wiksell 1969, 280 p., bibl.;
English summary: Prophet movements, their causes, import
and the conditions under which they arise, pp. 245-251.
> [A comparative study of medieval and modern movements in
> Europe and the U.S.A., and African, North American,
> Melanesian, Indian and Brazilian movements.]

54 LOWIE, ROBERT H. Primitive messianism and an ethnological
problem. <u>Diogenes</u> 19, Fall 1957, 62-72.

55 MONTGOMERY, ROBERT L. Domination versus an alternative route
of change. <u>Bulletin, Christian Institute for Ethnic
Studies in Asia</u> 3 (3-4), 1969, 13-18.
> [Orthodox Western Christianity - with inbuilt appeal to
> oppressed minorities - as alternative focus for accultura-
> tion in primal societies dominated by a non-Western culture;
> compare new religious movements as alternative to domina-
> tion by Western Christian forms.]

56 MÜHLMANN, WILHELM E[MIL]. Chiliasmus, Nativismus, Nationalismus,
in A. Busch (ed.), <u>Soziologie und moderne Gesellschaft</u>.
Stuttgart: Enke 1959, 223-242.

57 MÜHLMANN, WILHELM E[MIL], (ed.). <u>Chiliasmus und Nativismus:
Studien zur Psychologie, Sociologie und Historischen
Kasuistik der Unsturzbewegungen</u>. Berlin: D. Reimer
(1961) 1964, 472 p. Fr. trans.: <u>Messianismes révolu-
tionnaires du tiers monde</u>. Paris: Gallimard 1968, 389 p.
[Some case studies in German original not included.]
> [Includes modern millennial phenomena in Africa, with
> roots both in frustrations consequent on culture contact
> and in the "mutation" from mythical to historical thought
> resulting from the impact of the biblical viewpoint. See
> also case studies: Sulzmann, item 954; Knoob, 1594.]

58 PEEL, J[OHN] D[AVID] Y[EADON]. Understanding alien belief
    systems. British Journal of Sociology 20 (1), 1969,
    69-84.
    [With illustrations from the aladura movement, and
    various theories of African etc. movements.]

59 PEREIRA DE QUEIROZ, MARIA ISAURA. Aspectos gerais do
    messianismo. Revista de Antropologia (São Paulo) 8 (1),
    1960, 63-76.
    [A general account of messianism, prophets, etc.]

60 POSERN-ZIELINSKI, ALEKSANDER. Antropologiczna interpretacja
    Ruchow Spoleczno-Religijnych Trzeciego Swiata. Oceny I
    Propozycje. [An anthropological interpretation of socio-
    religious movements in the Third World. Evaluation and
    comments.] Lud (Warsaw) 55, 1971, 83-113.
    [Problems of research into socio-religious movements in
    the Third World.]

61 QUECHON, MARTINE. Réflexions sur certains aspects du
    syncrétisme dans l'Islam ouest-africain. Cahiers d'Études
    Africaines 11 (2), 1971, 206-230.
    [Uses Lanternari's theoretical framework for examining
    Islamic phenomena parallel to African Christian syncretisms.]

62 RYAN, BRYCE. Die Bedeutung der Revitalizationsbewegungen für
    den Sozialen Wandel in den Entwicklungsländern, in
    R. König (ed.), Aspekte der Entwicklungssoziologie
    (Kölner Zeitschrift für Soziologie und Sozialpsychologie,
    Sonderheft 13). Cologne and Opladen: Westdeutscher
    Verlag 1969, 37-65.

63 SHAREVSKAYA, B. I. K voprosu o tipologii antikolonial 'nyh
    religiozno-politiceskih dvizenij v tropiceskoj Afrike
    [The typology of anti-colonial politico-religious move-
    ments in Africa] Narody Azii i Afriki (Moscow) 4, 1974,
    16-26.

64 SIERKSMA, FOKKE. Een nieuwe hemel en een nieuwe aarde:
    messianistische en eschatologische bewegingen en
    voorstellingen bij primitieve volken. The Hague: Mouton
    1961, 312 p.
    [Messianic ideas among primitive peoples - Africa
    mentioned, pp. 211-212.]

65 SMITH, MARIAN W. Towards a classification of cult movements.
    Man 59 (art. 2), Jan. 1959, 8-12.

Theory

> [Surveys the anthropological contributions to this
> problem between 1943 (Linton, item 52) and 1958, and sug-
> gests three basic classifications as nativistic, vital-
> istic, or synthetist.]

66 SYMMONS-SYMONOLEWICZ, KONSTANTIN. Nativistic movements and
modern nationalism. Transactions, Illinois State Academy
of Science (Springfield, Illinois) 59 (3), 1966, 236-240.

67 TALMON, YONINA. Pursuit of the millennium: the relation
between religious and social change. Archives Européenes
de Sociologie (Paris) 3 (1), 1962, 125-148. Repr. in
B. McLaughlin (ed.), Studies in social movements. New
York: Free Press 1969, 400-427. Also repr. (abridged)
in J. R. Gusfield (ed.), Protest, reform and revolt: a
reader in social movements. New York: John Wiley & Sons
1970, 436-452.
> [Comparative study of some of the literature on millen-
> nial movements including discussion of Balandier's
> Sociologie actuelle d'Afrique noire, item 920.]

68 TALMON, YONINA. Millenarism. International Encyclopedia of
the Social Sciences. New York: Macmillan 1968, Vol. 10,
349-362, bibl.
> [History, characteristics, functions.]

69 THRUPP, SYLVIA L[ETTICE] (ed.). Millennial dreams in action:
essays in comparative study (Comparative Studies in Society
and History, Supplement II). The Hague: Mouton 1962,
229 p. Reprint, New York: Schocken Books 1970.
> [Conference papers, Chicago 1960 - case studies drawn
> from different societies and historical periods, relating
> these to a more general perspective. Specifically on
> Africa: George Shepperson, item 364.]

70 TIRYAKIAN, EDWARD A. A model of societal change and its lead
indicators, in S. Z. Klausner (ed.), The study of total
societies. Garden City, N. Y.: Doubleday 1967, 69-97.
> [Pp. 92 ff., one of three indicators which "seem to be
> significantly related to the outbreak of a revolution",
> with a lead time of about 10-30 years, involves "signifi-
> cant increases in the outbreak of non-institutional reli-
> gious phenomena", with specific mention of African
> independent movements.]

71 TIRYAKIAN, EDWARD A. Le sacré et le profane dans la destruc-
tion coloniale et la construction nationale. Revue de
l'Institut de Sociologie (Université Libre de Bruxelles)
2-3, 1967, 203-216.

[Spiritual renewal as basic to de-colonization, largely
assisted by independent religious movements as early modern-
izers and Africanizers, illustrating the theses of Durkheim
and Weber in an African context; economic effects especially
treated; parallels drawn with the Reformation and 19th
century American revivals.]

72 TURNER, H[AROLD] W[ALTER]. Methodology for modern African
religious movements. Comparative Studies in Society and
History 8 (3), 1966, 12-25.
[The location and identification of the phenomena and
the allocation to the most relevant disciplines.]

73 TURNER, H[AROLD] W[ALTER]. A typology for modern African
religious movements. Journal of Religion in Africa
(Leiden) 1 (1), 1967, 1-34.
[A suggested terminology and classification, revising
the outline given in Hayward, item 235.]

74 TURNER, H[AROLD] W[ALTER]. The contribution of studies on
religion in Africa to western religious studies, in
M. E. Glasswell and E. W. Fasholé-Luke (eds.), New Testament Christianity for Africa and the world: essays in
honour of Harry Sawyerr. London: S.P.C.K. 1974, 169-178.
[As exemplified in the study of African independent
churches.]

75 TURNER, VICTOR W[ITTER]. The ritual process: structure and
anti-structure. Chicago: Aldine Publishing Co. 1969,
213 p.
[Pp. 111-112, egalitarian and communal features of
millenarian movements; pp. 188-191, South African separatism and Melanesian millenarianism as examples of "religions of humility and status reversal".]

76 VAN BAAL, JAN. The political impact of prophetic movements,
in J. Matthes (ed.), International Yearbook for the
Sociology of Religion. Cologne and Opladen: Westdeutscher
Verlag, 5, 1969, 68-88, German summary.
[Includes a six-group typology, and examines the relation to colonialism and nationalism; by a former colonial
governor, later an anthropologist.]

77 WALKER, SHEILA S. Ceremonial spirit possession in Africa
and Afro-America. Forms, meanings and functional significance for individuals and social groups (Supplements to
Numen, 2nd series, 4). Leiden: E. J. Brill 1972, 179 p.,
bibl.

Theory

> [With special reference to Candomblé (Brazil), Voodoo
> (Haiti and Dahomey), Zar (Ethiopia), Winti (Surinam),
> Shango (Trinidad), and Songhay (Niger; note p. 95, new
> Haouka cult associated with colonial experience); ch. 5,
> peyote cult.]

78   WALLACE, ANTHONY F. C. Revitalization movements. American
     Anthropologist 58 (2), 1956, 264-281.
       [A theoretical framework for religious and other move-
     ments, viewing them as a response to strain and an attempt
     to remake culture to relieve the strain.]

79   WALLACE, ANTHONY F. C. Mazeway disintegration: the individ-
     ual's perception of socio-cultural disorganization. Human
     Organization 16 (2), 1957, 23-27 (Special issue, human
     adaptation to disaster).
       [P. 24, social movements (crisis cults and revitalization
     movements) precipitated by socio-economic pressures, partly
     similar to the disaster syndrome.]

80   WALLACE, ANTHONY F. C. Culture and personality (Studies in
     Anthropology 1). New York: Random House 1961, 213 p.
       [Ch. 4, the psychology of culture change, especially
     pp. 143-152, revitalization processes in five stages:
     steady state, increased individual stress, cultural dis-
     tortion, revitalization (six functions distinguished, from
     formulation of a new code to routinization), new steady
     state.]

81   WALLACE, ANTHONY F. C. Religion: an anthropological view.
     New York: Random House 1966, xv + 300 p.
       Pp. 157-166, "religion as revitalization" with a
     typology of revitalization movements; pp. 209-215, "func-
     tions of revitalization rituals".]

82   WALLACE, ANTHONY F. C. Revitalization movements in develop-
     ment, in Richard J. Ward (ed.), The challenge of develop-
     ment theory and practice. Chicago: Aldine Publishing
     Co. 1967, 448-454.

83   WALLACE, ANTHONY F. C. Nativism and revivalism. International
     Encyclopedia of the Social Sciences. New York: Macmillan
     1968, Vol. 11, 75-80, bibl.

84   WALLACE, A[NTHONY] F.C., VOGET, F. W., and SMITH, M[ARIAN] W.
     Towards a classification of cult movements: some further
     contributions. Man 59 (articles 25-27), Feb. 1959, 25-28.

[Continues the discussion from Smith, item 65. Voget distinguishes cultural, socio-psychological and socio-logical "referents".]

85 WELBOURN, F[REDERICK] B[URKEWOOD]. A note on types of religious society, in C. G. Baëta (ed.), item 112, 131-138.
[A suggested typology of "separatist" churches.]

86 WELBOURN, F[REDERICK] B[URKEWOOD]. A metaphysical challenge.
African Ecclesiastical Review 12 (4), 1970, 301-304.
[Comments on D. B. Barrett's views on causes of independent churches, and on the influence of cultural forms
on all religions.]

87 WERBLOWSKY, R[APHAEL] J[EHADAH] ZWI. Messianism in primitive
societies. The Listener (London) no. 1647=64, 1960,
684-686, illus.
[As a sign of dissatisfaction with the present; examples
from North America, and Pacific cargo-cults.]

88 WERBLOWSKY, R[APHAEL] J[EHADAH] ZWI. "A new heaven and a new
earth": considering primitive messianisms. History of
Religions 5 (1), 1965, 164-172.
[Review article on F. Sierksma, 1961 (item 64), with
theoretical discussion.]

89 WILSON, BRYAN R. An analysis of sect development. American
Sociological Review 24 (1), 1959, 3-15. Fr. trans.,
Typologie des sectes dans un perspective dynamique et
comparative. Archives de Sociologie des Religions 16=8
(juillet-déc.), 1963, 49-63.
[Sects as organizations attempting to preserve their
original value orientations; four types of sects dis-
tinguished. No direct reference to Africa.]

90 WILSON, BRYAN R. Millennialism in colonial perspective.
Comparative Studies in Society and History 6 (1), 1963,
93-114.
[Review article on Thrupp (ed.), item 69, and Mühlmann
(ed.), item 57, etc.]

91 WILSON, BRYAN R. Magic and the millennium: a sociological
study of religious movements of protest among tribal and
Third-World peoples. London: Heinemann/New York: Harper
and Row, 1973, 547 p; Frogmore, St. Albans: Granada
Publishing Co. 1975.
[Pp. 50-53, Aiyetoro; pp. 54-57, Tigare; pp. 61-63,
Mgijima; pp. 84-91, anti-witchcraft; pp. 94-100, Lenshina;

Theory

> pp. 136–141, Shembe; pp. 152–154, Déima cult; pp. 176–195,
> Church of the Lord Aladura; pp. 236–240, Makanna and Xhosa
> prophets; pp. 241–242, Yakan cult; pp. 264–268, Mau Mau;
> pp. 368–373 and 456–458, Kimbanguism; pp. 374–375, Matswa,
> pp. 376–379; and many lesser references, see Index of
> Movements.]

92   YINGER, J[OHN] MILTON.   The scientific study of religion.
     New York: Macmillan/London: Collier-Macmillan 1970,
     x + 593 p., illus.
       [Ch. 15, Religion and minority status; includes sections
     on revitalization movements, cargo cults (pp. 317–319),
     North American Indian movements (pp. 319–324) and among
     Afro-Americans (pp. 324–326.]

General

93   ADEGBOLA, EMMANUEL A. ADEOLA. <u>Working with Christ for Church renewal in Africa today</u>. Paper delivered to All Africa Conference of Churches, Abidjan Assembly, 1969. Mimeo.
[Pp. 5-6. section on "A church of one's own?"] Also in <u>South African Outlook</u> 99 (No. 1182) 1969, 174-177.
[Pp. 176-177, "Independent Churches."]
[Fr. trans. of this section in <u>Flambeau</u> (Yaoundé) 24, nov. 1969, 253-254.]

94   ADEGBOLA, EMMANUEL A. ADEOLA. An interview with Rev. A. Adegbola. <u>Presence</u> (Nairobi) 5 (3), 1972, 13-16, illus.
[Pp. 13-14, on preference for term 'indigenous' rather than 'independent' for the new African churches, as expressed earlier in his paper at Abidjan, 1969.]

95   ADEJUNMOBI, T. A. Polygamy, in V. W. Hayward (ed.), item 235, 52-59.
[Reference to the attitude of independent churches towards polygamy.]

96   AFRICAN STUDIES ASSOCIATION. Report of the sixth annual meeting...San Francisco, 1963. <u>African Studies Bulletin</u> (New York) 6 (4), 1963.
[Pp. 7-8, summary of papers given in a session on the topic "African religious movements". Topics included typology, Holy Water movement among the Suku (Zaïre) and the Aladura movement among the Yoruba (Nigeria).]

97   AFRICAN STUDIES ASSOCIATION. Report of the seventh annual meeting...Chicago, 1964. <u>African Studies Bulletin</u> (New York) 7 (4), 1964.
[Pp. 27-29, references to Musama Disco Christo Church (Ghana), to Mau Mau, and to the "sects".]

98   <u>AFRICA RESEARCH BULLETIN</u> (Exeter) Political, Social and Cultural Series. News summaries and reports, e.g. 2 (1-6), Jan.-June 1965, p. 267A, Lenshina movement; p. 325B, Jehovah's Witnesses; 2 (9), Sep. 1965, pp. 372C-373A, Zimbabwe Church of the Orphans, and Lenshina movement, in Zambia.

17

General

>   [Includes a regular section on religion, and covers a
>   large range of African and other newspapers not included
>   in the standard abstracting services.]

99   AJAYI, JACOB F. ADE and AYANDELE, EMMANUEL AYANKANMI. Writing
      African church history, in P. Beyerhaus and C. F.
      Hallencreutz (eds.), The Church crossing frontiers.
      Essays...in honour of Bengt Sundkler (Studia Missionalia
      Upsaliensia XI). Lund: Gleerup 1969, 90-108.
         [Pp. 102-108, the importance of the independent churches
      for African history, with reference especially to Sundkler,
      Turner and Haliburton.]

100   ALEXANDRE, PIERRE [HIPPOLYTE HENRI CHARLES]. Une esquisse
      sociologique des religions en l'Afrique noire. Revue de la
      Défense Nationale avr. 1958, 608-629.
         [Pp. 622-3, "fetish sects" such as Tigare; pp. 623-4,
      628, "syncretistic churches", especially the Ngol cult;
      p. 621, comment on Hamallism.]

101   ALEXANDRE, P[IERRE HIPPOLYTE HENRI CHARLES]. Marxisme et
      tradition culturelle africaine. Afrique et Asie (Paris)
      67, été 1964, 8-25.
         [Includes analysis of syncretistic cults in terms of
      their relationship to the influence of Communism in
      Africa.]

102   ALL AFRICA CONFERENCE OF CHURCHES. Reports and statements at
      Second Assembly, Abidjan 1969. The Conference, 1969.
      Mimeo.
         [See especially Report of the Chairman of the General
      Committee, p. 2; Report of Section III, esp. Appendix on
      four suggested criteria for membership of independent
      churches in AACC and recommended AACC initiatives. Fr.
      trans. of section III in Flambeau (Yaoundé) 24, nov. 1969,
      283-284.]

103   ALLIER, RAOUL [SCIPION PHILIPPE]. La psychologie de la
      conversion chez les peuples non-civilisés. Paris: Payot
      1925.
         [Vol. I, pp. 465-6, revivals at Thaba-Bossiou in Lesotho,
      1887-8, and among the Betsiléo, Madagascar, 1905.]

104   ANSON, PETER [FREDERICK]. Bishops at large. London: Faber
      1964, 593 p., illus.
         [Pp. 264-9, the African Orthodox Church and African Greek
      Orthodox Church, and the source of their episcopal orders
      in J. R. Vilatte; latter Church based on Welbourn;

pp. 278-9, Bresi-Audo's African Universal Church in Ghana;
p. 541, n.2, lists the names and founders of 4 churches in
Nigeria and 1 in Ghana.]

105 APPIAH-KUBI, KOFI. The independent African churches: fore-
    runners to authenticity. A.A.C.C. Bulletin 7 (2), 1974,
    31-36, illus.
        [Concrete examples of African culture being related to
    Christianity - in naming ceremonies, marriage matters, and
    music.]

106 ASSIMENG, JOHN MAXWELL. A sociological analysis of the impact
    and consequences of some Christian sects in selected
    African countries. Oxford University, D.Phil. thesis,
    1968, x + 583 p.
        [Pp. 133-161, Watch Tower Society and syncretist off-
    shoots in Central Africa; pp. 162-212, West Africa, esp.
    pp. 177-189 on the God's Kingdom Society schism; pp. 251-
    319, Pentecostalism, esp. pp. 262-311, Nigeria as a case
    study; pp. 447-454, causes of African separatism; pp. 455-
    514, passim, independent movements; appendices E, F, G,
    lists of independent "sects" in Nigeria, Ghana, Zambia;
    pp. 535-537, lists of files in Ibadan, Accra and Lusaka
    archives, many on independents.]

107 ASSIMENG, [JOHN] MAX[WELL]. Religious and secular messianism
    in Africa. Research Review (Legon, Ghana) 6 (1), 1969,
    1-19.
        ["Messianic movements"; non-logical and non-rational,
    exemplified by nativistic and proto-religious cults, and
    by Nkrumah's Volta River scheme.]

108 ASSIMENG, [JOHN] MAX[WELL]. The dynamics of religious sects.
    Ghana Bulletin of Theology 3 (8), 1970, 32-42.

109 AVERY, ALLEN WADE, JR. African independency: a study of the
    phenomena of independency and the lessons to be learned
    from it for greater church growth in Africa. Fuller
    Theological Seminary School of World Mission (Pasadena,
    California), M.A. thesis (Missions) 1969, 157 p.

110 AYANDELE, EMMANUEL AYANKANMI. External influences on African
    society, in J. C. Anene and G. N. Brown (eds.), Africa in
    the nineteenth and twentieth centuries. Ibadan: Ibadan
    University Press 1966, 133-148.
        [Pp. 140-4, "Ethiopianism" as a "nationalistic conse-
    quence of missionary activity".]

Bibliography of New Religious Movements in Primal Societies

General

111 BAËTA, C[HRISTIAN] G[ONÇALVES KWAMI]. Conflict in mission: historical and separatist churches, in G. H. Anderson (ed.), The theology of the Christian mission. New York: McGraw-Hill 1961, 290-299.
        [Theological analysis of the relationship between mission-created and independent churches; by a Ghanaian theologian.]

112 BAËTA, C[HRISTIAN] G[ONÇALVES KWAMI] (ed.). Christianity in tropical Africa. Studies presented and discussed at the Seventh International African Seminar, University of Ghana, April 1965. London: Oxford University Press for the International African Institute 1968, xiii + 449 p.
        [Pp. 139-143, methodology; see also under Welbourn, item 85; Webster, item 890; Shepperson, item 368; Bureau, item 477.]

113 BAËTA, CHRISTIAN GONÇALVES [KWAMI]. Prophetische Bewegungen und der Kampf um echte Kirche in Afrika. Evangelisches Missions Magazin 114 (3), 1970, 99-117.
        [English summary: Missionaria, 3 (2), 1971, 43.]

114 BAËTA, CHRISTIAN G[ONÇALVES KWAMI]. Some aspects of religious change in Africa. Ghana Bulletin of Theology 3 (10), 1971, 9-22.
        [The Christian attitude to African culture; pp. 17-19, new religious movements - their positive and negative influence.]

115 BALANDIER, GEORGES. Les conditions sociologiques de l'art nègre. Présence Africaine 10-11, 1951, 58-71.
        [Reference to independent religious movements and their abstract symbolism.]

116 BALANDIER, GEORGES. Contribution à une sociologie de dépendance. Cahiers Internationaux de Sociologie (Paris) n.s. 12, 1952, 47-69.
        [Reactions to the colonial situation, including African religious movements.]

117 BALANDIER, GEORGES. Messianismes et nationalismes en Afrique noire. Cahiers Internationaux de Sociologie (Paris) n.s. 14, 1953, 41-65. Eng. trans., Messianism and nationalism in Black Africa, in P. L. van den Berghe, (ed.), Africa: social problems of change and conflict. San Francisco: Chandler Publishing Co. 1965, 443-460.
        [Illustrated from the Congo area.]

118   BALANDIER, GEORGES.   Contribution à l'étude des nationalismes
           en Afrique noire.   Zaïre 8 (4), 1954, 379-389.
           [Pp. 387-389, Mau Mau, Kimbanguism and the role of mes-
           sianic movements in nationalism.]

119   BALANDIER, GEORGES.   Les mythes politiques de colonisation et
           de décolonisation en Afrique.   Cahiers Internationaux de
           Sociologie (Paris) n.s. 33, juillet-déc. 1962, 85-96.
           [Pp. 91-92, on new religious movements with revolutionary
           aims.]

120   BALANDIER, GEORGES.   Réflexions sur le fait politique: le cas
           des sociétés africaines.   Cahiers Internationaux de
           Sociologie (Paris) n.s. 37, juillet-déc. 1964, 23-50.
           [P. 37, messianic leaders in modern political
           developments.]

121   BANTON, MICHAEL [PARKER].   African prophets.   Race 5 (2), 1963,
           42-55.   Repr. in John Middleton (ed.), Black Africa, its
           people and their cultures today.   New York and London:
           Macmillan 1970, 222-233.
           [General article, indicating that prophets' functions
           are more than political.]

122   BANTON, MICHAEL [PARKER].   Race relations.   London: Tavistock
           Publications 1967, xiv + 434 p., maps, tables, diagrams.
           [Ch. 9, Colonial Africa; the interrelation of political
           and religious factors.]

123   BARRETT, DAVID BRIAN.   The African independent churches and
           the Bible, United Bible Societies Bulletin 72 (4), 1967,
           184-192.   German trans., Die selbständigen Kirchen in
           Afrika und die Bibel, Die Bibel in der Welt (Berlin) 11,
           1968, 40-50; Fr. trans., Les églises indépendantes d'Afrique
           et les possibilités qu'elles offrent comme partenaires
           dans la diffusion des Saintes Écritures, Cahiers de
           l'Alliance Biblique Universelle 2, 1967, 20-29.
           [A paper read at the U.B.S. Africa Regional Conference,
           Ghana, March 1967.]

124   BARRETT, DAVID BRIAN.   The African independent churches, in
           H. Wakelin Coxill and K. Grubb (eds.), World Christian
           Handbook 1968.   London: Lutterworth, for Survey Applica-
           tion Trust 1967, 378 p.
           [Pp. 24-28, survey; pp. 98-99, 227-228, statistics
           pp. 254-256, directory.]

General

125   BARRETT, DAVID BRIAN. L'évolution des mouvements religieux
          dissidents en Afrique (1862-1927). Archives de Sociologie
          des Religions no. 25=13, jan.-juin 1968, 111-140.
              [Fr. trans. by M. F. Perrin Jassy of some material from
          Chs. 1 and 10, and of Ch. 15, of his item 126 (1968).]

126   BARRETT, DAVID BRIAN. Schism and renewal in Africa: an
          analysis of six thousand contemporary religious movements.
          Nairobi and London: Oxford University Press 1968. xx +
          363 p., diagrams, tables, maps, illus.
              [A survey of some 250 tribes revealing the factors that
          correlate with the emergence of independent religious
          movements in order to explain their rise, and predict
          future movements.]

127   BARRETT, DAVID BRIAN. Séparatisme et renouveau en Afrique.
          Le Monde Non-Chrétien n.s. no. 88, oct.-déc. 1968, 3-22.
              [Fr. trans. of Ch. 18 of his item 126 (1968).]

128   BARRETT, DAVID B[RIAN]. AD 2000 - 350 million Christians in
          Africa: an analysis of some alternative futures (Com-
          mission on World Mission and Evangelism, Research Pamphlet).
          Geneva: World Council of Churches 1970, 70 p.; shorter
          version, same title, in International Review of Mission
          no. 233=59 (Jan.), 1970, 39-54. Fr. trans., L'an 2000 en
          Afrique: 350 millions de chrétiens. L'Eglise Vivante 22
          (2), 1970, 137-156. Even more briefly, as: The expansion
          of Christianity in Africa in the twentieth century. Church
          Growth Bulletin (Pasadena) 5 (5), 1969, 362-366.
              [Projections for growth of independent churches, passim.]

129   BARRETT, DAVID [BRIAN] (ed.). Who's who of African independent
          church leaders. Risk (Geneva) 7 (3), 1971, 23-34, illus.
              [Biographical notes on 56 leaders, with 31 photographs.]

130   BARRETT, LEONARD E. Religious rejuvenation in Africa: some
          impressions from West Africa. Journal of Ecumenical
          Studies 7 (1), 1970, 23-36; study questions, 203-204.
              [A survey, especially of causes, largely based on
          D. Barrett (1968).]

131   BEATTIE, JOHN H. M. and MIDDLETON, JOHN (eds.). Spirit medium-
          ship and society in Africa. London: Routledge and Kegan
          Paul, New York: Africana Publishing Corp., 1969, xxx +
          310 p., illus.
              [13 essays giving the traditional background to similar
          phenomena in new religious movements; for specific refer-
          ences to these see under Colson, item 1532; Field, 529;
          Lee, 1769; Middleton, 1387; Southall, 1397; Welbourn, 1219.]

132 BECKEN, HANS-JÜRGEN. Afrikanische unabhängige Kirche. Gibt
es einen zeitgemässen Missionsdienst in Afrika?
Evangelische Missions-Zeitschrift N.F. 28 (4), 1971,
177-180.
[In relation to missionary service.]

133 BECKEN, HANS-JÜRGEN. The experience of healing in the Church
in Africa. Contact (Geneva) 29, Oct. 1975, 7-11.

134 BEETHAM, T[HOMAS] A[LLEN]. Christian discipline: law and
gospel, in V. W. Hayward (ed.), item 235, 60-64.
[Reference to independent churches.]

135 BEETHAM, THOMAS A[LLEN]. Christianity and the new Africa.
London: Pall Mall 1967, 206 p., maps, appendices, bibl.
[Pp. 19-21, 46, 127-128, independent churches; pp. 163,
169, their statistics.]

136 BENDER, ROSS THOMAS. The people of God. A Mennonite inter-
pretation of the Free Church tradition. Scottdale, PA.:
Herald Press 1971, 208 p.
[Pp. 46-49, African independent churches; pp. 43-46,
East African Revival Fellowship.]

137 BENZ, ERNST (ed.). Messianische Kirchen, Sekten und Bewegungen
im Heutigen Afrika. Leiden: E. J. Brill 1966, 127 p.,
bibl.
[With an introduction by E. Dammann, and see items 217,
459, 1413, 1603.]

138 BENZ, ERNST. Neue Religionen. Stuttgart: Ernst Klett Verlag
1971, 179 p.
[Ch. 9: "Messianische Religionen in Afrika", 140-168;
other chapters on movements in Vietnam, North America, and
Melanesia.]

139 BEYERHAUS, PETER. What is our answer to sects? Ministry
(Morija, Lesotho) 1 (4), 1961, 4-13. German trans., Was
ist unsere Antwort auf die Sekten? Evangelische Missions-
Zeitschrift (Stuttgart) 18, 1961, 65-80.
[A missionary theologian evaluates independent movements.]

140 BEYERHAUS, PETER. Unüberwundenes Heidentum als innere Bedrohung
der afrikanischen Kirche. Evangelische Missions-Zeitschrift
N.F. 21, 1964, 114-131.

141 BEYERHAUS, PETER (ed.). Begegnungen mit messianischen
Bewegungen in Afrika (Weltmission Heute, 33/34). Stuttgart:
Evangelischer Missionsverlag 1967, 73 p.

General

> [Two essays by Beyerhaus on the church and these move-
> ments; H. Häzelbarth on Lekganyane's Zion Christian Church;
> Sundkler on messiah as healer; Oosthuizen on Shembe's
> Church and the Zulu world view; M.-L. Martin on African
> and biblical messianism; similar to their essays in item
> 1797.]

142   BEYERHAUS, PETER. Der schwarze Messias. Der Ruf (Berliner
      Missionsberichte) 4, Juli-August 1967, 267-276.

143   BEYERHAUS, PETER. Heilung bei synkretistischen Kultgemein-
      schaften in Afrika, in H.-J. Greschat and H. Jungraithmayr
      (eds.), item 218, 243-254.

144   BOER, HARRY R. Africa's other churches. The Reformed Journal
      (Grand Rapids, Michigan) 24 (5), 1974, 14-17.
      [A review article on Barrett (1968) and Oosthuizen
      (1968).]

145   BOOTH, JOSEPH. Africa for the African. Baltimore, Maryland:
      published by Joseph Booth, Press of the Educator of Morgan
      College 1897.
      [An important book by a man who was a force towards
      Ethiopianism in Central and South Africa. See Shepperson
      and Price, item 1473, for a summary of its contents.]

146   BOSCH, DAVID J[ACOBUS]. Review of F. F. Bruce, The spreading
      flame. Missionaria (Pretoria) 4 (4), 1972, 96-98.
      [P. 97, suggested parallels between earlier Christian
      history and recent history of Christianity in Africa as
      subjects for research.]

147   BOUCHAUD, J[OSEPH]. Aspects modernes du paganisme africain.
      Annales Spiritaines (Paris) no. 66=7, 1956, 93-99.
      [Includes discussion of messianism.]

148   BRANDRETH, HENRY R[ENAUD] T[URNER]. Episcopi vagantes and
      the Anglican Church. London: S.P.C.K. 1961, 140 p.,
      illus., bibl. (1st. ed. 1947).
      [Pp. 56-57, McGuire's consecration of D. W. Alexander
      as Primate of African Orthodox Church in South Africa, and
      Alexander's ordination of Reuben Spata (sic); p. 67,' con-
      secration of Ebenezer Johnson Anderson (Mar Kwamin Ntsetse-
      Bresi Ando) as Primate of Autonomous African Universal
      Church etc., 1935; p. 128, bibliography on African Ortho-
      dox Church in the Vilatte succession.]

149 BRISBANE, ROBERT HUGHES. Some new light on the Garvey move-
    ment. Journal of Negro History (Washington, DC) 36 (1),
    1931, 53-62.
    [Pp. 56-57 claims Garvey had discussions with followers
    of Chilembwe and Kimbangu.]

150 BROU, ALEXANDRE. Afrique - le Prophétisme protestant.
    Études [de Théologie de Philosophie et d'Histoire] (Paris)
    no. 184=24, 20 sep. 1925, 730-747.
    [Based on Dufonteny, see item 192. African prophet
    movements are blamed on Protestantism; pp. 739-747,
    Kimbanguism, a Protestant Anglo-Saxon-inspired political
    movement.]

151 BROU, ALEXANDRE. Le prophétisme dans les églises protestantes
    indigènes d'Afrique. Revue d'Histoire des Missions 8 (1),
    1931, 71-84; repr. in part in Congo (Brussels) 12 (1, v),
    juillet 1931, 708-720.
    [Draws on Buell (1928); includes Harris.]

152 BROWN, KENNETH J. (sic) [IRVING]. Joyous baptism among the
    African independent churches. Risk (Geneva) 7 (3), 1971,
    50-55, illus.
    [A survey of the varieties of baptism in independent
    churches, and of the meanings attached; from direct obser-
    vation.]

153 BROWN, KENNETH I[RVING]. Forms of baptism in the African
    independent churches of tropical Africa. Practical Anthro-
    pology 19 (4), 1972, 169-182.

154 BRULS, JEAN. Prophètes bantous en Afrique du Sud. L'Eglise
    Vivante (Louvain: Société des Auxiliaires des Missions)
    1 (3), 1949, 341-353.
    [Review article on Sundkler, 1st. ed., 1948, with con-
    cluding comment on importance of the indigenization of
    the Church in Africa.]

155 BUELL, RAYMOND LESLIE. The Native Problem in Africa. New
    York: Macmillan 1928; London: F. Cass 1965, 2 vols.
    [Vol. I: pp. 120-124, Ethiopianism; pp. 242-249, Watch
    Tower and Chilembwe; pp. 363, 368, 373-376, Thuku in
    Kenya; pp. 612f., Malaki in Uganda; pp. 745-749, Nigerian
    movements in the 1920s. Vol. II: pp. 66-68, Harris;
    pp. 302-305, United Native Church, Nigeria; p. 563, Faith
    Tabernacle, Kinshasa, Bel. Congo; pp. 601-609, the prophet
    movement Bel. Congo; pp. 730-733, the Garvey movement and
    Liberia. One of the earliest comprehensive treatments.]

General

156   BUERKLE, HORST W. The message of the "False Prophets" of the
       independent churches of Africa. Makerere Journal
       (Kampala) 11, Dec. 1965, 51–55; also German trans., Die
       Rebellion der Magie. Afrikas Kirchen und die falschen
       Propheten. Christ und Welt (Stuttgart) 39=18, 24 Sep.
       1965, 14.
       [A popular summary, with suggestions for the older
       churches.]

157   BÜHLER, ALFRED. Die messianischen Bewegungen der Naturvölker
       und ihre Bedeutung für probleme der Entwicklungsländer.
       Acta Tropica (Basel) 21, 1964, 362–382.
       [A general article including reference to Africa.]

158   BUREAU, RENÉ. Syncrétismes et messianismes en Afrique noire.
       Parole et Mission no. 24=7, 15 jan. 1964, 132–135.
       [Report on Bouaké conference, 1963.]

159   BUREAU, RENÉ. Sorcellerie et prophétisme en Afrique noire.
       Études (Paris) avr. 1967, 467–481.

160   CARTER, GWENDOLEN M[ARGARET]. Five African states. Ithaca,
       N. Y.: Cornell University Press 1963, xiv + 643 p., maps.
       [Pp. 83–85, messianic movements and Kitawala in Congo;
       p. 203, 'messianic cults' in Dahomey; p. 402, Chilembwe.]

161   CHESNEAUX, JEAN. Les hérésies coloniales. Leur rôle dans le
       développement des mouvements nationaux d'Asie et d'Afrique
       à l'époque contemporaine. Recherches Internationales à la
       Lumière du Marxisme (Paris) 6, mars-avr. 1958, 170–188.

162   CHESNEAUX, JEAN. Hérésies coloniales et millénarismes de
       libération nationale, in La naissance des Dieux. Paris:
       Edition de l'Union Rationaliste n.d. [1966], 237–271.
       [Pp. 249–252, 270, survey of African movements.]

163   CHODAK, SZYMON. Niektóre Socjologiczne aspekty funkcji
       religii w Czarnej Afryce (Some sociological aspects of
       the functions of religion in Black Africa). Studia
       Socjologiczne (Warsaw) 2, 1961, 212–243.
       [Includes new religious movements.]

164   CHURCH CONFERENCE ON AFRICAN AFFAIRS. Christian action in
       Africa. New York: Africa Committee of the Foreign Mis-
       sions Conference of North America 1942.
       [Pp. 62–64 on independent churches.]

165   COLEMAN, JAMES S[MOOT]. Current political movements in Africa,
        in W. O. Brown (ed.), The Annals of the American Academy
        of Political and Social Sciences (Philadelphia) 298,
        March 1955, 95-108.
          [Pp. 99-100, 'messianic politico-religious movements',
        distinguished as 'puritanical', 'chiliastic' and
        'nativistic'.]

166   COMHAIRE, JEAN L. Religious trends in African and Afro-
        American urban societies. Anthropological Quarterly
        (Washington D.C.) n.s. 1 (4), 1953, 95-108.
          [Pp. 95-99, Kimbanguism at Léopoldville; pp. 100-104,
        Lagos and 'West African nationalism'.]

167   COOK, LLOYD ALLEN. Revolt in Africa. Journal of Negro
        History, (Washington D.C.) 18 (4), 1933, 396-413.
          [Pioneer comparative study of prophet risings.]

168   CRONON, EDMUND DAVID. Black Moses. The story of Marcus
        Garvey and the Universal Negro Improvement Association.
        Madison: University of Wisconsin Press 1955; repr. 1962;
        xiv + 278 p., illus.
          [Pp. 177-183, Garvey's ideas on religion, and the
        African Orthodox Church.]

169   CRONON, EDMUND DAVID. Marcus Garvey. (Great Lives Observed).
        Englewood Cliffs, N. J.: Prentice-Hall Inc. 1973. 176 p.
          [Pp. 107-111, 132, African Orthodox Church; pp. 107-111
        are a reprint of G. A. McGuire's defence of Garveyism in
        the preface to A. J. Garvey (1926), vol. 2, pp. v-viii.]

170   CRUISE O'BRIEN, DONAL B[RIAN]. The Mourides of Senegal: the
        political and economic organization of an Islamic brother-
        hood (Oxford Studies in African Affairs). Oxford:
        Clarendon Press, 1971, xiv + 321 p., maps, tables, illus.
          [Pp. 286-293, the Mourides compared with African
        Christian movements.]

171   DAMBORIENA, PRUDENCIO. Tongues as of fire. Pentecostalism in
        contemporary Christianity. Washington and Cleveland:
        Corpus Books 1969, 256 p.
          [Pp. 123-24, 147-51, 174-75, Pentecostalism in Africa,
        both among independent and "imported" churches; expresses
        uncertainty about application of the term to the former.]

172   DAMMANN, ERNST. Das Christusverständnis in nachchristlichen
        Kirchen und Sekten Afrikas, in Jesus Christus. Das
        Christusverständnis im Wandel der Zeiten (Marburger

General

Theologische Studien I). Marburg: N. G. Elwert Verlag 1963, 135-148. Also in E. Benz (ed.), item 137, 1-22.

173 DAMMANN, ERNST. Bezeichnungen für die Führer nachchristlicher Kirchen und Sekten Afrikas, in Tagung für Allgemeine Religionsgeschichte 1963. Jena: Wissenschaftlichen Zeitschrift der Freidrich-Schiller Universität 1964, 113-117.

174 DAMMANN, ERNST. Die Religionen Afrikas. Stuttgart: Kohlhammer 1963, 302 p. Fr. trans., Les religions de l'Afrique. Paris: Payot 1964, 272 p.
[Pp. 276-280, post-Christian movements (253-257 in French trans.); and pp. 60, 80, 125, 149, 265, 267, Reformed Ogboni Fraternity, Nigeria.]

175 DAMMANN, ERNST. Weihnachten in den nachchristlichen Sekten Afrikas. Afrika Heute (Bonn) 24, 1964, 340-342.
[On the comparative neglect of Christmas celebration.]

176 DAMMANN, ERNST. Das Christentum in Afrika. Munich and Hamburg: Siebenstern Taschenbuch 116, 1968, 190 p.
[Pp. 160-169. independent churches as "post-Christian movements".]

177 DAMMANN, ERNST. Grundriss der Religionsgeschichte (Theolog-ische Wissenschaft: Sammelwek für Studium und Beruf). Stuttgart etc.: Verlag W. Kohlhammer 1972, 127 p.
[Pp. 93-99, survey of independent churches in South and Central Africa; pp. 99-101, Muslim movements: Mourides and Black Muslims.]

178 DAMMANN, ERNST. Das Problem einer Afrikanischen Theologie (Oberurseler Hefte. Studien und Beitrage fur Theologie und Gemeinde, Heft 3). Oberursel: Oberurseler Hefte 1975, 40 p.
[Case studies include Kimbanguism and Prophet Wovenu, Ghana.]

179 D'ANCY, M. Itinéraire syncrétiste. Parole et Mission (Paris) 1 (2), 15 juillet 1958, 219-251.
[The large number of "syncretist sects" and the possible causes - dissatisfaction with Christian forms, incomplete conversion, or residual paganism, not peculiar to Africa (but must be taken seriously). Pp. 239-246 on Congo movements; p. 240, Kitawala.]

180   DANEEL, M[ARTHINUS] L[OUIS]. The Christian gospel and the
       ancestor cults, Missionalia (Pretoria) 1 (2), August
       1973, 46-73.
       [Pp. 64-69 et passim, independent churches in relation
       to ancestors.]

181   D'ANNA, ANDREA. Da Cristo a Kimbangu. Bologna: Ed. Nigrizia,
       1964, 158 p. Sp. trans., De Christo a Kimbangu Madrid:
       Ediciones Combonianas, 1966, 146 p.
       [Popular survey of the main movements in South, Central,
       East and West Africa, based on secondary sources; not
       always accurate.]

182   DAVIDSON, BASIL. The Africans: an entry to cultural history.
       Harlow: Longmans, 1969, 367 p., illus., maps. American
       ed., The African genius. An introduction to social and
       cultural history. Boston: Atlantic Monthly Press, 1970.
       [Ch. 28, Twilight of the old gods - popular survey of
       the indigenous cults revived, sometimes with messianic
       aspects, in support of movements resisting European
       intrusion; including Shona, Ndebele, Herero, Nama, Maji-
       Maji and Mumbo. Ch. 29, New Redeemers, surveys Enoch
       Mgijima, Mhlakaza, Ethiopianism, Kamwana, Chilembwe,
       Nyirenda, Kimbangu.]

183   DAVIS, J[OHN] MERLE (ed.). Modern industry and the African.
       London: Macmillan 1933, xviii + 425 p., maps.
       [The Rand and the Copper Belt; pp. 4-5, 371, brief
       references to separatist churches and their causes;
       pp. 408-414, list of registered 'separatist churches' in
       South Africa.]

184   DE SAINT-CHARMANT, JEAN. Sectes et christianisme en Afrique
       noire. La Revue des Deux Mondes (Paris) no. 15, 1962
       (1 août), 339-353. Repr. in La Dépêche (Elisabethville)
       6 oct. 1964. Eng. trans., Sects and prophets in Black
       Africa, in Translations on Africa (Washington D.C.) 121,
       28 Oct. 1964, 13-16. Germ. trans., Sekten und Propheten
       im schwarzen Afrika. Schweizerische monatshefte für
       Politik und Kultur (Zurich) Jan. 1964, 1034-1046.
       [The relations between religion, tribal tradition and
       politics, set in the wider context of the contemporary
       situation, with some first-hand acquaintance with
       Harrisism, Lassyism, etc.]

185   DESCHAMPS, HUBERT. Les religions de l'Afrique noire. Paris:
       Presses Universitaires de France 1954.
       [Pp. 114-119, a brief survey of independent churches,
       prophetism and new cults.]

General

186   DESROCHE, HENRI [CHARLES]. Syncrétisme et messianisme en
      Afrique noire. Archives de Sociologie des Religions
      no. 16=8, juillet-déc. 1963, 105-108.
      [Report on the seminar under this title at Bouaké,
      Ivory Coast, October 1963.]

187   DILLON-MALONE, CLIVE. Towards an understanding of modern
      African religious movements. University of Birmingham,
      M. Soc. Sc. thesis (Sociology), 1973, 39 p., diagrams.
      [A typology of the synchronous evolutionary dynamics.]

188   DOS SANTOS, EDUARDO. Precursores do messianismo africano?
      Ultramar (Lisbon) no. 9= julho-setembro 1962, 134-137.
      [Examples of what the writer terms political ambitions
      and xenophobia.]

189   DOS SANTOS, E[DUARDO]. Profetismos africanos e situação
      colonial. Ultramar 3°trim. 1972, 33-52.

190   DOUGALL, JAMES W[ATSON] C[UNNINGHAM]. African separatist
      churches. International Review of Missions No. 179=45,
      July 1956, 257-266.
      [General review of the origins and causes from a
      missionary point of view.]

191   DOUGALL, JAMES W[ATSON] C[UNNINGHAM]. Christians in the
      African revolution (The Duff Missionary Lectures 1962).
      Edinburgh: Saint Andrew Press 1963, 114 p.
      [Pp. 61-74, analysis of major literature from the
      point of view of mission policy.]

192   DUFONTENY, [G]. Les sorciers comme chefs de rébellion, in
      Semaine de Missiologie XIV, La sorcellerie dans les pays
      de Mission. Brussels: L'Edition Universelle 1937, 70-88.
      [General article - new religious movements as Protestant
      and "politico-religious", and continuing the use of magic
      for healing; p. 37, special discussion of Kimbangu. By a
      Roman Catholic missionary.]

193   DU PLESSIS, JOHANNES C. The evangelization of pagan Africa.
      Cape Town and Johannesburg: Juta 1929, xii + 408 p.
      [Pp. 121-122, Harris; pp. 349-351, Chilembwe;
      pp. 350-351, Ethiopianism and separatism; ch. 15, Malaki.]

194   ECUMENICAL PRESS SERVICE (Geneva). The phenomenon of inde-
      pendent churches in Africa. Ecumenical Press Service 1
      (1), 1970, 11-14; Fr. trans., La phénomène des Eglises
      indépendantes en Afrique, Service Oecuménique de Presse

et d'Information 1 (1), 1970, 13-15; similar version, The
phenomenon of independent churches, African Ecclesiastical
Review (Masaka, Uganda) 12 (2), 1970, 120-122.

195   ELLENBERGER, HENRI F.   Les mouvements de libération mythique.
      Critique (Paris) no. 190=19, mars 1963, 248-267.
      [Review article on Mühlmann (1961), Lanternari (1962)
      and Worsley (1957); pp. 264-266, account of the Xhosa
      cattle-killing episode of 1856-57.]

196   EPELLE, E[MMANUEL] M. T[OBIAH].   The sects.   West African
      Religion (Nsukka, Nigeria) 13-14, Sep.-Dec. 1972, 42-51;
      also in Report of seminar on "The religious situation in
      Nigeria today"...1972...Nsukka.   Nsukka: Department of
      Religion, University of Nigeria, 1972, 41-50.

197   FABIAN, JOHANNES [N.].   Führer und Führung in den prophetisch-
      messianischen Bewegungen der (ehemaligen) Kolonialvölker.
      Anthropos (Freiburg) 58 (5-6) 1963, 773-809, bibl.
      [On the role of charismatic leaders, with many African
      examples.]

198   FERNANDEZ, JAMES W[ILLIAM].   Revitalized words from "The
      Parrot's Egg" and "The Bull that crashes in the Kraal":
      African cult sermons, in: American Ethnological Society,
      Essays on the verbal and visual arts (1966 annual meeting
      proceedings).   Seattle, Washington: University of
      Washington Press 1967, 45-63.
      [Analysis of sermons by a preacher of the Bwiti move-
      ment in Gabon, and a Zionist preacher in South Africa.]

199   FERNANDEZ, JAMES WILLIAM.   Contemporary African religion:
      confluents of enquiry, in G. M. Carter and A. Paden (eds.),
      Expanding horizons in African studies (Proceedings, 20th
      Anniversary Conference, Program of African Studies, 1968).
      Evanston: Northwestern University Press, 1969, 27-45.
      [Problems of enumeration, typology, cross-cultural
      comparative study, and acculturation, from an anthro-
      pological viewpoint.]

200   FERNANDEZ, JAMES WILLIAM.   Independent African Christianity:
      its study and its future.   Journal of African and Asian
      Studies 4 (2), 1969, 132-147.
      [A review article of Turner (1967), with some reference
      to S. G. Williamson, Akan religion and the Christian faith
      (1965), from an anthropological viewpoint.]

General

201 FERNANDEZ, JAMES WILLIAM. Microcosmogony and modernization
     in African religious movements (Occasional Papers Series,
     3). Montreal: McGill University Centre for Developing-
     Area Studies 1969, 21 p.
       [A lecture in a series on "modernization and protest"
     given in 1967.]

202 FERNANDEZ, JAMES W[ILLIAM]. The ethnic communion: inter-
     ethnic recruitment in African religious movements.
     Journal of African Studies (Los Angeles) 2 (2), 1975,
     131-147.
       [Based on Bwiti (Gabon), Amakhehleni or Old Man's Cult
     (Natal), Church of God in Christ (Natal), Christianisme
     Céleste (Benin), Apostolic Revelation Society (Ghana).]

203 FORTES, MEYER, and DIETERLEN, GERMAINE. African systems of
     thought. London: Oxford University Press for the
     International African Institute 1965. viii + 392 p.
       [See papers by Doutreloux, item 20; Stenning, 1399; and
     Sundkler, 1604.]

204 FOSTER, PETER G. An evaluation of approaches to the study of
     some modern religious movements in Africa. University of
     Manchester, M.A. thesis, 1967, 68 p.

205 FRASER, DONALD. The future of Africa. London: Church
     Missionary Society 1911, 309 p., illus. Fr. trans.,
     L'Afrique d'hier et l'Afrique de demain. Lausanne: La
     Concorde 1913, 241 p., illus.
       [Pp. 236-237, Ethiopianism, as "native Christian revolt
     against the control of the European" which "is righting
     itself".]

206 FROELICH, JEAN-CLAUDE. Animismes. Les religions païennes de
     l'Afrique de l'Ouest. Paris: Ed. de l'Orante 1964.
     254 p.
       [Ch. 10, "Le dynamisme religieux", includes pp. 214-217
     on the San cult (Mali), pp. 217-222 on the Goro-Atingali
     cult (S. Dahomey), pp. 221-227 on syncretisms and
     messianisms in general.]

207 FROELICH, JEAN-CLAUDE. Importancia del Islam, el
     Christianismo y las sectas en Africa negra. Actualidad
     Africana (Madrid) 143, Mar. 1964, 2ff.

208 FROELICH, JEAN-CLAUDE. L'Afrique se cherche des Dieux. Revue
     de Défense Nationale (Paris) 23, mai 1967, 822-833.
       [The appearance of new religions; features of the most
     important ones.]

209   FROELICH, JEAN-CLAUDE. Les nouveaux dieux d'Afrique. Paris:
      Prismes/Orante 1969. 127 p.
         [Chs. 3-4, messianism and syncretism, with special
      reference to Kimbanguism and prophet Harris, with Annexes
      (pp. 108-113) containing extracts from their documents;
      pp. 113-115, classification (based on Guariglia); p. 116,
      note on Croix Koma.]

210   FÜLLING, ERICH, and DEDEKIND, ECKART. Synkretistische
      Strömungen in Lateinamerika, Mittel-und-Südafrika.
      Lutherisches Missionsjahrbuch 1964, 54-67.
         [Pp. 62-66 on Africa.]

211   GARVEY, AMY JACQUES (ed.). Philosophy and opinions of Marcus
      Garvey, or, Africa for the Africans. 2 vols. New York:
      Universal Publishing House, 1923-1925. Repr.: New York:
      Arno Press, 1968-1969; London: F. Cass, 1967, in one vol.,
      xxxvi, 78, xvii, 412 p., illus., plates.
         [Pp. 27-33, Garvey's view of Christ and true
      Christology.]

212   GLUCKMAN, MAX. Order and rebellion in tribal Africa. London:
      Cohen and West, 1963, 273 p.
         [Ch. 4, "The magic of despair"; pp. 143-145 on Mau Mau,
      nativistic cults and separatist sects, based on Sundkler;
      pp. 212, 223, comparison with "sects" of early 19th
      century England; p. 217, as aspects of the colour-bar.]

213   GOLLOCK, GEORGINA A. Sons of Africa. London: Student
      Christian Movement, 1928, 247 p. German trans., Sohne
      Afrikas. Berlin: Heimatdienst Verlag, 1930, 156 p.
      Fr. adaptation, N. Poire, Fils et filles d'Afrique.
      Paris: Société des Missions Évangéliques, 1946.
         [Ch. 13 (=pp. 119-140 in Fr. adaptation), "Among the
      Prophets - a study of African heretics" - includes
      Malaki of Uganda, Braide of Nigeria, Kimbangu of the
      Congo, and South African movements; pp. 198-202 on Harris.]

214   GRANGETTE, G. Syncrétismes et messianismes en Afrique noire.
      Parole et Mission (Paris) 4 (4) 1961, 343-370.
         [Sympathetic approach to cause of such movements by a
      Dominican missionary in Senegal. Pp. 346-349, specific
      references to "religion de san"; pp. 349-350, Harrisism;
      pp. 350-352, messianic sects.]

215   GRAVRAND, HENRI. Meeting the African religions. Rome:
      Editora Editrice Ancora for the Secretariat for Non-
      Christians, 1969, 189 p.

General

[Pp. 117-121, syncretism and messianism in Africa; ch. 3, African religious dynamism.]

216   GRESCHAT, HANS-JÜRGEN. Die originalsprachliche Literatur des christlichen Syncretismus in Afrika. Afrika und Übersee (Hamburg) 48 (4), 1964, 254-261.
       [A general survey of oral and printed religious litera- ture in African languages.]

217   GRESCHAT, HANS-JÜRGEN. Eine vorläufige Bibliographie zum Problem nachchristlicher Kirchen, Sekten und Bewegungen in Africa, in E. Benz (ed.), item 137, 106-119, 158-165.

218   GRESCHAT, HANS-JÜRGEN and JUNGRAITHMAYR, HERRMANN (eds.). Wort und Religion - Kalima na Dini. Studien zur Afrikanistik, Missionswissenschaft, Religions-wissenschaft. Ernst Dammann zum 65. Geburtstag. Stuttgart: Evangelischer Missionsverlag 1969, 384 p., photo.
       [See items 143, Beyerhaus; 389, Turner; 1257, Greschat.]

219   GROVES, C[HARLES] P[ELHAM]. The planting of Christianity in Africa. London: Lutterworth Press, Vol. III, 1955, Vol. IV, 1958; reissued 1964.
       [Vol. III, p. 179, Ethiopianism in South Africa; Vol. IV, pp. 45-46, 123-124, Harris; pp. 62-63, Ethiopianism (Booth and Chilembwe); pp. 124-126, the Malakites of Uganda; pp. 126-127, Braide of Nigeria; pp. 127, 192, Kimbanguism in the Congo; pp. 128-130, 324, Ethiopianism in South Africa; p. 188, African Universal Church, Ghana; p. 189, Babalola in Nigeria; pp. 236-237, separatism; pp. 352-354, separatism illustrated in the Apostolic Revelation Society of Ghana and Cherubim and Seraphim of Nigeria.]

220   GUARIGLIA, GUGLIELMO. Prophetismus und Heilserwartungs- Bewegungen bei den Niedrigen Kulturen. Numen (Leiden) 5 (3) 1958, 180-193.
       [A classification of religious movements.]

221   GUARIGLIA, GUGLIELMO. Prophetismus und Heilserwartungs- Bewegungen als völkerkindliches und religionsgeschtichtliches Problem. Vienna: F. Berger 1959, xvi + 332 p., maps, bibl.
       [General world survey; esp. pp. 197-239, African move- ments, in terms of syncretist, millennialism, vitalism, etc.; extensive bibliography.]

222   GUARIGLIA, GUGLIELMO. I movimenti profetico-salvifici e le missioni. Le Missioni Cattoliche (Milan) 89 (8-9), 1960, 258-269.

223   GUARIGLIA, GUGLIELMO. Movimenti profetico-salvifici a livello
        etnologico: appunt storico-culturali ad un' interpretazione
        storicistica. Studi e Materiali per la Storia della
        Religioni (Rome) 32 (2), 1961, 248-284.
        [A critique of Lanternari, item 267.]

224   GUARIGLIA, GUGLIELMO. Movimenti profetico-salvifici in Africa
        e chiese separatiste nere, in La Chiesa e le trasformazioni
        sociali, politiche e culturali dell' Africa Nera. Milan:
        Vita e Pensiero 1961, 133-152.

225   GUARIGLIA, G[UGLIELMO]. Les grandes caractéristiques des
        sectes modernes (mouvements prophético-salvifiques) dans
        les terres de mission, in Devant les sectes non-chrétiennes,
        item 312, 13-27.

226   GUARIGLIA, GUGLIELMO. Gli aspetti etno-sociologici della fame
        nel mondo, in Il problema della fame nel mondo. Milan:
        Vita e Pensierio 1964, 248 p.
        [Pp. 57-61 on prophetic-salvation movements, in Africa
        as elsewhere, as reactions to economic distress.]

227   GUARIGLIA, GUGLIELMO. Pour une nouvelle typologie des
        "mouvements prophétiques" au niveau ethnologique, in Actes
        du VIe Congres international des Sciences anthropologiques
        et ethnologiques. Paris: Musée de l'Homme, Tome 2 (2),
        1964, 393-398.

228   HARRIS, JOHN H[OBBIS]. Dawn in darkest Africa. London:
        Smith Elder 1912, xxxvi + 308 p. Facs. repr. London:
        F. Cass 1968. Plates, illus., maps.
        [Pp. 287-289, on African secession churches and their
        dangers.]

229   HASTINGS, ADRIAN. Church and mission in modern Africa.
        London: Burns and Oates 1967, 263 p.
        [Pp. 140, 144, 234-235, causes of Protestant secession.]

230   HASTINGS, ADRIAN. Independent churches: short reading list.
        African Ecclesiastical Review 11 (4), 1969, 417-419.

231   HASTINGS, ADRIAN. Mission and ministry. London and Sydney:
        Sheed and Ward 1971, 214 p.
        [The concluding chapter, pp. 192-214, is a good summary
        of African independency.]

General

232   HASTINGS, ADRIAN. African Christianity. An essay in inter-
      pretation. London and Dublin: Geoffrey Chapman 1976,
      vi + 105 p.
      [Independent churches discussed as integral part of
      African Christianity. See index for individual leaders
      and bodies; e.g. Kimbangu and Kimbanguists, pp. 1, 11-12,
      17-19, 26, 27, 32, 53, 71; Church of the Lord (Aladura),
      27-28, 72; Isaiah and J. G. Shembe, 26-27, 71.]

233   HATZIMICHALI, N. L'église orthodoxe grecque et le messianisme
      en Afrique. Social Compass (Louvain) 22 (1), 1975, 85-95.

234   HAYWARD, VICTOR E. W. (ed.). African independent church move-
      ments. Ecumenical Review 15 (2), 1963, 192-202. Also
      International Review of Missions, no. 206=52, April 1963,
      163-172. Fr. trans., Mouvements ecclésiastiques
      indépendentes en Afrique. Église vivante (Paris-Louvain)
      15 (1), 1963, 18-32.
      [The Mindolo Consultation Statement of 1962; a sympathetic
      evaluation of these movements by the older churches.]

235   HAYWARD, VICTOR E. W. (ed.). African independent church move-
      ments. London: Edinburgh House Press, 1963, 94 p., bibl.
      [Some of the papers given at an Ecumenical Consultation
      on African Independent Churches held at Kitwe, Zambia, in
      September 1962. Includes the consultation's statement and
      a classification of modern African religious groups by
      H. W. Turner. See items: Adejunmobi, 95; Beetham 134;
      Lehmann 276; Mitchell 304; Sundkler 373; Pauw, 1820.]

236   HELANDER, GUNNAR. Must we introduce monogamy? Pietermaritz-
      burg: Shuter and Shooter 1958, 69 p.
      [Sympathetic study of polygamy as a mission problem in
      South Africa, but of general relevance to independent
      movements.]

237   HERSKOVITS, MELVILLE J[EAN]. The human factor in changing
      Africa. New York: Knopf 1962, 1v + 500 p.
      [Pp. 215-216, 417-429, separatist churches, messianic
      movements etc., and their causes.]

238   HEWITT, GORDON. The problems of success: a history of the
      Church Missionary Society 1910-1942. I: In tropical
      Africa, the Middle East, at Home. London: S.C.M. Press
      (for the Church Missionary Society) 1971, xx + 506 p.
      [Pp. 37-39, outline of the "African" and "Prophet"
      churches; p. 91, the Garrick Braide prophet movement;
      pp. 64-65, Reformed Ogboni Fraternity, in Nigeria; pp. 138,

142, the Revival in Kenya; pp. 239-241, 252 in Uganda;
pp. 271-272 in Rwanda; pp. 215-217, the independent Malakite
and African Orthodox Churches.]

239 HODGKIN, THOMAS [LIONEL]. Nationalism and colonial Africa.
London: Frederick Muller 1956, 216 p.
[Pp. 93-114, role of prophets and priests; p. 153, as
Protestant phenomena.]

240 HOEKENDIJK, JOHANNES C. "Ontwakend Afrika" en de Zending.
Wending: Maandblad voor Evangelie en Cultuur (The Hague)
15, 1960, 281-301.
[Pp. 283-287, new religious movements and Negritude as
signs of a long-continuing development rather than as an
"awakening"; brief characterizations based on Sundkler and
Schlosser.]

241 HOLAS, B[OHUMIL THÉOPHILE]. Sur la position des religions
traditionelles dans l'Ouest africain. Monde Non-Chrétien
(Paris) n.s. 26, juin-juillet 1953, 183-192.
[On the cartography and classification of religions in
Africa; pp. 190-192, on 'new cults'.]

242 HOLAS, B[OHUMIL THÉOPHILE]. Ouvrages et articles 1944-1962.
Paris: Paul Geuthner 1962, 69 p.
[A digest of the works of Holas, many of which are in-
cluded in this bibliography.]

243 HOLAS, BOHUMIL [THÉOPHILE]. L'Afrique noire. Paris: Bloud
and Gay 1964, 115 p., illus.
[Includes separatist churches and prophet movements
concerned with a "black Christ" and escapist in tendency.]

244 HOLAS, BOHUMIL [THÉOPHILE]. Les dieux d'Afrique noire. Paris:
Librairie Orientaliste Paul Geuthner S. A. 1968, 284 p.
[Pp. 236-249, "Mouvements séparatistes dérivés du
Christianisme" - secession and prophet-founded forms;
surveys of South Africa, Congo and West Africa.]

245 HOLLENWEGER, WALTER J. Handbuch der Pfingstbewegung. Zürich
University, doctoral dissertation (Theology) 1965, 10 vols.
[Vol. 2, 325 pp., on Africa, includes all independent
churches influenced by Pentecostals. See also item 247.

246 HOLLENWEGER, WALTER J. Ministry to ministers: an outreach
to African independent churches. The Christian Minister
(Rondebosch, Cape Town) 3 (5), 1967, 15f. Also in
United Church Review (Kharar, North India) June 1967,
129-132.

Bibliography of New Religious Movements in Primal Societies

General

[A plea for the theological education of ministers in African independent churches.]

247 HOLLENWEGER, WALTER J. Enthusiastisches Christentum. Die Pfingstbewegung in Geschichte und Gegenwart. Wuppertal: Theologischer Verlag R. Brockhaus, and Zurich: Zwingli Verlag, 1969, 640 p., illus. Eng. trans., The Pentecostals: the Charismatic movement in the Churches. London: S.C.M. Press; Minneapolis: Augsburg Publishing House 1972, 572 p.
[Abridged version of item 245; pp. 68-70, 406-407, African material; and on South Africa - Ch. 9 on Andrew Murray, J. A. Dowie and the beginnings; Ch. 10 on Nicholas Bhengu; Ch. 11 on "Latter Rain" movement; Ch. 12 on the Spirit in the Bantu independent churches as a general survey.]

248 HOLLENWEGER, WALTER J. Pentecostalism and the Third World. Dialog (Minneapolis) 9 (2) 1970, 122-129.
[P. 124, comment on pentecostal features in African independent churches, seen in their actions rather than in their theology: pp. 125-126, the Kimbanguist reasons for joining the World Council of Churches.]

249 HOOD, GEORGE. In whole and in part: an examination of the relation between the selfhood of churches and their sharing in the universal Christian mission. (A report to the Conference of British Missionary Societies). London: the Conference, 2nd. edn. 1971, 103 p. and 51 p., appendices. Mimeo.
[Pp. 32-33, 35-36, 75, relationships with "independent-indigenous" churches, and what may be learned from them.]

250 HOPKINS, RAYMOND F. Christianity and socio-political change in sub-Saharan Africa. Social Forces 44 (4), 1966, 555-562.
[Mainly on effect of missions; explains the growth of independent churches by a learning theory model.]

251 HUP, WALTER. Sekten und Splitterkirchen in Afrika. Kirchenblatt für die Reformierte Schweiz (Basel) 120, 1964, 257-262.

252 INTERNATIONAL REVIEW OF MISSION. World survey, 1967-68: Africa. International Review of Mission no. 229=58, 1969, 33-47.
[Pp. 35, 38-40, "schism and renewal through African independent church movements", with special reference to the Kimbanguist Church.]

253 IRVINE, CECILIA. Report of a trip to Africa to investigate
   some Christian churches. Bulletin, Aberdeen University
   African Studies Group, 7, September 1971, 11–18.
      [A visit in early 1970; pp. 13–18 on independent
   churches – brief information on 15 countries.]

254 JAFFREYS [sic – for JEFFREYS] M. D. W. African tarantula or
   dancing mania. The Eastern Anthropologist (Lahore) 6 (2),
   1952–53, 98–105.
      [The Makka movement of the 1930s, in Bamenda Division,
   compared with other similar movements in Madagascar
   (Imanenjana, 1963), Kenya (Chesu, 1906, among Kamba),
   Nigeria (Spirit movement, Ibibio, 1927), and England (the
   Shakers).]

255 JANOSIK, ROBERT J. Religion and political involvement: a
   study of black African sects. Journal for the Scientific
   Study of Religion 13 (2), 1974, 161–175.
      [The greater political involvement of Kikuyu movements;
   analysis of explanatory factors such as "ideological
   purity".]

256 JOHNSON, WILLIAM W. The harvest work in Africa. The Watchtower 32 (2), 1911.
      [Jehovah's Witnesses' history of their early work in
   Africa.]

257 JUNG, H. Die Entchristlichung unter den Negervölkern.
   Aussenpolitik (Stuttgart) 11 (11), 1960, 750–757.
      [The transformation of Christianity among the Negro
   peoples of Africa, Central and S. America, etc., into
   'sects, spiritism and fetishism'.]

258 KAMPHAUSEN, HANNES. Bermerkungen zur geistigen Situation
   afrikanischer Eliten aus der Sicht der akkulturations-und
   Heilservartungspróblematic, in R. König (ed.), Aspekte der
   Entwicklungssoziologie (Kölner Zeitschrift für Soziologie
   und Sozialpsychologie, Sonderheft 13). Cologne and
   Opladen: Westdeutscher Verlag 1969, 93–121.

259 KARSTEDT, [FRANZ] OSKAR. Probleme afrikanischer
   Eingeborenpolitik. Berlin: Mittler und Sohn, 1942 vi +
   162 p.
      [Pp. 95–104, Watch Tower, and Ngunzism in Angola; p. 112,
   Thuku, a Kikuyu.]

260 KARSTEDT, [FRANZ] OSKAR and VON WERDER, PETER. Die
   afrikanische Arbeiterfrage. Berlin: de Gruyter 1941.

General

[Pp. 148-151, Watch Tower; p. 154, Chilembwe; p. 194f.,
Thuku in Kenya; p. 234, Enoch Mgijima.]

261   KIMBLE, GEORGE H[ERBERT] T[INLEY]. Tropical Africa. New York:
       Twentieth Century Fund 1960, 2 vols., illus., maps.
       [Vol. I, p. 275 and II, pp. 205-206 on Aiyetoro; Vol. II,
       pp. 90, 275-276 on syncretist and separatist movements;
       p. 279 on Watch Tower and p. 280, Garvey's African Ortho-
       dox Church as nationalist influence.]

262   KNOOB, WILLI J. Die Rolle des Propheten in den
       afrikanischchristlichen Sekten. Ethnologica (Cologne) 2,
       1960, 398-406.
       [Charismatic prophets correspond to traditional diviners,
       and fulfil political and economic as well as religious
       functions.]

263   KNOOB, WILLI J. Die afrikanisch-christlichen Bewegungen unter
       den Bantu. Ein Akkulturationsproblem. University of
       Cologne, doctoral dissertation, 1962. 80 p.
       [A dissertation on independent churches, based on
       secondary sources.]

264   LAGERWERF, LENY. Women in the Church: from influence to
       responsibility. Exchange (Leiden) 12, Dec. 1975, 2-79,
       bibl.
       [Pp. 43-53, women's roles in African independent
       churches.]

265   LAMONT, VICTOR (ed.). ...And some fell on good ground, Risk
       (Geneva) 7 (3), 1971, 62 p., illus. Fr. adaptation,
       Graines d'Evangile: Aperçu des Églises indépendantes
       africaines. Yaoundé: CLE 1973, 63 p.
       [Special theme – African independent churches; and see
       under contributors: W. B. Anderson; D. Aoko; D. B.
       Barrett; D. R. Jacobs; O. O. Okite; M. F. Perrin Jassy;
       K. I. Brown.]

266   LANTERNARI, VITTORIO. Fermenti religiosi e profezie di
       libertà dei popoli coloniali. Nuovi Argomenti (Rome) 37,
       1959, 54-92.

267   LANTERNARI, VITTORIO. Movimenti religiosi di libertà e di
       salvezza dei popoli oppressi. Milan: Feltrinelli 1960,
       366 p., bibl. 2nd. ed., 1974, xxix + 366 p. Fr. trans.,
       Les mouvements religieux de liberté de salut des peuples
       opprimés. Paris: Maspero 1962, 399 p. Eng. tr., The
       religions of the oppressed: a study of modern messianic

cults. London: MacGibbon & Kee 1963, xx + 343 + xiii p.;
New York: Knopf 1963 and Mentor Books 1965, xvi + 286 p.
Sp. trans., Movimentos religiosos de libertad y salvación
de los pueblos oprimides. Barcelona: Ed. Seix Barral
1965. German trans., Religiöser Freiheits-und
Heilsbewegungen unterdruckter Völker. Neuwied/Berlin:
Hermann Luchterhard Verlag 1966, 538 p.
 [Ch. 1, "Nativistic-religious movements in Africa":
p. 22-39, the Congo; pp. 39-49, South Africa; pp. 49-50,
Nyasaland; pp. 50-56, West Africa; pp. 56-58, "other movements. Religious movements in colonial areas are reactions
against oppression, anxiety and frustration, aggravated by
alienation of lands and race relations. New Italian impres-
sion, 1974, has new preface and updated bibliography. See
also: A book review.... Current Anthropology 6 (4), 1965,
447-465: fifteen reviews of Religions of the oppressed
together with a précis of the book, and reply to the
reviewers by Lanternari.]

268   LANTERNARI, VITTORIO. La chiesa e le religioni dissidenti
      d' Africa, d'Asia, Oceania e America. Ulisse (Rome) 15
      (7), 1962, 127-143.

269   LANTERNARI, VITTORIO. Convegno internazionale di Bouaké sui
      sincretismi e messianismi dell' Africa Nera. Rivista di
      Antropologia (Rome) 50, 1963, 213-230, bibl. (With
      English summary).
       [Important for the summaries of papers presented by
      Balandier, Desroche, Lanternari, Verger, Dieterlen, De
      Heusch, Raymaekers, Rouch, Bureau, Perrot and Baëta, at
      this conference held in October 1963; the papers have not
      been published elsewhere.]

270   LANTERNARI, VITTORIO. Profeti Negri e movimenti di liberazione
      in Africa. Sapere (Milan) Dec. 1964, 689-695.

271   LANTERNARI, VITTORIO. Syncrétismes, messianismes, néo-
      traditionalismes en Afrique noire. Archives de Sociologie
      des Religions (Paris) no. 19=10, jan.-juin 1965, 99-116,
      bibl.

272   LANTERNARI, VITTORIO. Syncrétismes, messianismes, néo-
      traditionalismes. Postface à une étude des mouvements
      religieux de l'Afrique noire. II. La situation post-
      coloniale. Archives de Sociologie des Religions no. 21=11,
      jan-juin, 1966, 101-110.
       [Continues item 271. Especially the Legio Maria in
      Kenya; the Lumpa rebellion in Zambia; the Songhay of Niger;

General

Lumumba cult in Zaïre; and Harris derivatives in Ivory
Coast and Ghana; a general movement to less Christian
neo-traditional forms.]

273   LANTERNARI, VITTORIO. Occidente e terzo mundo. Bari: Dedalo
           Libri, 1967, 539 p.
           [Chs. 4-6, passim, especially pp. 157-163, Mulélism;
           pp. 178-182, Kimbanguism; pp. 202-206, Legio Maria;
           pp. 208-211, Lumpa Chruch; ch. 7, general survey of other
           movements.]

274   LEDOUX, MARC-ANDRÉ. Les églises séparatistes d'Afrique et de
           Madagascar. Revue Française d'Études Politiques
           Africaines (Paris) 32, août 1968, 30-36.
           [Three types (Ethiopian, Zionist and Messianic), the
           changing attitudes of the older churches.]

275   LEENHARDT, R.-H. Schisme et responsibilités missionaires. Le
           Monde Non-Chrétien n.s. 88, oct.-déc. 1968, 23-27.
           [Review article on Barrett (1968).]

276   LEHMANN, DOROTHEA A. Women in the independent African churches,
           in Hayward, item 235, 65-69.
           [The appeal to women, in Southern and Central Africa.]

277   LEHMANN, J. P. La fonction thérapeutique du discours
           prophétique. Psychopathologie Africaine 8 (3), 1972,
           355-383.

278   LESSING, PIETER. Only hyenas laugh. London: Michael Joseph,
           1964 263 p.
           [Pp. 181-184, "new religions": separatist churches as
           "pseudo-Christianity" and playing an "increasingly impor-
           tant" part for African nationalism.]

279   LEWY, GUENTHER. Religion and revolution. New York: Oxford
           University Press 1974, 674 p.
           [Pp. 194-220, African "separatism" and millenarian
           movements: outline of the Israelites of Mgijima,
           Kimbanguism, Matswa, Kitawala, Lumpa Church as examples.]

280   LEYS, NORMAN [MACLEAN]. Kenya. London: Hogarth Press 1924,
           423 p. 4th. edition, with introduction by G. A. Shepperson,
           London: F. Cass 1973, xv + 425 p.
           [Pp. 212f., Thuku in Kenya; pp. 341-350 on Chilembwe, an
           important early source and the basis for subsequent
           accounts.]

281 LIENHARDT, R[ONALD] G[ODFREY]. Some African "Christians".
     Blackfriars (Oxford) No. 382=33, Jan. 1952. 14-21.
     [A positive approach to separatists, with a penetrating
     account of causes.]

282 LINZ, M. 'Black Muslims' und Bantukirchen. Evangelische
     Missions Zeitschrift 20 (1), 1963, 21-26.

283 LOWIE, ROBERT [H.]. Primitive messianism and an ethnological
     problem. Diogenes (Chicago) 19, Fall 1967, 62-72. (See
     also parallel editions in French, German, etc.)
     [An interpretation of messianism and nativism;
     pp. 67-68, brief references to Africa.]

284 LUNTADILA [MUSIANGANI] JEAN-CL. LUCIEN. Has Christianity a
     future in present-day Africa? Ministry (Morija, Lesotho)
     9 (4), 1969, 155-157.
     [The General Secretary of the Kimbanguist Church on
     Africanization, and on involvement with the State and with
     war.]

285 LUYKX, BONIFACE. Christian worship and the African soul.
     African Ecclesiastical Review (Masaka, Uganda) 7 (2),
     April 1965, 133-143.
     [Pp. 136, 143, a Roman Catholic missionary on 'the
     sects' in Africa, caused by demand for a congenial ritual;
     but are 'deviations from normal worship and even from
     human culture'.]

286 LYNCH, HOLLIS R[ALPH]. Edward Wilmot Blyden, Pan-Negro
     patriot, 1832-1912. (W. African History Series). London
     and New York: Oxford University Press 1967, xvi + 272 p.,
     3 plates.
     [Pp. 98-100, 221-227, Blyden's influence on the first
     "African" churches; pp. 238-240, his influence on
     M. Agbebi.]

287 MACKIE, STEVEN G. (ed). Can churches be compared? Reflections
     on fifteen study projects. (Research Pamphlet 17).
     Geneva: World Council of Churches; New York: Friendship
     Press; 1970, 101 p.
     [Ch. 5: Changes in self-definition: p. 57, East
     African revival; p. 62, Kimbanguism; pp. 67-69, "heresy",
     e.g. Etoism in Solomon Islands.]

288 MACONI, VITTORIO. Il profetismo in Africa. La Missione
     (Milan), giugno 1956, 19-27.

43

BIBLIOGRAPHY OF NEW RELIGIOUS MOVEMENTS IN PRIMAL SOCIETIES

General

289   MAIR, LUCY [PHILIP]. Independent religious movements in three
       continents. Comparative Studies in Society and History
       1 (2), 1959, 113-136. Reprinted in John Middleton (ed.),
       Gods and rituals. Garden City, N.Y.: American Museum of
       Natural History 1967, 307-335; and in her Anthropology and
       social change. London: Athlone Press, New York;
       Humanities Press, 1969, 144-172.
       [American Indian, Melanesian and African movements com-
       pared. See also Mead, item 302.]

290   MAIR, LUCY [PHILIP]. New nations. London: Weidenfeld and
       Nicolson, Chicago: University of Chicago Press, 1963,
       235 p.
       [Ch. 6: "New religions": pp. 172-173, 181, causes
       surveyed; 176-182, African messiahs (Kimbangu, Matswa,
       Mpadi); 182-185, independent churches and their causes;
       185-191, new magicans and witchfinders.]

291   MAIR, LUCY P[HILIP]. Witchcraft as a problem in the study of
       religion. Cahiers d'Études Africaines (Paris) no. 15=4
       (3), 1964, 335-348.
       [Pp. 347-348, the relation between anti-witchcraft and
       messianic movements.]

292   MAIR, LUCY [PHILIP]. Witchcraft (World University Library).
       London: Weidenfeld and Nicolson 1969, 254 p.
       [Pp. 164. 177-179, witchfinding in independent churches;
       pp. 172-177, witchfinding movements - Bamucapi,
       ChiNg'ang'a, Atinga.]

293   MARGULL, HANS JÖCHEN. Aufbruch zur Zukunft. Messianische
       Bewegungen in Afrika und Südostasien. Gütersloh: Gerd
       Mohn 128 p.
       [A theological study of chiliastic and messianic move-
       ments in Africa and S.E. Asia as post-Christian; Section 3,
       Kimbanguism and Matswa.]

294   MARTIN, MARIE-LOUISE. Le Messianisme en Afrique. Flambeau
       (Yaoundé) no. 12, nov. 1966, 201-212.
       [Pp. 207ff. on the Lumpa church.]

295   MARTIN, MARIE-LOUISE. Les églises indépendantes d'Afrique et
       l'Église de Jésus-Christ sur le terre par le prophète
       Simon Kimbangu, en particulier. Flambeau (Yaoundé) no. 29,
       fév. 1971, 41-49.

296   MAURIER, HENRI. Religion et développement. Traditions
       africaines et catéchèses (Esprit de Mission). Tours:
       Maison Mame 1965, 190 p.

44

[Pp. 28-32, "une solution imparfaite: les messianismes africaines", interpreted as neopagan movements; by a Roman Catholic.]

297   MAYATULA, VICTOR MASHWABADA. African independent churches' contribution to a relevant theology, in H.-J. Becken (ed.), Relevant theology for Africa. Durban: Lutheran Publishing House for Missiological Institute at LTC Mapumulo 1973, 174-180.
        [P. 186, report of discussion on this paper; see also pp. 189-190.]

298   MBITI, JOHN S[AMUEL]. Afrikanische Beiträge zur Christologie, in P. Beyerhaus et al. (eds.), Theologische Stimmen aus Asien, Afrika und Lateinamerika. III. Munich: Chr. Kaiser Verlag 1968, 72-85. Eng. trans., Some African concepts of Christology, in G. F. Vicedom (ed.), Christ and the younger churches. Theological contributions from Asia, Africa and Latin America (Theological Collection 15). London: S.P.C.K. 1972, 51-62.
        [Pp. 74-79, uses Turner (1965), item 463, for data in discussing African christological ideas.]

299   MBITI, JOHN S[AMUEL]. African religions and philosophy. London: Heinemann 1969, 290 p.
        [Pp. 28, 232-236, 255, independent churches; pp. 255-257, Bayudaya, an African Judaism.]

300   MBITI, JOHN [SAMUEL], et al. Faith, hope and love in the African independent church movement. Study Encounter 10 (3), 1974, 1-19.
        [Includes his experience in the Kanisa ya Isa Mesia; an African theologian's interpretation of independent churches, with reactions by four scholars.]

301   MBITI, JOHN S[AMUEL]. God, dreams and African militancy, in J. S. Pobee (ed.), Religion in a pluralistic society (Supplements to the Journal of Religion in Africa, 2). Leiden: E. J. Brill 1976, 38-47.
        [Pp. 39-41, 43, illustrate the place of dreams in independent African churches.]

302   MEAD, MARGARET. Independent religious movements. Comparative Studies in Society and History 1 (4), 1959, 324-329.
        [Commentary on Mair, item 289.]

General

303   MENDELSOHN, JACK. God, Allah and Juju: religion in Africa
        today. New York: Nelson 1962, 245 p.
        [Pp. 156-165 on "rebel churches in a restless land."
        Popular account.]

304   MITCHELL, ROBERT CAMERON. Christian healing, in V. Hayward
        (ed.), item 235, 47-51.
        [Healing as a widespread characteristic of independent
        churches with examples from the Aladura churches of
        western Nigeria.]

305   MITCHELL, ROBERT CAMERON. Africa's prophet movements. The
        Christian Century 81 (47), 18 Nov. 1964, 1427-1429. Germ.
        trans., Prophetische Sekten in Afrika. Zeitwende 36,
        1965, 193-196.
        [The Lumpa uprising in Zambia, 1964, in the general
        context of African prophet movements.]

306   MITCHELL, ROBERT CAMERON. Towards the sociology of religious
        independency. Journal of Religion in Africa 3 (1), 1970,
        2-21.
        [A critique of D. B. Barrett (1968). See Barrett's
        response in same issue, pp. 22-44.]

307   MIZAN NEWSLETTER, THE. Soviet views on the Christian churches
        in Africa. The Mizan Newsletter (Oxford) 3 (7), 1961,
        16-23.
        [Pp. 17-18, 22, summarizes Sharevskaya's and
        Lavretskiy's views on independent churches.]

308   MONTEIL, VINCENT. L'Islam noir (Collections Esprit "Frontière
        Ouverte"). Paris: Editions du Seuil 1964, 368 p., maps.
        [Pp. 189-192, Syncrétisme et prophétisme, a brief
        survey, chiefly with reference to the Ivory Coast and
        Kimbanguism, and with final reference to syncretisms in
        Brazil.]

309   MOORHOUSE, GEOFFREY. The missionaries. London: Eyre Methuen
        1973, 368 p., illus., maps.
        [Ch. 18, A Black Reformation - on independent churches,
        including pp. 313-319 on the Church of the Lord (Aladura)
        based on Turner (1967).]

310   MUCHABAIWA, ALEXIO. Christian adaptation in Africa, in D.
        Lucas (ed.), Church and African values. Kampala: Gaba
        Publications 1974, 1-14.
        [Pp. 7-10, Adaptation and the African independent
        churches - new church structures, brotherly love, ancestor
        cult.]

311   MURRAY, FRANK. The witness of a servant-church. African
      Ecclesiastical Review (Masaka) 13 (1), 1971, 3-10.
         [P. 3, acknowledges the loss of many Roman Catholic
      church members to "breakaway movements" in Kenya and
      Zambia.]

312   MUSEUM LESSIANUM. Devant les sectes non-chrétiennes.
      Louvain: Desclée de Brouwer n.d. [1962], 318 p.
         [Pp. 62-163 on African independent religious movements.
      Papers at the 31st Semaine de Missiologie, by Roman
      Catholic scholars; see items Van Bulck, 637; (Anon), 980;
      (Anon), 1145; Guariglia, 224; Wagner, 1883; Pich, 1309.]

313   MVENG, ENGELBERT. Traditional remnants in modern African
      sects. Bulletin, Secretariat for Non-Christians (Vatican
      City) 7 (2), 1972, 45-55. Fr. trans., Les survivances
      traditionelles dans les sectes chrétiennes africaines.
      Cahiers des Religions Africaines, no. 13=7, 1973, 63-76.

313   NEILL, STEPHEN [CHARLES]. A history of Christian missions.
      Harmondsworth, England; Baltimore, Pennsylvania: Penguin
      Books 1964, 622 p.
         [Pp. 497-502, challenge of independent churches to
      Christianity in Africa.]

315   NEILL, STEPHEN [CHARLES]. Christianisme et orientations
      syncrétiques, in: Centre d'Histoire de la Réforme et du
      Protestantisme, Université Paul Valéry, Montpellier, Les
      Missions Protestantes et l'Histoire: Actes du IIe
      Colloque (4-9 octobre 1971). Paris: Société de l'Histoire
      du Protestantisme Français (Etudes des Colloques, 2) n.d.
      [1972?], 23-45.
         [Pp. 32-36, independent African churches: African
      Brotherhood Church, Legio Maria, Kimbanguism, Shembe's
      Church, as non-Christian (based on Oosthuizen).]

316   NIDA, EUGENE A[LBERT]. Message and mission: the communication
      of the Christian faith. New York: Harper and Bros. 1960,
      253 p., illus.
         [Pp. 139-142, "nativistic movements" as including inde-
      pendent churches. By a Protestant missionary
      anthropologist.]

317   NIKLEWICZ, PIOTR. Religie synkretyczne czarnej Afryki i ich
      rola w tworzeniu nowej afrykańskiej świadomości
      ponadplemiennej [Syncretist religions of Black Africa -
      their role in formation of the new African supra-tribal
      consciousness]. Przeglad Socjologiczny (Łodz) 23, 1969,

General

260-283 (digest in Africana Bulletin [Warsaw] 14, 1971, 232-233).

318   OKITE, ODHIAMBO W.   The politics of African church indepen-
       dency.   Risk (Geneva) 7 (3), 1971, 42-45.

319   OKITE, ODHIAMBO W.   Politics of Africa's independent churches,
       in D. B. Barrett et al. (eds.), Kenya Churches Handbook.
       Kisumu: Evangel Publishing House 1973, 118-123.

320   OMONIYI, PRINCE BANDELE.   A defence of the Ethiopian movement.
       Edinburgh: 1908, xi + 124 p.
       [By a Yoruba.]

321   OMOYAJOWO, J[OSEPH] AKINYELE.   An African expression of Chris-
       tianity, in M. Motlabi (ed.), Essays on Black Theology.
       Braamfontein, Transvaal: University Christian Movement
       1972, 60-70; repr. in B. Moore (ed.), Black Theology: the
       South African Voice.   London: C. Hurst 1973, 81-92.
       [A survey article, indicating African features of inde-
       pendent churches, with reference to West African sources.]

322   O'NEILL, PATRICK.   Religious pluralism in Africa.   Worldmission
       26 (1), 1975, 10-15.
       [Pp. 12-13, "fringe groups of Christian schismatics or
       Pentecostals" - a conservative Catholic viewpoint.]

323   OOSTERWAL, GOTTFRIED.   Modern Messianic Movements as a theo-
       logical and missionary challenge (Missionary Studies, 2).
       Elkhart, Indiana: Institute of Mennonite Studies 1973,
       55 p.
       [By a Seventh Day Adventist missiologist, with the strong
       eschatological emphasis of his own tradition; proposes a
       "holistic understanding" in which theology provides the
       "creative center"; pre-contact movements are recognised
       since messianism is a widespread feature of religions.]

324   OOSTHUIZEN, GERHARDUS CORNELIS.   Die Konfrontasie met die
       onafhanklike kerklike bewegings ("Separatiste") in Afrika
       in die jongste sendingsteologie, in Sendingswetenskap
       Vandag - n'Terreinverkenning (Lux Mundi I).   Pretoria:
       N. G. Kerk-Boekhandel 1968, 197-225.
       [Lectures of the South Africa Missiological Society,
       1st Missiological Congress, 1968.]

325   OOSTHUIZEN, GERHARDUS C[ORNELIS].   The church among African
       forces.   Practical Anthropology (Tarrytown, N. Y.) 11 (4),
       1964, 161-179.

[Pp. 162, 164-165, generalizations about political,
millennial and healing aspects of separatist movements, by
a South African theologian.]

326   OOSTHUIZEN, G[ERHARDUS] C[ORNELIS]. Independent African
churches: sects on spontaneous development? A reply to
Dr. Alex Van Wyk. Ministry (Morija, Lesotho) 5 (3), 1965,
99-107.
[A theological examination leading to classification as
"post-Christian or anti-Christian cult communities".]

327   OOSTHUIZEN, GERHARDUS C[ORNELIS]. The misunderstanding of the
Holy Spirit in the independent movements in Africa, in
Christusprediking in de Wereld. Kampen, Holland: Kok
1965, 172-197.

328   OOSTHUIZEN, G[ERHARDUS] C[ORNELIS]. Causes of religious
independentism in Africa. \Fort Hare Papers (Fort Hare,
Cape Province) 4 (2), 1968, 13-28; repr., Fort Hare Uni-
versity Press, 1968. Reprinted also in Ministry (Morija,
Lesotho) 11 (4), 1971, 121-133.
[A comprehensive survey; reprint in Ministry contains
additional material on Nehemiah Tile as the "father of
Black theology", pp. 123-125.]

329   OOSTHUIZEN, G[ERHARDUS] C[ORNELIS]. Post-Christianity in
Africa. London: C. Hurst & Co. 1968, 273 p., illus.
[Chs. 2-4, 7-8, primarily on independent movements -
general survey, classification, main features, and theological critique of the eschatology, christology, pneuma-
tology and ecclesiology.]

330   OOSTHUIZEN, GERHARDUS CORNELIS. The independent religious
movements versus orthodoxism. A study of the theological
aspect. African Ecclesiatical Review 12 (4) 1970,
289-300.
[A more sympathetic survey than his previous writings;
the theological lessons for the older churches.]

331   PADMORE, GEORGE. How Britain rules Africa. London: Wishart
1936, 402 p. Ger. trans., Afrika unter dem Joch der
Weissen. Leipzig: Erlenbach-Zurich n.d., 458 p.
[Pp. 365-367 on "tribal 'religious' organizations"
especially Chilembwe, and Enoch Mgijima in South Africa
(pp. 417-421 in Germ. trans.).]

332   PADMORE, GEORGE. Pan Africanism or Communism? London:
Dobson 1956, 463 p., illus.

General

[Pp. 87-104, Marcus Garvey's African Orthodox Church
under Archbishop Alexander McGuire (West Indian) in U.S.A.,
with Black Christ and Black Madonna; influence alleged on
dissident nationalist churches in Africa.]

333   PARRINDER, E[DWARD] GEOFFREY [SIMONS]. Witchcraft: European
      and African. London: Faber and Faber (1958) 1963. 215 p.
          [Pp. 170-180, Bamucapi in Central Africa and a first
      hand account of Atinga movement in Benin (Dahomey) and
      Nigeria, c. 1950.]

334   PARRINDER, [EDWARD] GEOFFREY [SIMONS]. Traditional religions
      and modern culture (Africa) Proceedings of the XIth Inter-
      national Congress of the International Association for the
      History of religions. Vol. I. Leiden: Brill, 1968,
      99-113.
          [Pp. 105-108, survey of causes and general features of
      "independent African churches"; pp. 112-113, Islamic
      separatism.]

335   PARRINDER [EDWARD] GEOFFREY [SIMONS]. Religion in Africa.
      Harmondsworth: Penguin 1969, 253 p., map. Second edition
      published as Africa's three religions. London: Sheldon
      Press 1976.
          [Pp. 114-115, 138f., 146, 149-163, "independency", a
      general historical survey.]

336   PEREIRA DE QUEIROZ, MARIA ISAURA. O messianismo no Brasil e
      no mundo. (Ciências Socias, Dominus 5). São Paulo:
      Editôra de Universidade de São Paulo 1965, 374 p.
          [Pp. 35-50, "Movimentos messiânicos africanos". Based
      largely on Balandier, Eberhardt and Sundkler.]

337   PEREIRA DE QUEIROZ, MARIA ISAURA. Messianic myths and move-
      ments. Diogenes (Paris) no. 90, Spring 1975, 78-99.
          [Messianism caused by crises due to oppression of in-
      justice, or to internal disorganization and anomie, in
      societies based on lineage; actual movements depend on
      presence of an individual as leader; examples from Africa
      etc., but more valuable from Brazil.]

338   PERRIN JASSY, MARIE-FRANCE. Women in the African independent
      churches. Risk (Geneva) 7 (3), 1971, 46-49, illus.

339   PHILIPPS, J. E. T. The tide of colour. I. Pan-African and
      anti-White. Journal of the African Society no. 82=21,
      Jan. 1922, 129-135.

[P. 130, brief reference to 1915 "Ethiopian rising" in
Nyasaland, and Nabingi society in Rwanda; pp. 133-134,
American connections with Ethiopianism; p. 134, Congo
secret sects.]

340   QUÉCHON, MARTINE. Réflexions sur certaines aspects du syn-
       crétisme dans l'islam ouest-africain. Cahiers d'Etudes
       Africaines 11 (2), 1971, 206-230.
       [Islamic-African syncretism examined by Lanternari's
       theories as worked out for Christian syncretism; p. 227,
       Laye sect.]

341   RANGER, TERENCE O[SBORN]. Connections between "primary
       resistance" movements and modern mass nationalism in East
       and Central Africa. Journal of African History 9 (3),
       1968, 437-453; 9 (4), 1968, 631-641. Also abridged in
       Robert O. Collins (ed.), Problems in the history of Colo-
       nial Africa 1860-1960. Englewood Cliffs, N. J.: Prentice-
       Hall, Inc., 1970, 351-360.
       [Includes "millennial" movements such as Maji Maji,
       Nyabingi, Mumbo, Dini ya Msambwa, Shona-Ndebele, and Kwilu
       rebellion.]

342   RANGER, TERENCE O[SBORN]. African attempts to control educa-
       tion in East and Central Africa, 1900 to 1939. Past and
       Present no. 32, Dec. 1965, 57-85.
       [Independent schools and their connection with indepen-
       dent churches.]

343   REHWALDT, HERMANN. Geheimbunde in Afrika. Munich: Ludendorff
       1941, 67 p.
       [Pp. 15ff., a national church for the Pedi; p. 17, Watch
       Tower; p. 21, Thuku; pp. 53f., Kausapala in Angola c. 1928.]

344   RETIF, ANDRÉ. Pullulement des 'églises' nègres. Études
       (Paris) no. 302=7, sep. 1959, 186-195. Germ. trans.,
       Religiöser Wildwuchs in Africa. Die Katholischen Missionen
       (Freiburg) 80, 1961, 43-47.
       [A Roman Catholic survey of various areas; interpretation
       as mixtures of paganism and Christianity, and as anti-
       white and political in nature.]

345   REYBURN, WILLIAM D. Quelques réflexions sur les mouvements
       ecclésiastiques indépendants en Afrique. Flambeau
       (Yaoundé) no. 22, mai 1969, 95-100.

346   REYBURN, WILLIAM D. Schism and renewal in Africa ..by David
       Barrett.......Review Article. Practical Anthropology
       (Tarrytown, N. Y.) 17 (3), 1970, 137-144.

General

347   RICHTER, JULIUS. Geschichte der evangelischen Mission in
        Afrika. Gütersloh: C. Bertelsmann 1922, viii + 813 p.
        [P. 111, Harris; pp. 141f., Braide; pp. 274f., Ntsikana;
        pp. 364F., Ethiopianism; pp. 566-568, Booth; pp. 572-573,
        Chilembwe; et passim.]

348   RISK (Geneva) 7 (3), 1971. See under LAMONT, VICTOR, item
        265.

349   ROTBERG, ROBERT I. Resistance and rebellion in British Nyasa-
        land and German East Africa, 1888-1915: a tentative com-
        parison, in P. Gifford and W. R. Louis (eds.), Britain and
        Germany in Africa: imperial rivalry and colonial rule.
        New Haven, Conn.; Yale University Press, 1967, 667-690.
        [Pp. 676-678, Booth, Chilembwe and Kamwana; pp. 678-683,
        689, Maji-Maji; p. 683-690, the Chilembwe rising.]

350   SASTRE, ROBERT. Christianisme et cultures africaines. Tam-
        Tam (Paris) 6 (7), 1957, 12-23. Eng. trans., Theology and
        African culture. Présence Africaine (Paris) 24-25, Feb.-
        May 1959, 142-152.
        [A Roman Catholic priest interprets messianism and
        independent churches as a response to Christianity in terms
        of spiritual emancipation.]

351   SCHLOSSER, KATESA. Propheten in Afrika. Braunschweig:
        A. Limbach 1949, 426 p., bibl., map.
        [Important survey of sixty-eight African prophets,
        divided into three types: traditional, Muslim, and Chris-
        tian. Extensive bibliography.]

352   SCHLOSSER, KATESA. Der Prophetismus in niederen Kulturen.
        Zeitschrift für Ethnologie (Berlin) 75, 1950, 60-72.

353   SCHOLZ, DIETER. The sociological background of African inde-
        pendent churches, in Rhodesian Mission Seminar (Berlin
        Kladow, August 1967). Heythrop, England: Heythrop College,
        1967, 90-96. Mimeo.
        [Pp. 90-94, Kimbanguism; pp. 94-95, Lumpa Church;
        pp. 95-96, South African movements.]

354   SCHUTTE, ANDRIES GERHARDUS. Die nativistischen Bewegungen als
        Handlungsabläufe. Eine Untersuchung nach den Ablaufsregeln.
        University of Heidelberg, Phil. Doc. dissertation, 1969.
        235 + 21 p., bibl.
        [A comparative sociological study of Mau Mau and
        Kimbangu/Ngunza movements, and the Paliau movement in the
        Admiralty Islands, New Guinea.]

355 SEMI-BI, ZAN. Messianismes et retour aux sources religieuses
     africaines (évolution historique). L'Afrique Littéraire
     et Artistique (Paris) 28, avril 1973, 36-41.
        [A survey; comments on a-political nature in West Africa.]

356 SHAREVSKAYA, B. I. Religioznaya politika Angliyskogo
     imperializma v Angliyshikh koloniyakh Afriki. [The reli-
     gious policy of British imperialism in British possessions
     in Africa.] Moscow: Gos-Politizdat 1950.
        [Includes African Christian sects interpreted from an
     Orthodox Soviet viewpoint as protest movements, by the
     leading Soviet writer on religion in Africa.]

357 SHAREVSKAYA, B. I. Staryye i Novyye Religi Tropicheskoy i
     Yushnoy Afriki. [Old and new religions of tropical and
     southern Africa.] Moscow: Izdatelstvo Nauka 1964, 387 p.,
     bibl.
        [Ch. 6, South Africa: section 2, the "Ethiopian movement".
     Ch. 7, Congo Basin: section 2, Kimbanguism and other move-
     ments, 1920-1950. Ch. 8, Tropical East Africa: includes
     "anti-colonial religio-political movements". Ch. 9,
     Tropical West Africa: Section 2, the formation of inde-
     pendent churches and sects. A major Russian study with
     extensive bibl., incl. Russian works.]

358 SHEJAVALI, ABISAI. The influence of the concept of the tradi-
     tional African leadership on the concept of the Church
     leadership. Africa Theological Journal (Makumira,
     Tanzania) 1, Feb. 1968, 75-82.
        [P. 80, critical account of independent churches by a
     Tanzanian Lutheran.]

359 SHENK, WILBERT R. Mission agency and African Independent
     churches. International Review of Mission no. 251=63,
     Oct. 1974, 475-491.
        [On the attitude and activities of American Mennonite
     Missions.]

360 SHEPHERD, R. H. W. The Separatist churches of South Africa.
     International Review of Missions No. 104=26, Oct. 1937,
     453-463.
        [A brief outline, with general comments on causes.]

361 SHEPPERSON, GEORGE [ALCOTT]. Ethiopianism and African nation-
     alism. Phylon (Atlanta) 14 (1), 1953, 9-18, bibl. Repr.
     in I. Wallerstein (ed.), Social change. The colonial
     situation. New York: J. Wiley, 1966, 478-488.

General

[Uses Ethiopian and Zionist categories in a general
treatment of the political role of independent churches.]

362   SHEPPERSON G[EORGE ALCOTT]. Notes on Negro American influ-
      ences on the emergence of African nationalism. Journal of
      African History 1 (2), 1960, 299-312. Repr. in W. J. Hanna
      (ed.), Independent Black Africa: the politics of freedom.
      Chicago: Rand McNally, 1964, 192-207.
      [Pp. 304-307 on Ethiopianism in South and Central Africa;
      pp. 309-310 on the African Church of Majola Agbebi in
      Nigeria.]

363   SHEPPERSON, GEORGE A[LCOTT]. External factors in the develop-
      ment of African nationalism, with particular reference to
      British Central Africa. Phylon (Atlanta) 22 (3), 1961,
      207-225.
      [Short discussion of prophets' role, mentioning
      Chilembwe, Harris, etc.]

364   SHEPPERSON, GEORGE A[LCOTT]. The comparative study of mil-
      lenarian movements, in S. L. Thrupp (ed.), item 69, 44-52.
      [Various terms currently used of African movements are
      distinguished.]

365   SHEPPERSON, GEORGE [ALCOTT]. Pan-Africanism and 'pan-
      africanism'. Phylon (Atlanta) 25 (4), 1962, 351-352,
      355, 357.
      ["Ethiopianism", the origins and applications of the
      term.]

366   SHEPPERSON, GEORGE [ALCOTT]. Church and sect in Central
      Africa. Rhodes-Livingstone Journal, 33, June 1963, 82-94.
      [A review article: Taylor and Lehmann (1961), item 1579;
      Sundkler (1961), item 1866; Welbourn (1961), item 1217;
      with further information.]

367   SHEPPERSON, GEORGE ALCOTT. Religion and the city in Africa:
      a historian's observations, in Urbanization in African
      social change, item 398, 141-150.
      [Pp. 147-149 on separatism.]

368   SHEPPERSON, G[EORGE ALCOTT]. Ethiopianism: past and present,
      in C. G. Baëta (ed.), item 112, 249-268.

369   SHORTER, AYLWARD. African culture and the Christian church:
      an introduction to social and pastoral anthropology.
      London: Geoffrey Chapman 1973, xi + 229 p., illus.

[Pp. 23-24, 206-212, independent churches, their typologies, causes and contributions, based on Sundkler,
Welbourn, Barrett, Turner, Oosthuizen and Murphree.]

370 SIK, ENDRE. Histoire de l'Afrique noire. Vol. II. Budapest:
Akademia Kiado 1964, 346 p., illus., bibl.
[Interprets African religious movements as having
"important role in organization of peasant movements"
which were an early expression of class consciousness.
P. 52, Chilembwe; p. 59, Malaki; p. 71, Braide; p. 78,
Harris; pp. 292-293, also pp. 130-131, Kimbangu. French
translation of Hungarian original.]

371 SPAZNIKOV, G. A. Religii stran Afriki. Moscow: Samma förlga
1967, 210 p.
[With summaries in Eng. and Fr.; includes "Christian-
African churches and sects", which "combine Christianity
with local traditional cults, especially with the cult of
ancestors".]

372 SUNDKLER, B[ENGT GUSTAF MALCOLM]. Sektenwesen in den jungen
Kirchen, in Die Religionen in Geschichte und Gegenwart.
Tubingen: Mohr, 3rd. ed. 1961, vol. V, columns 1664-1666.
[Independent churches in Africa.]

373 SUNDKLER, BENGT [GUSTAF MALCOLM]. What is at stake? (2) in
V. W. Hayward (ed.), item 235, 30-32.
[General statement on relationship of mission churches
to independent churches; special reference to Nyanza
independents in Kenya.]

374 SUNDKLER, BENGT [GUSTAF MALCOLM]. The one church and the
challenge of the independent churches, in: Association of
East African Theological Colleges, Christ and culture.
Report on conference at Limuru, 1964, 65-69. Mimeo.

375 SUNDKLER, BENGT G[USTAF] M[ALCOLM]. Historical factors in the
development of various forms of ministry in Africa. Credo
(Durban) 18 (1), 1971, 17-25.
[Includes the exercise of church discipline in independent churches as an example of team ministry.]

376 SUNDKLER, BENGT GUSTAF MALCOLM. Frälsningsförväntan i Afrika
[Salvation and expectation in Africa]. Svensk Missions
Tidskrift 60 (4), 1972, 172-182.
[Salvation as related to African thought and experience;
African independent churches, passim; his later interpre-
tation of messianic figures as God's "eikons", rather than
as "Black Christs".]

General

377   SURET-CANALE, JEAN. Afrique noire occidentale et centrale –
      l'ère coloniale (1900-1945). Paris: Editions Sociales
      1964, 640 p.
         [P. 543ff., on religious movements.]

378   TAMBARAN CONFERENCE SERIES. Vol. IV. The life of the church.
      London: Oxford University Press 1939.
         [Pp. 404-407, on the importance of reckoning with
      independency.]

379   TAYLOR, JOHN V[ERNON]. Saints or heretics? in J. Hermelink
      et al. (eds.), Basileia. Stuttgart: Evangelische
      Missionsverlag 1959, 305-312.
         [On the Cherubim and Seraphim, Lagos; the Lumpa Church
      and Emilio's "Children of the Sacred Heart", Zambia.]

380   TAYLOR, JOHN V[ERNON]. An African Christianity. CMS News-
      letter (London) 331, October 1969, 1-4.
         [Review article on Barrett, item 127.]

381   TERRY-THOMPSON, A[RTHUR] C[ORNELIUS]. The history of the
      African Orthodox Church. New York: Beacon Press 1956,
      139 p., illus.
         [On Garvey's church, which influenced African Churches
      in South and East Africa. Pp. 81-82, Archbishop
      Alexander.]

382   THOMAS, L. V. L'Eglise chrétienne d'Afrique noire. Tam-Tam
      (Paris) 7-8, déc. 1963, 7-21.
         [Includes "deformations" of the church found in syn-
      cretist movements and independent churches.]

383   THWAITE, DANIEL. The seething African pot. A study of black
      nationalism, 1882-1835. London: Constable 1935, 248 p.
         [Pp. 64ff. on African prophets, especially in Zaïre and
      Angola; by an opponent of African nationalism.]

384   TURNER, HAROLD W[ALTER]. African prophet movements. Hibbert
      Journal (London) no. 242=61, Apr. 1963, 112-116.
         [A general survey of causes.]

385   TURNER, H[AROLD] W[ALTER]. Modern African religious movements:
      an introduction for the Christian churches. Nsukka:
      Department of Religion, University of Nigeria, revised
      edn. 1965, 10 p. Mimeo.

386   TURNER, H[AROLD] W[ALTER]. Politics and prophets: a Nigerian
       test-case. Bulletin of the Society for African Church
       History (Aberdeen) 2 (1), 1965, 97-118.
            [The conflict between governments and prophets, with
       special reference to the prosecution of Garrick
       Braide.]

387   TURNER, H[AROLD] W[ALTER]. Monogamy: a mark of the church?
       International Review of Missions no. 219=55 (July), 1966,
       313-321.
            [Theological refutation of the view that polygamy dis-
       qualifies African groups from acceptance as Christian
       churches.]

388   TURNER, H[AROLD] W[ALTER]. Problems in the study of African
       independent churches. Numen (Leiden) 13 (1), 1966,
       27-42.
            [The problem of evidence in religion, and of partici-
       pation, commitment, objectivity and detachment, in the
       African context.]

389   TURNER, HAROLD W[ALTER]. African religious movements and
       Roman Catholicism, in H. J. Greschat and H. Jungraithmayr
       (eds.), Wort und Religion..., item 218, 255-264.
            [A critique of the thesis that these movements are
       solely Protestant phenomena; new material on the Holy Face
       Church and the prophetess Veronica in Eastern Nigeria.]

390   TURNER, HAROLD W[ALTER]. The place of independent religious
       movements in the modernization of Africa. Journal of
       Religion in Africa (Leiden) 2 (1), 1969, 43-63.

391   TURNER, HAROLD [WALTER]. Dynamic religion in Africa. Learning
       for Living (London) 12 (5), 1973, 3-7.
            [Pp. 5-7 on African independent churches, in the context
       of new movements elsewhere and of Christian history as a
       whole.]

392   TURNER, HAROLD W[ALTER]. A further dimension for missions:
       new religious movements in the primal societies. Inter-
       national Review of Mission no. 247=62 (July), 1973,
       321-337.

393   TURNER, HAROLD WALTER. Tribal religious movements, new.
       Encyclopaedia Britannica 1974, vol. 18, 697-705; also same
       title in Micropaedia series, 1974, vol. 10, 115, for
       location of brief articles on individual movements -
       African Greek Orthodox Church, Aiyetoro, Aladura, Braide,

General

Ethiopianism, Harris movement, Kimbanguist Church, Lumpa
Church, Maria Legio, Shembe's Nazarite Church, Zionist
churches.
[A theoretical and historical survey.]

394   TURNER, HAROLD W[ALTER]. African independent churches and
      education. Journal of Modern African Studies 13 (2),
      1975, 295-308.

395   TURNER, H[AROLD] W[ALTER]. New religious movements in primal
      societies. World Faiths no. 95, 1975, 5-10.

396   TURNER, HAROLD W[ALTER]. The study of new religious movements
      in Africa, 1968-1975. Religion. Journal of religion and
      religions 6 (1), 1976, 88-98.
      [A survey article.]

397   UGONNA, NABUENYI. The rise of creative Ethiopianism: the
      pan-Africanist literary influence. Pan African Journal
      (Nairobi) 6 (1), 1973, 1-14.
      [The rise of the Ethiopian movement in Africa and its
      progression from churches to politics.]

398   URBANIZATION IN AFRICAN SOCIAL CHANGE. Edinburgh: Centre of
      African Studies, University of Edinburgh, 1963, Mimeo.
      [See Hair, item 908; Shepperson, item 367; Mayer,
      item 1792.]

399   VAN CAMPENHOUDT, ANDRÉ. Séparatisme et pastorale en Afrique
      noire. L'Eglise Vivante (Louvain) 22 (5), 1970, 352-365.
      [A sympathetic approach, with willingness to learn from
      independency and to understand its causes; suggestions for
      the assistance which the Catholic Church may be better
      placed to offer than some other bodies; draws especially
      upon Barrett (1968).]

400   VAN DER POORT, CORNELIS. Anciennes at nouvelles tendances dans
      la littérature socio-religieuse. Revue-Congolaise des
      Sciences Humaines (Kisangani), juillet 1970, 79-88.
      [Review article on E. Andersson (1968) on Congo-
      Brazzaville churches, and D. B. Barrett (1968) on African
      independent churches.]

401   VAN LANGENHOVE, FERNAND. Consciences tribales et nationales
      en Afrique noire. The Hague: N. Nijhoff, Brussels:
      Institut Royal des Relations Internationales, 1960, 465 p.,
      bibl.

[Pp. 195-221, "Réactions politico-religieuses": based largely on Balandier, also Van Wing, Kenyatta and Paulus; pp. 368-374, Mau Mau.]

402 VAZ, JOSÉ. Do paganismo pré-christão ao neo-paganismo anti-christão. Portugal em Africa (Lisbon) no. 151=26, 1969, 19-32.
[Pp. 26-32, Os movimentos salvificos e de libertação.]

403 VERSTRAELEN, F. J. Assistentie aan en door onafhankelijke kerken. Wereld en Zending (Amsterdam) 2 (1), 1973, 35-45.
[Includes a discussion of the African Independent Church Conference in Rhodesia (associated with M. L. Daneel) and of M.-F. Perrin Jassy's study of Luo independency.]

404 VILAKAZI, ABSOLOM. African religious concepts and the separatist movements. Paper read to the Second Annual Conference, American Society of African Culture, New York, 1959, 10 p. Mimeo.
[Based on field work among his own people, the Zulu; sympathetic.]

405 VON SICARD, SIGVARD. Is he not the God of Africa also? Bulletin, Evangelical Fellowship for Missionary Studies no. 4, n.d. [1974], 14-21.
[Pp. 16-17, the significance of the independent churches for African theology.]

406 WAINWRIGHT, GEOFFREY. The localization of worship. Studia Liturgica 8 (1), 1971-72, 26-41.
[Pp. 38-41 specifically on Kimbanguist worship; otherwise relevant to all independent churches.]

407 WALLERSTEIN, IMMANUEL. Voluntary associations, in J. S. Coleman and C. G. Rosberg, Jr., (eds.), Political parties and national integration in tropical Africa. Berkeley and Los Angeles: University of California Press, 1964, 308-339.
[Pp. 329-330 on new religious groups.]

408 WALLS, A[NDREW] F[INLAY]. African church history: some recent studies. Journal of Ecclesiastical History 23 (2), 1972, 161-169.
[Review article: includes Turner (1967), Barrett (1968), Haliburton (1971).]

General

409   WARREN, MAX A. C.   In the CMS Newsletter, London.   No. 240,
        July 1961, 3-5, reflections on Field, item 528 and
        Welbourn 1217; No. 254, Nov. 1962, on Pentecostalism, with
        reference to Turner, items 458 and 459; No. 259, Apr.
        1963, on the Holy Chapel of Miracles, Nigeria.

410   WATT, W. W. (Chairman).   Religion in Africa.   Edinburgh:
        Centre for African Studies, University of Edinburgh, 1964,
        130 p.   Mimeo.
        [See H. J. Fisher, item 432; T. O. Ranger, item 1514;
        G. Shepperson, item 1476.]

411   WEBSTER, J[AMES] B[ERTIN].   Independent Christians in Africa.
        Tarikh (London) 3 (1), 1969, 56-81, illus.
        [A general survey, from a position that is especially
        critical of missionaries and whites.]

412   WELBOURN, F[REDERICK] B[URKEWOOD].   The missionary culture, in
        D. M. Paton (ed.), Essays in Anglican Self-Criticism.
        London: S.C.M. Press 1958, 238 p.
        [Pp. 65-68, brief references to independent churches, in
        connection with polygamy, nationalism and culture.]

413   WEMAN, HENRY.   The new praise in ancient tunes, in P. Beyerhaus
        and C. F. Hallenkreutz (eds.), The church crossing
        frontiers.   Essays...in honour of Bengt Sundkler (Studia
        Missionalia Upsaliensia XI).   Lund: Gleerup 1969,
        177-188.
        [P. 187, the "folk-music" of independent churches.]

414   WERNER, ALICE.   Myths and legends of the Bantu.   London:
        Harrap 1933, 335 p., illus.
        [Pp. 239-246 on traditional prophets and Chaminuka in
        Mashonaland, Mohlomi of the Basuto, and the religious
        origins of the Maji Maji rebellion in Tanganyika.]

415   WILLIAMS, DENNIS and VERRYN, TREVOR.   Pentecostalism.   A
        research report.   Waterkloof, Pretoria: Ecumenical
        Research Unit, n.d. [1972?], 44 p.   Mimeo.
        [Pp. 27-29, attempt to present Zionist African inde-
        pendent Churches as examples of world Pentecostalism.]

416   WILLIS, ROY.   The magical roots of African political power.
        New Society no. 328=13, 9 Jan. 1969, 47-49.
        [Chikanga and subsequent Tanzanian healing/witchfinding
        movements, early 1960s; Rice Kamanga's "church" among Lozi
        in Zambia (1960s?); Nuer prophets; Kimbangu and A. Matswa;
        Mau Mau; all as examples of mystical powers.]

417   WILLOUGHBY, W[ILLIAM] C[HARLES]. The soul of the Bantu. New
      York: Doubleday Doran 1928, 476 p.
      [Pp. 104-112, revelation by "possession"; 112-135,
      revelation by "prophets" - Chibisa, Makana, Mhlakaza,
      Marethe, Mgijima, Kimbangu, etc.; et passim: see
      "prophets" in index.]

418   WILSON, MONICA. The changing society, in P. Beyerhaus and
      C. F. Hallencreutz (eds.), The Church crossing frontiers.
      Essays...in honour of Bengt Sundkler (Studia Missionalia
      Upsaliensia XI). Lund: Gleerup 1969, 83-89.
      [The significance of African independent religious
      movements for the churches and the student of society with
      tribute to Sundkler's pioneering work.]

419   WORSLEY, PETER M. Millenarian movements in Melanesia. Rhodes-
      Livingstone Journal, 21, 1957, 18-31. Repr. in
      J. Middleton (ed.), Gods and Rituals. Garden City, N.Y.:
      American Museum of Natural History 1967, 337-352. Fr.
      trans. in J. Middleton (ed.), Anthropologie religieuse.
      Les dieux et les rites, textes fondamentaux. Paris:
      Larousse 1974, 167-180.
      [Includes comparative reference to millenial movements
      in Africa.]

420   ZAJĄCZKOWSKI, ANDRZEJ. Ruchy religijne w Afryce [The syncretic
      movements of Africa]. Przeglad Socjologiczny (Łodz) 23,
      1969, 284-306, digest in Africana Bulletin (Warsaw) 14,
      1971, 229-230.
      [Mainly on Harris and Déima movements; main value is to
      give security in an era of transformation.]

421   ZARETSKY, IRVING I. (comp.). Bibliography on spirit possession
      and spirit mediumship. Evanston: Northwestern University
      Press 1966, xvi + 106 p.
      [Primarily on sub-Saharan Africa, and traditional
      religions, but includes some prophet and similar movements.]

422   ZEITZ, LEONARD. Some African Messianic movements and their
      political implications. Paper read to the second Annual
      Conference, American Society of African Culture, New York
      1959, 42 p. Mimeo.
      [A general account of South African movements; brief
      accounts of Harris and the Watch Tower Society; longer
      treatment of Kimbanguism.]

West Africa

423 AGBEBI, MOJOLA. Inaugural sermon delivered at the celebration
     of the first anniversary of the "African Church", Lagos,
     West Africa, December 21, 1902. Yonkers, N. Y.: E. F.
     Horworth, printer n.d. [1903], 31 p.
        [Pp. 1-15, the sermon; p. 16, author's note; pp. 17-20,
     "The religion for the African", letter from "the Hon.
     E. W. Blyden, LL.D. Prince of Negro prophets"; pp. 21-31,
     press and other comments on the sermon. In the Schomburg
     Collection, N.Y.C.]

424 AGBEBI, MOJOLA. An account of Dr. Mojola Agbebi's work in
     West Africa, comprising Yorubaland, Fantiland, the Ekiti
     country, Central Nigeria, Southern Nigeria and the
     Cameroons. n.p. [New Calabar]: n.d. [?1904], 40 p.,
     illus.
        [Reprints of letters and press articles.]

425 AGBEBI, MOJOLA. The West African problem, in G. Spiller (ed.),
     Papers on inter-racial problems communicated to the First
     Universal Races Congress ... 1911. London: P. S. King
     & Co., 1911, 341-348. Pp. 343-348 repr. in H. S. Wilson,
     Origins of West African nationalism. London: Macmillan
     1969, 304-308.
        [A rationale for African practices, including secret
     societies, human sacrifice, cannibalism and polygamy; by
     the notable independent Baptist.]

426 AGBEBI, MOJOLA (comp.), assisted by Chief James Horsfall,
     Prince Charles Batabo, Chief Sokari Amakri and others.
     The Christian Handbook. New Calabar, West Africa: n.p.
     n.d., [17 p.]
        [Contents: Lord's Prayer, Creed, Ten Commandments,
     Church Covenant, passages from the Bible, Hymns,
     Benediction.]

427 ALEXANDRE, PIERRE [HIPPOLYTE HENRI CHARLES]. A West African
     Islamic movement: Hamallism in French West Africa, in
     R. I. Rotberg and A. A. Mazrui (eds.), Protest and power

West Africa

in Black Africa. New York: Oxford University Press
1970, 497–512.
[Includes comparisons with Chilembwe, Kimbangu, and
Matswa.]

428 BLYDEN, EDWARD WILMOT. The return of the exiles and the West
African Church (A lecture at Breadfruit School House,
Lagos, 2/1/91). London: W. B. Whittingham 1891, 39 p.
See also African Repository 68, 1892, 1–18. Pp. 24–33
repr. in part in H. R. Lynch (ed.), Black spokesman.
London: F. Cass 1971, 191–194.
[An independent church that would make its own serious
mistakes, but had Crowther's work to encourage it.]

429 COOKSEY, JOSEPH JAMES and McCLEISH, ALEXANDER. Religion and
civilization in West Africa: a missionary survey of
French, British, Spanish and Portuguese West Africa with
Liberia. London: World Dominion Press 1931, vi + 277 p.
[Pp. 55–71, 135–141, 251, Harris; p. 678, Prophet
Loxzema at Sassandra; p. 141, Oppong.]

430 ECUMENICAL REVIEW (Geneva), The Church of the Lord (Aladura).
The Ecumenical Review 24 (2), 1972, 121–129; repr. in
Ecumenical Exercises III (Faith and Order Paper, 61),
Geneva: W.C.C. 1972, 3–11.
[One of the World Council of Churches surveys, based on
materials from Church members.]

431 EDWARDS, ADRIAN C. The study of religion in West Africa,
1959–69. Religion: Journal of Religion and Religions 2
(1), 1972, 42–56.
[Places the study of independency within the wider context, with special references to Baëta (1962), Webster
(1964), Turner (1967), Peel (1968).]

432 FISHER, HUMPHREY J[OHN]. Muslim and Christian separatism in
Africa, in W. M. Watt (ed.), Religion in Africa, item 410,
9–23.
[Description of West African Muslim separatism and comparison with some characteristics of Christian separatism.]

433 FISHER, HUMPHREY J[OHN]. Separatism in West Africa, in
J. Kritzeck and W. H. Lewis (eds.), Islam in Africa. New
York: Van Nostrand-Reinhold Co. 1969, 127–140, bibl.
[Pp. 139–140. comparisons of Christian and Muslim sepa-
ratism; otherwise on four examples of Muslim separatism –
the Murids, Hamallists, "coastal fever", and Ahmadiyya.]

434 FISHER, HUMPHREY J[OHN]. Independency and Islam: the Nigerian aladuras and some Muslim comparisons. Journal of African History 11 (2), 1970, 269-277.
[A review article on J. D. Y. Peel (1968) and H. W. Turner (1967), together with detailed Islamic (especially Ahmadiyya) comparisons.]

435 THE FOREIGN FIELD. The challenge of West Africa. The Foreign Field (London: Wesleyan Methodist), September 1922, p. 221.
[On the movements derived from Harris and Oppong.]

436 FROELICH, JEAN CLAUDE. Review of Le séparatisme religieux en Afrique noire (B. Holas, 1965). Revue de Psychologie des Peuples (The Hague) 20 (4), 1965, 474-482.

437 GOUILLY, ALPHONSE. L'Islam dans l'Afrique Occidentale française. Paris: Ed. Larose 1952, 318 p., map, illus.
[Pp. 134-161 (and see index), Hamallism; pp. 167-169, "la secte Layenne" of Limahou Laye (1843-1909).]

438 GRESCHAT, HANS-JURGEN. Westafrikanische Propheten. Morphologie einer religiösen Spezialisierung (Marburger Studien zur Afrika-und Asienkunde, Serie A: Afrika - Band 4). [Berlin: Dietrich Reimer] 1974, 113 p.

439 HALIBURTON, GORDON MacKAY. The prophet Harris, a study of an African prophet and his mass-movement in the Ivory Coast and the Gold Coast, 1913-1915. Harlow: Longman 1971, xxii + 250 p., maps, illus.; New York: Oxford University Press 1973, xv + 155 p., illus. [Shortened version]
[A definitive historical study.]

440 LITTLE, KENNETH. West African urbanization: a study of voluntary associations in social change. Cambridge: Cambridge University Press 1965, 179 p.
[Pp. 35-47, 93-95, et passim, "syncretist cults" and independent churches, especially in Ghana (after Fiawoo, item 523).]

441 LLOYD, PETER CUTT. Africa in social change: changing traditional societies in the modern world. Harmondsworth: Penguin 1967, 364 p.
[Pp. 255-263, witchfinding movements and "new sects", with West African examples.]

442 LYNCH, HOLLIS R. Edward Blyden, Pan-Negro Patriot 1832-1912 (West Africa History Series). London: Oxford University Press 1967, 290 p., 3 plates.

West Africa

[Pp. 98-100, 221-227, Blyden's influence on the first "African" churches; pp. 238-240, his influence on M. Agbebi.]

443 MITCHELL, HUGH (ed.). The vision glorious. A report of the work of the Apostolic Church missionary movement. Bradford: Apostolic Church n.d. (c. 1949), 41 p., illus.
[Pp. 20-23, Nigeria (photo of Pastor G. Perfect); pp. 28-30, Gold Coast (photos of Pastors J. McKeown and J. Anaman etc.) with reference to Faith Tabernacle Church.]

444 MUSSON, MARGARET. Prophet Harris: the amazing story of Old Pa Union Jack. Wallington, U.K.: Religious Education Press 1950, 111 p., illus.
[Popular, imaginative, inaccurate reconstruction.]

445 PARRINDER, [EDWARD] GEOFFREY [SIMONS]. West African religion. London: Epworth Press 1949, xii + 223 p., map. 2nd edition, revised and enlarged, London: Epworth Press 1961, xv + 203 p.
[Pp. 190, 193, "separatist churches; pp. 191-193, neo-pagan movements.]

446 PILKINGTON, F. W. "Old Man Union Jack": William Wade Harris, prophet of West Africa. West African Review (London) no. 293=23, Feb. 1952, 122-125.

447 PLATT, W[ILLIAM] J. An African prophet. The Ivory Coast Movement and what became of it. London: S.C.M. Press 1934, 157 p.
[Prophet Harris of the Ivory Coast; pp. 81-83, some reference to Kimbangu; pp. 84-86, to Sampson Oppong; by the Methodist missionary who "discovered" the Harris movement.]

448 QUECHON, MARTINE. Réflexions sur certains aspects du syncrétisme dans l'Islam ouest-africain. Cahiers d'Études Africaines no. 42=11 (2), 1971, 206-230.
[Uses Lanternari's theoretical framework for examining Islamic phenomena parallel to African Christian syncretisms.]

449 RINGWALD, WALTER. Westafrikanische Propheten. Evangelische Missions-Zeitschrift (Stuttgart) 1 (4), 1940, 118-122; idem 1 (5), 1940, 145-155.
[In Nigeria and, particularly, in Ghana.]

450 RYTZ, O. Das wiederwachende reliogiöse Selbstbewusstein der
     nichtchristlichen Völker und die Mission in Afrika.
     Evangelisches Missions Magazin (Basel) 91, 1947, 12-18.

451 SARPONG, PETER K[WASI]. Why the Aladura? A thoughtful
     answer. Pastoral Institute Newsletter (Bodija, Ibadan)
     no. 66, 31 August 1974, p. 7.
     [Repr. from the Ghana Standard no. 26, 1974; on the
     African demand for immediate results from divine action;
     by a Ghanaian Roman Catholic bishop.]

452 SAWYERR, HARRY ALFONSO EBUN. Creative evangelism. London:
     Lutterworth Press 1968, 183 p.
     [P. 97, Ghana "spiritual churches" as Judaistic Chris-
     tianity; pp. 97-100, support for this view from the text
     of seven "divinations" or messages to individuals in
     Sierra Leone - probably by a Church of the Lord (Aladura)
     prophet.]

453 SCHUTZ, L[OUIS]. William Wade Harris und seine Massenbewegung.
     Evangelisches Missions Magazin (Basel) 86 (3), 1942,
     83-92.

454 SMITH, [J.] NOEL. The Presbyterian Church of Ghana 1835-1960:
     a younger church in a changing society. Accra: Ghana
     Universities Press 1966, 304 p., illus., maps.
     [Pp. 132-133, the 1906 Aberewa cult in Ivory Coast;
     pp. 255-261, "semi-orthodox 'African' healing churches",
     based largely on Baëta (1962); pp. 261-266, new forms of
     traditional cults and shrines, such as Tigare.]

455 SPIESS, K. Religiöse Verirrungen unter Heidenchristen. Neue
     Allgemeine Missionszeitschrift 3, 1926, 137-142.

456 SYLLA, ASSANE. Les persécutions de Seydina Mouhamadou
     Limamou Lâye par les autorités coloniales. Bulletin IFAN
     Sér. B, 33 (3), 1971, 590-641.
     [A Senegal Islamic movement in the 1880s.]

457 TASIE, G[ODWIN] O[NYEMEACHI] M[GBECHI]. Christian awakening
     in West Africa 1914-1918: a study of the significance of
     native agency. West African Religion (Nsukka) 16 (2),
     1975, 45-60.
     [On Harris of Liberia and Braide of Eastern Nigeria.]

458 TURNER, HAROLD W[ALTER]. The litany of an independent West
     African church. Sierra Leone Bulletin of Religion 1 (2),
     1959, 48-55. Also in Practical Anthropology (Tarrytown,
     N. Y.) 7 (6), 1960, 256-262.

West Africa

> [An analysis of a Church of the Lord (Aladura) text –
> see item 459.]

459   TURNER, HAROLD W[ALTER]. The catechism of an independent West
       African church. Sierra Leone Bulletin of Religion 2 (2),
       1960, 45–57. Also in Occasional Papers (International
       Missionary Council, London) 9 April 1961, 10 p. Also
       Germ. trans., Katechismen unabhängiger westafrikanischer
       Kirchen, in E. Benz, item 137, 72–88.
       [An analysis of a text from the Church of the Lord
       (Aladura); comparisons with two Ghanaian and two Kimbanguist
       catechisms.]

460   TURNER, HAROLD W[ALTER]. Searching and syncretism: a West
       African documentation. International Review of Missions
       no. 194=49 (April), 1960, 189–194. Also in Practical
       Anthropology (Tarrytown, N. Y.) 8 (3), 1961, 106–110.
       [An analysis of the religious literature possessed by a
       member of an aladura church.]

461   TURNER, HAROLD W[ALTER]. The Church of the Lord: the expan-
       sion of a Nigerian independent church in Sierra Leone and
       Ghana. Journal of African History 3 (1), 1962, 91–110.

462   TURNER, H[AROLD] W[ALTER]. Pagan features in West African
       independent churches. Practical Anthropology (Tarrytown,
       N. Y.) 12 (4), 1965, 145–151.
       [Such features are not confined to the independent
       churches, nor derived entirely from indigenous religions.]

463   TURNER, H[AROLD] W[ALTER]. Profile through preaching. A
       study of the sermon texts used in a West African indepen-
       dent church (C.W.M.E. Research Pamphlets No. 13). London:
       Edinburgh House Press 1965, 88 p.
       [The Church of the Lord (Aladura): visual profiles
       derived from an analysis of 8,000 texts.]

464   TURNER, HAROLD WALTER. African independent church. Vol. 1,
       History of an African independent church: the Church of
       the Lord (Aladura). Vol. 2, African independent church:
       the life and faith of the Church of the Lord (Aladura).
       Oxford: Clarendon Press 1967, 217 and 391 p., illus.,
       maps.
       [A comprehensive study in depth, including phenomeno-
       logical description and theological analysis; extension
       of a Nigerian church into West Africa.]

465 WALKER, F[RANK] DEAVILLE. The day of harvest in the white
fields of Africa. London: Cargate Press n.d. [1925],
80 p., illus.
[Ch. 1, prophet Harris, with photo; pp. 16-18, Sampson
Oppong, with photo; pp. 71-79 on Platt and the Harris
movement.]

466 WALKER, F[RANK] D[EAVILLE]. Harris le prophète noir. Privas
(Ardèche): Pasteur Delattre, 1931, 191 p., illus.

467 WESLEYAN METHODIST MISSIONARY SOCIETY, London. Reports. See
No. 101 (1914), 1915, 163-166; no. 102 (1915), 1916, 149-
150; no. 106 (1919), 1920, 73-74; no. 107 (1920), 1921,
80-81; no. 112 (1925), 1926, 81-85; and others from 1923
to 1928.
[The Harris movement, first in Apollonia, Gold Coast,
then in Ivory Coast.]

468 WILSON, H[ENRY] S[UMMERVILLE]. E. W. Blyden on religion in
Africa. Sierra Leone Bulletin of Religion 2 (2), 1960,
58-66.
[Esp. pp. 64-65 on Africanizing Christianity, and his
role in the foundation of the United Native African Church
in Lagos.]

469 WOLD, JOSEPH CONRAD. God's impatience in Liberia (Church
Growth Series). Grand Rapids, Michigan: W. B. Eerdmans
1968, 226 p.
[Pp. 117-122, the Harris movement as an example of a
"people" or mass movement.]

470 YATES, WALTER LADELL. The history of the African Methodist
Episcopal Zion Church in West Africa: Liberia, Gold Coast
(Ghana) and Nigeria, 1900-1939. Hartford Seminary Founda-
tion, Ph.D. dissertation 1967, xiv + 398 p.
[Ch. 4 includes the schism and re-union of the African
National Church.]

471 ZARWAN, JOHN. William Wade Harris: the genesis of an African
religious movement. Missiology (Pasadena) 3 (4), 1975,
431-450.

BENIN (DAHOMEY)

472 LOMBARD, J. Cotonou, ville Africaine. Études Dahoméennes
(Porto Novo, Benin) 10, 1953, 179-187.

West Africa

>   [Pp. 186-188, on new religious movements imported from
>   Nigeria including the Cherubim and Seraphim Society and
>   the United Native African Church.]

473   PARRINDER, E[DWARD] GEOFFREY [SIMONS]. Les sociétés
      religieuses en Afrique occidentale. Présence Africaine
      n.s. 17-18, fev.-mai 1958, 17-22.
      [A brief account of several independent churches in
      Porto Novo.]

See also items 160, 202, 206, 333, 805.

CAMEROON

474   BRITISH GOVERNMENT. Report on Cameroons under British mandate
      for the year 1930. London: HMSO 1931. Colonial No. 64.
      [Pp. 9, 12, brief account of prophetess Makaiya in
      Bamenda and Manfe Divisions in 1930.]

475   BRUTSCH, L. R. Origine et développement d'une église
      indépendante africaine. L'Eglise Baptiste Camerounaise.
      Le Monde Non-Chrétien (Paris) n.s. 12, oct.-déc. 1949,
      408-424.

476   BUREAU, RENÉ. Flux et reflux de la christianisation
      camerounaise. Archives de Sociologie des Religions
      no. 17=9 (jan.-juin), 1964, 97-112. Repr. (abbr.) in
      Jeunes Églises (Bruges) no. 23=7, 1965, 28-32.
      [P. 110 on the relative lack of syncretisms in the
      Cameroon.]

477   BUREAU, RENÉ. Influence de la Christianisation sur les
      institutions traditionelles des ethnies côtières du
      Cameroun, in Baëta, item 112, 165-181.
      [The crisis after the first impact of Christianity,
      producing a situation in which some synthesis of the new
      religion and traditional culture is required.]

478   CHRISTOL, FRANK. Quatre ans au Cameroun. Paris: Société des
      Missions Evangéliques de Paris 1922, 246 p., illus.
      [Letters from a French missionary. Brief description
      of the Native Baptist Church.]

479   COLIGNON, A. Le véritable histoire de Marie aux Léopards.
      Paris, 1933.
          [Prophetess Sombe or Maria among the Kundu, 1915. Viewed
      as a charlatan.]

480   HODGKIN, THOMAS [LIONEL]. The French Cameroons. West Africa
      (London) 27 Nov. 1954, p. 1109, and 4 Dec. 1954, p. 1133.
          [Native Baptist Church in Doula, including reference to
      role of the Garvey movement.]

481   HORNER, NORMAN A. Cross and crucifix in mission. New York:
      Abingdon 1965, 223 p.
          [Pp. 51-52, the "Ngoumba Independent Church" (correct
      name: Église protestante africaine) among the Ngoumba, a
      secession from the Presbyterian Church of Cameroon on the
      issue of their vernacular.]

482   HUGHES, W[ILLIAM]. Dark Africa and the way out or a scheme
      for civilizing and evangelizing the dark continent.
      London: Sampson Low 1892, 155 p.; facs. repr., New York:
      Negro Universities Press 1969.
          [Pp. 31, 71, 72, brief description of the Native Baptist
      Church.]

483   JADOT, J.-M. Sous les Manguiers en fleurs. Histoires de
      bantous. Paris: Ed. de Belles-Lettres 1922, 225 p.
          [Includes reference to prophetess Sombe or Maria, among
      the Kundu 1915, as a genuine seer.]

484   KWAST, LLOYD EMERSON. West Cameroon Baptist Church growth.
      Fuller Theological Seminary, School of World Mission, M.A.
      thesis 1968, 319 p.; also, abbreviated, as The discipling
      of West Cameroon. Grand Rapids: Eerdmans 1971, 205 p.
          [Pp. 218-221 of thesis: separatistic and syncretistic
      religious movements - Baptist Church of Cameroon (polyg-
      amous), "prayer cults", and Cherubim and Seraphim from
      Nigeria.]

485   MALLO, EUGÈNE. Rapports entre jeunes églises. Flambeau
      (Yaoundé) 5, fév. 1965, 37-39.
          [Brief definitions of two kinds of independent churches -
      formed by secession, or as new formations; brief evalua-
      tion of independents in the Cameroon context.]

486   MARTIN, FLAVIUS. Ebenezer Baptist Church, Victoria, West
      Cameroon, 1858-1965. Victoria, Cameroon: Basel Mission
      Press 1965.
          [A brief study, includes the secession and return.]

West Africa

487 MVENG, ENGELBERT. Histoire du Cameroun. Paris: Présence
    Africaine 1963, 533 p.
    [Pp. 457-458, the Native Baptist Church and other
    independents.]

488 RUDIN, HARRY R. Germans in the Cameroons 1884-1914 (Yale
    Historical Publications: Studies 12). New Haven: Yale
    University Press 1938, 456 p.
    [Pp. 361-363, Native Baptist Church - various divisions
    1888 to 1898.]

THE GAMBIA

489 The GAMBIA OUTLOOK (Banjul). Three cheers! For Prophet John:
    the saboteurs and confusionists failed. (See also letter
    to the Editor). The Gambia Outlook, 17 July 1973, p. 1
    etc.
    [Enthusiastic reports on a visiting Ghanaian healer.]

490 The PROGRESSIVE NEWSPAPER (Banjul). Editorial: By their
    fruits ye shall know them. The Progressive Newspaper
    no. 500, 23 July 1973, 1-2.
    [A highly critical report on Prophet John Yeboah, a
    Ghanaian healer. See also in subsequent issue: Beware,
    "Prophet" John Yeboah - reporting enquiries being made
    from the Ghanaian authorities.]

GHANA

491 ACQUAH, IONÉ. Religion. Accra survey. London: University
    of London Press 1958. 176 p.
    [Pp. 148-150, a brief survey with statistics of churches
    in Accra founded by Africans.]

492 ANQUANDAH, JAMES R. The Christian torn between the world and
    his faith, in God's mission to Ghana. Accra: Asempa
    Publishers 1974, 48-59.
    [Text of an address at a church leaders' conference 1973;
    reasons why members of "orthodox" churches seek the help
    of independent churches.]

493 APEA-ANIM, PETER NEWMAN. The history of how Full Gospel Church
    was founded in Ghana (then Gold Coast Colony). n.p.
    [Accra?]: the author, n.d., 13 p., photo.

72

[The Ghanaian parallel to the Nigerian influence of the American Faith Tabernacle and the British Apostolic Church on an indigenous movement, from 1917 to the Ghana Apostolic Church of 1953.]

494 ARMSTRONG, CHARLES W. The appeal of Apolonia. The Foreign Field (London: Wesleyan Methodist) April 1915, 209-211.
     [The Harris movement.]

495 ARMSTRONG, CHARLES W. The winning of West Africa. London: Wesleyan Methodist Missionary Society 1920, 64 p.
     [Ch. 4, "The Apolonian movement"; a summary of the work of Harris in West Ghana.]

496 BAËTA, C[HRISTIAN] G[ONÇALVES KWAMI]. Prophetism in Ghana: a study of some 'spiritual' churches. London: SCM Press 1962, 169.
     [Includes the Church of the Twelve Apostles, Musama Disco Christo Church, the Saviour Church, the Apostolic Revelation Society and the Prayer and Healing Society of the Evangelical Presbyterian Church.]

497 BAËTA, C[HRISTIAN] G[ONÇALVES KWAMI]. Christianity and heal-ing. Orita (Ibadan) 1 (2), 1967, 51-61.
     [Ghanaian "healing sects" and their methods, set in the context of Christian history.]

498 BAËTA, C[HRISTIAN] G[ONÇALVES KWAMI]. Aspects of religion, in W. Birmingham et al. (eds.), A study of contemporary Ghana, Vol. 2, Some aspects of social structure. London: George Allen and Unwin 1967, 240-250.
     [Pp. 247-248, brief outline of "spiritual churches"; p. 249, some statistics for African Methodist Episcopal Zion, Apostolic, and African Christian groups.]

499 BARKER, PETER. Glimpses into Ghana. Outreach (Guildford, USCL) 9 (2), 1973, p. 1.
     [Brief description of the Saviour Church.]

500 BARTELS, F. L. The roots of Ghana Methodism. Cambridge: Cambridge University Press 1965, 368 p.
     [P. 82, the Akonomnsu ("water drinkers") of the 1860s; pp. 161-163, Majola Agbebi in 1902, early Ethiopianism and the Basel Mission in 1905, the African Methodist Episcopal Zion Church under Pinanko; pp. 174-178, prophet Harris; p. 188, African Methodist Episcopal Zion Church. By a Ghanaian historian.]

West Africa

501   BECKMANN, DAVID M. Eden Revival. Spiritual Churches in Ghana.
      St. Louis, MO; London: Concordia Publishing House 1975,
      144 p.
            [Published version of a Concordia Seminary B.D. disserta-
      tion based on personal participation in the Eden Revival
      Church (1962-) of Yeboah-Korie, earlier published in off-
      set form, 1973, by World Mission Institute, Concordia
      Seminary, St. Louis. (Name changed to Feden Church, 1975).]

502   BREIDENBACH, PAUL S[TANLEY]. Sunsun Edwuma, the spiritual
      work: forms of symbolic action and communication in a
      Ghanaian healing movement. Northwestern University, Ph.D.
      dissertation 1973, 430 p., maps, tables.
            [Church of the Twelve Apostles, in southwestern Ghana.]

503   BREIDENBACH, PAUL S[TANLEY]. Spacial juxtaposition and belief
      orientations in a ritual of a Ghanaian healing movement.
      Journal of Religion in Africa 7 (2), 1975, 92-110.
            [Church of the Twelve Apostles.]

504   BROKENSHA, DAVID W. Social change at Larteh, Ghana. Oxford:
      Clarendon Press 1966, 249 p., illus.
            [Pp. 25-32, the churches, including five independents,
      and their relations to traditional customs.]

505   BRUCE, ERNEST. I grew up with history. African Challenge
      (Lagos) 7 (4), April 1957, 6-10.
            [Personal reminiscences of Prophet Harris by a Ghanaian
      Methodist minister (d. 1963).]

506   CARSTAIRS, G. M. A view from the shrine. The Listener
      (London) no. 1666=65 (2 Mar.), 1961, 387-389, illus.
            [Comparison of modern West African and Indian shrines
      and their priests, using M. J. Field, item 528.]

507   CERULLI, ERNESTA. La setta dei Water Carriers. Studi e
      Materiali per la Storia delle Religioni (Rome) 34 (1),
      1963, 27-29.
            [A syncretist Harris derivative among the Nzemba (sic,=
      Nzima) with healing emphasis.]

508   CHING, D[ONALD] S. Ivory tales. London: Epworth Press 1950,
      126 p.
            [Pp. 95-124, a summary account of Harris, by a Methodist
      missionary.]

509   CHRIST APOSTOLIC CHURCH OF GHANA. Constitution. The Church,
      n.d. [1964], 31 p.

510   CHRISTENSEN, JAMES BOYD. The Tigare cult of West Africa.
      Papers of the Michigan Academy of Science, Arts and Letters
      (Chicago) 39, 1954, 389-398.
      [A neo-traditional cult.]

511   CHRISTENSEN, JAMES BOYD. The adaptive functions of Fanti
      priesthood, in W. Bascom and M. J. Herskovits (eds.),
      Continuity and change in African cultures. Chicago:
      University of Chicago Press 1959, 257-278.
         [Concise analysis of the impact of Christianity on tra-
      ditional Fanti religion, with concluding section on "new
      cults" - Tigare.]

512   CHRISTIAN MESSENGER (Accra). See: 6 (3), March 1965, pp. 1,
      6; 6 (5), May 1965, p. 2.
         [Report of a debate in Ghana National Assembly on
      "prophets" and "sects".]

513   DEBRUNNER, HANS W[ERNER]. Witchcraft in Ghana. London: Brown
      Knight and Truscott (1959) 1961, 209 p., illus.
         [Chs. 20 and 21, "African healing churches and witch-
      craft" and "A witch-hunting prophet".]

514   DEBRUNNER, HANS W[ERNER]. The story of Sampson Oppong, the
      prophet. Accra: Waterville Publishing House 1965, 37 p.,
      illus.
         [Based on a personal interview.]

515   DEBRUNNER, HANS W[ERNER]. A history of Christianity in Ghana.
      Accra: Waterville Publishing House 1967, xi + 375 p.,
      illus., maps, bibl.
         [P. 33, Yota Mission of P. Chei as a new community;
      pp. 269-277, Harris and derivative churches; pp. 310-311,
      Sampson Oppong; pp. 319-320, new cults; pp. 321-327, pen-
      tecostal and similar churches; pp. 329-333, 345-348, heal-
      ing churches.]

516   DE WILSON, GEÓRGE. The biography of Prophet John Mensah.
      Cape Coast (Ghana): the author n.d. [ca. 1960], 42 p.
         [On the founder of the "Church of Christ (Spiritual
      Movement)" 1959, at Cape Coast. By a Ghanaian.]

517   DICKSON, KWESI A. The "Methodist Society": a sect. Ghana
      Bulletin of Theology (Legon) 2 (6), 1962, 1-7.
         [A short-lived secession in Ghana in the 1860s.]

518   EDEN REVIVAL CHURCH. The Edenian (Accra) 1 (1-2), 1968; then
      as The Torch 1 (3), June 1968 - .
         [The Church journal. (From 1975, Feden Church).]

West Africa

519   EDEN REVIVAL CHURCH. Handbook: Christianity original re-
      enacted. Accra: the Church 1971, 68 p., illus.
         [A comprehensive account – history of the church and of
      its founder, Yeboa-Korie; doctrine, worship, organization,
      social activities, testimonies. (From 1975, Feden Church).]

520   EPHSON, ISAAC S. Gallery of Gold Coast Celebrities 1632-1958.
      Vol. 1. Accra: Ilen Publications Ltd., 1969, 147 p.
         [Pp. 75-78, M. C. Hayford (1863-1935); pp. 110f.
      Frank A. O. Pinanko (1875-1945), a founder of the A.M.E.
      Zion Church in Ghana.]

521   FAITH BROTHERHOOD PRAYING CIRCLE. Constitution and aims.
      Accra: the Circle n.d. [1967?], 16 p.
         [Founded 1967 by Prophet F. A. Mills.]

522   FERNANDEZ, JAMES W[ILLIAM]. Rededication and prophetism in
      Ghana. Cahiers d'Etudes Africaines 10 (2), 1970,
      228-305, illus.
         [The Apostolic Revelation Society of C. K. Wovenu.]

523   FIAWOO, D. K. The influence of contemporary social changes on
      the magico-religious concepts and organization of Southern
      Ewe-speaking people of Ghana. Edinburgh University, Ph.D.
      dissertation (Social Anthropology) 1959, 374 p.
         [Reference to various neo-traditional movements; Atike,
      Elekete and their role in social change. See Little,
      item 440.]

524   FIAWOO, D. K. Urbanization and religion in Eastern Ghana.
      Sociological Review (Keele) n.s. 7 (1), 1959, 83-97.
         [Pp. 93-94, the communal life of the Apostolic Revela-
      tion Society at Tadzewu.]

525   FIAWOO, D. K. From cult to church: a study of some aspects
      of religious change in Ghana (Ewe examples). Ghana
      Journal of Sociology (Legon) 4 (2), 1968, 72-87.
         [Atike or medicine cults as syncretistic adjustment
      movements, similar to Christian cults and including both
      Christians and non-Christians.]

526   FIELD, M[ARGARET] J[OYCE]. Some new shrines of the Gold Coast
      and their significance. Africa (London) 13 (2), 1940,
      138-149.
         [Revival of traditional methods to deal with new
      problems.]

527   FIELD, M[ARGARET] J[OYCE]. Akim-Kotoku, an 'oman' of the Gold
      Coast. London: Crown Agents for the Colonies 1948, viii
      + 211 p.
        [Pp. 171-197, on new cults relating traditional prac-
      tices to modern life.]

528   FIELD, M[ARGARET] J[OYCE]. Search for security: an ethno-
      psychiatric survey of rural Ghana. London: Faber and
      Faber 1960, 478 p.; repr..New York: Norton 1970.
        [Pp. 87-104, Ashanti healing shrines from a psycho-
      logical perspective.]

529   FIELD, M[ARGARET] J[OYCE]. Spirit possession in Ghana, in
      J. Beattie and J. Middleton (eds.) Spirit mediumship and
      society in Africa. London: Routledge and Kegan Paul
      1969, 3-13.
        [Pp. 9-10, possession by "the Holy Spirit" in Christian
      "spiritual" communities.]

530   GHANA, GOVERNMENT OF. Parliamentary debates. Official
      reports, Vol. 5. Accra: Government Printing Department
      1965.
        [Columns 228-266, a debate on the "Spiritual Churches"
      in the National Assembly on 22 January 1965.]

531   GHANA, GOVERNMENT OF. Proceedings of the Committee appointed
      by Government: vide Commissioner for Education and Cul-
      ture Letter No. SCR-087 of 31st May 1974. Hayford-
      Benjamin Committee (Church of the Lord - Aladura).
      Seventh Sitting Thursday 4th July 1974. Witness:
      Apostle E. A. Ofosu. Accra: the Committee 69 p. Mimeo.

532   GOOD NEWS TRAINING INSTITUTE (Accra). Newsletter. 1- ,
      1971 - . Reports and Memoranda, 1971 - .
        [A co-operative training programme linking the older
      and many independent churches.]

533   GOODY, JACK. Anomie in Ashanti? Africa (London) 27 (4),
      1957, 356-362.
        [A criticism of Ward, item 568, which asserts that
      increased malaise due to European contacts is not proven.]

534   HALIBURTON, GORDON M[acKAY]. The Anglican Church of Ghana
      and the Harris movement of 1914. Bulletin of the Society
      for African Church History (Nsukka) 1 (3-4), 1964, 101-
      106.
        [On John Swatson, mulatto evangelist in West Ghana,
      influenced by Harris.]

West Africa

535   HALIBURTON, GORDON M[acKAY]. The calling of a prophet:
      Sampson Oppong. Bulletin of the Society for African
      Church History (Aberdeen) 2 (1), 1965, 84-96.

536   HALIBURTON, GORDON M[acKAY]. The late Sampson Oppong, Ashanti
      prophet. West African Religion (Nsukka) no. 5, Feb. 1966,
      1-3.
      [An obituary notice.]

537   HARTENSTEIN, KARL. Anibue: die "Neue Zeit" auf der Goldkuste
      und unsere Missionsausgabe. Stuttgart: Evangelische
      Missionsverlag, 1932, 127 p. Dutch trs., Anibue: de
      "Niewe Tijd" op de Goudkust en enze zendingstaak.
      Culumborg: 1935, 175 p.
      [Pp. 83-86 on prophet Chei among the Ewe.]

538   HAYFORD, JOSEPH EPHRAIM CASELY. William Waddy Harris: the
      West African reformer. The man and his message. London:
      C. M. Phillips 1915; 2nd. impression 1916, 19 p.
      [Hayford's impression of Harris through personal con-
      tact with his preaching at Axim; by a Gold Coast lawyer
      and nationalist.]

539   HAYFORD, MARK CHRISTIAN (ed.). The year-book and report of
      the Baptist Church and Mission and the Christian Army of
      the Gold Coast. London: the Church, n.d. [1913], 127 p.
      [The independent church founded by the author, ordained
      in 1898 by Majola Agbebi.]

540   HORLER, EDMUND C. Stretching out her hands to God. The For-
      eign Field (London: Wesleyan Methodist) July 1917, p. 153.
      [A missionary on the opportunity provided in Apolonia
      (W. Ghana) by the Harris converts.]

541   JAHODA, GUSTAV. Traditional healers and other institutions
      concerned with mental illness in Ghana. International
      Journal of Social Psychiatry (London) 7 (4), 1961, 245-268.
      [Includes examination of a prayer healing church as a
      new institution to deal with new problems.]

542   JEHU-APPIAH, J[EMISIMIHAM]. Musama Disco Christo Church his-
      tory. Koforidua, Ghana: Fanzaar Press n.d. [1943].
      [Original in Fanti.]

543   JEHU-APPIAH, MATAPOLY MOSES (comp.). The constitution of the
      Musama Disco Christo Church. Mazano, P. O. Box 3, Gomoa
      Eshiem, via Swedru, Ghana: the Church, 1959, 58 p.

544 JENKINS, PAUL. A comment on M. P. Frempong's History of the
    Presbyterian Church at Bompata. Ghana Notes and Queries
    12, June 1972, 23–27.
    [P. 24, comments on Sampson Oppong's influence in pro-
    ducing converts for a Presbyterian Church in the late
    1920s, based on Frempong, idem, p. 22.]

545 JENKINS, PAUL. Überlegungen zu den anlässlich der Volkszählung
    in Ghana von 1960 gemachten Angaben über die
    Religionszugehörigkeit. Evangelische Missions-Zeitschrift
    (Stuttgart) 31 (4), 1974, 170–189.
    [Independent churches were only 1.5% of the population
    in 1960 but have probably increased since.]

546 KIMBLE, DAVID. A political history of Ghana: the rise of
    Gold Coast nationalism 1850–1950. Oxford: Clarendon
    Press 1963, xviii + 587 p., illus., maps.
    [Pp. 86, 163–166, A.M.E. Zion, Church of Gold Coast,
    Nigritian Church, Musama Disco Christo, Harris and
    Oppong.]

547 KOTEY, G. N. A sketch of the life and works of Prophet John
    Mensah, founder and leader of the Church of Christ (S.M.)
    Ghana. Accra: the author, n.d. [ca. 1972] 46 p., photo.

548 MEERTS, H. C. G. De 'Nazarene Healing Church of Ghana'. Een
    studie van een onafhankelijke kerk in Ghana als faktor in
    het proces van religieuze verandering. Stichting
    Teologische Fakulteit Tilburg, doctoral dissertation 1974,
    255 p., maps, bibl.
    [Includes short English autobiography (pp. 219–220) of
    D. K. Mensah, founder of this church in 1960.]

549 MERTENS, (FR.) [A study of the Catholic Church in Ghana.]
    Accra: The Pastoral Institute [ca. 1973].
    [Ch. 12 (26 pp.), independent religious movements.]

550 METHODIST RECORDER, The (London). See: 6 May 1915, 4 May
    1916, 3 May 1917, for missionary reports on the Harris
    mass movement in west Ghana.

551 MUSTAPHA-TAYLOR, PRINCE. [History of the Musama Disco Christo
    Church, Ghana.] Cape Coast, Ghana: the author, 1969,
    63 p.

552 NATIONAL PASTORAL CENTRE, ACCRA. Good News Training Institute
    (Ghana). Information Service 73/30 [1973], 2 p.
    [Roman Catholic centre reports on Independent Churches'
    Training Centre.]

West Africa

553 NTIFORO, S. R. and RUTISHAUSER, PAUL. Report on "Prayer groups and sects". Report to Synod, Presbyterian Church of Ghana, 1966. Accra: Presbyterian Church of Ghana 1966, 16 p.
[A careful and influential report.]

554 OPOKU, K[OFI] A[SARE]. Traditional religious beliefs and spiritual churches in Ghana: a preliminary statement. Research Review (Legon, Ghana) 4 (2), 1968, 47-60.
[A survey, with details of sacrifice and childnaming in the Church of the Messiah.]

555 OPOKU, K[OFI] A[SARE]. The Universal Prayer Group "Mpaebo Kuw" (Adoagyiri Nsawam), the call of the prophet. Research Review (Legon, Ghana) 5 (1), 1968, 101-107.
[Founded by the blind Odiyifo Dompreh in 1950.]

556 OPOKU, K[OFI] A[SARE]. Kingdom: a religious community. Research Review (Legon, Ghana) 6 (1), 1969, 66-69.
[A Utopian community in Ashantiland, 1967-68.]

557 OPOKU, K[OFI] A[SARE]. A directory of "spiritual churches" in Ghana. Research Review (Legon, Ghana) 7 (1), 1970, 98-115.
[Names, addresses, founders and dates for 107 bodies, and incomplete information on a further 106.]

558 OPOKU, K[OFI] A[SARE]. Letters to a spiritual father. Research Review (Legon, Ghana) 7 (1), 1970, 15-32.
[24 letters to Brother Lawson, founder of the Divine Healer's Church, reproduced from the Church's Easter Convention Reports of 1967 and 1968, with introduction and comments.]

559 PRO MUNDI VITA. The church in Ghana. Pro Mundi Vita no. 53 1975.
[Pp. 26-29, Roman Catholics and independent churches in Ghana.]

560 ROTH, WILLARD E. Ghana: not too independent to welcome help. World Encounter (Philadelphia) 13 (1), 1975, 18-19, illus.
[Report on the first missionary from the Lutheran Church in America to independents in Ghana, 1974.]

561 RUTISHAUSER, PAUL. Auf der Suche nach Heilung Geborgenheit Gottes-Dienst. Auftrag (Basel) June 1974, 7-10, illus.

562 SACKEY, ISAAC. A brief history of the A.M.E. Zion Church, West Gold Coast District. Ghana Bulletin of Theology (Legon, Ghana) 1 (3), 1957, 16-20.

["Ethiopian" type of independent church founded under
American auspices 1903. By a Ghanian clergyman of this
church.]

563 SARPONG, P[ETER] K[WASI]. Success of faith and healing churches
     in Ghana. Worldmission 25 (2), 1974, 22-26.
     [By the Roman Catholic archbishop of Ghana.]

564 SCHNELLBACK, J[ÖRG]. Ghana in Zählen. Evangelische Mission
     1975. Hamburg: Verlag der Deutschen Evangelischen
     Missionshilfe 1975, 185-202.
     [Statistical details of churches in Ghana, including
     independent churches.]

565 SOUTHON, A. E. Gold Coast Methodism: the first hundred years
     1835-1935. London: Cargate Press; Accra: Methodist Book
     Depot, 1934, 158 p., illus.
     [Pp. 141f., on Sampson Oppong.]

566 STOEVESANDT, G. The sect of the Second Adam. Africa (London)
     7 (4), 1934, 479-482.
     [A defunct community in Ghana, ca. 1911, which sought a
     return to primitive paradise.]

567 VAN TRIGT, F. De Profeet Harris. Afrika Ontwaakt (Oosterbeck,
     Tafelberg) 19 (4), 1948, 59-61.
     [An account of Harris derived from the journal of
     Fr. Stauffer, the Roman Catholic priest at Axim, when
     Harris visited there.]

568 WARD, BARBARA E. Some observations on religious cults in
     Ashanti. Africa (London) 26 (1), 1956, 47-61.
     [Reasons for dissatisfaction with the church in Ashanti,
     and development of new witchfinding cults in the 1940s.]

569 WEAVER, EDWIN and WEAVER, IRENE. From Kuku Hill: among
     indigenous churches in West Africa (Missionary Studies 3).
     Elkhart, Indiana: Institute of Mennonite Studies 1975,
     128 p., illus., map.
     [Full account of the Good News Training Institute;
     Mennonite mission policy concerning independent churches;
     appendix by Prophet F. A. Mills. A companion volume to
     The Uyo Story on Nigeria.]

570 WEINBERG, S. KIRSON. "Mental healing" and social change in
     West Africa. Social Problems (Spencer, Indiana) 11 (3),
     1964, 257-299.

West Africa

[Pp. 264-268, role of Christian "faith healers" in
supplanting the native doctors' position in traditional
society.]

571   WESLEYAN METHODIST MISSIONARY SOCIETY (London). Reports:
No. 107 for 1920, 1921, 79-80; no. 108 for 1921, 1922,
p. 79; no. 112 for 1925, 1926, 86-87.
[On Sampson Oppong.]

572   WIEGRABE, P. Un nouveau culte indigène à la Côte d'Or.
Journal des Missions Evangéliques 5 (21), 1950, 378-380.
[The Tigare cult.]

573   WITTER, T. On the fringe of the Ashanti mass movement. The
Foreign Field (London: Wesleyan Methodist) September 1922,
223-225; see also p. 221.
[On the Sampson Oppong movement.]

574   WOVENU, CHARLES KWABLA NUTONUTI. Adzogbedede na mawu.
Tadzewu, Ghana: Apostolic Revelation Society, 1963, 24 p.
Eng. trans., Vowing to God. Tadzewu: Apostolic Revela-
tion Society 1963, 24 p.

575   WYLLIE, R[OBERT] W. Pastors and prophets in Winneba, Ghana:
their social background and career developments. Africa
(London) 44 (2), 1974, 186-193.

576   WYLLIE, ROBERT W. Pioneers of Ghanaian Pentecostalism:
Peter Anim and James McKeown. Journal of Religion in
Africa 6 (2), 1974, 109-122.

See also items 97, 104, 106, 107, 148, 178, 202, 227, 429, 435, 438,
440, 443, 447, 449, 451, 454, 459, 460, 470, 489, 490, 915, 1394.

IVORY COAST

577   ALLÉGRET, ELIE. The missionary question in the French colonies.
International Review of Missions 46=12 (April), 1923,
161-181.
[Pp. 173-174, the Harris movement, with two extracts
from administrators' reports.]

578   AMON D'ABY, F[RANÇOIS]-J[OSEPH]. La Côte d'Ivoire dans la
cité africaine. Paris: Larose 1951, 208 p., illus, map.
[Pp. 151f., Prophet Harris, by an Ivory Coast scholar.]

BLACK AFRICA

579   AMOS-DJORO, ERNEST. Les mouvements marginaux du protestantisme
      africain: les Harristes en Côte d'Ivoire. Paris: Ecole
      Pratique des Hautes Etudes, section des sciences religieuses,
      1956, 315 p. Mimeo.

580   AMOS-DJORO, ERNEST. Les églises harristes et le nationalisme
      ivoirien. Le Mois en Afrique (Paris) 5, mai 1966, 26-47.
      [By the then ambassador of the Ivory Coast to Germany.]

581   AUGÉ, MARC. Les métamorphoses Vampire. Nouvelle Revue de
      Psychanalyse no. 6, 1972, 129-146.
      [Pp. 129-130 on witchcraft and anthropophagy. Confes-
      sions made to Acho, the Harris prophet, and recorded at
      Bregbo.]

582   AUGÉ, MARC. Théorie des pouvoirs et idéologie. Etude de cas
      en Côte d'Ivoire (Collection Savoir). Paris: Hermann
      1975, 440 p., map.
      [Pp. 247-249, Harris, Ahui, Aké, Atcho, and Niaba's
      "Papa Nouveau" church (1953-), their place in society and
      world views, with some local texts reproduced; pp. 289-307,
      sociological reflections.]

583   BERNUS, EDMOND. Ahouati, notes sur un village Dida. Études
      Eburnéenes (Abidjan), 6, 1957, 213-230.
      [Pp. 217-219, on a Harris church, Chratchoche.]

584   BIANQUIS, JEAN. Le prophète Harris, ou dix ans d'histoire
      religieuse á la Côte d'Ivoire (1914-1924). Paris:
      Société des Missions évangéliques de Paris, 1924, 40 p.
      Also in Foi et Vie (Paris), 16 nov. and 1 déc. 1924.
      [A Protestant missionary compares several contemporary
      views of the Harris movement.]

585   BOULNOIS, JEAN. Gnon-Sua, dieu des Guérés. Paris: Fournier
      1933, 132 p.
      [Pp. 168ff., prophet Harris in the Ivory Coast.]

586   BUREAU, RENÉ. Le Prophète Harris et la religion harriste
      (Côte d'Ivoire). Abidjan: Institut d'Ethno-Sociologie
      1971, 193 p., and in Annales de l'Université d'Abidjan
      (Série F) 3, 1971, 31-196, illus., bibl.

587   DE BILLY, EDMOND. En Côte d'Ivoire, mission protestante de
      AOF. Paris: Société des Missions Evangéliques 1931,
      182 p., illus.
      [Pp. 13-19, 27, 36-43, on Harris, by a Protestant
      missionary.]

West Africa

588 DECORVET-BLOCHER, JEANNE. Les matins de Dieu. Nogent-sur-
     Marne: Mission Biblique en Côte d'Ivoire n.d. [?1972],
     252 p., maps, illus.
          [On the establishment of the Mission Biblique in Ivory
     Coast from 1927; ch. 3 (= pp. 25-34) Les Églises du
     prophète Harris; see also pp. 5, 7.]

589 DESANTI, DOMINIQUE. Attio le guérisseur. Constellation
     (Paris) 166, fév. 1962.
          [A young healer at Bregbo, Ivory Coast, in the Harris
     tradition.]

590 DESANTI, DOMINIQUE. Côte d'Ivoire. L'Atlas des voyages.
     Lausanne: Rencontre 1962, 286 p., illus.
          [Has a chapter on Harris churches, and an interview with
     Jonas Ahui (or Awi), the older Ebrié leader.]

591 DIETERLEN, GERMAINE (ed.). Textes sacrés de l'Afrique noire.
     Paris: Gallimard 1965, 287 p.
          [Pp. 98-106: 'Cantiques harristes', with introduction
     by, and reprinted from, J. Rouch, 1963.]

592 ETIENNE, PIERRE. Phénomènes religieux et facteurs socio-
     économiques dans un village de la région de Bouaké
     (Côte d'Ivoire). Cahiers d'Etudes Africaines 6 (3), 1966,
     367-401.
          [Pp. 371-393, the Tete Kpa and Tigali (=Tigare) cults.]

593 FENTON, THOMAS. Black harvest. London: Cargate Press 1956,
     160 p.
          [Pp. 39-76, reconstruction of the actual development of
     a Protestant church subsequent to Harris, by the former
     Methodist Mission superintendent.]

594 FOREIGN FIELD, The (London: Wesleyan Methodist Missionary
     Society). Issues for: Dec. 1924, 59-62, illus.; Oct.
     1926, 25; Jan. 1927; Feb. 1927, 107-112, illus.; Mar. 1927,
     136-141, illus.; July 1927; Aug. 1927.
          [The Harris movement, including accounts of missionaries'
     interviews with Harris himself.]

595 GIRARD, JEAN. Déima. Vol. 1: Prophètes paysans de
     l'environnement noir. Vol 2: Les évangiles selon la
     prophétesse Bogué Honoyo (Collection Actualité-recherche).
     Grenoble: Presses Universitaires de Grenoble 1974 and
     1973 (sic), 492 and 263 p., maps, illus., tables, bibl.
          [A comprehensive study, requested and checked by the
     large Déima syncretistic movement (1922-) founded by

prophetess Bague Honoyo (=Marie Lalou) (1892-1951); vol. 2
consists of the first written expression of the extensive
oral teaching of Déima.]

596   GORJU, JOSEPH. Un prophète de la Côte d'Ivoire. Les Missions
      Catholiques no. 2400, 4 juin 1915, 267-268.
         [Account of prophet Harris by a Roman Catholic
      missionary.]

597   GRIVOT, R. Le cercle de Lahou. Bulletin de l'Institut
      Français d'Afrique Noire (Dakar), 4 (1-4), 1942, 7-154.
         [Pp. 82-89, Harris, Botto Adaye, Nianga and other "cults"
      in the Ivory Coast.]

598   HALIBURTON, G[ORDON] M[acKAY]. The development of Harrisism.
      International Review of Mission no. 252-63 (Oct.), 1974,
      499-506.

599   HARRINGTON, PETER. An interview with the "Black Prophet".
      The African Missionary (Cork, Ireland) 18, Mar.-Ap. 1917,
      13-16. Fr. trans., Une intervue avec le Prophète noir.
      Echo des Missions Africaines de Lyon 16 (6), 1917, 191-195.
         [A Roman Catholic missionary describes a meeting with
      Harris in 1916.]

600   HARTZ, JOSEPH. Ein sonderbarer schwarzer Prophet.
      Afrikanisches Missions-Glocklein (St. Pierre, Bas-Rhin,
      France) 3 (3), 1925, 56-60.
         [By the Superior of the Missions Africaines de Lyon,
      who knew Harris.]

601   HAWING, G. Article in Alleluia (Diocese of Conakry), repr.
      in Afrique Nouvelle (Dakar) no. 891, 4/10 sept. 1964, 12.
      Eng. tr., Africanization of the Christian cult. Trans-
      lations on Africa (Washington D.C.) no. 111, 8 Oct. 1964,
      6-9.
         [General remarks; p. 7, reference to a "Harriste" group
      in Ivory Coast succeeding because indigenized.]

602   HIMMELHEBER, H[ANS]. Massa-Fetisch der Rechtschaffenheit.
      Tribus (Stuttgart) 4-5, 1954-55, 56-62.
         [The Massa cult in Ivory Coast among the Senoufo.]

603   HOLAS, BOHUMIL [THÉOPHILE]. Bref aperçu sur les principaux
      cultes syncrétiques de la basse Côte d'Ivoire. Africa
      24 (1), 1954, 55-60.
         [Harris and subsequent prophet cults, especially Déima.]

West Africa

604   HOLAS, BOHUMIL [THÉOPHILE]. Changements modernes de la pensée
       religieuse baoulé (Côte d'Ivoire). Monde Non-Chrétien
       (Paris) 31, juillet-sep. 1954, 265-275.
       [A new cult, 'L'Ayéré kpli' or tétékpan, hostile to
       ancestral beliefs, and of universal outlook.]

605   HOLAS, BOHUMIL [THÉOPHILE]. Note sur l'apparition du 'vide
       spirituel' en Côte d'Ivoire et sur ces conséquences. Revue
       de Psychologie des Peuples (The Hague) 9 (4), 1954, 398-404.
       [Includes cults 'de Massa' or 'de la Corne'; emphasizes
       the impossibility of a spiritual vacuum in African society,
       as a background to new religious movements.]

606   HOLAS, BOHUMIL [THÉOPHILE]. Fondements spirituels de la vie
       sociale sénoufo (Region de Korhogo, Côte d'Ivoire). Journal
       de la Société des Africanistes (Paris) 26 (1-2), 1956, 9-32.
       [Pp. 28-32, new cults - 'de la Corne' (Massa) and Nya.]

607   HOLAS, BOHUMIL [THÉOPHILE]. Le prosélytisme en Côte d'Ivoire.
       La Vie Intellectuelle (Paris) no. 87=28 (déc.), 1956,
       31-41. Also in Rencontres (Paris) no. 48, 1957, 155-167,
       and in Vitalité actuelle des religions non-chrétiennes.
       Paris, 1957.
       [The Harris movement on the coast; the Ayéré kpli cult
       among the Baoulé of the centre; the Massa cult of the
       Senoufo in the north.]

608   HOLAS, BOHUMIL [THÉOPHILE]. Changements sociaux en Côte
       d'Ivoire. Paris: Presses Universitaires de France 1961,
       119 p., plates, figs.
       [Pp. 59-64, new 'cults' in traditional societies,
       especially the Oubi of the south-west.]

609   HOLAS, BOHUMIL [THÉOPHILE]. Le séparatisme religieux en
       Afrique noire (L'exemple de la Côte d'Ivoire). Paris:
       Presses Universitaires de France 1965, 410 p., bibl.,
       illus.
       [Major study of the cult of the prophet Boto Adai, with
       texts; the Harris movement and its successors; new cults,
       especially Ayéré kpli, and Massa. Indices of vernacular
       terms, and of 'Prophets and cults' in Africa; extensive
       bibliography. The index of cults and the bibliography
       need correction.]

610   JACOBS, DONALD R. Sunday in Africa - let's go to church:
       church and symbol. Risk (Geneva) 7 (3), 1971, 36-41.
       [An Aladura church in Abidjan.]

BLACK AFRICA

Ivory Coast

611 JOSEPH, GASTON. La Côte d'Ivoire: le pays, les habitants.
        Paris: Fayard (1917) 1944, xii + 234 p., maps.
        [Pp. 97-104, Harris and followers.]

612 JOSEPH, GASTON. Une atteinte à l'animisme chez les populations
        de la Côte d'Ivoire. Annuaire et Mémoires du Comité d'Études
        Historiques et Scientifiques de l'Afrique Occidentale Française
        1916. Gorée: Un primeire du governement général [de l'Afrique
        occidentale française] 1916, 344-348.
        [Which item is also listed in a bibliography of Annuaire
        et Mémoires... of 1917, p. 497.]

613 KOMOROWSKI, ZYGMUNT. Geneza ruchów reformatorskich na
        Wybrzeżu Kości Słoniowej [The origin of reform movements
        in the Ivory Coast]. Kultura i Społeczeństwo (Warsaw) 1
        (2), 1966, 167-175.
        [New "religious sects" placed alongside other modernizing
        agents.]

614 LÄDRACH, O. Der Sturz eines afrikanischen Lügengottes. Basler
        Missionsbuchhandlung 1919, 36 p.
        [Pp. 11-16, the Aberewa cult at Bonduku, Ivory Coast,
        1906; a female spirit offering protection and success and expos-
        ing evil-doers; and on other new forms of traditional cults.]

615 LEHMANN, J.-P., and MEMEL-FOTÉ, HARRIS. Le cercle du prophète
        et du sorcier. Réflexions à propos d'une paralyse
        fonctionelle hystérique chez un enfant de 13 ans.
        Psychopathologie Africaine (Dakar) 31 (1), 1967, 81-119;
        Eng. summary, p. 6.
        [Pp. 82-85, 110-119, 'le prophète' Josué Edjro, a healer
        recognised by the Methodist church.]

616 LeJEUNE, ADOLPHE. Religions nouvelles. Echo des Missions
        Africaines de Lyon (Lyon) 46 (5), 1947, 11-13.
        [The Adai and Déima cults of the Ivory Coast; a critical
        account of their beginnings by a local Roman Catholic
        missionary in the Divo area.]

617 MARTY, PAUL. Études sur l'Islam en Côte d'Ivoire. Paris:
        E. Leroux 1922, 496 p., maps.
        [Pp. 13ff. on the Harris movement.]

618 MEMEL-FOTÉ, HARRIS. Un guérisseur de la basse Côte d'Ivoire:
        Josué Edjro. Cahiers d'Etudes Africaines 7 (4), 1967,
        547-605.
        [An independent Christian healer with a biblical empha-
        sis, from 1965, in Adjoukrou area.]

87

West Africa

619   METHODIST RECORDER, The (London). No. 3491=65, 9 Oct. 1924,
       10 and 11, illus.
       [Two articles referring to the Harris movement, with
       photos of Harris.]

620   NIANGORAN-BOUAH, G. Echos de voyage. Bulletin d'Information
       et de Liaison (Abidjan) 1, 1968, 38.
       [Anyama's Harris-type church founded near Bakouma in
       1956.]

621   PAULET, MIREILLE. Les mouvements prophétiques ivoiriens.
       Spiritus no. 49=13 (mai), 1972, 177-190.
       [With special reference to Marie Lalou, Raphael Mihin,
       to the future of such movements in Africa and the atti-
       tudes of missions towards them.]

622   PAULME, DENISE. Une religion syncrétique en Côte d'Ivoire:
       le culte déima. Cahiers d'Études Africaines (Paris) 3
       (1), 1962, 5-90, bibl., illus.
       [Déima, founded by Marie Lalou, who was inspired by the
       doctrine of prophet Harris. Translation (and commentary)
       of 12 texts of the cult; prayers, catechism, testaments
       and doctrine.]

623   PAULME, DENISE. Une société de Côte d'Ivoire hier et
       aujourd'hui: Les Bété. The Hague: Mouton 1962, 200 p.,
       illus.
       [Pp. 180-194 on "Culture nouveaux", Asye and Tetegba.]

624   PAULME, DENISE. Sur un myth africain récent d'origine de la
       mort, in Actes du VIe Congrès international des Sciences
       anthropologiques et ethnologiques. Paris: Músee de
       l'Homme, Tome II, 2e. vol., 1964, 449-452.
       [A myth in the Marie Lalou cult, with biblical and
       Islamic features.]

625   PIAULT, COLETTE, et al. Prophétisme et thérapeutique. Albert
       Atcho et la communauté de Bregbo (Collection Savoir).
       Paris: Hermann 1975, 324 p., map, illus.
       [A detailed study of one of the most charismatic prophet
       healers in the Harriste churches: ch. 1, Atcho and his
       village community (C. Piault); ch. 2, his religion
       (R. Bureau); ch. 3, the confessions of malice and killing
       predominant in patients (Piault and L. Saghy); ch. 4,
       personal responsibility replacing persecution beliefs as
       cause of one's troubles (A. Zempléni); ch. 5, the signifi-
       cance of this change for modern development (M. Augé);
       appendices: case studies of confessions.]

626 PLATT, WILLIAM J. (ed.). News Notes from West Africa (England)
     1, Jan. 1926, 1-5; 2, Apr. 1926, 2-3; 3, July 1926, 3.
     Also Fr. trans., Courrier de l'A.O.F.
        [The continuing Harris movement as taken up by the
     Methodists, and reported in a circular letter to mission-
     ary supporters.]

627 PLATT, WILLIAM J. From fetish to faith. London: Cargate
     Press 1935, 159 p., map.
        [Ch. 5, "The Prophet Movements", a first-hand account of
     the Harris movement as it existed in the 1920s.]

628 PRITCHARD, JOHN R. Le prophète Harris et le Méthodisme
     ivoirien. Flambeau (Yaoundé) 37, fév. 1973, 62-64.
        [Review of Haliburton (1971).]

629 PRITCHARD, JOHN R. The Prophet Harris and Ivory Coast.
     Journal of Religion in Africa 5 (1), 1973, 23-31.
        [Review article on Haliburton's The prophet Harris
     (1971) and Roux's L'Évangile dan la Forêt (1971) with
     respect to Harris, and comparing discrepancies in their
     accounts.]

630 ROUCH, JEAN. Introduction à l'étude de la communauté de
     Bregbo. Journal de la Société des Africanistes (Paris)
     33 (1), 1963, 129-202, illus., bibl. (Section entitled
     "Cantiques harristes" repr. with introduction by Rouch in
     G. Dieterlen (ed.), Textes sacrés d'Afrique noire.
     [Paris]: Gallimard 1965, 98-106.)
        [Description of the community of Albert Atcho, a young
     healer in the Harris tradition, on Ebrié Lagoon, east of
     Abidjan. By a French anthropologist.]

631 ROUX, ANDRÉ. Un prophète: Harris. Présence Africaine
     (special number, Le Monde Noire) 8-9, 1950, 133-140.
        [Anecdotal account of Harris and his role in bolstering
     Protestant strength in the Ivory Coast.]

632 ROUX, ANDRÉ. L'Evangile dans la forêt: Naissance d'une
     Eglise en Afrique noire. Paris: Editions du Cerf 1971,
     195 p.
        [By a former Methodist missionary; the Methodist take-
     over of the Harris churches.]

633 SEAMANDS, JOHN T. Pioneers of the younger churches. New York
     and Nashville: Abingdon Press 1967, 221 p.
        [Pp. 164-180, "William Wade Harris of the Ivory Coast" -
     a factual account.]

West Africa

634   SIRVEN, PIERRE. Les conséquences géographiques d'un nouveau
       syncrétisme religieux en Cote d'Ivoire: le kokambisme.
       Les Cahiers d'Outre-mer (Bordeaux) no. 78=20, 1967,
       127-136, illus.
            [Founded by Koba Yao, from 1956, with change from yam to
       cassava cultivation.]

635   SOUTH AFRICAN OUTLOOK (Lovedale). West African prophet found.
       South African Outlook no. 672=57 (2 May), 1927, 97-98.
            [The French Protestant missionary Benoit's "discovery"
       of Harris.]

636   THOMPSON, E. W. The Ivory Coast: a study on modern mission-
       ary methods. International Review of Missions no. 68=17
       (Oct.), 1928, 630-644.
            [An account of the Methodist takeover of the Harris
       churches.]

637   VAN BULCK, G. Le prophète Harris vu par lui-même. (Côte
       d'Ivoire 1914), in Museum Lessianum, item 312, 120-124;
       Eng. trans. by J. D. Hargreaves, The prophet Harris in
       his France and West Africa. London: Macmillan 1969,
       247-252 (with notes).
            [Important extracts from the journal of a Roman Catholic
       missionary, Joseph Hartz, who interviewed Harris.]

638   VORC'H, ALINE. Anthropophagie. L'Anthropophagie comme langage.
       Albert Atcho prophète harriste de Bregbo (Côte d'Ivoire).
       Perspectives 7: Bulletin de l'Association du 7e Art
       (Cotonou, Dahomey) no. 2, juillet-août-septembre 1974,
       40-41.

639   WALKER, F. DEAVILLE. The story of the Ivory Coast. London:
       Cargate Press 1926, 82 p., illus.
            [Chs. 2 and 3 and Addendum: a popular account of the
       Harris movement and the later takeover by the British
       Methodists. By a Methodist missionary historian. (Third
       revised ed., 1930).]

640   YANDO, EMMANUEL. L'évolution du Harrisme en Côte d'Ivoire.
       Faculté Libre de Théologie Protestante, Paris, thèse,
       1970, 126 p.

641   ZOLBERG, ARISTIDE R. One party government in the Ivory Coast.
       Princeton: Princeton University Press 1964, xiv + 374 p.
            [Pp. 37-38, "no evidence" that Harrism has had any
       contemporary political significance.]

BLACK AFRICA

Liberia

See also items 91, 151, 184, 193, 209, 213, 214, 227, 308, 347, 420,
429, 435, 438, 444, 447, 453, 454, 457, 466, 467, 471, 514, 515, 540,
550, 651, 652, 653.

LIBERIA

642   BROWN, KENNETH I[RVING]. Aladura baptism. Hibbert Journal
      (London) no. 245=62 (Jan.), 1964, 64-67.
      [Account of Church of the Lord (Aladura) baptism in
      Monrovia.]

643   BROWN, KENNETH I[RVING]. Worshipping with the Church of the
      Lord (Aladura). Practical Anthropology (Tarrytown, N.Y.)
      13 (2), 1966, 59-84.
      [The author participated in river baptism, churching of
      twins, circumcision, etc., at the Monrovia headquarters
      branch of this Nigerian church.]

644   CASON, JOHN WALTER. The growth of Christianity in the
      Liberian environment. Columbia University, Ph.D. disser-
      tation 1962, 561 p., maps.
      [Pp. 296-297, Harris; pp. 450-453, Church of the Lord
      (Aladura).]

645   FRAENKEL, MERRAN. Tribe and class in Monrovia. London:
      Oxford University Press for the International African
      Institute 1964, xii + 244 p., tables, figs., maps, plates.
      [Pp. 151-195 (Ch. 5), "Churches and societies", dis-
      cusses the increasing number of "independent local
      churches" founded in Monrovia since World War II.]

646   HALIBURTON, GORDON MacKAY. The prophet Harris and the Grebo
      rising of 1910. Liberian Studies Journal (Greencastle,
      Indiana) 3 (1), 1970-71, 31-39.

647   KORTE, WERNER. A note on independent churches in Liberia.
      Liberian Studies Journal (Greencastle, Indiana) 4 (1),
      1971, 81-87.
      [Surveys the few existing inadequate studies, and the
      information about an itinerant prophet, who might have
      been W. W. Harris.]

648   KORTE, WERNER. Organisation und gesellschaftliche Funktion
      unabhängiger Kirchen in Afrika. Beispiele aus Liberia

91

West Africa

und Ansatze zu einer allgemeinen Theorie. Justus-Liebig
University, doctoral dissertation 1974, 588 p., maps,
diagrams, tables.
[Includes a list of independent churches in Liberia and
two texts collected from local churches.]

649   KORTE, WERNER. Religiöse Dissidenten, Propheten und
Kultgrundungen im südostlichen Liberia im 19. und 20.
Jahrhundert. Sociologus, Frühl 1976.
[Revised from chapter 4 of his dissertation.]

650   KORTE, WERNER, and MASSING, ANDREAS. Institutional change
among the Kru, Liberia - transformational response to
change, in Dieter Oberndorger (ed.), Africana Collecta II
(Materialen des Arnold-Bergstraesser-Instituts,
Düsseldorf) 30, 1971, 117-140, Germ. summary.
[Pp. 130-133, 138-139, religious associations including
independent churches.]

651   MARTIN, JANE JACKSON. The dual legacy: government authority
and mission influence among the Grebo of eastern Liberia,
1834-1910. Boston University, Ph.D. dissertation (History)
1968, 490 p.
[The milieu of the prophet Harris; the Cavalla rebellion;
a small secession from the Protestant Episcopal mission
in the 1880s, influenced by Jehovah's Witnesses.]

652   WILLIAMS, WALTER B. God's avenging sword. Sinoo-Kroo Coast
District, no pub., 1928, 8 p.
[An American Methodist missionary who met Prophet
Harris.]

653   WILLIAMS, WALTER B., and WILLIAMS, MAUDE WIGFIELD. Adventures
with the Krus in West Africa. New York: Vantage Press
1955, 147 p.
[Pp. 141-142, "the real story of the 'Prophet Movement'"
- i.e. Harris.]

See also items 155, 429, 444, 469, 470.

MALI

654   CARDAIRE, MARCEL. L'Islam et le terroir africain. Bamako-
Koulouba: IFAN, 1954, 30-46.

[Especially pp. 37-38, the origin of the "religion de
l'homme de Wolo", San District, Mali.]

655   HOLAS, B[OHUMIL THÉOPHILE].   Le Nya: changements spirituels
      modernes d'une société ouest-africaine.   Acta Tropica
      (Basel) 12 (2), 1955.   97-122, illus.
         [The Minianka, a Senoufo group; the cults of Nya and of
      massa.]

See also items 206, 214, 602, 605, 606, 607, 609.

NIGER

656   MONFOUGA-NICOLAS, JACQUELINE.   Ambivalence et culte de posses-
      sion.   Contributions à l'étude du Bori Hausa.   Paris:
      Editions Anthropos 1972, 384 p.
         [Bori cult among the Hausa of Niger - an all-female
      spirit possession cult which is in effect a third religion,
      the others being the traditional system and orthodox Islam,
      both male-dominated.]

See also item 77.

NIGERIA

657   ABDUL, M. O. A.   Syncretism in Islam among the Yoruba.   West
      African Religion (Nsukka) 15, Mar. 1974, 44-56.

658   ABERNETHY, DAVID BEAVER.   Education and politics in a develop-
      ing society: the Southern Nigerian experience.   Harvard
      University Ph.D. dissertation (Political Science) 1965,
      565 p.
         [Pp. 55-57, role of the African churches.]

659   ADAMS, R. F. G.   Oberi Okaime: a new African language and
      script.   Africa (London) 17 (1), 1947, 24-34.
         [A "revealed" language in a section of the Spirit Move-
      ment, Eastern Nigeria, from 1927; now the Oberi Okaime
      Church.]

West Africa

660 ADEDEJI, J. A. The church and the emergence of the Nigerian
theatre, 1866-1914. Journal of the Historical Society of
Nigeria 6 (1), 1971, 25-45.
[Pp. 39-43, the contribution of the "African" churches
of Lagos to African music and drama.]

661 ADEDIPE, R. A. Igbeyawo mimo [Holy Marriage]. Ado Ekiti,
Western Nigeria: Ilori Press 1949, 48 p.
[One of several books in Yoruba by a leader of the Christ
Apostolic Church.]

662 ADEDIPE, R. A. Itan Igbesi Aiye Apostle Ayo Babalola. Christ
Apostolic (Lagos, Christ Apostolic Church) no. 8, June
1969, 13-14, photo.
[An outline of Apostle Babalola's life and teaching.]

663 ADEFOPE, J. O. Isipaya fun odun 1972, lati owo J. O. Adefope.
Ibadan: Abiodun Printing Works 1972, 18 p.
[Visions and prophecies.]

664 ADEJOBI, EMMANUEL OWOADE ADE. The observances and practices
of the Church of the Lord (Aladura) in the light of Old
and New Testament. Lagos: the author 1965, 14 p.
[Biblical warrants for the Church practices, with a
general apologetic, by the leading minister of the Church.]

665 ADEMAKINWA, J. A. Iwe itan ijo wa lati egbe Okuta-iyebiye Ijo
Faith Tabernacle Apostolic Church de Christ Apostolic
Church [History of our church from Diamond Society, Apos-
tolic Church]. Lagos: Pacific Printing Works 1945, 180 p.
[By a member of this Church, in Yoruba.]

666 AFRICAN CHURCH (Incorporated). Revised Constitution of the
African Church (Incorporated). Lagos: the African Church
Inc., n.d. [1951?], 45 p.

667 AFRICAN CHURCH ORGANIZATION. Report of proceedings of the
African Church Organization for Lagos and Yorubaland,
1901-1908. Liverpool: African Church Organization 1910,
104 p.
[Origins, history and some statistics.]

668 AGBABIAKA, TUNDE. A night with Bar Beach Aladuras. Sunday
Daily Times (Lagos) 10 November 1974, 1 p., illus.

669 AINA, J. ADE. Odun medogbon Ijo Aladura ni ilu Ibadan [Silver
Jubilee of the establishment of the Aladura Church in
Ibadan.] Ibadan: the author n.d. [1949] 27 p.

[Includes a general history of the early Aladura movement, by one of its leaders. In Yoruba.]

670 AINA, J. ADE. Present day prophets and the principles upon
   which they work. Ibadan: the author n.d. [ca. 1932],
   16 p.; reprinted Nsukka, Nigeria: Department of Religion,
   University of Nigeria 1964, with introduction by
   H. W. Turner, 10 p. Mimeo.
      [A defence of the Aladura movement by an early leader,
   with an attempt at a theology of the place of holy water
   in the movement.]

671 AITALEGBE, R. M. E. Oba Akenzua II, C.M.G.; personality profile. Apapa: Ministry of Information, Mid-West Nigeria
   [1965?], 6 p.
      [The founder of the Aruosa cult or Edo National religion.]

672 AJAYI, J[ACOB] F. A[DE]. Christian missions in Nigeria 1841-
   1891. The making of a new elite. London: Longmans 1965,
   317 p.
      [Pp. 266-273, E. W. Blyden's advocacy of an independent
   African church.]

673 AKINYELE, ISAAC BABALOLA. Akanse awon eko ati alaye kikun lori
   ofin mewa [Special lessons and elucidations on the Ten
   Commandments]. Ibadan: Iranlowo Press 1953, 103 p.
      [One of the earliest of a series of more than twelve
   pamphlets in Yoruba on religious subjects, written by one
   of the founders of the large Christ Apostolic Church in
   Nigeria. (In Library of University of Ibadan).]

674 AKIWOWO, AKINSOLA A. The place of Mojola Agbebi in the African
   nationalist movements, 1890-1917. Phylon (Atlanta) 26 (2),
   1965, 122-139.

675 AKPAN, NTIEYONG UDO. The wooden gong. London: Longmans 1965,
   118 p.
      [Fiction: pp. 76-86 on the advent of an Ethiopian-type
   church and of the Spirit movement to an east Nigerian
   village.]

676 ALEXANDER, D. A. R. Report of the Commission appointed to
   enquire into the Owegbe Cult: including statement by the
   Government of the Mid-Western group of Provinces. Benin
   City: Ministry of Internal Affairs and Information 1966,
   159 p.

West Africa

677   ALUKO, T. M. Kinsman and foreman. London: Heinemann Educational Books 1966, 203 p.
      [Fiction; includes an "Alasotele" prophet movement which predicts judgment day on a certain date; see especially chs. 11, 15, 24.]

678   ALUTU, JOHN O. A groundwork of Nnewi history. Nnewi, Eastern Nigeria: Homeland Information Service 1963.
      [Pp. 298-303, on the National Church of Nigeria.]

679   ANYIAM, FREDERICK UZOMA. Among Nigerian celebrities. Yaba (Lagos): the author 1960, 71 p.
      [Pp. 15-17 on Garrick Sokari Braide, "Nigeria's greatest prophet".]

680   APOSTOLIC HERALD (British Apostolic Church). See nos. 5, 1932, p. 9, and 13, 1932, pp. 8-9, on the tour of the British Apostolic Church delegation in Nigeria.

681   AUTHORITY, S. O. A. The Happy City "Aiyetoro". Okitipupa (Western Nigeria): the Holy Apostles Community, 2nd. ed. 1960, 77 p., map; enlarged ed., Lagos: Eruobodo Press n.d. [1966?], 116 p., illus.
      [Official history of the Community, by one of their leaders. Enlarged edition has important photographs.]

682   AWAKE (New York: Watchtower Bible and Tract Society). I was an "aladura" (as told to Awake correspondent in Nigeria). Awake 52 (17), 8 Sept. 1971, 16-18.
      [Testimony of a convert, first to the Cherubim and Seraphim, and then to Jehovah's Witnesses.]

683   AYANDELE, E[MMANUEL] A[YANKANMI]. An assessment of James Johnson and his place in Nigerian history. Journal of the Historical Society of Nigeria (Ibadan), 2 (4), 1963, 486-516; 3 (1), 1964, 73-101.
      [Discusses his role in the formation of the "African" churches in Lagos.]

684   AYANDELE, E[MMANUEL] A[YANKANMI]. The missionary impact on modern Nigeria 1842-1914. A political and social analysis. London: Longmans Green 1966, 393 p., illus.
      [Ch. 6, the rise of Ethiopianism, 1875-1890; Ch. 7, the successes and failures of Ethiopianism, 1890-1914; pp. 270-278, Reformed Ogboni Fraternity; 254-255 et passim, Mojola Agbebi.]

685 AYANDELE, E[MMANUEL] A[YANKANMI]. The Nigerian church and the
Reformed Ogboni Fraternity. Nigerian Baptist, June 1966,
19-23.

686 AYANDELE, E[MMANUEL] A[YANKANMI]. The aladura movement among
the Yoruba. The Nigerian Christian (Ibadan), 3 (7), 1969,
15-16; 3 (9), 1969, 14.
[A review article of Peel (1968), item 855.]

687 AYANDELE, E[MMANUEL] A[YANKANMI]. Holy Johnson: pioneer of
African nationalism 1836-1917 (Africana Modern Library
13). London: F. Cass 1970; New York: Humanities Press
1970; 417 p., maps, illus.
[Pp. 355-363, relations with the Braide movement;
M. Agbebi, see index.]

688 AYANDELE, E[MMANUEL] A[YANKANMI]. A visionary of the African
Church: Mojola Agbebi (1860-1917) (Religion in Africa 1).
Nairobi: East African Publishing House 1971, 32 p.

689 AYORINDE, J. A. Oba Sir Isaac Babalola Akinyele, Kt.,
Olubadan-Ibadan. Odu - Journal of African Studies
(Ibadan), 1 (2), 1965, 78-82.
[Obituary on early leader and later President of the
Christ Apostolic Church; in Yoruba.]

690 BABALOLA, J[OSEPH] A[YO]. Iwe imototo ati iwa mimo [The book
of hygiene and holy living]. Ilesha, Western Nigeria:
Ola-Iya Printing Works 1959, 50 p.
[By the prophet leader of the 1930 Aladura revival;
edited by D. O. Babajide; in Yoruba.]

691 BANFIELD, A. W. Report. The Church Missionary Review,
no. 808=67 (Aug.-Sept.), 1916, p. 477. Also in The Bible
in the World (London: BFBS), 12, July 1916, 137-138.
[On the Braide movement, from the Bible Society's agent
in West Africa.]

692 BARRETT, STANLEY R. God's Kingdom on stilts: a comparative
study of rapid economic development. University of Sussex
Ph.D. dissertation (Social anthropology) 1971, 603 p.,
maps.
[On the Holy Apostles' Community, Aiyetoro.]

693 BARRETT, STANLEY R. Crisis and change in a West African
Utopia, in Edward B. Harvey (ed.), Perspectives on Modern-
ization: essays in memory of Ian Weinberg. Toronto:
University of Toronto Press 1972, 160-181.

West Africa

[A revised version appears as ch. 7., The new economy, in his dissertation of 1971.]

694   BARRETT, STANLEY R. Two villages on stilts: economic and family change in Nigeria (Social and Economic Change Series). New York and London: Chandler Publishing Company 1974, 115 p., illus.
[Aiyetoro and neighbouring religious settlements – from communalism to capitalism; suppression and re-emergence of the family.]

695   BATUBO, A. B. The dawn of Baptist work in Eastern Nigeria. Port Harcourt: the author 1964, 52 p.
[Especially on Dr. Mojola Agbebi's work, and Baptist secessions, by a Nigerian Baptist layman.]

696   BENIN, OBA OF. Addresses in connexion with Aruosa (Edo National Church of God...). Benin City (Nigeria): the Church 1946, 17 p.
[A neo-primal "church".]

697   BERRY, S[ARAH] S[HEPHERD SWEEZY]. Christianity and the rise of cocoa-growing in Ibadan and Ondo. Journal of the Nigerian Historical Society 4 (3), 1968, 439–451.
[Pp. 440-445, the Agege planters, mostly members of the "african" churches, and their possible influence on Ondo.]

698   BEYIOKU, AKIN FAGBENRO [HORATIO ANTUS WILLIAMS]. The origin of Ijo Orunmila organization. Lagos: Alafin Press 1944, ca. 10 p.
[A Nigerian "nativist church" based on traditional Yoruba religion's Ifa cult. Traces the various offshoots of this group. By its founder.]

699   BILL, MRS. S. A. [GRACE]. The Revival. Qua Iboe Mission Quarterly (Belfast) no. 136, Feb. 1928, 4–5.
[On the "spirit movement" in Ibibioland 1927; by the wife of the founder of the Qua Iboe Mission.]

700   BOLAJI, SIMEON LABANJI. Anatomy of corruption in Nigeria. Ibadan: Daystar Press 1970, 144 p.
[Pp. 16-19, corrupt prophets and founders of independent churches.]

701   BRADBURY, R[OBERT] E[LWYN]. The Benin Kingdom and the Edo-speaking peoples of South-western Nigeria (Ethnographic survey of Africa, Western Africa series, part 13). London: International African Institute 1957, 212 p., plates, maps, bibl.

[Pp. 163-164, new semi-Christian cults, from 1929;
p. 52, Aruosa Cult.]

702   BRADBURY, R[OBERT] E[LWYN]. Continuities and discontinuities
in pre-colonial and colonial Benin politics (1897-1951),
in I. M. Lewis (ed.), History and social anthropology
(A.S.A. Monographs 7). London: Tavistock Publications
1968, 193-252. Reprinted in his Benin Studies. London:
Oxford University Press for the International African
Institute 1973, xxi + 293 p., ill.
[Pp. 243-247, Reformed Ogboni Fraternity as a political
factor; pp. 245-246, Aruosa cult as an Edo reply to the
Reformed Ogboni Community.]

703   BRITISH GOVERNMENT: Colonial Reports, Annual. No. 1435.
Nigeria. Report for 1928. London: HMSO 1929, 39 p.,
map.
[P. 10, decline of the Spirit Movement of 1927 in
Ibibioland.]

704   BROTHERHOOD OF THE CROSS AND STAR. The light of the World.
[Calabar]: the Church [Irregularly from 1, Aug. 1964,
from 23 to 46 pp., continuing.]
[The magazine of the Church, containing testimonies,
articles, and many sermons of the founder, O. O. Obu.]

705   BUCKLEY, ANTHONY DAVID. The idea of evil in Yoruba traditional
religion and its development in three aladura churches.
University of Leicester M.A. dissertation (religion)
1969, 140 p.
[Both Yoruba religion, and the Cherubim and Seraphim,
the Christ Apostolic Church, and the Church of the Lord
(Aladura) seek to remove man's alienation by restoring
the Holy to the centre of their worlds.]

706   BY THE LAGOON (Lagos, the Cathedral). Spurious! [and] Who
gave thee this authority? By the Lagoon October 1952,
pp. 13 and 14.
[On the Church Army of Africa founded in 1952 by Jones
and Oladunjoye, ex-Salvation Army officers.]

707   BY THE LAGOON (Lagos, the Cathedral). The return of Igbololo
seceders. By the Lagoon January 1954, p. 23.
[From the Remo Independent Christ Church, formed from
the Anglican congregation at Igbololo in December 1946.]

West Africa

708   CALABAR AND OWERRI PROVINCES, Commission of Enquiry. Report
of the Commission of Enquiry appointed to Inquire into the
Disturbances in the Calabar and Owerri Provinces,
December 1929. Lagos: Government Printer 1930, 159 p. +
appendices.
    [Pp. 19-20, 106, religious aspects of the "Aba riots";
the Spirit Movement of 1926, see Appendix III, (i),
pp. 10-11; the Dancing Women of 1925, idem, pp. 10-11.]

709   [CAMPBELL, JAMES GEORGE]. The origin, the thirty-six articles
of faith, and the constitution and other regulations, of
the West African Episcopal Church. Lagos: the author
1942, 4 + 22 p.
    [The church founded by the author in 1903.]

710   CHAMBERS, MICHAEL. Jesus of Oyingbo. New Society (London)
no. 80=3 (9 April), 1964, 13-15, illus.
    [Emmanuel Odumosu and the Universal College of Regen-
eration in Lagos; development from "simple messianism" to
complex economic organization.]

711   CHERUBIM AND SERAPHIM, ETERNAL SACRED ORDER OF. Holy Hymn
Book. Lagos: the Order, n.d. [after 1957], 197 p.
    [201 hymns and 9 canticles selected from a larger
Yoruba hymnbook of this aladura church, one of a number of
Cherubim and Seraphim groups.]

712   CHERUBIM AND SERAPHIM, ETERNAL SACRED ORDER OF. The "Order":
rules and regulations, duties of workers, and forty days
Lenten programme. Lagos: the Order n.d. [ca. 1959], 76 p.
    [Rules, officers, teaching, orders of service for
various occasions, lectionaries and Bible study helps.]

713   CHERUBIM AND SERAPHIM, SACRED ORDER OF. Daily Bible reading
pamplet 1965. Lagos: the Order 1965, 52 p.
    [The 14th edition of a yearbook of this church (not the
same as that in items 711 and 712) containing lectionary,
directory of officers and centres, and a history.]

714   CHICK, JONATHAN. Reformation without conversion: the impact
of Christianity on the Bini peoples of West Africa.
Church Quarterly Review (London) Oct.-Dec. 1967, 466-480.
    [Pp. 473-479, the Oba of Benin's Aruosa cult as a
Christian-influenced revival of traditional religion.]

715   CHRIST APOSTOLIC CHURCH. Orin ihinrere: Gospel songs.
Ibadan: the Church 3rd ed. 1961, 687 p.

[803 hymns, mostly chosen from a wide range of English
Hymnbooks, together with some original compositions; all
in Yoruba, for the largest aladura church.]

716 CHRIST APOSTOLIC CHURCH. Iwe ilana ati ti Ijo Aposteli Kristi
nigi grogbo. Ibadan: the Church, revised ed. 1968, 75 p.
[Constitution, orders and teaching.]

717 CHRIST CHURCH OF THE LORD. Iwe orin mimo. Ibadan: the
Church, 2nd. ed. n.d., 452 p.
[364 hymns and 29 choruses, in Yoruba, for an aladura
church.]

718 "CHURCHMAN". 5th year of our 1st President's Homecall. Christ
Apostolic (Lagos, Christ Apostolic Church) no. 8, June
1969, p. 2, photo.
[Commemorating I. B. Akinyele, with a long quotation
from his letter of 27 January 1930 to D. O. Odubanjo in
which Pastor Myers of Canada is mentioned.]

719 CHURCH MISSIONARY SOCIETY (Anglican). Proceedings. London:
the Society, annually.
[E.g.: 1916-1917, pp. 3-4, 26-27, and 1918-1919, p. 32,
on the Braide movement in the Niger Delta; 1932, pp. 5-6,
the aladura movement and Joseph Babalola.]

720 CHURCH OF THE LORD (ALADURA). Hymn Book. Ogere (Western
Nigeria): the Church n.d. [1958], 344 p.
[300 hymns, some original, for an aladura church; in
English and Yoruba editions. At least three smaller
churches derivative from this church have their own hymnbooks.]

721 CHURCH OF THE LORD (ALADURA). The Voice of the Spirit. A
monthly magazine of the Church of the Lord (Aladura).
Lagos: the Church, 1 (1), 1968, 21 p.
[A revival of a magazine begun in the 1940s.]

722 COKER, E[KUNDAYO] O[LUSEGUN]. The order: constitutions and
bylaws of the Eternal Sacred Order of the Cherubim and
Seraphim. Enugu: Dek's Press, n.d., 37 p.
[One of a number of aladura constitutions, orders of
worship etc., published in Nigeria.]

723 COKER, J[ACOB] K[AYINDE]. The African Church. Lagos: 1913.
[By a leader of the "African Church" secession in Lagos.]

West Africa

724   COKER, JACOB KAYINDE. Polygamy defended. Lagos: Karaole
      Press 1915, 22 p.
          [A scholarly defense of polygamy against the Minute of
      the Church Missionary Society which condemned it.]

725   COKER, S[IMEON] A. Three sermons on the Christian ministry.
      London: Unwin 1904, 32 p.
          [A theological statement by the Superintendent, African
      Church, Lagos, in support of the episcopacy.]

726   COKER, S[IMEON] A. The rights of Africans to organise and
      establish indigenous churches unattached to and uncon-
      trolled by foreign church organizations. Lagos: Tikatore
      Press 1917, 48 p.
          [A lecture delivered by Coker, an "African" churchman,
      occasioned by his defence of the Christ Army Church.]

727   COLEMAN, JAMES S[MOOT]. Nigeria, background to nationalism.
      Berkeley and Los Angeles: University of California Press
      1958, xiv + 510 p., illus., maps.
          [Pp. 174-178, 302-303, "nativistic" and secession movements
      as aspects of nationalism; concentrates on those connected
      with white domination and on National Church of Nigeria.]

728   COMHAIRE, J[EAN]. La vie religieuse à Lagos. Zaïre (Brussels)
      3 (5), 1949, 549-556.
          [Pp. 552-556, the "African Churches", "prophetic sects" and
      neo-traditional groups - Ijo Orunmila and Reformed Ogboni.]

729   CUYPERS, PAUL. The Catholic answer to the independent
      churches. Uyo, Eastern Nigeria: Uyo Inter-church Study
      Group 1966, 2 p. Mimeo.

730   DAFIDI, [A. A. ABIOLA-JACOBS]. Ifan, igbe aiye alagba Wm.
      Folarin Sosan. Ibadan: Lisabi Press 1957, 17 p.
          [A biography of the Rev. W. F. Sosan, a leader of the
      Cherubim and Seraphim in Western Nigeria; in Yoruba.]

731   DALBY, DAVID. The indigenous scripts of West Africa and
      Surinam: their inspiration and design. African Language
      Studies 9, 1968, 156-197.
          [Pp. 156-169, includes the Obere Okaime "revealed" script.]

732   DALBY, DAVID. Further indigenous scripts of West Africa:
      Manding, Wolof and Fula alphabets and Yoruba "Holy" writing.
      African Language Studies 10, 1969, 161-181.
          [Pp. 174-177, 180, Oshitelu's holy writing and revealed
      words, in the Church of the Lord (Aladura).]

733   DALLIMORE, H[ENRY]. The Aladura movement in Ekiti. Western
      Equatorial Africa Church Magazine no. 443=36 (May, 1931,
      93-97, illus.
      [Contemporary account of the Babalola prophet movement
      by a C.M.S. missionary who initially attempted to work
      with it.]

734   DALLIMORE, HENRY. Aftermath of the prophet movement. Church
      Missionary Outlook (London) Oct. 1938, 220-22.
      [The aladura and Babalola revival.]

735   DELANO, ISAAC O. Notes and comments from Nigeria. London:
      USCL 1944, 64 p.
      [Pp. 31-34, the "African" church; pp. 34-36, the original
      Faith Tabernacle Church; Ch. 9, the Order of Cherubim and
      Seraphim; a Nigerian's descriptive account, with questions
      as to the adequacy of such forms of Christianity for the
      future.]

736   DUCKWORTH, E. H. A visit to the Apostles and the town of
      Aiyetoro. Nigeria Magazine (Lagos) 36, 1951, 386-440,
      illus., map.
      [Based on a five-day visit by the editor of Nigeria;
      little on the religious features.]

737   ECHUERO, MICHAEL J. C. The religious culture of 19th century
      Lagos. West African Religion (Nsukka) 12, July 1972, 16-25.
      [Pp. 22-24, the background to the formation of inde-
      pendent churches in the 1890s.]

738   EDO NATIONAL CHURCH OF GOD. The book of the Holy Aruosa,
      according to the ancient Binis. Benin City (Nigeria):
      Edo National Church of God 1946, vol. 1, 19 p.; 1948,
      vol. 2, 6 p.
      [The mythology and legends of the Aruosa or Edo
      National Church, "re-established" in 1945 by the Oba (King)
      of Benin.]

739   EKEZIE, JOSIAH OKWUOBASI. Spiritual renaissance in Nigeria.
      n.p. [Nsukka]: the author (Ministry of Education,
      Nsukka) n.d. [1970?], 104 p., illus.
      [By the "founder and leader of the Society for Right
      Human Relations in Nigeria", "launched since 1965";
      detailed astringent comment on the moral and social situ-
      ation, with suggested remedies.]

740   EKIT, RICHMAEL (ed.). Do you know the Spirit movement of 1927
      in Ibibioland? Edem Urua Ibiono (Itu, Eastern Nigeria):
      the author n.d. [1964], 54 p.

West Africa

        [Biographical account of Ekit and other leaders in the
Spirit movement, published for the Oberi Okaime Church.]

741   EKWENSI, CYPRIAN [O. D.]. Iska. London: Hutchinson 1966,
       222 p.
       [Fiction; especially Book 4, a prophet of the "Prayer
       People".]

742   EMMANUEL, CHRISTIANAH A[BIODUN AKINSOWON]. Iwe itan tabi
       isipaya orun ti Olorun fi han [Book of vision or revela-
       tions of heaven shown by God]. Lagos: Bethel Press 1940,
       9 p.
       [An account of the visions received in 1925 by one of
       the founders of the Cherubim and Seraphim. In Yoruba.]

743   ENANG, KENNETH. Community and salvation in the Nigerian
       independent churches. Zeitschrift für Missionswissenschaft
       und Religionswissenschaft (Munster) 59 (4), 1975, 255-268.
       [Among the Annang people, south-eastern Nigeria, and set
       against the traditional religious background.]

744   ENANG, K[ENNETH] N. The Holy Spirit in the Nigerian inde-
       pendent churches. Africana Marburgensia 9 (2), 1976,
       3-31.

745   ENYINDAH, ALEX O. The Pentecostal Churches as I see them.
       Report of Seminar on "The Religious Situation in Nigeria
       Today"...1972...Nsukka. Nsukka: Department of Religion,
       University of Nigeria 1972, 100 p. Mimeo.
       [Pp. 94-96, especially on the "prayer houses" of eastern
       Nigerian states; a critical survey.]

746   EPELLE, E[MMANUEL] M. T[OBIAH]. The Church in the Niger
       Delta. Aba, Eastern Nigeria: Niger Delta Diocese 1955,
       128 p.
       [Pp. 51-54 on the Braide Movement, by a Nigerian Angli-
       can historian.]

747   EPELLE, E[MMANUEL] M. T[OBIAH]. The Church in Opobo. Opobo,
       Eastern Nigeria: St. Paul's Church Parochial Committee,
       n.d. [1958], 69 p.
       [Especially chs. 4 and 5 on Braide and other secessions.]

748   EPELLE, E[MMANUEL] M. T[OBIAH]. Bishops in the Niger Delta.
       Aba, E. Nigeria: Niger Delta Diocese 1964, 196 p.
       [Pp. 136-139, Bishop James Johnson and the Braide
       movement.]

749   ERIVWO, S. U. Christian churches in Urhoboland. Orita
      (Ibadan) 7 (1), 1973, 32-45.
         [Pp. 43-45, the African Church. Based on his Ibadan
      University Ph.D. dissertation, Christianity in Urhoboland
      1901-1961, 1972.]

750   ERIVWO, S. U. The Holy Ghost Devotees and Demonday's minis-
      try - an evaluation. West African Religion (Nsukka)
      no. 15, March 1974, 19-31.
         [G. A. Ebifeya's church, founded at Jos in 1958; and
      Monday Uzoechi, a healer of the insane.]

751   FERGUSON, JOHN. Christian byways: deviations from the Chris-
      tian faith. Ibadan: Daystar Press 1968, 60 p.
         [Pp. 17-21, "The sects" in Nigeria - brief accounts of
      five, and of their common features; pp. 42-46, "Secret
      societies" - account and criticism of the Reformed Ogboni
      Fraternity.]

752   FLAMINGO (Nigeria). Nigeria's rich woman - (magic) doctor
      meets the witches. Flamingo 1973, 28-31, illus.
         [Olufunmilaye Komaya, a member of St. Stephen's West
      African Episcopal (independent) Church in Lagos; her
      African Science Herbal Hospital at Bariga.]

753   GODFREY, PETER B. A Lagos diary. The Unitarian (Bala)
      no. 830, January 1973, 1-4, 12, illus.
         [A visit to the Lagos Unitarian Brotherhood Church in
      1972.]

754   GOD'S KINGDOM SOCIETY. Theocratic Songs of Praise. Warri,
      Mid-West Nigeria: the Society n.d. [1954], 184 p.
         [193 hymns, etc., mostly original, together with psalms
      and other biblical material adapted for an African society
      derived from Jehovah's Witnesses; in English.]

755   GOERNER, H. CORNELL. Africa, in Baker J. Cauthen et al. (eds.),
      Advance: a history of Southern Baptist Foreign Missions.
      Nashville, Tennessee: Broadman Press 1970, 136-186.
         [Pp. 144-148, the Baptists in Lagos, Moses Stone and
      Mojola Agbebi, and the independence movement; from the
      official Southern Baptist viewpoint.]

756   GRESCHAT, HANS-JÜRGEN. The National Church of Nigeria:
      Beispiel des religiösen Nationalismus. Evangelische
      Missions-Zeitschrift (Stuttgart) 25 (2), 1968, 86-97.

West Africa

757 GRIMLEY, JOHN D., and ROBINSON, GORDON E. Church growth in
    Central and Southern Nigeria. Grand Rapids, Michigan:
    W. B. Eerdmans 1966, 386 p., illus., maps, tables, bibl.
        [Ch. 4, pp. 299-317, "Prophetism and church growth",
    surveys the Braide movement, Cherubim and Seraphim, Christ
    Apostolic Church and Church of the Lord (Aladura). By a
    Baptist missionary.]

758 GROVES, W. T. A Nigerian prophet. The Herald (London, Prim-
    itive Methodist Missionary Society) 9 (6), June 1916,
    84-87, illus.
        [An illiterate prophet of the Braide movement at Azumini,
    Eastern Nigeria, 1916; by a Methodist missionary.]

759 HAU, K. Ecriture, textes et comput Oberi Okaime. Bulletin
    IFAN (Dakar), série B, 23 (1-2), 1961, 291-308.
        [The revealed script and language of a section of the
    Spirit movement in Eastern Nigeria from 1927.]

760 HOLY CHURCH OF THE LORD. Ilana isin mimo (constitution) ati
    awon ofin Ijo Mimo Olluwa (Aladura). The Holy Church of
    the Lord ni gbogbo agbaiye. Ife, Nigeria: the Church
    n.d. 34 p., illus.
        [Almost identical with J. O. Oshitelu's Constitution
    (1938) for the Church of the Lord (Aladura); leader,
    Prophet S. O. Ogundiya.]

761 HOLY SAVIOUR'S CHURCH. The rules and regulations, observances
    and the constitution of the New Salem Holy Saviour's
    Church (Aladura). Ife, Nigeria: the Church n.d. [1966?],
    40 p.
        [Founded in 1946 by J. O. Denton (or Ogunde) by
    secession from the Church of the Lord (Aladura).]

762 IDOWU, E. BOLAJI. Olodumare: God in Yoruba belief. London:
    Longmans 1962, 222 p.
        [Pp. 211-215, "syncretistic sects", especially
    Orunmilaism and Reformed Ogboni Fraternity.]

763 IDOWU, E. BOLAJI. Towards an indigenous church. London:
    Oxford University Press 1965, viii + 60 p.
        [A Nigerian Methodist theologian gives a positive eval-
    uation of the role of independent churches in making
    Christianity indigenous. P. 9, the National Church of
    Nigeria and the Aruosa Church in Benin City; pp. 41-47,
    the appeal of the aladura churches.]

764   IFEKA-MOLLER, C[AROLINE VICTORIA MARGARET]. White power:
       socio-structural factors in conversion to Christianity,
       Eastern Nigeria, 1921-1966. Canadian Journal of African
       Studies (Montreal) 8 (1), 1974, 55-72, tables, map,
       résumé fr.
          [Discusses both mission and aladura bodies, with Onitsha
       as a case study.]

765   IGE, OYE. Joseph Babalola - a twentieth century prophet. The
       African Historian (Ibadan, University of Ife) 1 (3), 1965,
       38-42.
          [An account of the aladura prophet, Babalola, based on
       Mediayese, item 795. In a student journal.]

766   IJOMAH, B. I. C. and UMEH, NAT. This woman saw Jesus?
       Veronica - fake or stigmatist? Eagle (Onitsha, Nigeria)
       May 1964, 16-17.
          [A Roman Catholic prophetess at Nsukka, Eastern Nigeria.]

767   IKECHIUKU, J[OSEPH]. The characteristics, office and duty of
       the Holy Spirit. Sapele: Good News Printers, n.d., 26 p.,
       photo.
          [By the founder of St. Joseph's Chosen Church of God.]

768   IKECHIUKU, JOSEPH. The immutable rules and conducts of St.
       Joseph's Chosen Church of God selected through the reve-
       lation of God. Sapele, Mid-West Nigeria: the author,
       n.d., 55 p., photo.
          [Contains a creed, rule for worship, baptism, various
       festivals, marriage, burial and the organisation of the
       Church.]

769   ILOGU, EDMUND [C. O.]. Christ Healing Church - a study of
       the sociology of one independent African church. West
       African Religion (Nsukka) no. 8, July 1970, 12-19.
          [Founded by Prophet S. Ogola of Opobo in 1936, with
       some twenty branches; Anglican and Igbo backgrounds.]

770   ILOGU, EDMUND [C. O.]. Christianity and Ibo culture. Leiden:
       E. J. Brill 1974, 262 p., map, illus.
          [Pp. 59, 61, G. Braide; pp. 60-61, growth of independent
       churches; p. 100, Ihiala churches; p. 102, Nsukka churches;
       pp. 110-115, Aba churches and reasons for joining inde-
       pendents.]

771   IWUAGWU, AUGUSTINE O. The "Spiritual Churches" in the East-
       ern States of Nigeria (A selected study). University of
       Ibadan, Ph.D. dissertation (Religious Studies) 1971,
       xi + 541 p., map.

West Africa

[Christ Army Church; "Faith" Churches; "Apostolic" Churches; Mount Zion Churches; and others. Includes list of "Spiritual Church" publications, 16 p. Ch. 9 as extract reprint in Exchange (Leiden) 9, Dec. 1974, 12-26, on the Onu Uzo Ndu Christ Apostle Church since 1953 (pp. 271-301 in dissertation).]

772   IWUAGWU, A[UGUSTINE] O. Church Prayer Band - its formation and organization. Outreach: the Magazine of the Diocese of Owerri 2 (1), 1974, 15-18; 2 (12), 1974, 12-14.
      [Pp. 14 and 17, prayer bands as alternative to resort to (independent) "prayer houses", and the need to avoid developing into the latter; Anglican context.]

773   IWUANYANWU, SAMUEL. Searching for the healing churches - but did I find any? Outreach: the Magazine of the Diocese of Owerri 2 (9), 1973, 18-20.
      [Experience in a "healing church" and in Jehovah's Witnesses.]

774   IYALLA, N. B. The most Rev. James George Campbell, D.B.P., Senior Patriarch of the West African Episcopal Church and the presiding Patriarch of the Christ Army Church G.B.C. Nigeria: a brief account of his missionary labours. Lagos: Oluwole Press 1945, 16 p.
      [On the founder of the West African Episcopal Church, by one of his ministers; pp. 6-11 on the Braide movement.]

775   JAHN, JANHEINZ. Through African doors: experiences and encounters in West Africa. London: Faber and Faber 1962, 232 p., maps, illus.
      [Pp. 219, a baptism by "Irvingites"; p. 221, plural belonging; pp. 223-225, Holy Chapel of Wisdom. Calabar; pp. 225-227, Jehovah's Witnesses, Benin; pp. 227-229, new movements in Africa.]

776   JOHNSON, JAMES. Elijah II. Church Missionary Review (London) no. 808=67 (Aug.), 1916, 455-462.
      [On Garrick Braide, Eastern Nigeria 1915-1916, by the Nigerian Anglican assistant bishop concerned.]

777   JUWE, SYLWE MUBUNDU. The dawn of a new day. [East Nigeria]: the author n.d. [1950s?], 26 p., photo.
      [An exhortation to go forward with the guidance Christ gave towards restoring the ancient faith of a paradisal African civilization which had its own true prophets and already knew about Jesus.]

778   JUWE, SYLWE MUBUNDU. The Western Ibo people. Port Harcourt,
      Eastern Nigeria: the author n.d. [1953?] 54 p.
      [An account of a "missionary tour" by a Nigerian after a
      visionary experience, to preach a national religion in
      place of western Christianity and commercialized forms of
      traditional religion.]

779   JUWE, SYLVE MUBUNDU. Why [sic] is the National Church of
      Nigeria and the Cameroons and the God of Africa. Asaba,
      Nigeria: the author n.d., 41 p.
      [An apologia for this movement.]

780   KAKA, G. A. Biography of late Dr. J. O. Oshitelu. The
      Guardian (Lagos) 1 (6), 1966, 25-30, illus.
      [Obituary article on the founder of the Church of the
      Lord (Aladura).]

781   KALU, OGBU U. The politics of religious sectarianism in Africa.
      West African Religion (Nsukka) 16 (1), n.d. [1975], 15ff.
      [With special reference to Nigerian aladura groups and
      their political attitudes.]

782   LAGOS, [ANGLICAN] DIOCESE OF. Reports and Minutes of Pro-
      ceedings...of the Synod. Lagos: the Diocese.
      [E.g.: 1920, p. 11, itinerant prophets; 1922, pp. 11-14,
      the clash with the first aladura society; 1924, p. 78;
      1928, p. 23, the "Seraphim" movement; 1931, pp. 8-10,
      "fancy sects"; 1933, pp. 10-11, non-fraternization with the
      "so-called African Churches"; 1935, p. 16, prophet move-
      ments in Bassa country; 1936, pp. 25-26, questions the
      "African" claims of independents, and maintains a stand
      against polygamy; 1948, p. 81, reports return of earlier
      seceders; 1958, p. 48, a new attitude of cooperation with
      the African Church Bethel.]

783   LANGLEY, JABEZ AYODELE. Garveyism and African nationalism.
      Race 11 (2), 1969, 157-172.
      [Pp. 159, 160, Patriarch J. G. Campbell's rejection of
      political Garveyism, but sympathy for the economic
      proposals.]

784   LEITH-ROSS, SYLVIA. African women. London: Faber 1939;
      Routledge and Kegan Paul 1965, 367 p.
      [East Nigeria: pp. 299-301 on "sects" as spiritually
      dangerous and anti-government; pp. 250-253, denominations
      in Port Harcourt.]

West Africa

785   LUCAS, J. OLUMIDE. Lecture on the history of St. Paul's
       Church, Breadfruit, Lagos (1852-1945). Lagos: St. Paul's
       Church n.d. [1946?], 72 p., illus.
       [Pp. 26-29, background to the secession of 1891 and the
       United Native African Church; pp. 35-38, the 1901 seces-
       sion of the Anglican Church, by the minister of the
       Anglican parish most involved.]

786   MACAULAY, HERBERT. The history of the development of mission-
       ary work with special reference to the United African
       Church. Lagos: Adedimeta Printing Works 1942, 37 p.
       [By a leading Nigerian nationalist who was not a member
       of the church. In English and Yoruba.]

787   McCLELLAND, ELIZABETH M. The experiment in communal living at
       Aiyetoro. Comparative Studies in Society and History 9
       (1), 1966, 14-28.
       [On the Aiyetoro Holy Apostles' Community.]

788   McDONALD, T. R. Aspects of religious sectarianism and syn-
       cretism in African urban settings, with special reference
       to Port Harcourt. Oxford University, B.Litt. thesis
       1968-69, 149 p.

789   McKENZIE, PETER R. Religion in an African city. The Outlook
       (Christchurch, New Zealand - Presbyterian Church) July
       1973, 12-14, illus.
       [Pp. 13-14, description of a Christ Apostolic Church
       service at Oke-Iyanu, New Ibadan, in 1972.]

790   MACLEAN, UNA. Magical medicine. A Nigerian case-study.
       London: Allen Lane 1971, 167 p.
       [Pp. 108-112, Samson Tella of Ibadan, aladura prophet,
       and his asylum for the insane.]

791   MARIOGHAE, MICHAEL and FERGUSON, JOHN. Nigeria under the
       cross. London: Highway Press 1965, 126 p.
       [Pp. 51-60, discussion of causes and character of
       Nigerian "sects", and description of the Aiyetoro
       Community.]

792   MARTIN, SAMUEL W[ADIEI]. Where Jesus found me. [U.S.A.]:
       the author n.d. [1921], 32 p.
       [The life history and apologia for missions in Africa,
       of the founder of the Pilgrim Baptist Mission of Nigeria
       (Inc.), ca. 1938, at Issele-Uku. An appendix contains
       testimonials from prominent U.S. citizens.]

793 MARTIN, SAMUEL WADIEI. The autobiography of the Rev. Samuel
     Wadiei Martin. [Issele Uku]: the author n.d. [ca. 1966?]
     281 p., illus.

794 MAXWELL, J[OHN] LOWRY. Nigeria. The land, the people and
     Christian progress. London: World Dominion Press n.d.
     [ca. 1927], 164 p.
     [Pp. 83-84, survey of the earlier secession churches,
     and the Braide movement; pp. 112-113, statistical survey
     of "independent churches", based on 1921 census.]

795 MEDAIYESE, J. A. Itan igbedide woli J. A. Babalola fun ise
     ihinrere [The rise of prophet Babalola for the work of the
     Gospel]. Ibadan: Christ Apostolic Church n.d. [ca. 1960],
     104 p., illus.
     [A biography by the General Superintendent of Babalola's
     Church, and his contemporary; in Yoruba.]

796 MESSENGER, JOHN C., JR. The Christian concept of forgiveness
     and Anang morality. Practical Anthropology (Tarrytown,
     N.Y.) 6 (3), 1959, 97-103.
     [The acceptance of the Christian doctrine of a forgiving
     deity, found in prayer churches, is a factor behind
     immorality.]

797 MESSENGER, JOHN C., JR. Religious acculturation among the
     Ibibio, in W. R. Bascom and M. J. Herskovits (eds.),
     Continuity and change in African cultures. Chicago:
     University of Chicago Press 1959, 279-299.
     [Pp. 286-299, the Spirit movement of 1930-1938 and its
     effects as seen in 1951; nativist reactions and ensuing
     syncretism in all churches.]

798 MESSENGER, JOHN C., JR. Reinterpretation of Christian and
     indigenous belief in a Nigerian nativist church. American
     Anthropologist 62 (2), 1960, 268-278. Repr. in John
     Middleton (ed.), Black Africa: its people and their cul-
     ture today. N.Y. and London: Macmillan 1970, 212-221.
     [The Christ Army Church among the Anang Ibibio of south-
     east Nigeria, 1950; its organization and beliefs.]

799 MITCHELL, ROBERT CAMERON. Religious change and modernization:
     the aladura churches among the Yoruba in southwestern
     Nigeria. Northwestern University, Ph.D. dissertation
     (sociology), 1970, 457 p.
     [With special reference to Ibadan; aladura as religious
     protest, seeking to indigenize Protestant forms of
     Christianity.]

West Africa

800   MITCHELL, ROBERT CAMERON. Religious protest and social change:
      the origins of the aladura movement in western Nigeria,
      in R. I. Rotberg and A. A. Mazrui (eds.), Protest and
      power in Black Africa. New York: Oxford University Press
      1970, 458-496.

801   MITCHELL, ROBERT CAMERON. Witchcraft, sin, divine power and
      healing: the aladura churches and the attainment of life's
      destiny among the Yoruba, in The traditional background to
      medical practice in Nigeria (Occasional Paper no. 25).
      Ibadan: University of Ibadan Institute of African Studies
      1971, 61-78.
      [Paper given at a conference held in 1966.]

802   MOLLER, CAROLINE [VICTORIA MARGARET] [IFEKA-]. Some aspects
      of belief in the Eternal Sacred Order of Cherubim and
      Seraphim (Onitsha Branch). Uyo, E. Nigeria: Uyo Inter-
      Church Study Group 1966, 4 p. Mimeo.

803   MOLLER, CAROLINE V[ICTORIA] M[ARGARET] [IFEKA-]. An aladura
      church in Eastern Nigeria. London University, Ph.D.
      dissertation (social anthropology) 1968, 281 p.
      [The Cherubim and Seraphim, Eternal Sacred Order Mt.
      Zion, in Onitsha from 1949.]

804   MORRILL, WARREN T. Two urban cultures of Calabar. University
      of Chicago, Ph.D. dissertation (anthropology), 1960,
      309 p.
      [Includes the differential impact of independent churches
      upon the Ibo and Efik groups.]

805   MORTON-WILLIAMS, PETER. The Atinga cult among the south-
      western Yoruba: a sociological analysis of a witch-finding
      movement. Bulletin IFAN (Dakar), série B, 18 (3-4),1956,
      315-334.
      [Analysis of the impact a witchfinding movement had
      among the western Yoruba in the early 1950s.]

806   NATIONAL CHURCH OF NIGERIA AND THE CAMEROONS. Catechism of
      the National Church professing the natural religion of
      Africa. Aba: Research Institute of African Religion,
      n.d., 20 p.
      [Catechism, creed, and a few hymns.]

807   NATIONAL CHURCH OF NIGERIA AND THE CAMEROONS. Hymns and
      prayers for use in the...Church... Aba: the Church, n.d.
      [1948], 54 p.

[57 hymns, some original, together with prayers and a creed, expressing the beliefs of an associate of the early Zik political movement; in English.]

808 NEWTON, KENNETH and NEWTON, ANNA. Aiyetoro, community of co-operators. Africa Today (New York) 11 (4), 1964, 4-6. (Reprinted from Peace News.)
[A descriptive account by British teachers.]

809 NIGER, [ANGLICAN] DIOCESE ON THE. Reports of Proceedings...of the Synod... Onitsha: the Diocese.
[E.g.: 1931, p. 55; 1940, pp. 4, 9, 18, 19; on various secession groups.]

810 NIGER DELTA CHURCH BOARD (ANGLICAN). Reports or minutes of proceedings of the...Church Board.... Lagos: C.M.S. for the Board.
[E.g.: 1916, pp. 60-85, the three-day discussion of the Braide movement; 1917, pp. 53-63; 1918, pp. 8-9, 17; 1919, pp. 35, 39, 50, all on the same topic; 1921, printed in Diocesan Magazine (see item 896) and 1921-1931 (again published separately) passim, on the later effect of the movement, especially 1929, p. vi.]

811 NIGERIA, CHRISTIAN COUNCIL OF. Annual reports. Lagos: the Council.
[E.g.: 1934, p. 17, faith healing; 1947, p. 23, invitations from two "secessionist groups" in East Nigeria to the American Church of the Nazarene; 1964, pp. 34-35, relations with three independent churches; pp. 50-54, see Turner, item 875.]

812 NIGERIA MAGAZINE (Lagos). Cherubim and Seraphim. Nigeria Magazine no. 53, 1957, 119-134, illus.
[Popular account of history and main features of an aladura church.]

813 NIGERIA MAGAZINE (Lagos). Aiyetoro. Nigeria Magazine no. 55, 1957, 356-386, illus.
[Pictorial account of a visit to the Holy Apostles' Community. Sequel to Duckworth, item 736.]

814 NIGERIAN CHRISTIAN, THE (Ibadan). The Christ Apostolic Church: a summary of its history and structure. The Nigerian Christian 3 (5), 1969, 4-5.

815 NIGERIAN CHRISTIAN, THE (Ibadan). Citation (Rev. Samuel Wadiei Martin). The Nigerian Christian 7 (1), 1973, 1, 3, illus.

West Africa

> [On the occasion of the conferment of the honorary
> D.Litt. degree on the founder of the Pilgrim Baptist
> Church.]

816   NIGERIAN CHRISTIAN, THE (Ibadan). Prophet Demonday Zeachi
      (the new "Saviour"). The Nigerian Christian 8 (5), 1973,
      pp. 1, 4, 6, illus.; Editorial [on Demonday Zeachi], idem
      8 (6), 1973, 2.
      [A current healer of the insane, etc., formerly of the
      Assemblies of God, Umuahia. Editorial compares his influ-
      ence in forcing the state government to care for the
      mentally ill to the social record of the "established
      churches".]

817   NIGERIAN CHRISTIAN, THE (Ibadan). The United Native African
      Church in Nigeria. The Nigerian Christian 9 (7), 1974,
      14-15, illus.
      [A popular history, contributed by the Church.]

818   NWANGORO, BOB. The city of Salem. Drum (Lagos) Oct. 1956,
      7-9, illus.
      [A journalistic account of Gideon Urhobo and his God's
      Kingdom Society, with headquarters at Warri.]

819   NWANGWU, JONATHAN. I am Jesus Christ. Eagle (Onistsha) Sep.
      1964, 7-10, 12-13, illus.
      [Odili Nwanjuani, an Igbo messianic founder of the
      "Uwaoma Church".]

820   NWOSU, V[INCENT] A. (ed.). Prayer houses and faith healing.
      No place, no publisher [Printed by Tabansi Press,
      Onitsha] n.d. [1971], 52 p.
      [By four Roman Catholic seminarians; special attention
      to Omenma Central Prayer House, Cherubim and Seraphim Holy
      Prayer Houses, and the All Christian Praying Band at
      Ufuma.]

821   OBU, O. O. Seven sermons published in three booklets: What
      is Brotherhood? What is Cross? What is Star? Calabar:
      Brotherhood [of the Cross and Star] Press, n.d.
      [1967-68?], 80 p. total.

822   O'CONNELL, JAMES. Government and politics in the Yoruba
      African churches: the claims of tradition and modernity.
      Odu. University of Ife Journal of African Studies 2 (1),
      1965, 92-108
      [A review article on Webster, item 888.]

823 ODUBANJO, D. O. Recommendations by Pastor D. O. Odubanjo of
     Lagos to the Nigerian Council in July 1936, on the matter
     of founding schools and colleges for the Apostolic Church
     in Nigeria. Christ Apostolic (Lagos, Christ Apostolic
     Church) no. 8, June 1969, p. 8, illus.
     [A sophisticated statement of the case.]

824 OGEDEGBE, PETER IRABOR. Origin and causes of independent
     churches, with special reference to Edo. Ibadan Univer-
     sity, Department of Religious Studies, B.A. (Hons.)
     Extended Essay 1969, 119 p., illus.
     [Includes U.N.A., Benin United Baptist Mission, United
     Church of Cherubim and Seraphim Organization, Edo
     Cherubim and Seraphim Church, St. Joseph Chosen Church of
     God, Christ Apostolic Church, Holy Aruosa Church.]

825 OGEDEGBE, PETER I[RABOR]. The Holy Aruosa Church. Orita
     (Ibadan) 4 (2), 1970, 149-154.
     [Extract from his essay, above.]

826 OGUNBIYI, THOMAS A. J. Awon Adura Banuso ati ti Oto. Ibadan:
     Lishabi Press 1932, 15 p.
     [Private prayers for each day of the week, and for
     personal problems, each prefaced by Hebrew names of God
     with Yoruba equivalents. By the Anglican founder of the
     Reformed Ogboni Fraternity.]

827 OJI, B. A. Originality of religion revealed. Aba: Research
     Institute of African Mission Press 1960, 58 p.
     [An apology for the "National Church of Nigeria" espe-
     cially in relation to Christianity and Islam; prefaced by
     report of a lecture by Azikiwe in 1951 with special
     reference to "the God of Africa".]

828 OKE, G[ABRIEL] A. A short history of the United Native
     African Church. Part I, 1891-1903. Lagos: Shalom Press
     1918, 17 p.
     [By an "African" churchman.]

829 OKE, G[ABRIEL] A. A short history of the United Native
     African Church. Part II, 1904-1924. Lagos: Ijaiye Press
     1936, 67 p.

830 OKE, S. ADENIRAN. The Ethiopian National Church: a neces-
     sity. Ibadan: Lisabi Press 1923, 32 p.

West Africa

831 OKOJIE, XTO G. In Comments [on] Materials for a history of
       studies of crisis cults: a bibliographic essay, by Weston
       LaBarre. Current Anthropology 12 (1), 1971, 31-32.
         [Outline of Osenuwegbe's cult in Benin area, 1926-31,
         and persisting; hostile both to Christianity and to
         traditional practices.]

832 OKOLUGBO, EMMANUEL O. The problem of syncretism with partic-
       ular reference to Christianity in Aboh District. Ibadan
       University, Department of Religious Studies, B.A. (Hons.)
       Extended essay 1968, 77 p., illus.

833 OKPALAOKA, C. I. (ed.). A report on the Holy City of Aiyetoro.
       Nsukka: Sociological Association, University of Nigeria
       1962, 23 p. Mimeo.
         [A descriptive report by students after a visit to the
         community.]

834 OLA, C. S. Foundations of the African Church. Nigerian
       Christian (Ibadan) 9 (3), 1974, 3-4, illus.; 9 (4), 1974,
       14-15, illus.
         [The independent church founded ca. 1903.]

835 OLADUNJOYE, D. A. A short history of the Church Army in
       Africa. Ibadan: the author, n.d. 6 p.
         [Founded by the author in 1952, after he left the
         Salvation Army.]

836 OLAYEMI, SAM. I am Jesus. Drum (Lagos) July 1957, 22-23,
       illus.
         [A journalistic account of the "Spiritual Kingdom" of
         Ededem Bassey, Ikot Ekpene.]

837 OLOWOKURE, JACOB OLABODE KEHINDE. Christianity in Ijeshaland
       1858-1960. Ibadan University, M.A. thesis, Department of
       Religious Studies 1970, 324 p.
         [Pp. 174-234, the aladura movement, especially
         Babatope, Babalola, and the Apostolic Churches;
         pp. 234-237, Jehovah's Witnesses; pp. 238-239, 281,
         Reformed Ogboni Fraternity.]

838 OLUYIMIKA, ISAAC A. The concept of the Holy Spirit in the
       Christ Apostolic Church, Nigeria. Ibadan University,
       Department of Religious Studies, B.A. (Hons.) Extended
       essay 1973, 49 p., illus.
         [General history, plus "sermons".]

116

839   OMOYAJOWO, J[OSEPH] A[KINYELE]. Your dreams. Ibadan: Daystar
      Press 1965, 57 p.
      [Pp. 24-29, account of how aladura prophets interpret
      dreams; by a Methodist minister.]

840   OMOYAJOWO, JOSEPH AKINYELE. The Christian Church and sec-
      tarian movements: Montanism and the independent church
      movement of Yorubaland. Ibadan University, Department of
      Religious Studies, B.A. (Hons.) Extended essay 1966, 51 p.

841   OMOYAJOWO, JOSEPH AKINYELE. The Cherubim and Seraphim Move-
      ment - a study in interaction. Orita (Ibadan) 4 (2),
      1970, 124-139.

842   OMOYAJOWO, JOSEPH AKINYELE. Cherubim and Seraphim Church in
      Nigeria. Ibadan University Ph.D. dissertation 1971,
      827 p., illus., maps, diagrams.
      [Includes pp. 718-725 on Aiyetoro "Holy City of the
      Apostles".]

843   ONYIOHA, K. O. K. The National Church of Nigeria: its
      catechism and credo. Ebute Metta, Lagos: the author
      1951, 52 p.

844   ONYIOHA, K. O. K. Christianity, Islam and Godianism in
      Nigeria. Enugu: the author 1964, 15 p., illus.
      [A lecture at the University of Nigeria by the leading
      figure in Godianism, successor to the National Church of
      Nigeria.]

845   OROGUN, J. B. The Order of Service of Christ Apostolic
      Church, Nigeria and Ghana. Akure, Nigeria: the author
      1966, 70 p.
      [An English version of the main services with full texts
      of hymns.]

846   OSHITELU, JOSIAH OLUNOWO. Awon asotele ohun ti yio bere si
      sele tabi inu odun 1931 [Prophecies that will happen in
      1931]. Ibadan: Lisabi Press n.d. [ca. 1930], 16 p.
      [The first of a series of printed prophecies by the
      founder of the Church of the Lord (Aladura).]

847   OSHITELU, JOSIAH OLUNOWO. Catechism of the Church of the
      Lord...and the Holy Litany...with the Church Prayer Drill.
      Ogere, W. Nigeria: the author 1948, 22 p.
      [See Turner, items 458 and 459 for analysis of these
      texts.]

West Africa

848   OTONG, D. U. The development of Christ Faith Prayer Fellow-
      ship Ministry in Nigeria: an appeal for help. Port
      Harcourt: Goodwill Press for the author, n.d. [1965],
      10 p.
          [By the founder of the Christ Faith Church, Abak, E.
      Nigeria.]

849   OTTAH, NELSON. The Apostle of "Godianism". Drum (Lagos)
      Oct. 1962, pp. 15, 17.
          [On K. O. K. Onyioha of the former National Church of
      Nigeria.]

850   OWERRI, [ANGLICAN] DIOCESE OF. Renewal: the story of the
      Third Session of the Fifth Synod of the Diocese of
      Owerri...1972. [Owerri: the Synod n.d. (1972?)] 72 p.
          [Pp. 28-30, report on "the challenge of the sects";
      pp. 34-35, 41, development of church "Prayer Bands" as an
      "answer".]

851   PARRATT, JOHN K[ING]. Religious change in Yoruba society - a
      test case. Journal of Religion in Africa 2 (2), 1969,
      113-128.
          [P. 117, aladuras' reason for Christian conversion;
      pp. 121-125, causes of aladura churches' growth;
      pp. 125-7, their future; p. 128, growth statistics.]

852   PARRATT, JOHN K[ING] and DOI, AHMAD RAHMAN I. Some further
      aspects of Yoruba syncretism. Practical Anthropology
      (Tarrytown, N. Y.) 16 (6), 1969, 252-266.
          [Pp. 253-255, substantial rejection of traditional
      divining but some residual use of "native medicine" among
      aladura churches.]

853   PARRINDER, [EDWARD] GEOFFREY [SIMONS]. Indigenous churches in
      Nigeria. West African Review no. 394=31 (Sept.), 1960,
      87, 89, 91, 93, illus.
          [A sympathetic general survey.]

854   PARRINDER, [EDWARD] GEOFFREY [SIMONS]. Religion in an African
      city. London: Oxford University Press 1953, 211 p;
      reprint, New York: Negro Universities Press, 1974.
          [Pp. 107-132, "The Cross: separatist sects", in
      Ibadan.]

855   PEEL, J[OHN] D[AVID] Y[EADON]. Aladura: a religious movement
      among the Yoruba. London: Oxford University Press for
      the International African Institute 1968, xiii + 338 p.,
      diagrams, maps, tables, bibl.

118

[Based on his London Ph.D. dissertation, 1966; pp. 316-324, bibliography of some 150 publications of the Cherubim and Seraphim Society and the Christ Apostolic Church.]

856 PEEL, J[OHN] D[AVID] Y[EADON]. Syncretism and religious change. Comparative Studies in Society and History 10 (2), 1968, 121-141.
[The Yoruba background of tolerance based on plurality of Orisha cult groups; the "African" and aladura churches, especially the latter, as remarkably non-syncretist; comparisons with syncretist "ethiopian" churches; criticism of the "acculturation model".]

857 PHILLIPS, SAMUEL CHARLES. Egbe Ogboni Keferi. Ti Nwon Npe Ni R.O.F. Ibadan: Temidayo Press (printer), n.d. 8 p.
[An Anglican bishop on the Reformed Ogboni Fraternity; in Yoruba.]

858 PHILLIPS, S[AMUEL] C[HARLES]. The heathen cult called Reformed Ogboni Society. Ibadan: the author 1956.

859 PILTER, M. T. More about Elijah II. Church Missionary Review (London) no. 815=68 (Mar.), 1917, 142-145.
[A missionary on the Braide movement 1915-1916.]

860 QUA IBOE MISSION QUARTERLY (Belfast). On the aftermath of the 1927 "spirit movement" in E. Nigeria, see no. 145, May 1930, p. 160.

861 RICHES OF GRACE (British Apostolic Church). Ethiopia's cry for help. Riches of Grace 6, 1931, p. 215.
[The appeal from Faith Tabernacle.]

862 SAHLMANN, HERBERT. Der Stadtstaat Aiyetoro - eine Siedlung der Holy Apostles Community in Nigeria. Geographische Rundschau (Braunschweig) 18 (10), 1964, 399-404, illus.
[Seen as an "un-African" development, based on old tribal traditions and ancient Christian customs, and led by a young elite.]

863 SHEPPERSON, GEORGE A[LCOTT]. Comment on E. M. McClelland's "The experiment of communal living at Aiyetoro". Comparative Studies in Society and History 9 (1), 1966, 29-32.

864 SHIRER, WILLIAM L. The story of a remarkable pentecostal outpouring in Nigeria. Pentecostal Evangel (Springfield,

West Africa

Missouri) no. 1294, 25 Feb. 1939. Germ. trans., Die
Geschichte einer bemerkenswerten pfingstlichen
Ausgiessung in Nigeria. Die Verheissung des Vaters
(Zurich, Schweiz Pfingstmission) 32 (4), 1939, 1-4; idem
32 (5), 1939, 4-5.
[The influence of Faith Tabernacle, Philadelphia in a
revival movement in E. Nigeria in 1935.]

865   SIMPSON, C. E. E. B. An African village undertakes community
development on its own. Mass Education Bulletin (London)
2 (1), 1950, 7-9.
[The earliest published account of Aiyetoro, by the
local administrative officer.]

866   SIMPSON, GEORGE EATON. Religious changes in Southwestern
Nigeria. Anthropological Quarterly 43 (2), 1970, 79-92.
[Pp. 80-82, Ijo Orunmila and its secessions; pp. 83-85,
Reformed Ogboni Fraternity and Atinga Cult; pp. 85-86, the
aladura.]

867   SKLAR, RICHARD L. Nigerian political parties. Princeton,
N.J., Princeton University Press 1963, 578 p.
[Pp. 253-255, 466, 494, the Reformed Ogboni Fraternity
in Benin politics.]

868   SOYINKA, WOLE. The Jero Plays. The trials of Brother Jero.
Jero's metamorphosis. London: Eyre Methuen 1973, 92 p.
[The trials..., repr. of the 1964 edition, pp. 7-44;
Jero's Metamorphosis, pp. 45-92, first publication.
Humourous satires on an aladura prophet, by Nigeria's
leading playwright.]

869   STEPHENS, A. JOHN (ed.). African attitudes to health and
healing. Ibadan: the author 1964, 71 p. Mimeo.
[A documentation prepared for Nigerian Christian Council
study on health and healing, containing covering letters
from H. W. Turner and R. C. Mitchell; Turner's chapter on
healing from African Independent Church vol. II, 1967;
J. Ade Aina, Present day prophets...; R. C. Mitchell's
paper in the Mindolo Consultation Report 1963 (abbreviated); R. C. Mitchell, The Aladura movement among the
Yoruba 1918-1931; J. Babalola, The Book of Hygiene and
Holy Living; A. J. Ogunbiyi, Various types of prayers.]

870   TALBOT, P[ERCY] AMAURY. The peoples of Southern Nigeria.
London: Oxford University Press 1926, 4 vols.; reprint,
London: F. Cass (Library of African Studies) 1969.

[Vol. II, p. 275; vol. IV, contains official 1921 census
returns; pp. 118-123, reference to the Braide and other
independent movements.]

871   TAMUNO, TEKENA and HORTON, [W.] ROBIN [G.]. The changing
       position of secret societies and cults in modern Nigeria.
       African Notes (Ibadan) 5 (2), 1969, 36-62.
           [Pp. 48-49, 54-55, Atinga cult, Reformed Ogboni Frater-
       nity and Owegbe cult.]

872   TASIE, GODWIN ONYEMEACHI MGBECHI. Christianity in the Niger
       Delta 1864-1918. Aberdeen University, Ph.D. dissertation
       (Church history) 1969, 544 p.
           [Ch. 6, the prophet Garrick Sokari Braide, very
       favourably interpreted by a fellow-countryman; ch. 4,
       Niger Delta Pastorate, as background.]

873   TIMES BRITISH COLONIES REVIEW, THE. Third quarter 1957,
       p. 19, on the Holy Apostles' Community at Aiyetoro,
       illus.

874   TURNBULL, THOMAS N[APIER]. What God hath wrought: a short
       history of the Apostolic Church. Bradford: Puritan
       Press 1959, 186 p.
           [An official history; pp. 71-87, how the Apostolic
       Church in Nigeria developed in connection with the aladura
       movement.]

875   TURNER, H[AROLD] W[ALTER]. The relationship of churches in
       the renewed church in Nigeria, in A renewed church in
       Nigeria, 14th Report, Christian Council of Nigeria. Lagos:
       the Council 1964, 50-54.
           [Includes discussion of relations between older and
       independent churches; this section reprinted by the
       Institute of Church and Society, Ibadan.]

876   TURNER, H[AROLD] W[ALTER]. The late Sir Isaac Akinyele,
       Olubadan of Ibadan. West African Religion (Nsukka, E.
       Nigeria), no. 4, July 1965, 1-4.
           [An obituary of an outstanding leader in the aladura
       movement from 1925-1964.]

877   TURNER, H[AROLD] W[ALTER]. Religious groups in Eastern
       Nigeria. West African Religion (Nsukka) no. 5, February
       1966, 7-18; no. 6, August 1966, 10-15.
           [A provisional check-list of materials on independent
       churches, prophets, etc., in the National Archives,
       Enugu.]

West Africa

878 TURNER, HAROLD WALTER. Nigerien, in W. J. Hollenweger (ed.),
    Die Pfingstkirchen Selbstdarstellungen, Dokumente,
    Kommentare (Kirchen der Welt, 7). Stuttgart:
    Evangelisches Verlagswerk 1971, 115-124; rev. Eng. trans.,
    Pentecostal movements in Nigeria, Orita (Ibadan) 6 (1),
    1972, 39-47.
    [A survey of pentecostal forms of Christianity in
    Nigeria, both indigenous independent and missionary.]

879 UYO SURVEY TEAM. The Abak Story. Uyo, E. Nigeria: the Team
    1967, v + 44 p. Mimeo. (For private circulation).
    [A survey of 33 independent and 17 mission-connected
    churches within a five-mile radius of Abak, with brief
    history and description of 81 congregations, and analysis
    of results.]

880 WARD-PRICE, H[ENRY] L[EWIS]. Dark subjects. London: Jarrolds
    1939, 287 p.
    [Pp. 241-243, sympathetic account of the early Babalola
    movement, by the British colonial officer concerned with
    it.]

881 WEAVER, EDWIN I. A leadership training programme (for inde-
    pendent churches in Eastern Nigeria), and: Nigeria
    Mennonite Church. Messages and Reports, African Mennonite
    Fellowship, Bulawayo 1965. 1965, 33-37, and 60-63.
    [Independent churches and co-operation in eastern
    Nigeria.]

882 WEAVER, EDWIN I. and WEAVER, IRENE. The Uyo Story. Elkhart,
    Indiana: Mennonite Board of Missions 1970, 127 p., illus.,
    appendices.
    [American Mennonite missionaries describe their pio-
    neering work assisting independent churches in eastern
    Nigeria 1959-1967. Covers material in articles published
    by Weavers under same title in Gospel Herald (Scottdale,
    Pennsylvania) 55 (34, 35, 36), 1962 and 56 (6), 1963.]

883 WEBSTER, DOUGLAS. A "Spiritual Church". Frontier 6 (2),
    1963, 116-120, illus. Also in Practical Anthropology
    (Tarrytown, N.Y.) 11 (5), 1964, 229-232, 240.
    [The Holy Chapel of Miracle; a description of a service
    and its atmosphere, by an Anglican theologian.]

884 WEBSTER, J[AMES] B[ERTIN]. Agege plantation and the African
    Church, 1901-1920. Nigerian Institute of Social and
    Economic Research Conference Proceedings, March 1962,
    124-130. Mimeo.

885   WEBSTER, J[AMES] B[ERTIN]. The African Churches. <u>Nigeria</u>
      <u>Magazine</u>, no. 79, Dec. 1963, 254-266, illus.
      [The earlier independent churches in Lagos and
      Yorubaland; many good illustrations.]

886   WEBSTER, J[AMES] B[ERTIN]. The Bible and the plough. <u>Journal</u>
      <u>of the Historical Society of Nigeria</u> (Ibadan) 2 (4), 1963,
      418-434.
      [The development of commerce advocated by T. F. Buxton
      and Henry Venn, as attempted by mission societies in West
      Africa, and by independent churches at Ifako, Agbowa and
      Agege in Nigeria.]

887   WEBSTER, J[AMES] B[ERTIN]. Source material for the study of
      the African Churches. <u>Bulletin of the Society for</u>
      <u>African Church History</u> (Nsukka, E. Nigeria) 1 (2), 1963,
      41-49.

888   WEBSTER, JAMES BERTIN. <u>The African Churches among the Yoruba</u>,
      <u>1888-1922</u>. Oxford: Clarendon Press 1964, xvii + 217 p.,
      illus., bibl.
      [An historical study of secessions from mission churches;
      pp. 92, 94-96, the Braide movement, Niger Delta. Exten-
      sive bibliography of the writing of the African Church
      leaders themselves.]

889   WEBSTER, J[AMES] B[ERTIN]. Christianity in Nigeria. <u>Historia</u>
      (Ibadan) 2 (1), 1965, 48-55.
      [Pp. 51-52, the "African Churches"; p. 53, the aladura
      movement; pp. 53-55, revivals of traditional religion -
      Orunmila, and M. Ojike's attempt at a "national church".]

890   WEBSTER, J[AMES] B[ERTIN]. Attitudes and policies of the
      Yoruba African Churches towards polygamy, in C. G. Baëta
      (ed.), item 112, 224-248.

891   WELCH, J[AMES] W. Witchcraft and Christianity in the Niger
      Delta. <u>Church Overseas</u> (London) 4, 1931, 328-330.
      [On Igbe cult, started by Ubiosa of Ukhuokori, who was
      credited with healing powers; grew into distinct cult
      specializing in detection of witches.]

892   WELTON, MICHAEL R. The Holy Aruosa: religious conservatism
      in a changing society. <u>Practical Anthropology</u> (Tarry-
      town, N.Y.) 16 (1), 1969, 18-27.
      [The Edo National Church as nativistic in Linton's sense,
      not in Lanternari's; its history, creed and worship.]

West Africa

893   WESLEYAN METHODIST MISSIONARY SOCIETY, London. Reports
No. 117 (for 1930), 1931.
[Pp. 79-80, "strange prophets" in Ilesha and Ifeke areas.]

894   WESLEYAN METHODIST MISSIONARY SOCIETY. Annual Reports,
Nigeria District.
[E.g., 1931, pp. 18-19, 22, 26, 34; 1934, p. 20, on the aladura movement.]

895   WESTERN EQUATORIAL AFRICA, Anglican Diocese of. Reports and
Minutes of Proceedings...of the Synod.... Lagos: the Diocese.
[E.g., 1916, pp. 25-26, 43-46, Appendix I, 61-67, on the Braide prophet movement; 1917, pp. 23-24, 45, Appendix I, idem; 1918, pp. 53, 57, Appendix II, pp. 61-62, idem.]

896   WESTERN EQUATORIAL AFRICA DIOCESAN MAGAZINE (Anglican).
Reports on the Braide movement and other prophet movements:
No. 152=22 (Aug.), 1917, p. 212; no. 164=23 (Aug.), 1918, 194-196; no. 175=24 (July), 1919, 171-173; no. 197-198=26 (May-June), 1921, passim and p. 164; 36 (May) 1931, 89-91.

897   WESTGARTH, J. W. The movement at Uyo. Qua Iboe Mission
Quarterly (Belfast) no. 135, Nov. 1927, 260-264.
[On the "spirit movement of 1927 in Ibibioland; a first-hand account by a missionary involved.]

898   WESTGARTH, J. W. The Holy Spirit and the primitive mind.
London: Victory Press 1946, 64 p.
[A sympathetic missionary's account of the spirit movement in Ibibioland.]

899   WOBO, M. SAM. A brief resume of the life course of Dr. J. O.
Ositelu (Part 1). Ode Remo, W. Nigeria: Degosen Printing Works 1955, 15 p.
[Biography of the founder of the Church of the Lord (Aladura) by a former disciple.]

See also items 58, 91, 96, 104, 106, 166, 174, 213, 227, 232, 238, 261, 286, 304, 309, 333, 347, 362, 379, 386, 389, 409, 423, 424, 425, 426, 428, 433, 434, 438, 442, 443, 449, 457, 458, 459, 461, 468, 470, 472, 484.

BLACK AFRICA

SIERRA LEONE

900 BANTON, MICHAEL [PARKER]. An independent African church in
Sierra Leone. Hibbert Journal (London) 55 (1), 1956,
57-63,
[A service at the Church of the Lord (Aladura).]

901 BANTON, MICHAEL [PARKER]. West African city: a study of
tribal life in Freetown. London: Oxford University Press
for the International African Institute 1957,
xvii + 228 p., plates, maps, tables.
[Pp. 140-141, brief description of the Church of the
Lord and the reasons why Sierra Leone has relatively few
independents.]

902 FASHOLE-LUKE, EDWARD W. Christianity and Islam in Freetown.
Sierra Leone Bulletin of Religion 9 (1), 1967, 1-16.
[Pp. 2-3, 8-9, on the "negative instance" of Sierra
Leone.]

903 FASHOLE-LUKE, EDWARD W. Religion in Freetown, in C. Fyfe and
E. Jones (eds.), Freetown: a symposium. Freetown:
Sierra Leone University Press 1968, 127-142.
[Pp. 127-128, 131-133, 141, independent prophet-healing
churches.]

904 FYFE, CHRISTOPHER. The Countess of Huntingdon's Connexion in
nineteenth century Sierra Leone. Sierra Leone Bulletin of
Religion 4 (2), 1962, 53-61.
[Esp. pp. 57, 60, the secession of two congregations of
recaptives from the African settler-dominated Connexion in
1847; their joining the Wesleyan Mission in 1886.]

905 FYFE, CHRISTOPHER. The Baptist churches in Sierra Leone.
Sierra Leone Bulletin of Religion 5 (2), 1963, 55-60.
[Pp. 58-60, W. Jenkins and the African or Ibo Baptist
Church, from 1838; T. G. Lawson and the (Baptist) Church
of God.]

906 FYFE, CHRISTOPHER. The West African Methodists in the nineteenth century. Sierra Leone Bulletin of Religion 3 (1),
1961, 22-28.
[Secessions from mission-connected Methodism: by
Rawdon St. (1822); by O'Connor and the recaptives, as the
West African Methodist Church (1844); their renewal of
mission connections in 1861 and 1859.]

125

West Africa

907   FYFE, CHRISTOPHER. A history of Sierra Leone. London:
      Oxford University Press 1962, 773 p.
          [Pp. 232-233, 290, West African Methodist Church;
      p. 233, African Baptist Church; pp. 233, 469, secessions
      from Countess of Huntingdon's Connexion; pp. 286, 329,
      418, T. G. Lawson and the (Baptist) Church of God; all
      were nineteenth century independent developments.]

908   HAIR, P[AUL] E[DWARD] H. Christianity at Freetown from 1792
      as a field for research, in Urbanization in African
      Social change, item 398, 127-140.
          [Pp. 136-138 on new church groups; p. 133, an early form
      of "Ethiopianism"?]

909   LYNCH, HOLLIS R. The Native Pastorate controversy and cul-
      tural ethnocentrism in Sierra Leone, 1871-1874. Journal
      of African History 5 (3), 1964, 395-413.
          [The failure of an attempt to found an independent
      church in the 1870s.]

910   MARKWELL, MATEI. The Rev. Daniel Coker of Sierra Leone.
      Sierra Leone Bulletin of Religion 7 (2), 1965, 41-48.
          [Pp. 46-47, origins of the West African Methodist Church,
      1821.]

911   NDANEMA, I. M. The Martha Davies Confidential Benevolent
      Association. Sierra Leone Bulletin of Religion 3 (2),
      1961, 64-67.
          [One of the semi-independent women's movements in
      Freetown, founded 1910; by a Sierra Leone minister.]

912   OLSEN, GILBERT W. Church growth in Sierra Leone. Grand
      Rapids: Eerdmans 1969, 222 p., maps.
          ["Detailed analysis of several Creole churches, two
      African independent churches, and nine other mission-
      related churches."]

913   TUBOKU-METZGER, C. E. Sectarianism and divided Christendom:
      the African situation, in Report of Proceedings, Anglican
      Congress 1963. Toronto: Anglican Book Centre, London:
      S.P.C.K., New York: Seabury Press 1963, 38-40.
          [Sympathetic reference to independent groups in
      Freetown - Decker's Church, Mother Jane Bloomer, and the
      Church of the Lord - by a Sierra Leone minister.]

914   WALLS, ANDREW FINLAY. The Nova Scotia settlers and their
      religion. Sierra Leone Bulletin of Religion 1 (1), 1969,
      19-31.

[Pp. 28-31, on the independent chapels in Freetown,
first half of nineteenth century; and see further references given there.]

See also item 452.

TOGO

915   DEBRUNNER, HANS W[ERNER]. A church between colonial powers.
A study of the church in Togo. London: Lutterworth Press
1965, 368 p., maps, bibl.
[Pp. 269, 281, Prophet Doh's prayer movement and
Wovenu's Apostolic Revelation Society; pp. 281-282, healing
movement in Togo; pp. 283-284, Apostolic Faith Mission;
pp. 284-287, Sect of the Second Adam, in Ghana.]

West Central Africa

916 ANDERSSON, EFRAIM. Munkukusa, en nyhednisk folk-rörelse i
     Kong, Svensk Missionstidskrift 41 (4), 1953, 184-197.
     [Munkukusa anti-witchcraft purification movement of
     1951-53.]

917 ANDERSSON, EFRAIM. Messianic popular movements in the Lower
     Congo (Studia Ethnographica Upsaliensia XIV). Uppsala:
     Almquist and Wiksell; London: Kegan Paul, 1958, xiii +
     287 p., ill., bibl.
     [A major study; discusses the term "prophet" and the
     movements related to Kimbanguism in the French and Belgian
     Congos from 1921 to the 1950s; Ngunzism or the Kimbangu
     movement; Matswanism; the Ngunzist Salvation Army; Mpadi's
     Khaki Church; the Munkukusu movement. Also examines out-
     side influences, including Jehovah's Witnesses, the Salva-
     tion Army, and Marcus Garvey; pp. 244-245, Béatrice and
     the Antonians.]

918 AXELSON, SIGBERT. Culture confrontation in the Lower Congo
     from the old Congo Kingdom to the Congo Independent State
     with Special reference to the Swedish missionaries in the
     1880s and the 1890s (Studia Missionalia Upsaliensia XIV).
     Stockholm: Gummessons 1970, 340 p., maps, illus., bibl.
     [P. 102, F. Bullamatare; and pp. 102-103, F. Casolla -
     nativistic revolts; pp. 136-147, Kimpa Vita or prophetess
     Béatrice (based on Lorenzo da Lucca and Bernardo da Gallo
     as analysed by Cuvelier (1954) and Jadin (1961).]

919 BALANDIER, GEORGES. Messianisme des Ba-Kongo. Encyclopédie
     Coloniale et Maritime Mensuelle (Paris) 1 (12), 1951,
     216-220, illus.
     [Kimbanguism, Matswanism, Amicalism and Khakism.]

920 BALANDIER, GEORGES. Sociologie actuelle de l'Afrique noire.
     Dynamique des changements sociaux en Afrique centrale.
     Paris: Presses Universitaires de France (1955) 1963,
     xii + 532 p.; Eng. trans., The sociology of black Africa:
     social dynamics in Central Africa. New York: Praeger
     1970, 540 p.

West Central Africa

[Revised and enlarged edition: pp. 65-67, Ngol and
Mulifa cults; pp. 219-232, 270-276, etc., Bwiti; pp. 396-
416, Amicalism; 417-504, Congo Kimbanguism and messianism.
Comparison between Fang and Kongo messianism.]

921 BALANDIER, GEORGES. Naissance d'un mouvement politico-
religieux chez les "Ba-Kongo" du Moyen-Congo, in Proceedings of the III International West Africa Conference held
at Ibadan, Nigeria, December 1949. Lagos: Nigerian
Museum 1956, 324-336.
[Kimbanguism, Amicalism and Khakism.]

922 BALANDIER, GEORGES. Afrique ambigüe. Paris: Plon 1957,
211 p., illus. German trans., Zwielichtiges Afrika.
Stuttgart: Schwab 1959; also Eng. trans., Ambiguous
Africa: cultures in collision. London: Chatto and
Windus 1966, 276 p., illus.
[Ch. 7: "Mouvements contraires" - Matswanism and
Kimbanguism; descriptions of churches and rituals.]

923 BALANDIER, GEORGES. La vie quotidienne au royaume de Kongo du
XVIe au XVIIIe siècle. Paris: Hachette 1965, 286 p. Eng.
trans., Daily life in the Kingdom of the Kongo from the
16th to the 18th century. London: George Allen and Unwin
1968, 288 p.
[Pp. 261-268, the prophetess Béatrice and Antonian
movement, based on Jadin (1961) and Cuvelier (1953).]

924 BATSÎKAMA BA MAMPUYA MA NDWALA, R. Ndona Béatrice. Serait-
elle témoin du Christ et de la foi du vieux Congo?
Kinshasa: Editions du Mwanza 1970.

925 BUANA-KIBONGI, R. L'évolution du Kimbanguisme. Flambeau
(Yaoundé), 10, 1966, 75-81.
[An outline; pp. 80-81, a similar movement in the Nguedi
seminary has been kept from political developments and in
touch with the church. See item 991.]

926 CORNEVIN, ROBERT. Saint Antoine de Padoue, la secte
(congolaise) des Antoniens et le moderne culte antoiniste.
France Eurafrique no. 178=18 (nov.), 1966, 37-40.

927 CUVELIER, J. (ed.). Relations sur le Congo du Père Laurent de
Lucques (1700-1717). Brussels: Institut Royal Colonial
Belge, Sections des Sciences Morales et Politiques, 32 (2),
1953.
[The prophetess Béatrice, reincarnation of St. Anthony,
early 18th c.]

BLACK AFRICA

928　DA CAVASO, EMILIO. Culto antonianio negli antichi regni del
　　　Congo ed eresia dell' Antonianismo 1645-1834. Il Santo
　　　(Padua) 1 (1), 1961.

929　DADIÉ, BERNARD B. Béatrice du Congo. Paris: Présence
　　　Africaine 1970.
　　　　[An opera in three acts. See also item 936.]

930　DA GALLO, BERNARDO. Relazione dell'ultime guerre civili del
　　　Regno di Congo ...Come anche del scisma nella Fede per
　　　via d'una donna, che si fingeva S. Antonio.... Archivio
　　　della S.C. Propaganda Fide: Scritture originali riferite
　　　nelle Congregazioni Generali Vol. 576, 2-22 marzo 1711;
　　　repr. in T. Filesi, Nazionalismo e religione nel Congo...
　　　Rome: 1972, 55-90.
　　　　[A Capuchin missionary's first-hand report on the
　　　Antonians. See item 937.]

931　DA LUCCA, LORENZO. Lettera Annua del 1705; Lettera Annua del
　　　1706 in Filippo Bernardi da Firenze (recorder) Relazione
　　　d'alcuni Missionari Cappuccini Toscani, singolarmente del
　　　P. Lorenzo da Lucca...., held at Convent of Montughi,
　　　Provincial Archives of the Florentine Capuchins, vol. 2,
　　　516 p.
　　　　[Material on Antonianism, pp. 218-222 of 1705 letter,
　　　and pp. 261-289 of 1706 letter, which are reprinted in
　　　T. Filesi, item 937, pp. 91-93 and 93-111; pp. 111-113
　　　give a report of 5 October 1711 by Da Lucca to the Pope.]

932　DA SILVA RÊGNO, ANTÓNIO. Syncretic movements in Angola. Luso-
　　　Brazilian Review 7 (2), 1970, 25-44.
　　　　[The movement of Simon Toko, against the background of
　　　the history of the Kingdom of the Congo and of Kimbanguism,
　　　Mpadism and Matswanism; from a loyal Portuguese viewpoint.]

933　DE POSTIOMA, ADALBERTO. A heresia do Antonianismo. Portugal
　　　em Africa, 2nd. ser. no. 114=19, Nov.-Dec. 1962, 378-381.
　　　　[An expression of independency in the old Portuguese
　　　period of the Congo.]

934　DOS SANTOS, EDUARDO. Precursores do messianismo africano?
　　　Ultramar 9, July-Sept. 1962, 134-137.
　　　　[The Antonians, 1704-1706; Mona N'Engana Nzâmbi, 1890s.]

935　DOS SANTOS, EDUARDO. O Antonianismo. Uma página da História
　　　do Antigo Reino do Congo. Studia (Lisbon) 30-31, 1970,
　　　81-112.

131

West Central Africa

936   ENTENTE AFRICAINE (Abidjan). Béatrice du Congo. Entente
       Africaine, 8 déc. 1971, 42-49, illus.
           [Critical account of a play with this title, by Ivory
       Coast playwright Bernard Dadié, presented at the Festival
       of Avignon in 1971, with photos of the production; on the
       prophetess Béatrice and the Antonian movement.]

937   FILESI, TEOBALDI. Nazionalismo e religione nel Congo all'
       inizio del 1700: la setta degli Antoniani. Africa
       (Rome) 26 (3), 1971, 267-303, Part I; 26 (4), 1972, 463-
       508, Part II. Republished under same title in series:
       Instituto Italiano per L'Africa, Quaderini della Rivista
       "Africa" 1. Rome: A.BE.T.E. 1972, 119 p., 2 facs.
           [Based on original missionary documents of La Lucca and
       Da Gallo, here reproduced in appendices, together with a
       letter from F. Colombano da Bologna of 15 May 1706.]

938   FILESI, TEOBALDI. San Salvador. Cronache dei re del Congo
       (Collana Biblioteca Nigrizia, 2). Bologna: Editrice
       degli Instituti Missionari Italiani 1974, 325 p., illus.
           [Pp. 213-266, prophetess Béatrice and the Antonian
       movement.]

939   JADIN, LOUIS. Le Congo et la secte des Antoniens: restauration
       du royaume sous Pedro IV et las "Sainte-Antoine" congolais
       (1694-1718). Bulletin de l'Institut Historique Belge de
       Rome (Rome and Brussels) 33, 1961, 411-615.
           [The Italian Capuchin mission and the 17th century
       prophetess Béatrice.]

940   JADIN, LOUIS. Les sectes religieuses secrètes des Antoniens
       au Congo (1703-1709). Cahiers des Religions Africaines
       (Kinshasa) no. 3=2 (jan.), 1968, 109-120.
           [On the similarities between the Antonian movement and
       Kimbanguism.]

941   JANZEN, JOHN M. Vers une phénoménologie de la guérison en
       Afrique centrale. Etudes Congolaises (Kinshasa) 85=12 (2),
       1969, 97-114.
           [Includes theoretical discussion; pp. 101-106, a con-
       crete case of a prophet-healer among the Manianga.]

942   JANZEN, JOHN M. Kongo religious renewal: iconoclastic and
       iconorthostic. Canadian Journal of African Studies 5 (2),
       1972, 135-143.
           [Pp. 135-136, iconoclastic movements of 1506, 1704, ca.
       1850; p. 136, Kiyoka movement, ca. 1890; Kimbanguism;
       Matadi revival of 1930; pp. 138-139, Nguedi revival of

1947; pp. 139-40, Munkukusa anti-witchcraft movement,
1951-53; pp. 140-142, Croix-Koma movement of Malanda, late
1950s.]

943   JOSET, PAUL-ERNEST. Quelques mouvements religieux au Bas
      Congo et dans l'ex-Afrique Équatoriale Française. Journal
      of Religion in Africa 1 (2), 1967, 101-128.
         [Briefly on Ngunzism, Missions des Noirs, Tonsi, Bola-
      Mananga, Mayangi, Salutisme Congolais, Khakism, Amicalism;
      more fully, Kitawala, especially in Katanga.]

944   MacGAFFEY, WYATT. Comparative analysis of Central African
      religions. Africa (London) 42 (1), 1972, 21-31 (French
      summary).
         [Pp. 28-30, modern prophets and movements.]

945   MARIN, J. Une nouvelle secte: le "Mpevu Nzambi". Revue
      d'Histoire des Missions 9 (1), 1932, 607-608.
         [Founded by "Moanda Tsangu" in Belgian Congo - back-
      ground in Swedish protestant missions; based on report
      by Catholic missionary Heidet.]

946   MEIRING, P[IET] G[ERHARD] J[ACOBUS]. Donna Béatrice and
      twentieth-century theology Theologia Viatorum (Sovenga)
      3 (1), 1975, 62-72.
         [Reflections on the questions implicit in the movement
      of prophetess Béatrice.]

947   N'DIAYE, JEAN-PIERRE. Elites-africaines et culture occidentale.
      Assimilation ou résistance. Paris: Editions Présence
      Africaine 1969, 217 p.
         [Pp. 180-188, "L'animisme en face de la situation
      coloniale" - Bwiti, Kimbanguism, Ngol, Mpadi, Matswa,
      Lumumbaism; similar to Balandier's approach.]

948   NDOUNDOU, DANIEL. Nkunga Nsikumusu (1947-1963) Zaïre:
      [Ndoundou's colleagues] n.d. 281 p. Mimeo.
         [Hymns by a leader in the 1947 Nguedi revival, showing
      main themes of the latter; with anonymous introduction.]

949   NIGRIZIA (Verona). Nel nome del Padre, di André Matswa e di
      Simon Kibangu. Nigrizia 2, Fev. 1958, 2-4, illus.

950   NIPPGEN, J. Une société secrète chez les Ba-Congo de
      l'Afrique tropical: la société de la "mort" et de la
      "résurrection". Revue Anthropologique (Paris) 32 (3-4),
      1922, 119-121.

West Central Africa

951   PIACENTINI, R. Maboni. Le Père Joseph Bonnefont. Issy-les-
        Moulineaux: 1951, 192 p.
        [Pp. 73-83, account of contact with Ngunzism, by a
        Roman Catholic missionary.]

952   PINTASSILGO, ANTONIO RODRIQUES. Seitas secretas no Congo.
        Portugal em Africa (Lisbon) 10 (60), 1953, 361-371.
        [Kimbanguism in Congo influenced three prophetic-political
        movements in Cabinda - Ngwima (1916), Ngunza prophets, and
        Mayangi.]

953   SINDA, MARTIAL. Le messianisme congolais et ses incidences
        politiques - Kimbanguisme - Matsouanisme - autres
        mouvements. Paris: Payot 1972, 390 p., bibl.
        [Pp. 20-50, earliest movements including F. Kassola
        (1632), and Béatrice; Part III: Mpeve Nzambi, Lassyism,
        Moungoungouna, Croix-Koma, and Kindoki.]

954   SULZMANN, ERIKA. Die Bewegung der Antonier in alten Reiche
        Kongo, in W. E. Mühlmann, item 57, 81-85.
        [The cult of St. Anthony as the basis for a national
        church independent of Rome, early in the 18th century.]

955   TASTEVIN, C. Nouvelles manifestations du prophétisme en
        Afrique équatoriale et en Angola. Comptes Rendus de
        l'Académie des Sciences Coloniales (Paris) 16 (3), 1956,
        149-153.
        [Includes Kimbanguism, the "Religion du Salut", Toko's
        "Etoile rouge", and a "prophète du Christ" from the then
        French Congo.]

956   THOMPSON, VIRGINIA and ADLOFF, RICHARD. The emerging states
        of French Equatorial Africa. Stanford, California:
        Stanford University Press 1960, xii + 595 p., bibl.
        [Pp. 304-314, summary of role of "messianic cults";
        pp. 348-349, Bwiti; pp. 478-482, Matswa; see also pp.
        554-555, notes 21-28; also pp. 43-44, 490-492.

957   ZIEGLE, H. Notes sur la psychologie des Bantous
        de l'Afrique Centrale. Cahiers d'Outre-Mer (Bordeaux) 4
        (13), 1951, 23-38.
        [Includes the effects of Christianity on traditional
        religion, seen in the "heresy" of Kimbanguism, and in the
        continuation of ancestral rites in the Salvation Army of
        the Middle Congo.]

Black Africa

ANGOLA

958 BENTLEY, W[ILLIAM] HOLMAN. Pioneering on the Kongo. London: Religious Tract Society, 2 vols., 1900, 478, 448 p., illus. [Vol. 1, pp. 290-292, Kiyola, anti-fetish movement from 1872 in Northern Angola.]

959 CHILCOTE, RONALD H. Protest and resistance in Brazil and Portuguese Africa: a synthesis and classification, in R. H. Chilcote (ed.), Protest and resistance in Angola and Brazil: comparative studies. Berkeley and Los Angeles: University of California Press 1972, 243-302. [Many bibliographical references.]

960 CUNHA, JOAQUIM M[OREIRA] da S[ILVA]. Movimentos associativos no África Negra. Lisbon: Junta de Investigações do Ultramar 1956, 57 p., plates, bibl. [Sections 1-3, pp. 7-34, on classification, mystico-religious associations, and Watch Tower. English summary, pp. 55-56.]

961 CUNHA, JOAQUIM M[OREIRA] da S[ILVA]. Movimentos associativos no África Negra, vol. II, Angola. Lisbon: Junta de Investigações do Ultramar 1959, 90 p., illus., map. [Two types of movements in Angola: "de forma primitiva e conteudo novo" (Os Santos e Santas and Grupo do Espirito Santo) and "mistico-religiosas de forma e conteudo novos" (Tocoism, Lassyism, Dieudonné, and Watch Tower).]

962 CUNHA, JOAQUIM M[OREIRA] da S[ILVA]. Tocóismo. Ultramar (Lisbon) 5, 1961, 141-175. [Extract from previous item.]

963 DE OLIVEIRA, HERCULANO. Religiões acatólicas em Angola. Portugal em África (Lisbon) 73=13, 1956, 36-50. [Pp. 41-43, Kimbanguism; pp. 43-45, "Religião Salvadore" of Zacharias Bonzo; pp. 45-48, Simon Toco and the Red Star sect; pp. 48-50, an anti-European iconoclastic group.]

964 DE OLIVEIRA, HERCULANO. Movimento messiânico-cummunista Africano. Portugal em África 85=15 (1), 1958, 18-35. [Pp. 28-32 on religious messianic movements.]

965 DOS SANTOS, EDUARDO. Do sincretismo mágico e religioso nos fundamentos ideológicos do terrorismo no Nordeste do Angola. Garcia de Orta (Lisbon) 10 (1), 1962, 77-91, bibl.

135

West Central Africa

966   DOS SANTOS, EDUARDO. O Nordeste Angolano e os movimentos
       profético-salvíficos. Ultramar (Lisbon) no. 17=5 (1),
       1964, 32-73.

967   DOS SANTOS, EDUARDO. Maza. Elementos de etno-história para
       a interpretaçao do terrorismo no Nordeste de Angola.
       Lisbon: the author 1965, 373 p.
          [Pp. 259-315, ten prophet and other movements.]

968   DOS SANTOS, EDUARDO. Religiões de Angola (Estudos Missionários
       3). Lisbon: Junta de Investigações do Ultramar 1969,
       536 p., bibl.
          [Pp. 298-310, 449-510, expand his 1965 work, and repre-
       sent the official Portuguese attitude to some eighteen
       movements, from the Antonians to modern Baha'i.]

969   EDWARDS, ADRIAN C. The Ovimbundu under two sovereignties: a
       study of social control and social change among a people
       of Angola. London: Oxford University Press for the
       International African Institute 1962, xvii + 169 p.
          [Pp. 160-161, an account of a "contra-acculturative"
       movement which arose in 1955 combining features of cargo-
       cults and anti-witchcraft movements.]

970   ESTERMANN, CARLOS. O tocoísmo como fenómeno religiosos.
       Garçia de Orta 13 (3), 1965, 327-342.
          [Biography of Simon Toco; the beliefs of the cult and
       its syncretism with Bantu religion.]

971   GIL, MARIA HELENA. Les messianismes d'Angola. Contributions
       à l'inventaire des messianismes et millénarismes d'Afrique
       noire. École Pratique des Hautes Études, diplôme, VIe
       Section 1972, 191 + xxvii p. Mimeo.

972   GONCALVES, JOSÉ. O tocoísmo perante a sociedade angolana
       (Relatório de material recolhido). Bulletin IFAN (Dakar)
       29 (B) 3-4, 1967, 678-694, map. French summary.
          [A survey of Simon Toco's "Église de notre Seigneur
       Jésus-Christ", related to Catholics, Baptists, Salvation
       Army and Jehovah's Witnesses, and not to Angolan nation-
       alists; Toco's transference to the Azores.]

973   GRAHAM, ROBERT H. CARSON. Under seven Congo kings. London:
       Carey Press 1931, 293 p., illus.
          [By a Baptist missionary in Angola. Pp. 186, 188,
       Kimbanguism in the Portuguese area.]

974   MARGARIDO, ALFREDO. L'Église Toko et le mouvement de libéra-
       tion de l'Angola. Le Mois en Afrique (Paris) 5 (mai),
       1966, 80-97.
       [An Angolan sociologist surveys movements 1930-1966;
       Simon Toco and his "Kimbanguist" church of urbanized
       workers.]

975   MARGARIDO, ALFREDO. I movimento profetici e messianici
       angolesi. Rivista Storica Italiana (Naples) 80 (3), 1968,
       538-592, bibl.
       [A major survey from the Antonians onwards; some seven-
       teen movements including Kiyoka (1871), Tonsi, Tawa,
       Tokoism, Chipambule, Lassy, and the Santi of Nova Lisboa.]

976   MARGARIDO, ALFREDO. The Tokoist church and Portuguese colo-
       nialism in Angola, in R. H. Chilcote (ed.), Protest and
       resistance in Angola and Brazil: comparative studies.
       Berkeley and Los Angeles: University of California Press
       1972, 29-52.

977   MARTIN, MARIE-LOUISE. Fierce persecution of Kimbanguist
       Christians in Angola. Ministry (Morija, Lesotho) 10 (1),
       1970, 46-47.

978   MERCIER, EMMANUEL. La nuova ondata, ha nome cipambule.
       Nigrizia (Verona) 17 (11), 1959, 13-15, illus.
       [Some notes on a new "spirit" and the sect made up of
       its believers: Cipambule, among the Tshokwe of Angola.]

979   MONDE E MISSIONE (Milan). Il Tocoismo predica l'unità dei
       cristiani. Mondo e Missione 103 (24), 1974, 629-630.
       [Simon Toco (photo) returned to Angola on 31 August 1974
       from over ten years in exile.]

980   MUSEUM LESSIANUM. Sectes nouvelles en Angola, in Museum
       Lessianum, item 312, 140-143.
       [Prophets Simon Toco, Zacharias Bonzo, Mayange (of
       Cabinda) and, particularly, Lassy.]

981   NORDBY, JUEL MAGNAR ARNT. The role of the Methodist class
       meeting in the growth of an African city church: a
       historico-sociological study. Boston University School
       of Theology, Th.D. dissertation 1967, 279 p.
       [The class meeting serves as an alternative to African
       independency; cf. Roman Catholic "pious associations".
       Luanda, Angola, is referred to.]

West Central Africa

982   VAZ, JOSÉ M.   Do paganismo pré-cristão ao neo-paganismo anti-
        cristão. Portugal em África no. 151=26 (1), 1969, 19-32.
        [Pp. 26-32, "Os movimentos salvíficos e do libertação".]

983   VAZ, J[OSÉ] M.   No mundo do Cabindas: a sociedade africana
        em crise. Portugal em África no. 164=28, 1971, 81-96.
        ["Prophetic movements" in Cabinda mentioned.]

984   WHEELER, DOUGLAS L. and PÉLISSIER, RENÉ. Angola (Library of
        African Affairs). London: Pall Mall/New York: Praeger
        1971, 296 p., illus.
        [Pp. 152-155, 266, peasants and prophets. A brief
        survey of new religious movements.]

See also items 258, 343, 383.

CENTRAL AFRICAN REPUBLIC

985   BULLETIN DU COMITÉ DE L'AFRIQUE FRANÇAISE. Les événements de
        la Haute-Sangha. Bulletin du Comité de l'Afrique
        Française 2, 1929, 4, 171-173.
        [The Karinou revolt, a nativistic prophet movement,
        1928-1931.]

986   HEIJKE, JAN. Les Nzapa ti Azande. Diocese of Bougoussou,
        report dated 1971, 7 p. Typescript.
        [Memorandum by a Dutch Roman Catholic priest, based in
        part on an earlier report by Père G. Montemanni. A syn-
        cretist healing movement among the Azande dating from
        1933. (Copy in Dept. of Religious Studies, University
        of Aberdeen).]

987   MICHEL, MARC. Les débats du soulèvement de la Haute-Sangha
        en 1928. Annales du Centre de l'Enseignement Supérieur
        de Brazzaville 2, 1966, 33-48, map.
        [The first of a series of rebellions, under Karinou, a
        sorcerer-diviner; messianic, nativistic, anti-white and
        anti-Muslim.]

Black Africa

CONGO REPUBLIC

988   ANDERSSON, EFRAIM. Missionärernas ställning till inhemska
       väckelserövelser på missionsfälten. Svensk
       Missionstidskrift (Uppsala) 38 (4), 1950, 197-216.
       [Pp. 202-211, the 1947 Nguedi revival.]

989   ANDERSSON, EFRAIM. Churches at the grass-roots: a study in
       Congo-Brazzaville (World Studies in Mission). London:
       Lutterworth 1968, 296 p., tables, bibl.
       [See index for Kimbangu, munkukusa, ngunzism, revival
       movements, sects.]

990   BALANDIER, GEORGES. Sociologie des Brazzaville Noires. Paris:
       Armand Colin 1955, 274 p.
       [Pp. 224-226, a Matswanist follower.]

991   BUANA-KIBONGI, R. Le réveil spirituel au Congo-Brazzaville.
       Flambeau (Yaoundé) 11, août 1966, 143-157.
       [The revival of 1947 at the Nguedi seminary of the
       Swedish Evangelical Mission, and its subsequent evolution
       within the Eglise Evangélique du Congo.]

992   DURIEZ, M. J. Étude de Balalisme. Paris: Centre des Hautes
       Études d'Administration Musulmane, Section Islam-Afrique
       noire, 1950. Mimeo.
       [Amicalism or Matswanism, by a French administrator.]

993   HAFFMANS, ROBERT. Het fenomeen van de Afrikaanse sekten als
       aktueel missieprobleem in de Kongo. Het Missiewerk
       (Nijmegen) 40 (1), 1961, 31-42.
       [Includes brief accounts of Matswanism, Bougism,
       Dieudonnism, Khakism, and Nzobism.]

994   HAGENBUCHER-SACRIPANTI, FRANK. Les fondements spirituels du
       pouvoir au royaume de Loango (République Populaire du
       Congo) (Mémoires ORSTOM No. 67). Paris: O.R.S.T.O.M.,
       1973, 214 p., illus.
       [Appendices: 1. "Bougisme"; 2. "Devotees of God the
       Creator" - pp. 195-199.]

995   LARTEGUY, J. Quinze ans après sa mort, Matsoua est devenu le
       Christ noir du Congo. Paris-Presse l'Intransigeant (Paris)
       16 déc, 17 déc., 1956.

996   [MASSAMBA-DÉBAT, A.] Congo. De la révolution messianique à
       la révolution politique. Brazzaville: [Librairie
       Populaire] 1968, 107 p.

West Central Africa

[By a former president of the Congo Republic, with Kimbanguist sympathies.]

997 MBAMBI, A. C'etait en 1946.... Liaison (Brazzaville) 75, 1960, 56-60.
[By a Congolese; deals with the messianic promise of Matswanism - a cargo-cult?.]

998 MONDE NON-CHRÉTIEN. Matswa. Monde Non-Chrétien n.s. 26, juin 1953, 202-210. An extract from: Le problème le plus délicat du XXe siècle en A.E.F. La Lettre Ecarlate (Brazzaville), 3rd ed., 1 avril 1953.
[A summary of the career of André Matswa, with good documentation.]

999 RENAULT, L. Abbé Fulbert Youlou et Matsoua. Bulletin d'Information de la France d'Outre-Mer (Paris) no. 324, nov. 1956.

1000 THIEL [PÈRE]. Le Kakinisme (mouvement politico-religieuse en pays Balari). Annales Spiritaines (Paris) 59 (6), 1949, 91-92.
[Notes on a political-religious movement among the Lali.]

1001 VINCENT, JEANNE-FRANÇOISE. Le mouvement Croix-Koma: une nouvelle forme de la lutte contre la sorcellerie en pays kongo. Cahiers d'Etudes Africaines 6 (4), 1966, 527-564, illus.
[Pp. 534-535, Kimbanguism, Salvation Army, Matswanism, Lassyism, Mukunguna movement; pp. 536-564, the "Crucifixion Movement" of Victor Malanda, a pious Roman Catholic anti-witchcraft moral reformer, from 1964.]

1002 WAGRET, JEAN-MICHEL. Histoire et sociologie politiques de la République du Congo. Paris: R. Pichon et R. Durand-Auzias, 1963, 250 p., map.
[Places religious movements (founded by Kimbangu, Mpadi, Matswa, Lassy, etc.) in the context of the political evolution of the nation.]

1003 WEST AFRICA (London). Rise and fall. West Africa no. 2412, 24 Aug. 1963, p. 941, illus.
[A biographical account of the Abbé Fulbert Youlou and his inheritance of the support given Matswa.]

1004 YOULOU, FULBERT. La Matsouanisme. Brazzaville: Imprimerie Centrale 1955.
[By a national, the Abbé Youlou, a former Roman Catholic priest who became prime minister.]

Black Africa

See also items 184, 400, 1116.

EQUATORIAL GUINEA

1005   GONZALES DE PABLO, AQUILINO. La secta del "Mbueti" o "Mbiti".
       Actas y Memorias de la Sociedad Española de Antropología
       Etnografía y Prehistoria (Madrid) T., 19, 1944, 70-84.

1006   GONZALES DE PABLO, AQUILINO. El Mbueti y sus doctrinas.
       Cuadernos de Estudios Africanos (Madrid) 2, 1946, 69-92.
          [The situation and role of Bwiti in Equatorial Guinea;
          doctrines, a Bwiti vocabulary list, initiation rites and
          worship.]

1007   PERRAMON, RAMON. Al habla con los buetis. Guinea Española
       (Santa Isabel) no. 1554=159 (Mar.), 1962, 72-73; 1555=159
       (April), 1962, 109-110.
          [Description of a Bwiti service and shrine.]

1008   PINILLOS DE CRUELLS, MANUEL. La secta del' Mbueti. Africa
       (Madrid) no. 6=86 (Feb.), 1949, 10-12.
          [On the Bwiti cult and its penetration of Equatorial
          Guinea during the preceding sixty years.]

1009   VECIANA VILALDACH, ANTONIO de. Le secta del Bwiti en la Guinea
       Española. Madrid: Consejo Superior de Investigaciones
       Científicas, Instituto de Estudios Africanos, 1958, 63 p.,
       bibl.
          [First systematic study of Bwiti, including its tradi-
          tional and historical setting.]

GABON

1010   ADAM [PÈRE]. Le Ngol. Annales Spiritaines (Paris) 58 (4),
       1948, 57-59.
          [A new religion whose name was derived from "DeGaulle".]

1011   BALANDIER, GEORGES. Les Fan, conquérants en disponibilité.
       Tropiques (Paris) no. 316=47 (déc.), 1949, 23-26.
          [Includes discussion of the Bwiti cult as a politico-
          religious development among the Fang.]

141

West Central Africa

1012   BALANDIER, GEORGES. L'utopie de Benoît Ogoula Igugua. Les
        Temps Modernes (Paris) 84-85, oct.-déc. 1952, 771-781.
        [Messianism in Gabon.]

1013   BARBERET, J. Les Issogho. Revue d'Ethnographie et des
        Traditions Populaires (Paris) no. 15=4 (3), 1923.
        [One of the first explorations of the socio-religious
        significance of Bwiti.]

1014   BINET, JACQUES. Drugs and mysticism. The Bwiti cult of the
        Fang. Diogenes (Paris) no. 86, 1974, 31-54. Also parallel
        French and Spanish editions.

1015   BINET, JACQUES, GOLLNHOFER, OTTO, and SILLANS, ROGER. Textes
        religieux du Bwiti-fang et de ses confréries prophétiques
        dans leurs cadres rituels. Cahiers d'Études Africaines
        12 (2), 1972, 197-253, illus., bibl.

1016   BIRINDA de BOUDIÉGUY, MATHIEU. La Bible secrète des noirs
        selon le Bouity. Paris: Omnium Litteraire n.d. [1952],
        141 p., illus.
        [Valuable accounts of Bwiti's history, functions and
        religious philosophy, and especially of its initiation;
        attempted parallels with Greek and Judaeo-Christian cul-
        ture; by a member.]

1017   BULÉON [PÈRE]. Excursions au pays des Eshiras. Les Missions
        Catholiques (Lyon) 26, 1894.
        [P. 642, on the Bwiti as a secret society.]

1018   BUREAU, RENÉ. "Connais-tu la mort?" Les trois nuits
        rituelles du bwiti fang. Annales de l'Université
        d'Abidjan, série D Lettres, Tome 6, 1973, 231-303, maps,
        illus.
        [Extended discussion of symbolic structure of the
        place of worship; music; ritual.]

1019   BUREAU, RENÉ. La religion d'eboga. Vol. 1, Essai sur le
        Bwiti fang (323 p.). Vol. 2, Lexique du Bwiti fang
        (241 p.) (Thèse d'État, Paris, 1972). Abidjan:
        Institut d'Ethno-Sociologie, 2 vols. Mimeo.

1020   DANEY [PÈRE]. Sur les croyances des indigènes de la sub-
        division de Sindara (Gabon, A.E.F.). Revue Anthropologique
        (Paris) 34 (7-8), 1924.
        [Includes detailed descriptions with impressionistic
        interpretations of Bwiti.]

BLACK AFRICA

Gabon

1021 ESPARRE, PAUL-LOUIS. Quelques aspects métaphyiques du "bouiti mitshogo". Genève-Afrique 7 (1), 1968, 53-57, bibl.
[The similarities with Buddhism and Greek antiquity; the nine cosmic spheres of which knowledge is acquired during initiation.

1022 FERNANDEZ, JAMES W[ILLIAM]. The idea and the symbol of the Saviour in a Gabon syncretistic cult. (Basic factors in the mythology of messianism). International Review of Missions no. 211=53 (July), 1964, 281-289. Fr. trans., La notion et symbole du Sauveur dans un culte syncrétiste gabonais. Flambeau (Yaoundé) 16, nov. 1967, 208-217. Also résumé in X Internationaler Kongress fur Religionsgeschichte, Marburg 1960. Marburg: N. G. Elwert 1961, 84-85.

1023 FERNANDEZ, JAMES W[ILLIAM]. Symbolic consensus in a Fang reformative cult. American Anthropologist 67 (4), 1965, 902-929.
[Analysis of Bwiti symbols.]

1024 FERNANDEZ, JAMES W[ILLIAM]. Principles of opposition and vitality in Fang aesthetics. Journal of Aesthetics and Art Criticism (Cleveland) 25 (1), 1966, 53-64, illus.
[Pp. 62,63, on the traditional duality of Fang culture (expounded in the article) as continuing in the Bwiti cult.]

1025 FERNANDEZ, JAMES W[ILLIAM]. Unbelievably subtle words: representation and integration in the sermons of an African reformative cult. History of Religions (Chicago) 6 (1), 1966, 43-69.
[Includes detailed examination of one sermon in the Bwiti cult.]

1026 FERNANDEZ, JAMES W[ILLIAM]. The affirmation of things past: Alar Ayong and Bwiti as movements of protest in Central and Northern Gabon, in R. I. Rotberg and A. A. Mazrui (eds.), Protest and power in Black Africa. New York: Oxford University Press 1970, 427-457.

1027 FERNANDEZ, JAMES W[ILLIAM]. Equatorial excursions: the folk- lore of narcotic inspired visions in an African religious movement, in R. M. Dorson (ed.), African folklore. Garden City, N. Y.: Anchor Books 1972, 341-361.
[Effects of iboka during Bwiti initiations: visiting the lands of the dead, and of primeval origin, and hence the great gods.]

143

BIBLIOGRAPHY OF NEW RELIGIOUS MOVEMENTS IN PRIMAL SOCIETIES

West Central Africa

1028   FERNANDEZ, JAMES W[ILLIAM]. Fang representations under
       acculturation, in P. D. Curtin (ed.), Africa and the West.
       Intellectual responses to European culture. Madison:
       University of Wisconsin Press 1972, 3–48.
       [Bwiti cult, passim and pp. 30ff.; pp. 26–27, occult
       literature from France.]

1029   FERNANDEZ, JAMES W[ILLIAM]. Persuasions and performances: of
       the beast in every body...and the metaphors of Everyman.
       Daedalus, Winter 1972, 39–60.
       [Pp. 51–56, the creation of metaphors in the Bwiti cult.]

1030   FERNANDEZ, JAMES W[ILLIAM] and BEKALE, P. Christian accultura-
       tion and Fang witchcraft. Cahiers d'Etudes Africaines
       (Paris) 2 (6), 1961, 244–270.
       [Pp. 244–255, introduction and comment on Bekale's text,
       by Fernandez, pp. 256–270, text by Bekale, a Gabonese of
       Fang background; reference to Bwiti and other anti-
       witchcraft movements.]

1031   GOLLNHOFER, OTTO. Le Bwete des Fan, syncrétisme issue de
       nombreuses sources: mouvements messianiques et
       prophétiques. École Pratique des Hautes Études, Paris,
       dissertation 5e section, 1966–67.

1032   GOLLNHOFER, OTTO and SILLANS, ROGER. Recherches sur le
       mysticisme des Mitsogo--peuple de montagnards du Gabon
       central (Afrique équatoriale), in Réincarnation et vie
       mystique en Afrique noire. Paris: Presses Universitaires
       de France 1965, 143–173.
       [Bwiti cult in the Mitsogo.]

1033   GREBERT, F. Au Gabon. Paris: Société des Missions
       Evangéliques de Paris 1922.
       [Includes account of the sacred musical instruments etc.,
       used in Bwiti.]

1034   LASSERRE, GUY. Libreville: la ville et sa région. Paris:
       Colin 1958, 347 p.
       [Pp. 313–317, Bwiti in Libreville; firsthand account of
       Nydeya Kanya, a combination of Catholicism and Bwiti.]

1035   LE ROY, A. Les pygmées. Les Missions Catholiques (Lyon), 29,
       1897, 237–238; also as Les pygmées. Paris: 1928,
       pp. 200–201.
       [An important early description of initiation into Bwiti.]

1036   MBENG, JEAN-MARIE. Ella-Akou, prophète ou charlatan? Liaison
       (Brazzaville) 44, 1954, 25–26.

1037   OSCHWALD, P. La danse "De Gaulle" à Lambarene. Journal des
        Missions Évangéliques (Paris) 21, fév. 1950, 7-13.
        [The beginnings of the Ngol movement.]

1038   POUNAH, PAUL-VINCENT. Concept Gabonais. Monte-Carlo, Monaco:
        Société des Éditions Paul Bory, 1968, 88 p.
        [Pp. 11-18, religious beliefs; pp. 47-55, secret
        societies (including Bwiti).]

1039   RAPONDA-WALKER, [ANDRÉ]. Le Bouiti. Bulletin de la Société
        des Recherches Congolaises (Brazzaville) 4, 1924, 3-7.
        [By the first Gabonais Catholic priest.]

1040   RAPONDA-WALKER, [ANDRÉ]. La statue du Bouiti. Bulletin de la
        Société des Recherches Congolaises (Brazzaville) 8, 1927,
        142-143.

1041   RAPONDA-WALKER, A[NDRÉ]. Invitation à payer sa contribution
        au Bouiti. Liaison (Brazzaville) 46, 1955.

1042   ŚWIDERSKI, STANISLAW. Le Bwiti, société d'initiation chez les
        Apindji au Gabon. Anthropos 60 (5-6), 1965, 541-576,
        illus.
        [The Bwiti cult as syncretistic, with emphasis on the
        more traditional sections of the movement.]

1043   ŚWIDERSKI, STANISLAW. Refleksje na temat zycia i jego
        affirmacji w synkretycznych kultach Fangów [Thoughts on
        life and its assertion according to the Fang syncretistic
        cults]. Przeglad Socjologiczny (Łodz) 23, 1969, 233-259.
        Eng. digest in Africana Bulletin (Warsaw) 14, 1971,
        230-232, by the author.

1044   ŚWIDERSKI, STANISLAW. La harpe sacrée dans les cultes
        syncrétiques au Gabon. Anthropos 65 (5-6), 1970,
        833-857, illus.
        [Bwiti - as an esoteric secret initiation society rather
        than a religion.]

1045   ŚWIDERSKI, STANISLAW. Le symbolisme du poteau central au
        Gabon. Mitteilungen der Anthropologischen Gesellschaft
        in Wien 100, 1970, 299-315.
        [The symbolism of the centre post in Bwiti, in the paral-
        lel women's Ombwiri Societies, and in "syncretist sects"
        in general; relation to Christianity.]

1046   ŚWIDERSKI, STANISLAW. Notes sur le Ndeya Kanga, secte
        syncrétique du Bouiti au Gabon. Anthropos 66 (1-2), 1971,
        81-119, bibl., Eng. summary.

West Central Africa

[The more recent development of Bwiti in a Christian direction, with a shift from the biological and natural to the spiritual; includes a cult of the Virgin Mary in place of the Fang mythical woman.]

1047   ŚWIDERSKI, STANISLAW. L'Ombwiri société d'initiation et de guérison au Gabon. Studi e Materiali di Storia delle Religioni (Religioni e Civiltà 1) (Rome) vol. 40-41, 1971, 125-204.
        [The women's society corresponding to Bwiti.]

1048   ŚWIDERSKI, STANISLAW. L'adaptation du missionnaire au context anthropologique et culturel. Kerygma (Ottawa) 18=6, 1972, 67-77.
        [Pp. 75-77, examples from the Bwiti ceremonial.]

1049   ŚWIDERSKI, STANISLAW. Uwagi o wspólczisnej poezji religijnej Fangów (Gabon). Przeglad Socjologiczny (Łodz) 25, 1972, 259-274.
        [Modern religious poetry of the Fang, found in the Bwiti cult - syncretistic, and reformatory.]

1050   ŚWIDERSKI, STANISLAW. Die Sakrale Verzierung der Tempel in den synkretischen Sekten in Gabun. Mitteilungen der Anthropologishen Gesellschaft in Wien 102, 1973, 105-113, illus.

1051   ŚWIDERSKI, STANISLAW. Notes biographiques sur les fondateurs et les guides spirituels des sectes syncrétiques au Gabon. Anthropologica (Ottawa) N.S. 15 (1), 1973, 37-87, illus.

1052   ŚWIDERSKI, STANISLAW. Remarques sur la philosophie religieuse des sectes syncrétiques au Gabon. Canadian Journal of African Studies 8 (1), 1974, 43-53, illus.; Eng. summary.
        [The Bwiti ancestral cult as a synthesis of traditional and Christian world views progressively developing to meet new needs.]

1053   ŚWIDERSKI, STANISLAW. Aperçu sur la trinité et la pensée triadique chez les Fang au Gabon. Canadian Journal of African Studies 9 (2), 1975, 235-257, illus.

1054   ŚWIDERSKI, STANISLAW. Notions théologiques dans la religion syncrétique Bouiti au Gabon. Église et Théologie 6, 1975, 319-364, tables.

1055   ŚWIDERSKI, STANISLAW. Synkretyzm religijny w Gabonie (Religious syncretism in Gabon). Przeglad Socjologiczny (Łodz) 26, 1975, 133-174.

[Bwiti cult and other sects; discussion of the role of women within them.]

1056   ŚWIDERSKI, STANISLAW. La conception psycho-religieuse de l'homme dans le religion syncrétique Bouiti au Gabon. Africana Marburgensia 9 (2), 1976, 32-66, ill. German summary.

1057   VERINES [CAPITAINE]. Le Mbouiti. Religion secrète du Gabon. [No place]: Centre Militaire d'Information et de Spécialisation pour l'Outre-Mer, Section de Documentation, 1e trimestre, 1959, 521 p. Mimeo.
       [Especially on the relations with the ancestors, and on the socio-political importance of Bwiti, in relation to the administration and to the nationalist leader L. Mba.]

1058   WEINSTEIN, BRIAN. Gabon: nation-building on the Ogooué. Cambridge, Massachusetts: Massachusetts Institute of Technology Press 1966, 287 p.
       [Ch. 3, "Anomie and the motive force of the Fang", includes Fang witchfinding movements such as Mademoiselle, the new religious movements such as Bwiti and the Great Revival.]

See also items 101, 198, 202.

ZAÏRE

Note: In view of the approximately 600 items in A. Geun's bibliography on Kimbanguism and Congo prophetism (see item 1105 below), the entries here are confined to the major works and to some items not found in Geun's bibliography.

1059   ALTHABE, GÉRARD. Les fleurs du Congo (Cahiers Libres, 232-233). Paris: Maspero 1972, 376 p.
       [Pp. 138-172, a sociological analysis of Kimbanguism in terms of a new social stratification of literates and illiterates.]

1060   ANDERSSON, EFRAIM. Primitiva religiöse väckelser i Afrika, in Uppdrag in Afrika. Svenska missionsinsater i de svartas vårdsdel. Stockholm: Missions Forbundetsferlag 1947, 122-149.

West Central Africa

[Pp. 126ff., Ngunzism; pp. 133-138, revivals in Baptist
area, Kasai, 1932, and at Baloloa, 1935; pp. 142ff.,
Nguedi revival 1947.]

1061   ANDERSSON, EFRAIM. Nkita - en extatisk sekt hos Teke i Kongo.
       Svensk Missionstidskrift (Uppsala) 43, 1955, 15-25.
       [Nkita, at Teke in Congo.]

1062   ANYENYOLA [WELO], JACQUES-OSCAR. Leadership dans les
       mouvements prophétiques de la ville de Lubumbashi.
       Problèmes Sociaux Congolais 83 (déc.), 1968, 25-84.
       [Kimbanguism, Jehovah's Witnesses, Apostles (of John
       Maranke) discussed, with reference to leadership, doctrine
       and liturgy.]

1063   ANYENYOLA WELO [JACQUES-OSCAR]. Le mouvement Kitawala en
       République du Zaïre. Problèmes Sociaux Zaïrois
       (Lubumbashi) no. 96-97 = mars-juin 1972, 3-26, bibl.

1064   ANYENYOLA [WELO], J[ACQUES]-O[SCAR]. A propos du vandaisisme
       et de son fondateur. Extrait du Bulletin Trimestriel du
       CEPSI: Programmes sociaux et économiques 94-95, 1972,
       57-88.
       [L'Église des Dignes, founded by Emmanuel Vanda in the
       Kasai in the 1920s.]

1065   AZOMBO, SOTER. Quelques réflexions à propos de la "Jamaa" au
       Congo. Tam-Tam (Paris) 5-6, 1965, 79-87.
       [A critical survey.]

1066   BAZOLA, ETIENNE. Le Kimbanguisme. Cahiers des Religions
       Africaines (Kinshasa) no. 3=2 (jan.), 1968, 121-152 ibid.,
       no. 4=2 (juillet), 1968, 315-336.
       [Survey of ten Congo movements; Part 2, Kimbanguism in
       relation to traditional culture and nationalism; its
       Christian status.]

1067   BENA-SILU. Die Kimbanguisten-Kirche in Zaïre. Eine
       Selbstdarstellung. Evangelische Mission Jahrbuch.
       Hamburg: Verlag der Deutschen Evangelischen Missionshilfe
       1975, 51-66.
       [By the chief secretary to the Spiritual Head of the
       E.J.C.S.K.]

1068   BERNARD, GUY. La contestation et les églises nationales au
       Congo. Canadian Journal of African Studies 5 (2), 1971,
       145-156.
       [Independent churches since independence: Kimbanguist
       Church (E.J.C.S.K.), Église de la Foi, Missions des Noirs,

Fikambi-kambi, Église Dieu de Nos Ancêtres, Kitawala, and various self-contained communities - their diverse reactions.]

1069 BIEBUYCK, D[ANIEL]. La société kumu face au Kitawala. Zaïre (Brussels) 11 (1), 1957, 7-40.
[Shows the relationship between the Kitawala movement (Jehovah's Witnesses) and the political, social and religious aspects of Kumu society.]

1070 BOKA, SIMON [-PIERRE] and RAYMAEKERS, PAUL. 250 Chants de l'Église de Jésus-Christ sur la terre par le prophète Simon Kimbangu (E.J.C.S.K.) Première Série: 85 Chants de Nsambu André (Notes et Documents 3). [Kinshasa]: Institut de Recherches Economiques et Sociales, Université Lovanium 1960, 43 p.

1071 BOSSCHE, JEAN VANDEN. Sectes et associations secrètes au Congo belge. [Kinshasa]: Gouvernement Général, 2e, Direction générale, Direction des A.I.M.O. éd. du Bulletin Militaire 1954, 101 p.

1072 CAHIERS DE LA RÉCONCILIATION (Paris: Mouvement International de Réconciliation). 5-6, 1966, 1-52, bibl.
[Pp. 33-39, Kimbanguist hymns in French; whole issue records a visit of two delegates from the Movement in 1966 to explore co-operation.]

1073 C. C. Les événements du Kwango. La secte du Tupelepele, quelques épisodes tragiques. Bulletin Cercle Colonial (Luxembourg) 8, 1931, 169-171.
[The religious dimensions of the Pende revolt, 1931.]

1074 CHOMÉ, JULES. La passion de Simon Kimbangu 1921-1951. Brussels: Présence Africaine 1959, 134 p. bibl.
[A Belgian lawyer using local sources examines the trial of Kimbangu, criticizes the colonial government, and rehabilitates Kimbangu.]

1075 CHOMÉ, JULES. Le retour de Simon Mpadi. Remarques Congolaises (Brussels) 2 (21), 1960, 216-223.
[News reports of Mpadi's release after imprisonment without trial from 1939; history of Mpadi and his Église des Noirs; relations with Kimbanguism.]

1076 CONGO MISSION NEWS. Among the Kimbanguist deportees. Congo Mission News, 60, October 1927, 31.

West Central Africa

1077   CONGO: REVUE GÉNÉRALE DE LA COLONIE BELGE (Brussels). See
       issues: 2, 1921, 575-576; 3 (1), 1922, 63-64; 5 (ii, 5),
       déc. 1924, 747-748.
       [On Kimbangu etc.; 1924 item is an editorial replying to
       criticisms, in L'Étoile Belge of 10 nov. and 12 déc. 1924.]

1078   CORNELIS, JOS. FLOR. Lettera Pastorale dell' Arcivescovo di
       Elisabethville sul movimento africano della "Jamaa". Le
       Missioni Francescane (Rome) 41, 1965, 28-31.

1079   COURRIER AFRICAIN (C.R.I.S.P., Brussels). Documents de Simon
       Mpadi. Courrier Africain no. 80-81, 1968.

1080   CRANE, WILLIAM H. The Kimbanguist Church and the search for
       authentic catholicity. The Christian Century 87 (22),
       1970, 691-695. Repr. in Peter Kami et al. (eds.), Pente-
       costals and politics. Wick, Bristol: Student Christian
       Movement Publications 1975, 8-11. Dutch version, De Kerk
       der Kimbanguisten en het zoeken naar authentieke
       Katholiciteit. De Heerbaan 24 (4), 1974.

1081   CRUISE O'BRIEN, CONOR. To Katanga and back: a U.N. case
       history. London: Hutchison 1962, 371 p., illus; [N.Y.]:
       Simon and Schuster 1963, 370 p., illus; Fr. trans.,
       Mission au Katanga. Paris: Plon 1964, xiii + 442 p.
       [Pp. 118, 320-321, Tshombe's association with the
       Apostles, a Katangese "revivalist sect". Pp. 152, 163,
       violence fostered by Watch Tower.]

1082   DAYE, PIERRE. L'Empire colonial belge. Brussels - Paris: Ed.
       du Soir and Berger-Levrault 1923.
       [Pp. 206-225, the influence of Garveyism and pan-
       Africanism in Kinshasa when Kimbanguism began.]

1083   DEAUBECHIES. Le Kitawala. Tendances du Temps [Lubumbashi]
       no. 58=19, 1961, 5-18.
       [Translation of a publication in Kibemba.]

1084   DECHANET, J.-M. En marge du monachisme africain, la Jamaa.
       Parole et Mission (Paris) 5 (18), 1962, 429-436.
       [A Benedictine interprets Jamaa in monastic terms.]

1085   DE CRAEMER, WILLY, et al. Analyse sociologique de la Jamaa.
       Kinshasa: Centre de Recherches sociologiques (Épiscopat
       Catholique du Congo) 1965, 79 p. Mimeo.

Black Africa

1086 DE CRAEMER, WILLY. The Jamaa movement in the Katanga and
       Kasai regions of the Congo. Review of Religious Research
       10 (1), 1968, 11-23.
       [Based on field research since 1964.]

1087 DE CRAEMER, WILLY. Jamaa and Ecclesia. Harvard University,
       Ph.D. dissertation 1973.

1088 DE MOOR, VINCENT. Leur combat: essais de missiologie. Paris:
       Beauchesne 1937.
       [Pp. 141-154, Watch Tower.]

1089 DEPAGE, ANDRÉ. L'organisation du prophétisme Kongo. Cultures
       et Développement (Louvain) 2 (2), 1970, 407-425.
       [The various sections, including Kimbanguism, as at
       1967.]

1090 DIANGIENDA [KUNTIMA], J[OSEPH]. Le Kimbanguisme. Courrier
       Hebdomodaire (Centre de Recherche et d'Information
       Sociopolitique, Paris), 60, 29 jan. 1960, 16-17.
       [By one of Kimbangu's sons.]

1091 DIANGIENDA KUNTIMA, [JOSEPH]. Botschaft des Oberhauptes der
       Kimbangu-Kirche an die Christen in der Schweiz und in
       Europa. Auftrag (Basel) 7 (2), 1973, 16.
       [A letter from the spiritual head of the Kimbanguist
       Church.]

1092 DIANGIENDA [KUNTIMA], JOSEPH. Wer immer diesen Willen hat...,
       "ist uns jederzeit willkommen", Auftrag (Basel) 7 (6),
       1973, 8-9, photos.
       [The spiritual head of the Kimbanguist Church inter-
       viewed by the president of the Basel Mission.]

1093 DUVAL, ARMAND. Reflexion sur le charisme: à propos de
       l'article "La Jamaa et son avenir" [by P. Mukendi]. Revue
       du Clergé Africain (Mayidi, Zaïre) 26 (5), 1971, 307-312.
       [Compare item 1140, by P. Mukendi.]

1094 L'ÉGLISE DU JÉSUS CHRIST PAR LE PROPHÈTE SIMON KIMBANGU.
       Nsadulu yo Ntwadusulu ua Dibundu dia "Kimbanguisme". n.p.:
       the Church, 1961 or 1962, 53 p., + 4 p. contents, photos.
       [The constitution and ceremonies, in Kikongo; printed in
       Brazzaville.]

1095 EPP, FRANK H. The world's largest peace church. The
       Mennonite (North Newton, Kansas) 30 September 1969,
       578-580, illus.
       [The Kimbanguist church.]

West Central Africa

1096   FABIAN, JOHANNES. Dream and charisma. Theories of dreams in
        the Jamaa Movement (Congo). Anthropos 61 (3-6), 1966,
        544-560, bibl.
           [Roman Catholic "family" movement in Katanga and south-
        east Zaïre; texts and analyses of dreams.]

1097   FABIAN, JOHANNES. Tod dem Propheten - ein Document zu einer
        prophetischen Situation. Sociologus (Berlin) N.F. 17 (2),
        1967, 131-146, Eng. summary.
           [Includes analysis of a text from the Jamaa movement.]

1098   FABIAN, JOHANNES. An African gnosis - for a reconsideration of
        an authoritative definition. History of Religions (Chicago)
        9 (1), 1969, 42-58.
           [Pp. 45-56, outline of Jamaa movement in the light of a
        recent definition of Gnosticism.]

1099   FABIAN, JOHANNES. Charisma and cultural change: the case of
        the Jamaa movement in Katanga (Congo Republic). Compar-
        ative Studies in Society and History 11 (2), 1969,
        153-173, bibl. Fr. trans., Le charisme et l'évolution
        culturelle: le cas du mouvement Jamaa au Katanga. Études
        Congolaises (Kinshasa) 12 (4), 1969, 92-116.
           [The relation of charismatic movements to social studies;
        history of Tempels and the Jamaa; a text and its analysis.
        French version includes Swahili original of the text.]

1100   FABIAN, JOHANNES. Jamaa: a charismatic movement in Katanga.
        Evanston: Northwestern University Press 1971, 284 p.
           [Contains bibliographical sketch of Placide Tempels, and
        analysis of the ideology or world view of the Jamaa; based
        on Chicago University Ph.D. dissertation 1969.]

1101   FABIAN, JOHANNES. Kazi: conceptualizations of labor in a
        charismatic movement among Swahili-speaking workers.
        Cahiers d'Études Africaines 50=13 (2), 1973, 293-325,
        bibl.
           [In south Katanga, copper-mine-town workers and the
        Jamaa movement.]

1102   FOX, RENÉE C., DE CRAEMER, WILLY, and RIBEAUCOURT, JEAN-MARIE.
        La deuxième indepéndance: étude d'un cas: La rébellion
        au Kwilu. Études Congolaises (Brussels and Kinshasa) 8
        (1), 1965, 1-35. Eng. trans., The second independence: a
        case study of the Kwilu rebellion in the Congo. Comparative
        Studies in Society and History 8 (1), 1965, 78-110.
           [The background of the Kwilu rebellion of Jan. 1964 as
        found in "messianic syncretist cults" in Kwilu area since

the 1930s, often led by products of mission schools;
fuller treatment of Mulélisme, a political form of
messianism.]

1103   GERARD, JACQUES E. Les fondements syncrétiques du Kitawala
(Collection Etudes Africaines, 1). Brussels: Centre de
Recherche et d'Information Sociopolitiques (C.R.I.S.P.),
and Le Livre Africain 1969, 119 p., bibl.
[By a former Belgian colonial administrator concerned
with religious movements.]

1104   GÉRARD, O. A remarkable case of fruitful adaptation in Africa.
The "Jamaa" in the Congo. Christ to the World (Rome) 9
(1), 1964, 16-32, part 1; idem, 9 (2), 1964, 119-131,
part 2. Fr. trans., Un cas remarquable d'adaptation
féconde en Afrique. La "Jamaa". Le Christ au Monde (Rome)
9 (1), 1964, 18-36 and 9 (2), 1964, 129-142. See also
reply in Christ to the World 9, 1964.
[Incorporates editorial introduction, pp. 16-17;
[V.] Mulago, A visit to the Jamaa, pp. 17-19; [A.] Piette,
Fruits yielded by the Jamaa in a mission of the Archdiocese
of Luluabourg, pp. 19-21; [P.] Tempels, the "Jamaa" and
the reconciliation of the clans, p. 21; [O.] Gérard,
Christian life in the Jamaa, pp. 22-32 and 119-131.]

1105   GEUNS, ANDRÉ. Bibliographie-Commentée du Prophétisme Kongo
(Les Cahiers du CEDAF, 7/1973. Série 5: Bibliographie).
Brussels: Centre d'Etude et de Documentation Africaines
1973, 81 p.
[600 items, briefly annotated; mostly on Kimbanguism
and similar movements; index of subjects.]

1106   GEUNS, ANDRÉ. Chronologie des mouvements religieux indé-
pendants au Bas-Zaïre, particulièrement du mouvement fondé
par le prophète Simon Kimbangu 1921-1971. Journal of
Religion in Africa (Leiden) 6 (3), 1974, 187-222.
[Bibliography, pp. 189-191.]

1107   GILIS, CHARLES-ANDRÉ. Kimbangu, fondateur d'église. Brussels:
La Librairie Encyclopédique 1960, 126 p.
[A sympathetic survey based on existing publications;
questions whether any new material on Kimbangu remains to
be found.]

1108   GROSJEAN, JOSEPH. Jamaa, a spiritual adventure. White
Fathers - White Sisters (Sutton Coldfields) 182, 1972,
10-23.

West Central Africa

1109   HABARI, CHARLES. Le lumumbisme dévie en religion. Le
       Courrier d'Afrique (Kinshasa) 10 juillet 1963, 1 and 3.
       [An association of Lumumba and Kitawala supporters at
       Stanleyville, hostile to whites and their churches.]

1110   HEIMER, HALDOR E[UGENE]. The church suited to home needs: a
       look at the people of two churches in Luluabourg, Congo,
       in R. T. Parsons (ed.), Windows on Africa: a symposium.
       Leiden: E. J. Brill 1971, 21-37.

1111   HEIMER, HALDOR EUGENE. The Kimbanguists and Bapostolo: a
       study of two African independent churches in Luluabourg,
       Congo, in relation to similar churches and in the context
       of Lulua traditional religion and culture. Hartford
       Seminary Foundation, Ph.D. dissertation 1971, 478 p.

1112   HOLLENWEGER, WALTER J. Marxist and Kimbanguist mission: a
       comparison (Inaugural Lecture, 23 November 1972).
       Birmingham: University of Birmingham 1973, 14 p. Ger.
       trans., Marxistische und kimbanguistische Mission - ein
       Vergleich. Evangelische Theologie 34 (5), 1974, 434-447.
       [Inaugural lecture: Kimbanguism treated as more
       Christian than much orthodox Christianity and as dealing
       with African man's "alienation".]

1113   HOLLENWEGER, WALTER J. Pentecost between Black and White:
       five case studies on Pentecost and politics. Belfast:
       Christian Journals Ltd. 1974, 143 p.
       [Ch. 3 (= pp. 55-73), Pentecost of N'Kamba, considers
       Kimbanguist church relations to western Pentecostalists,
       its orthodoxy, its relation to Kimbanguist dissenters, and
       its future.]

1114   IRVINE, CECILIA. The birth of the Kimbanguist Movement in the
       Bas-Zaïre 1921, Journal of Religion in Africa 6 (1), 1974,
       23-76.
       [Introductory survey; detailed chronology and documenta-
       tion of events; texts of unpublished letters from Baptist
       missionaries.]

1115   JANSSEN, TH. M. De ontmoeting tussen Bantoe-religieuziteit en
       christelijk geloof. Tijdschrift voor Theologie (Breda-
       Bruges) 5 (4), 1965, 411-441 (Eng. summary, p. 441); Eng.
       trans., Religious encounter and the Jamaa. Heythrop
       Journal (Oxford) 8 (2), 1967, 129-151, bibl.
       [Pp. 129-145, Tempels' encounter with Bantu life;
       pp. 145-151, on Jamaa as an outcome of this.]

1116   JANZEN, JOHN M. and MacGAFFEY, WYATT. An anthology of Kongo
       religion: primary texts from lower Zaïre. (Publications
       in Anthropology 5). Lawrence, Kansas: University of
       Kansas 1974, x + 163 p., illus., tables, map.
           [Ch. 1 on literacy as introducing a new genre of sacred
       writings; many of the examples they give derive from
       independent churches, especially Kimbanguist, but also the
       Church of the Blacks (S. Mpadi); the Church of the Holy
       Spirit (Masemba Esiae); the Church of Jesus Christ of Two
       Witnesses (T. Ntwalani) and the Church of the Twelve
       Apostles (Isaac D.).]

1117   JEWSIEWICKI, B. La contestation sociale et la naissance du
       prolétariat au Zaïre au cours de la première moitié du XXe
       siècle. Canadian Journal of African Studies 10 (1), 1976,
       47-70.
           [African religious movement seen as one of several modes
       of social contestation of colonial rule in Zaïre.]

1118   JOSSE, [PÈRE]. Autour de Kitawala. Essor du Congo [Lubumba-
       shi] 25 sep., 6 and 27 oct., 10 nov., 1945.

1119   JULES-ROSETTE, BENNETTA. Song and spirit: the use of songs
       in the management of ritual contexts. Africa (London) 45
       (2), 1975, 150-166.
           [Data from a congregation of the Apostolic Church of
       John Maranke (Vapostori) in the Kasai area of Zaïre.]

1120   KANYINDA LUSANGA. Le facteur religieux comme agent de prise
       de conscience politico-nationaliste pendant la période
       coloniale au Zaïre: le cas des mouvements messianiques
       (Kimbanguisme, Kitawale...). Études Zaïroises (Kinshasa)
       2, mai-juin 1975, 41-69.

1121   KEIDEL, LEVI. Black Samson. An African's astonishing pil-
       grimage to personhood. Carol Stream, Illinois: Creation
       House 1975, 144 p.
           [Pp. 73-77, Simon Kimbangu's influence in the conversion
       of a fellow-prisoner; pp. 99-100, Kimbangu's death and
       its effect; autobiography of a prisoner.]

1122   KIKASA KIBASO. Le début du mouvement Kitawala au Katanga-
       Shaba (1923-1937). Mémoire de Licence, Department of
       History, National University of Zaïre, Lubumbashi, 1972.
       Mimeo.

1123   KOPYTOFF, IGOR. Suku religion: a study in internally induced
       reinterpretation. Northwestern University, Ph.D. disserta-
       tion (anthropology) 1960.

West Central Africa

[Pp. 141-167, three religious movements among the
Basuku in the Congo: Mbiande, 1924;
Lupambula 1944-45; Holy Water 1954-95.]

1124 LANZAS, A. and BERNARD, G[UY]. Les fidèles d'une "nouvelle
Église" au Congo. Genève-Afrique (Geneva) 5 (2), 1966,
189-216.
[The Kinshasa branch of the Apostolic Church of John
Malungu [sic; Maranke]; appendix of 11 hymns in Fr. trans.
from Tshiluba.]

1125 LEBEER, PAUL. In Belcopresse [Kinshasa] 1, 22 avril 1956,
16-19; 3, 6 mai 1956, 87-88 and 101-10s; 4, 13 mai 1956,
149-151; 5, 20 mai 1956, 169-170.
[Series of articles on Kitawala in the Congo.]

1126 LERRIGO, P. H. J. The "Prophet Movement" in Congo. International Review of Missions, no. 42=11 (April), 1922,
270-277.
[A first-hand account of the origin of Kimbanguism,
especially the call of Kimbangu and his healings, by a
Baptist medical missionary.]

1127 LUNTADILA [MUSIANGANI], LUCIEN J.-CL., YOWANI ALBERT, DIATA
NORBERT, WIKISI RAYMOND (signators). Mise au point sur le
Kimbanguisme. [Kinshasa?] [The Church] septembre 1957,
5 p. Mimeo.
[Defence during last period of severe persecution, by
"adeptes du Kimbanguisme". Extract published in
C.R.I.S.P., 47 (8), 8 jan. 1960.]

1128 LUSANGU SASA. Le messianisme congolais et ses incidences
politiques. Cahiers des Religions Africaines no. 12=6
(juillet), 1972, 235-238.
[A review article on M. Sinda's work of this title.]

1129 MacGAFFEY, WYATT. Kongo and the king of the Americans.
Journal of Modern African Studies 6 (2), 1968, 171-181.
[Includes the contributions of Kimbanguism and Kitawala
to popular Congolese images of America.]

1130 MacGAFFEY, WYATT. The beloved city: a commentary on a
Kimbanguist text. Journal of Religion in Africa 2 (2),
1969, 129-147. Germ. trans., H. J. Margull, Die geliebte
Stadt, oder: Wir gehoren dem neuen Jerusalem Eine
Erklarung aus dem kimbanguistischen Kirche im Kongo, in
J. Freytag and H. J. Margull (eds.), Junge Kirchen auf
eigenen Wegen: Analysen und Dokumente. Neukirchener
Verlag 1972, 21-31.

[A slightly abbreviated and edited translation of
K. S. Dialungana's Zolanga Yelusalemi, a basic Kimbanguist
publication.]

1131 MacGAFFEY, WYATT. Kimbanguism: an African Christianity.
Africa Report (Washington D.C.) 21 (1), 1976, 40-43, illus.

1132 MAKABZU, JEAN PERCE. Yesu Klisto evo Simon Kimbangu?
[Kinshasa]: Librairie Evangélique du Congo 1964, 14 p.
[A strong attack on Kimbanguism.]

1133 MAKENGERE [PSEUD.]. Vigilance! La Revue Coloniale Belge
(Brussels), 1 (8), 1946, 4-7.
[Watchtower in the Belgian Congo, by a Belgian colonial
official.]

1134 MARKOWITZ, MARVIN D. Cross and sword. The political role of
Christian missions in the Belgian Congo 1908-1960 (Hoover
Institution Publications 114). Stanford, California:
Hoover Institution Press, Stanford University, 1973,
223 p., bibl.
[Ch. 13, messianic and syncretistic sects; also pp. 154,
155, 159, on Kimbanguism.]

1135 MARTIN, MARIE-LOUISE. Prophetic Christianity in the Congo.
The Church of Jesus Christ on earth through the prophet
Simon Kimbangu. Johannesburg: Christian Institute for
Southern Africa n.d. [1968], 40 p., illus. Abridged Fr.
trans., L'Église Kimbanguiste, Congo-Afrique (Kinshasa) 9
(39), 1969, 441-450.
[Contains selected church documents in English trans-
lation, and "special considerations for missiology and
African church history".]

1136 MARTIN, MARIE-LOUISE. Kirche ohne Weisse. Simon Kimbangu und
seine Millionenkirche im Kongo. Basel: Friedrich Reinhardt
Verlag 1971, 279 p., maps, photos. Eng. trans., Kimbangu.
An African prophet and his church. Oxford: Basil Blackwell
1975, xxiv + 198 p.; Grand Rapids: Eerdmans 1976, 224 p.
[A survey of mission history and earlier movements
(Beatrice and Nongqause); history of Kimbanguism 1918-1960;
the present practice and political and theological
positions of the Church. See review by D. J. Bosch in
Missionalia 1 (2), 1973, 96-98.]

1137 MARTIN, MARIE-LOUISE. A la recherche d'un pastorat pleinement
africain. Flambeau (Yaoundé) no. 33, fev. 1972, 35-40.
[Address at opening of Kimbanguist School of Theology
1971.]

West Central Africa

1138   MELS, BERNARD. An example of fruitful adaptation in Africa:
        the Jamaa at Luluabourg. Christ to the World (Rome) 9 (6),
        1964, 500-504; Fr. version, Un exemple d'adaptation
        féconde en Afrique. La "Jamaa" à Luluabourg. Le Christ
        au Monde (Rome) 9 (6), 1964, 526-530. (Reprinted from
        Pastoralia 1 Aug. 1964).
        [By the Roman Catholic archbishop of Luluabourg.]

1139   MELS, BERNARD. Lettera pastorale dell' Arcivescovo di
        Luluabourg sul movimento africano della "Jamaa". Le
        Missione Francescane (Rome) 41, 1965, 32-34.

1140   MUKENDI, PLACIDE. La Jamaa et son avenir. Revue du Clergé
        Africain (Mayidi, Zaïre) 26 (2), 1971, 142-168.
        [A major criticism of Jamaa. See a reply by A. Duval,
        item 1093.]

1141   MUKENGE, GODEFROID. Le prêtre face à la Jamaa et à l'apostolat
        des laïcs. Orientations Pastorales (Limete-Kinshasa) 98,
        jan-fev. 1965, 24-33.

1142   MUKENGE, GODEFROID. Une spiritualité africaine de mariage
        chez les Bantus de l'Afrique centrale: la Jamaa. Revue
        du Clergé Africaine (Mayidi, Zaïre) 25 (2), 1970, 151-172.

1143   MULAGO [GWA CILALA MUSHARHAMINA], VINCENT. Autour du mouvement
        de la "Jamaa". Orientations Pastorales (Limete-Kinshasa)
        1, 1960, 3-28.
        [Records the "intentions" Jamaa members made when Tempels
        left.]

1144   MUNAYI, THOMAS. Le mouvement kimbanguiste dans le Haut-Kasai
        1921-1960. Thèse de Doctorat de 3ᵉ Cycle, Université de
        Provence 1974. Vol. I, 400 p.; vol. II, 133 p.
        ["Une contribution de haute valeur à l'étude du
        Kimbanguisme au Zaïre".]

1145   MUSEUM LESSIANUM. Sectes dans l'est du Congo ex-Belge. Devant
        les Sectes Non-Chrétiennes. Rapports et Compte rendu de
        la XXXIᵉ Semaine de Missiologie Louvain 1961. Paris:
        Desclee de Brouwer n.d. [1962?] 91-101.
        ["Sectes religieuses (Kitawala)" - pp. 96-98.]

1146   MWENE-BATENDE, [GASTON]. Le phénomène de dissidence des
        sectes religieuses d'inspiration Kimbanguiste. Les
        Cahiers du CEDAF 6, 1971 (Série 4: Religion), 37 p.
        [The Ntwalanist Church, based on prophet Thomas Ntwalani
        (1880-1942), by separation from Kimbanguist Church 1963,

under his son Kiamosi Simon Ntwalani; offical history,
rules and constitution, etc.]

1147 MWENE-BATENDE, [GASTON]. Quelques aspects du prophétisme au
      Zaïre. Cahiers des Religions Africaines (Kinshasa)
      no. 11=6 (jan.), 1972, 69-90.

1148 MWENE-BATENDE, [GASTON]. La dynamique socio-culturelle des
      mouvements prophétiques dans le Bas-Zaïre. Cahiers des
      Religions Africaines (Kinshasa) no. 13=7 (jan.) 1973,
      43-62.

1149 NGINDU [MUSHETE], [ALPHONSE]. En marge d'un colloque récent.
      Simon Kimbangu et le Kimbanguisme sous l'éclairage de
      l'histoire. Revue du Clergé Africain (Mayidi, Zaïre) 17
      (6), 1972, 631-645.

1150 NGINDU [MUSHETE], A[LPHONSE]. Simon Kimbangu et le
      Kimbanguisme. Une lecture historique à propos d'un
      colloque récent. Cahiers des Religions Africaines
      no. 11=6 (jan.), 1972, 91-103.

1151 NOTHOMB, DOMINIQUE M. Une nouvelle forme de catéchèse.
      Nouvelle Revue Théologique (Louvain) 86, 1964, 725-744.
      [A White Father on Jamaa, as already existing before
      Tempels' catechetical approach.]

1152 PAULUS, JEAN-PIERRE. Le Kitawala au Congo belge (mouvement
      indigène à caractère politico-religieux). Revue de
      l'Institut de Sociologie Solvay (Brussels) 2/3 1956,
      257-270.
      [The entry of Watch Tower from the Rhodesias via Katanga
      in 1951-52, prepared for by an earlier sect of Bereti
      Ambrasius; the anti-white and political nature varied in
      different areas of the Congo.]

1153 PEDERSEN, ODD KVAAL, AFRIKANSK MARTYRIUM. Randbemerkninger
      til presentasjon av "Jesu Kristi Kirke pa jorgen ved
      profeten Simon Kimbangu" Norsk Tidsskrift for Misjon 24
      (1), 1970, 3-24.

1154 PHILIPPE, RENÉ. Le secte "Nebele" chez les Mangbetu. Africa-
      Tervuren 8 (4), 1962, p. 98.
      [An anti-European religious group dating from the first
      years of colonization.]

1155 PHILIPPE, RENÉ. Les "nganga nzambe" ou prêtres de Dieu?
      Africa-Tervuren 11 (1), 1965, 23-25.
      [A neo-primal movement described by a missionary.]

West Central Africa

1156   PRÉSENCE AFRICAINE. Émeutes à Léopoldville. Présence
       Africaine 23, déc. 1958-jan. 1959, 113-122.
          [Pp. 119-121, relation between the Abako political
       movement and Kimbanguism in the 1959 riots.]

1157   RAYMAEKERS, PAUL. L'Église de Jésus-Christ sur la terre par
       le prophète Simon Kimbangu: contribution à l'étude des
       mouvements messianiques dans le Bas-Kongo. Zaïre
       (Brussels) 13 (7), 1959, 675-756, illus.
          [Substantial study of the independent church which
       resulted from the Kimbanguist movement.]

1158   RAYMAEKERS, PAUL (ed.). Histoire de Simon Kimbangu, prophète,
       d'après les écrivains Nfinangani et Nzungu (1921).
       Archives de Sociologie des Religions 31=16 (1), 1971,
       15-42, illus., also Kinshasa: Université de Kinshasa
       1971, 60 p.

1159   REMY, J. Kibango. Annales apostoliques des Pères du Saint-
       Esprit (Paris) mars-avril 1922, 45-48.
          [Acknowledges defections from the Roman Catholic
       community.]

1160   [REUNION DES PASTEURS KIMBANGUISTES.] Office du prophète
       Simon Kimbangu (Nkanda Bisambu bis tata Simon Kimbangu).
       [Kinshasa]: La Réunion des Pasteurs Kimbanguistes n.d.
       [1960-62?], 115 p., illus.
          [Contains a life of Kimbangu (in French); a liturgy for
       Kimbanguists (in French and KiKongo); ten hymns (in
       KiKongo). Not an official publication of the Kimbanguist
       Church.]

1161   REVUE DE DROIT ET DE JURISPRUDENCE DU KATANGA [Lubumbashi].
       On Mwana Lesa see 2 (8), 1926, 201-204; 2 (9), 1926,
       225-230; 2 (10), 1926, 242-247; 2 (11), 1926, 274-276; 3
       (1), 1927, 328-332. See also article by A. Sohier, Un
       prédécesseur de Mwana Lesa, in 2 (4), 1926, 97.

1162   REYBURN, WILLIAM D. Christianity and ritual communication.
       Practical Anthropology (Tarrytown, N.Y.) 10 (4), 1963,
       145-159.
          [P. 158, prophet movements as response to the chasm
       between Western and African ritual symbolism; mentions
       movement among the Bayanzi, Zaïre. By a missionary
       anthropologist.]

1163   RIDDLE, NORMAN GEORGE. Church growth [and the communication
       of the Gospel] in Kinshasa. Fuller Theological Seminary
       School of World Mission, M.A. thesis (Missions) 1971,
       196 p.
           [Pp. 38-67, independent churches - pp. 38-59, Kimbanguism;
       60-64, Holy Spirit church; 64-67, Jehovah's Witnesses and
       Watch Tower.]

1164   RYCKMANS, ANDRÉ. Les mouvements prophétiques Kongo en 1958:
       contribution à l'étude de l'histoire du Congo [Preface and
       notes by Paul Raymaekers.] Kinshasa: Bureau d'Organisation
       des Programmes Ruraux de l'Université Lovanium 1970, 55 p.
           [Historical outline of Kimbanguism and twelve other move-
       ments; the psychological, social and political character-
       istics of the lower Congo; characteristics of prophet
       movements; predictions of increasing paganization and
       politicization; appendix of letters and reports from the
       Belgian official who dealt with Kimbangu in 1921.]

1165   SALMON, PIERRE. Sectes secrètes Zande (République du Zaïre),
       in Mélanges Gourou: études de géographie tropicale
       offertes à Pierre Gourou. The Hague: Mouton 1972,
       427-440.
           [Five "secret societies" current in 1960 as millennial
       cults protesting against both the traditional and the
       colonial order.]

1166   SHANK, DAVID A. An indigenous African Church comes of age.
       Kimbanguism. Mennonite Life, June 1972, 53-55.
           [A description of the 50th anniversary celebrations at
       Nkamba "holy city" and of the first communion service.]

1167   SOMERS, EMILE. La Jamaa, une gnose sexuelle? Revue du
       Clergé Africain (Mayidi, Zaïre) 26 (5), 1971, 313-320.

1168   TANNER, RALPH E. S. The Jamaa movement in the Congo, a socio-
       logical comment on some religious interpretations.
       Heythrop Journal 9 (2), 1968, 164-178.
           [A criticism of Tempels' thought; pp. 175-178, the
       Jamaa.]

1169   TELEMA (Kinshasa-Gombe). Chrétien fier, africain inexorable:
       le destin du Kimbanguisme. Telema 2 (1), 1975.

1170   TEMPELS, PLACIDE and MEERT, JAQUES. La Jamaa. Orientations
       Pastorales (Limete-Kinshasa) 2, n.d. [ca. 1960], 1-32.

West Central Africa

1171   TEMPELS, PLACIDE. Notre rencontre. Limete - Kinshasa:
       Centre d' Etudes Pastorales n.d. [1962], 207 p.
       [A collection of essays that appeared in Orientations
       Pastorales 1960-62, discussing theological and missiological
       ideas, all of which relate to their expression in the Jamaa
       movement; essays specifically on Jamaa are: pp. 26-29, À
       propos de la Jamaa; pp. 84-89, Doctrine de la Jamaa.]

1172   THEUWS, THEODOR. Le mouvement "Jamaa" au Katanga, in Museum
       Lessianum, Familles anciennes, familles nouvelles. Rapports
       et compte rendu de la XXXe Semaine de Missiologie, Louvain
       1960. Bruges, 1961, 118.

1173   THOMAS, GEORGE. Kimbanguism: African Christianity. IDOC
       International (North American edn.) 21, 13 March 1971,
       2-29.

1174   TRANFO, LUIGI. Bianchi e Negri. Saggi di acculturazione
       Africana (Problemi Libri). Palermo: Palumbo Editore
       1972, 147 p.
       [Pp. 5-50, contemporary Kimbanguism.]

1175   TRUBY, DAVID W. Régime of gentlemen: personal experiences of
       Congolese Christians during the 1964 rebellion. London:
       Marshall Morgan and Scott 1971, 160 p.
       [Ch. 10, persecuted by the "Son of Man": a Simba
       insurrectionist who claimed to have risen from the dead,
       and his armed group of twelve disciples.]

1176   TURNBULL, COLIN M[acMILLAN]. The lonely African. New York:
       Simon and Schuster 1962; Doubleday Doran 1963. London:
       Chatto and Windus 1963, 223 p.
       [Pp. 200-204, 212, 217 (U.K. edition), Kitawala, from
       an African viewpoint.]

1177   TURNER, THOMAS. Mouvements de résistance chez les Mongo du
       Sankuru. Revue Congolaise des Sciences Humaines 2,
       jan. 1971, 59-84.
       [Pp. 78-79, "révoltes et mouvements religio-politiques" -
       Tonga-Tonga (1904), Loambo (1917-18), and the revolt of
       Basongo Meno (1919), both as "médicaments".]

1178   TURNER, THOMAS and WEMBOLUA KASONGO. Le Vandisme (Sankuru-
       Zaïre) et sa signification politique. Cahiers du C.E.D.A.F.,
       no. 5, 1974, 39 p.
       ["Political importance of a religious movement".]

1179 USTORF, WERNER. Africanisch Initiative. Das aktive Leiden des
Propheten Simon Kimbangu (Studien zur interkulturellen
Geschichte des Christentums, Band 5). Bern: Herbert
Lang; Frankfurt: Peter Lang 1975, 457 p., bibl., maps,
table.
[Historical study, with background in colonial Congo;
a "critical study".]

1180 VAN DER POORT, CORNELIS. Gamba, een onafhankelyke kerk in
Zaïre. Een onderzoek naar struktur en funktionering.
Free University of Amsterdam, doctoral dissertation
(Faculteit der Rechtsgeleerdheid) 1973, 513 p., maps,
tables.
[An independent church derived from the Heart of Africa
Mission in Haut-Zaïre in 1960, and now a constituent of
the Église du Christ au Congo. By a sociologist.]

1181 VAN WING, J. Le Kibanguisme vu par un témoin. Zaïre
(Brussels) 12 (6), 1958, 563-618.
[Historical assessment critical of Kimbangu and Mpadi;
claims Kimbangu became a Roman Catholic in 1951.]

1182 VRINDTS, F. Secte des Bena Nzambi wa Malemba. Port Francqui:
Belgian Government, 8 nov. 1951, 28 p., Mimeo. [Zaïre:
State Archives.]
[Founded by Mata, ex-army sergeant, in 1944; government
report in a document from the colonial archives.]

1183 WAINWRIGHT, GEOFFREY. Theological reflections on "The
Catechism concerning the prophet Simon Kimbangu", of 1970.
Orita (Ibadan) 5 (1), 1971, 18-35.

1184 WAUTHION, R. Le mouvement Kitawala au Congo belge. Bulletin
de l'Association des Ancients Étudiants de l'Institut
Universitaire des Territoires d' Outre-Mer (Anvers) 3
(8), 1950, 3-10.
[A good account.]

1185 WINDELS, A. Le secte secrète des Mani à Lukolela. Aequatoria
(Coquilhatville) 3 (2), 1940, 49-53, and idem 3 (3), 1940,
79-84.
[Written in 1936 by a missionary priest; a secret society
originating among the Zande c. 1900, imitating aspects
of Catholic ritual.]

West Central Africa

1186   WYMEERSCH, P. Les "Apostolos". Notes sur un mouvement
        syncrétique de la région de Lubumbashi (Rép. du Zaïre).
        Africa-Tervuren 19 (1), 1973, 6115; 19, illus. by Père
        Johan Everdert; map. Pp. 27-28, Flemish summary.
        [The "Apostles" of John Maranke, originating in
        Rhodesia.]

1187   ZABALA REZ.-PICABEA, XABIER. Étude sociologique de la Jamaa:
        le cas de Lubumbashi. National University of Zaïre,
        Mémoire de Licencié (Sociologie), juillet 1974, 133 p.
        Mimeo.

See also items 4, 6, 21, 27, 28, 29, 41, 91, 96, 117, 118, 149, 150,
155, 160, 166, 178, 179, 182, 192, 209, 227, 232, 244, 248, 252, 272,
293, 295, 308, 315, 353, 354, 357, 370, 383, 406, 416, 422, 459, 1412,
1419, 1425, 1427.

Eastern Africa

1188   BARRETT, DAVID B[RIAN] (ed.). African initiatives in religion.
       21 studies from East and Central Africa. Nairobi: East
       African Publishing House 1971, 288 p., illus., maps.
          [Revised papers from the Workshop in Religious Research,
       Nairobi, December 1967.   See under D. E. W. Smoker, M. L.
       Martin, T. O. Ranger, D. B. Barrett, M. L. Daneel,
       M. W. Murphree.]

1189   BESSELL, M. J. Nyabingi. Uganda Journal (Kampala) 6 (2),
       1938, 73-86.
          [The Nyabingi movement in Uganda and Rwanda.]

1190   CHURCH, J[OHN] E. Awake Uganda! The story of Blasio Kigozi
       and his vision of revival. 2nd rev. ed., n.p. [Kampala],
       n.d. [1957], ix + 53 p., illus. 1st. ed., London:
       Highway Press 1937, viii + 56 p., illus.; originally
       published in Luganda under title Buganda zukuku! 1936.
          [Memoir of the Ganda pastor who was one of the early
       leaders in the East African revival.]

1191   CHURCH, J[OHN] E. Jesus satisfies. Achimota, Dar es Salaam
       and Lusaka: African Christian Press 1969, 48 p.
          [The East African Revival conventions at Kabale in 1945
       and 1955, with outlines of addresses delivered.]

1192   DIRVEN, PETER J. The Maria Legio. The dynamics of a break-
       away church among the Luo of East Africa. Pontificia
       Universitas Gregoriana, dissertation for Doctorate in
       Missiology 1970, xxxii + 343 p., maps, illus.

1193   DOENS, IRÉNÉE. L'Église Orthodoxe en Afrique Orientale dans
       et hors le cadre patriarcat grec orthodoxe d' Alexandrie.
       Revue du Clergé Africain (Mayidi, Zaïre) 24 (5), 1969,
       543-576.
          [Includes the relations with Reuben Spartas.]

1194   FITZPATRICK, P. Heard any prophecies recently? Dini na Mila
       (Kampala) 3, April 1966, 5-11.

Bibliography of New Religious Movements in Primal Societies

Eastern Africa

> [Prophecies, including the coming of the white men or
> new religions, among "the Rwanda, Kigezi, Ganda, Bhambaa,
> and Fipa".]

1195   GOLDTHORPE, J. E. Outlines of East African society. Kampala:
       Department of Sociology, Makerere University 1958.
       [Ch. 8 (pp. 190-231), "Religious groups", has thorough
       coverage of the entire religious situation in the mid-
       1950s.]

1196   HARLOW, VINCENT and CHILVER, E. M. (eds.). History of East
       Africa Vol. II. Oxford: Clarendon Press 1965, 766 p.
       [Pp. 363-371, Kikuyu independent schools movement;
       pp. 371-373, Kikuyu sects; pp. 379-380, Nyanza movements;
       pp. 116, 509-510, Uganda; pp. 633-634, the absence of
       "sects" from Tanganyika.]

1197   HORNER, NORMAN A. An East African Orthodox Church. Journal
       of Ecumenical Studies 12 (2), 1975, 221-233.

1198   IMPERATO, P. J. Witchcraft and traditional medicine among
       the Luo of Tanzania. Tanzania Notes and Records 66,
       Dec. 1966, 193-201.
       [P. 201, faith-healing not traditional for Luo, but
       became popular through South Nyanza separatists, espe-
       cially G. Aoko of Maria Legio and her exorcism of evil
       spirits - many Luo travelled to her.]

1199   KIERAN, JOHN A. The Christian Church in East Africa in modern
       times (2). Neue Zeitschrift für Missionswissenschaft
       (Schoneck-Beckenried) 25 (4), 1969, 273-287.
       [Pp. 273-276, 278, historical survey of independent
       churches as a "third section of Christianity".]

1200   KING, KENNETH J[AMES]. Pan-Africanism and education: a study
       of race, philanthropy and education in the southern states
       of America and East Africa. Oxford: Clarendon Press 1971,
       xiii + 296 p., illus., maps.
       [Pp. 240-245, E. Kalibala's independent school, 1935;
       pp. 245-246, Molonket's independent church at Narok, ex-
       Africa Inland Mission, 1929; p. 248, Koinange and
       Githunguri independent school.]

1201   KING, NOEL Q[UINTON]. The East African revival movement and
       evangelism. Ecumenical Review 20 (2), 1968, 159-162.

1202   KITABU CHA KISIFU. [A book of praise]. Nairobi: Majestic
       Printing Works n.d.; also Nakuru: Uzima Press 1972.

166

[Printed hymnbook of the East African Revival Fellowship, with eight hymns including the Luganda Tukutendereza
[We praise Thee] translated into 20 languages.]

1203 LEMARCHAND, RENÉ. Rwanda and Burundi. London: Pall Mall/
      New York: Praeger 1970, 562 p., illus., maps.
      [P. 60, pp. 100-102, Nyabingi cult as a messianic
      movement.]

1204 MUGA, ERASTO. African response to Western Christian religion.
      A sociological analysis of African separatist religious
      and political movements in East Africa. Kampala: East
      African Literature Bureau 1975, 216 p.

1205 NANKYAMAS, THEODORUS. On the Orthodox Church in Uganda and
      Kenya. Porefthendes (Athens) 3, 1961, 43-44.

1206 PAPASARANTOPOULOS, CHRYSOSTOM. A report on the missionary work
      carried out in the Metropolis of Eirinoupolis (East Africa).
      Porefthendes (Athens) 5, 1963, 2-3
      [Concerns the African Orthodox Church. See also p. 34
      of same issue.]

1207 PARKIN, DAVID J. Medicines and men of influence. Man N.S.
      3 (3), 1968, 424-439.
      [Analysis of witchcraft eradication movements, especially
      in post-independent Africa, with examples from the Fipa of
      Tanzania (Kamcape) and Nyika of Kenya (Kajiwe, 1966);
      regarded as equivalent to cargo cults in Melanesia.]

1208 RANGER, T[ERENCE] O[SBORN]. Report on the conference for the
      historical study of East African religion, Limuru, June
      1974. African Religious Research (African Studies Center,
      UCLA) 4 (2), 1974, 6-46.
      [Pp. 33-45, "prophetism and conceptual change" - on the
      indigenous origins and history of prophets, even in move-
      ments also under Christian influence.]

1209 RUANDA MISSION (of the Church Missionary Society). Ruanda
      Notes (London) 1-. 1932?- . Quarterly intercession
      paper. Ruanda Mission Quarterly Prayer Paper (London)
      [no serial numbers]. Ruanda News Sheet (London) n.d.,
      illus. Front Line News (Kabale, Uganda) 1 (1-3), 1945-46;
      then as Revival News (Croydon, U.K.) 2 (1-3), 1947-51;
      also Junior Ruanda Notes and Annual Report.
      [The Revival Movement, passim, especially Ruanda News Sheet 5.]

1210 SMOKER, DOROTHY E. W. Decision-making in East African revival
      movement groups, in D. B. Barrett (ed.), item 1188, 96-108.

Eastern Africa

1211   STANLEY SMITH, ALGERNON C.   Road to revival: the story of the
       Ruanda Mission.   London: Church Missionary Society n.d.
       [1946?],   116 p., illus.
       [On the East African revival movement in Rwanda, passim;
       pp. 36-38, Nyabingi.]

1212   ST. JOHN, PATRICIA.   Breath of life.   London: Norfolk Press
       1971, 238 p., illus.
       [History of the Ruanda Mission and the East African Re-
       vival; see especially chapters 10-12 for the latter.]

1213   THOMSON, C. R.   Revival in Africa.   Calcutta: Evangelical
       Literature Depot 1952.
       [Description of the East African Revival, including the
       great conventions.]

1214   USHER-WILSON L[UCIEN] C.   Dini ya Misambwa.   Uganda Journal
       (Kampala) 16 (2), 1952, 125-129.
       [The "religion of the ancestors" in Kenya and, to a
       lesser extent in Uganda, from 1947. By an Anglican
       bishop.]

1215   WARREN, MAX [ADRIAN CUNNINGHAM].   Revival: an enquiry.
       London: SCM Press 1954, 123 p.
       [A theological analysis of the causes and meaning of
       the "revival" movement which affected mission church mem-
       bers in East Africa from ca. 1935 and remained (with a few
       minor exceptions) within the mission churches, without
       forming an independent church.]

1216   WELBOURN, F[REDERICK] B[URKEWOOD].   Independency in East
       Africa.   Ecumenical Review (Geneva) 11 (4), 1959, 430-436.
       [An outline of his method of approach, and evaluation.]

1217   WELBOURN, F[REDERICK] B[URKEWOOD].   East African rebels. A
       study of some independent churches.   London: SCM Press
       1961, xii + 258 p.
       [Reuben Spartas and the African Greek Orthodox Church;
       Joswa Mugema and the Society of the One Almighty God;
       Mabel Ensor and Mengo Gospel Church, all among the Ganda;
       and the Kikuyu independent church/schools movement in
       Kenya from the 1920s.]

1218   WELBOURN, F[REDERICK] B[URKEWOOD].   East African Christian.
       London: Oxford University Press 1965, vi + 226 p.
       [A general review of Christianity in East Africa; see
       especially chapters 12 and 13 on "spirit churches" and
       Ethiopian churches in East Africa.]

1219   WELBOURN, F[REDERICK] B[URKEWOOD]. Spirit initiation in Ankole
and a Christian spirit movement in Western Kenya, in
J. Beattie and J. Middleton (eds.), Spirit mediumship and
society in Africa. London: Routledge and Kegan Paul
1969, 290-306.
[P. 291, Mungu cult; pp. 295-300, African Israel Church
Nineveh; pp. 300-306, comparison with Nyoro spirit cult
in Ankole.]

1220   WENTINCK, DIRK E. The Orthodox Church in East Africa.
Ecumenical Review (Geneva) 20 (1), 1968, 33-43.
[History of the African Orthodox Church and of its rela-
tions with the Patriarch of Alexandria.]

BURUNDI

1221   FALAGUASTA, ANTONIO. Inamujandi profetessa del Burundi.
Nigrizia (Verona) 90 (21), 1972, 20-25, illus.
[A prophetess in conflict with the authorities in 1934.]

1222   RODEGEM, F. M. Nangayîvûza, une sect syncrétique au Burundi.
Cultures et Développement 2 (2), 1969-70, 427-434.
[Founded in 1950 by the prophet-healer, Bashahu, and
surviving his death in 1955; Roman Catholic milieu.]

ETHIOPIA

1223   CRUMMEY, DONALD. Shaikh Zakaryas: an Ethiopian prophet.
Journal of Ethiopian Studies (Addis Ababa) 10 (1), 1972,
55-66.
[The Addis Krestyan (New Christians) movement of
Zakaryas (ca. 1845-1920), a Muslim prophet converted by
visions, whose movement survived into the 1930s; it passed
from being a Muslim reform movement to acting as a Christian one.]

1224   HAMMERSCHMIDT, ERNST. Äthiopien: Christliches Reich zwischen
Gestern und Morgen. Weisbaden: Otto Harrassowitz 1967,
186 p., bibl.
[Pp. 97-99, Abba Walda Teñsa'e Gezaw of Walisso, a
prophet-healer interviewed in 1966.]

Eastern Africa

1225   IWARSSON, JONAS. A Moslem mass movement toward Christianity
       in Abyssinia. The Moslem World 14 (3), 1924, 286-289.
       Eng. trans. from Svensk Missionstidskrift (Uppsala) 1,
       1924.
       [Shaikh Zakaryas and his conversion.]

1226   SHACK, WILLIAM A. Religious strangers in the Kingdom of
       Ethiopia. Journal of Modern African Studies 13 (2), 1975,
       361-366.
       [A review article, with discussion of the absence of
       millenarianism, pp. 365-366.]

                              KENYA

Note: In view of Clough and Jackson's A bibliography on Mau Mau
with some five hundred entries (see item 1246 below), the material
given here on this subject is confined to a few items dealing more
specifically with the religious dimensions of the movement.

1227   ABONYO, AGNES A. Independent church "Johera" in Kasagam
       (Occasional Research Paper 96), in Occasional Research
       Papers Religion and Philosophy (Makerere University
       Department of Religious Studies and Philosophy) Vol. 10,
       1975, 16 p. Mimeo.
       [Church of Christ in Africa, among the Luo.]

1228   ANDERSON, JOHN [E.] The struggle for the school. The inter-
       action of missionary, colonial government and nationalist
       enterprise in the development of formal education in
       Kenya. London and Nairobi: Longman 1970, 192 p., illus.
       [Ch. 8 (pp. 112-131), The independent schools; p. 114,
       Nomiya Luo Mission, John Okwala's movement; p. 128, African
       Christian Church and Schools; otherwise describes the
       history of the Kikuyu Independent Schools Association and
       the African Independent Pentecostal Church, the Kikuyu
       Karing'a Educational Association and the African Orthodox
       Church, and the interaction of all four, 1929-1952.]

1229   ANDERSON, JOHN [E.] Self-help and independency: the political
       implications of a continuing tradition in African educa-
       tion in Kenya. African Affairs no. 278=70 (Jan.), 1971,
       9-22.
       [Pp. 9-14, independent church-school systems.]

                              170

1230 ANDERSON, WILLIAM B. Children of Jakobo. Risk (Geneva) 7 (3),
1971, 14-19, illus.
[History of the Holy Spirit Church of East Africa.]

1231 AOKO, DAVID. High Priest David Zakayo Kivuli. Risk (Geneva)
7 (3), 1971, 20-22, illus.
[Biography of the founder of the African Israel Church
Nineveh.]

1232 AOKO, DAVID. Language use in the independent churches of
Nairobi, in W. H. Whiteley (ed.), Language in Kenya.
Nairobi: Oxford University Press 1974, 253-262, tables.
[The range of vernaculars used in worship in 22 denomina-
tions, with tables showing founders and congregational
details.]

1233 ASHTON-GWATKIN, F[RANK TRELAWNY ARTHUR]. Dini ya msambwa.
Spectator (London) 11 August 1950, 173-174.
[Elijah Masinde's "Religion of the Ancestors".]

1234 BARNETT, DONALD L. and KARARI, NJAMA. Mau Mau from within.
London: MacGibbon and Kee 1966, 512 p., illus.; New York:
Modern Reader Paperbacks 1970.
[Pp. 38-39, 103-104, independent church-school movement
(African Independent Pentecostal Church and African Ortho-
dox Church); pp. 77-78, Beecher Report in relation to
independent church-schools.]

1235 BARRETT, DAVID B., MAMBO, GEORGE K., McLAUGHLIN, JANICE, and
McVEIGH, MALCOLM J. (eds.). Kenya Churches Handbook: the
development of Kenyan Christianity 1498-1973. Kisumu,
Kenya: Evangel Publishing House 1973, 349 p., illus., maps,
tables, figures, folding maps of Kenya and Nairobi, bibl.
[See under G. K. Mambo, O. W. Okite, E. Kinyanjui,
M. J. McVeigh, J. Murray, for sections on independent
churches in Kenya, see also p. 153, independent churches
organizations; maps 7 and 12, distribution; pp. 255-287,
directory entries; pp. 184-189, statistical tables;
pp. 193-210, photographic essay.]

1236 BEAVER R[OBERT] PIERCE. The Mau Mau movement in Kenya.
Occasional Bulletin Missionary Research Library (New York)
4 (2), 1953.

1237 BEECHER, LEONARD J. African separatist churches in Kenya.
World Dominion (London) 31 (1), 1953, 5-12. Fr. trans.,
Au Kenya: nationalisme et églises séparatistes africaines.
Monde Non-chrétien (Paris) n.s. 23, juillet-sep. 1952, 324-336.
[A good general survey of various types.]

Eastern Africa

1238   BERNARD, GLADNESS M.   The "Weni-Mwanguvu" Igange congregation
       (Occasional Research Paper 97), in Occasional Research
       Papers Religion and Philosophy (Makerere University
       Department of Religious Studies and Philosophy), Vol. 10,
       1975, 12 p.   Mimeo.
          [An independent pentecostal church in Taita, formed as a
       result of the T. L. Osborne campaign in Mombasa, 1957.]

1239   BERTOLINO, GIOVANNI.   La nuova setta auche nel Meru.   Missioni
       Consolata (Turin) 36 (6), 1934, 86.
          [Cf. item 1308, Pich (1934).]

1240   BEWES, T. F. C[ECIL].   The work of the Christian church among
       the Kikuyu.   International Affairs 29 (3), 1953, 316-325.
          [P. 321, independent schools; pp. 323-325, Mau Mau.]

1241   BEWES, T. F. C[ECIL].   The Christian revival in Kenya.   World
       Dominion (London) 34 (2), 1956, 110-114.

1242   BØGGILD, JENS.   Kristi kirke i Afrika.   Dansk Missionsblad,
       142 (1), 1975, 15-19, illus.
          [The Luo Church of Christ in Africa.]

1243   BROWN, GERALD G.   Christian response to change in East African
       traditional societies (Woodbrooke Occasional Papers, 4).
       London: Friends Home Service Committee for Woodbrooke
       College 1973, 52 p.
          [Pp. 26-43, 46-47, independent churches among the Luo
       and Luyia surveyed; the ecstatic features of early Quakers
       contrasted with the expulsions from Quaker missions for
       similar behaviour.]

1244   BUSTIN, E.   La décentralisation administrative et l'évolution
       des structures politiques en Afrique orientale britannique.
       Eléments d'une étude comparative.   Liège: Collections
       scientifique de la Faculté de Droit 1958.
          [Pp. 372-374, Dini ya Msambwa, Dini ya Jesu Kristo, etc.]

1245   CAGNOLO, CONSTANZO.   Uno schisma nella Chiesa protestante del
       Kikuyu.   Missioni Consolata (Turin) 46 (7), 1944, 55-57;
       idem, 46 (8), 1944, 69-72.
          [The African Orthodox Church.]

1246   CLOUGH, MARSHALL S. and JACKSON, KENNELL A., JR.   A bibliography
       on Mau Mau.   [Stanford, California] 1975, iii + 74 p.
          [Lists works treating the religious aspects of Mau Mau,
       e.g., Beecher, Leakey, Pich, Prins, Welbourn, etc.]

1247 CORFIELD, F. D. Historical survey of the origins and growth
of Mau Mau. Nairobi: Government Printer; London: Her
Majesty's Stationery Office 1960, 321 p., map.
[The official "Corfield Report": pp. 41, 45, the
African Orthodox Church; pp. 171-190, "Kikuyu Independent
Schools" and various independent religious developments.]

1248 DAY, TERENCE. White God or Black God: a question of identity.
Yes: the CMS Magazine no. 3, 1973, 10-11.
[A lecturer in the Department of Religion, University of
Nairobi, reports on his students' attitudes to missions,
and their "ideological support" for independent churches.]

1249 DIRVEN, PETER J. Katholische Sekte in Ostafrika: Die Maria-
Legio-Kirche. Die Katholischen Missionen (Freiburg)
Jan. 1970, 12-15, illus.

1250 DIRVEN, PETER J. The Maria Legio: the dynamics of a breakaway Church among the Luo in East Africa. Pontifica
Universitas Gregoriana (Rome), doctorate in Missiology
1970, 343 p.

1251 DIRVEN, PETER J. A protest and a challenge: the Maria Legio
breakaway church in West Kenya. African Ecclesiastical
Review (Masaka, Uganda) 12 (2), 1970, 127-133.

1252 DRUM (East African edition).
[Occasional illustrated reports on independent churches.
See, e.g., on Maria Legio, June 1971; Holy Ghost Coptic
Church of Africa, September 1972.]

1253 DUNDAS, CHARLES. History of Kitui. Journal of the Royal
Anthropological Institute 43, 1913, 480-549.
[Pp. 535-537, Kyesu (=Jesus) cult, here called Kesho.]

1254 ECUMENICAL REVIEW. The African Brotherhood Church. Ecumenical
Review 24 (2), 1972, 145-149; repr. in Ecumenical Exercise
III (Faith and Order Paper 61). Geneva: World Council of
Churches 1972, 27-41.
[A W.C.C. survey based on material from Kenya, on this
Kamba church.]

1255 FARSON, NEGLEY. Last chance in Africa. London: Gollancz
1949, 384 p.
[Pp. 127-130, Kikuyu independent schools and church;
pp. 218-239, Watu wa Mungu among the Kikuyu, Dini ya
J. Kristo (also Kikuyu), and the Dini ya Msambwa of Elijah
Masinde among the Luyia.]

Eastern Africa

1256   GICARU MUGO. Land of sunshine. Scenes of life in Kenya before
       Mau Mau. London: Lawrence and Wishart 1958, 175 p.
       [Pp. 109–111, the Arathi or "Seers" between the wars;
       pp. 111–112, Dini ya Msambwa; pp. 112–113, Andu a Ruri
       of Reuben Kahiko in the Rift Valley in the 1940s.]

1257   GRESCHAT, HANS-JÜRGEN. Dini ya Roho, in H.-J. Greschat and
       H. Jungraithmayr (eds.), Wort und Religion: Kalima na
       Dini. Stuttgart: Evangelischer Missionsverlag 1969,
       265–274.
       [Based on research in the Kenya National Archives; an
       independent church in Western Kenya.]

1258   GROENESTEIN, GONDOLPHUS. In Onder ons (Utrecht Fraters) 1966,
       117–119.
       [On Jeremiah Onditi (d. 1966), and his Dini ya Jeremiah
       Onditi, from 1956.]

1259   HOBLEY, C[HARLES] W[ILLIAM]. The ethnology of Akamba and
       other East African tribes. Cambridge: Cambridge Univer-
       sity Press 1910; reprinted: London: Lass 1971.
       [P. 10, Chesu or Ki-Jesu dancing movement of 1906.]

1260   HOBLEY, CHARLES WILLIAM. Bantu beliefs and magic, with par-
       ticular reference to the Kikuyu and Kamba.... London:
       H. F. and G. Witherby 1922, 312 p.
       [Pp. 255–258, Kathambi/Ngai cult of 1911 (Kamba).]

1261   HUXLEY, ELSPETH (JOSCELIN]. The rise of the African zealot.
       Corona (London) 2 (5), 1950, 163–166.
       [The Watu wa Mungu of the Kikuyu, and the Dini ya
       Msambwa of the Luyia; the roots of such movements in
       secret societies.]

1262   IRVINE, CECILIA. Towards a profile of the African independent
       churches (Separatist) in Nairobi city, July 1967. Columbia
       University, M.A. dissertation (Joint Committee on Graduate
       Instruction) 1968, 210 p.
       [Surveys 25 congregations of 17 churches, out of 22
       churches identified. Based on Barrett, and Welbourn and
       Ogot, with some field work.]

1263   KAGGIA, BILDAD [MWAGANU]. Roots of freedom 1921-1963. Nairobi:
       East African Publishing House 1975, 202 p., map, illus.
       [Biography; ch. 8 (pp. 69–77), Kaggia's challenge to the
       Anglican Church from 1946; the beginnings of the "Dini ya
       Kaggia".]

1264   KAUFMANN, HERBERT. Zwischen Zauberei und Christentum.
       Frankfurter Allgemeine Zeitung 134, 12 June 1965.
       [Legio Maria, a secession from the Roman Catholic
       church.]

1265   KENYA, GOVERNMENT OF. Report of the commission of inquiry
       into the affray at Kolloa, Baringo. Nairobi: Government
       Printer 1950, 21 p.
       [Elijah Masinde and the history of his Dini ya Misambwa;
       the disturbance among the Suk (Pokot) in 1950.]

1266   KENYA GOVERNMENT. National Assembly, House of Representatives
       Debates Official Report 3 (1). Nairobi: Government
       Printer 1964, Columns 512-516, 773-782, debates of 24 and
       30 June 1964.
       [O. Odinga, Minister for Home Affairs, interprets the
       Legio Maria as a non-political movement within the Roman
       Catholic Church.]

1267   KENYATTA, JOMO. Facing Mount Kenya: the tribal life of the
       Gikuyu. London: Secker and Warburg 1961 (1938); New York:
       Vintage Books, n.d., xxi + 326 p., illus.
       [Pp. 269-279 (259-269 in Vintage ed.), describes the
       Watu wa Mungu, "People of God".]

1268   KIBUE, C. K. The African Greek Orthodox Church in Kenya.
       Porefthendes (Athens) 3, 1961, 54-55; idem 4, 1962, 40-41.

1269   KIKUYU INDEPENDENT SCHOOLS ASSOCIATION. Report and constitu-
       tion of the Kikuyu Independent Schools Association con-
       nected with the African Independent Pentecostal Church
       1938. Nyeri: 1938 (1935).
       [In Kikuyu and English.]

1270   KIMILU, DAVID N. The separatist churches. Dini na Mila
       (Kampala) 2 (2-3), 1967, 11-61.
       [Pp. 15-17 compares Maria Legio and the (Kamba) Friends
       of the Holy Spirit; pp. 17-61, largely on the latter
       church, with the English text of fifty-nine hymns on
       pp. 26-48.]

1271   KING, KENNETH [JAMES]. The Kenya Maasai and the protest
       phenomenon. Journal of African History 12 (1), 1971,
       117-138.
       [Pp. 128-131, the break from the Africa Inland Mission
       at Narok, 1929-30.]

Eastern Africa

1272   KINYANJUI, ELIJAH. The rise and persecution of the Aroti
       prophets 1927-48, in D. B. Barrett et al. (eds.), item
       1235, 124-127, photo.
          [Beginnings of the Kikuyu Spirit churches, by an early
       member.]

1273   KITAGAWA, DAISUKE. African independent church movements in
       Nyanza Province, Kenya. Nairobi: Christian Council of
       Kenya 1962. Mimeo.
          [A private report to the Council.]

1274   KUSHNER, GILBERT. An African revitalization movement: Mau
       Mau. Anthropos (Freiburg) 60 (5-6), 1965, 763-802,
       bibl.
          [As more than an anti-Christian or anti-European
       movement.]

1275   LAMBERT, H. E. The background to Mau Mau. Widespread use of
       secret oaths in Kenya. The Times British Colonies Review
       (London) 8, Winter 1952, 21, illus.
          [Refers to the "cult of the secret society", "prophets",
       "People of God", etc.]

1276   LANGFORD SMITH, N[EVILLE]. Revival in East Africa. Inter-
       national Review of Missions no. 169=43 (Jan.), 1954, 77-81.
          [Primarily on Kenya.]

1277   LEAKEY, L[OUIS] S[EYMOUR] B[AZETT]. Mau Mau and the Kikuyu.
       London: Methuen 1952, 115 p. Ger. trans., Mau Mau und die
       Kikuyu. Munich: C. H. Beck 1953, 139 p.
          [Especially pp. 89-92, the two main separatist churches
       and their schools.]

1278   LEAKEY, L[OUIS] S[EYMOUR] B[AZETT]. The religious element in
       Mau Mau. African Music (Roodepoort, Transvaal) 1 (1),
       1954, 77.
          [Extracted from the Manchester Guardian Weekly, 1 July
       1954, Mau Mau hymnbooks setting new words to Christian
       tunes.]

1279   LINDBLOM, [KARL] GERHARD. The Akamba in British East Africa:
       an ethnological monograph (Archives d'Études orientales,
       17). Uppsala: Appelberg, 2nd enlarged edition 1920,
       607 p.
          [Pp. 238-240, Kijesu [= Jesus] cult; pp. 230-234,
       Kathambi/Ngai cult as in 1911.]

176

1280   LONSDALE, JOHN M. A political history of Nyanza 1883-1945.
        University of Cambridge, Ph.D. dissertation (History) 1964,
        ix + 405 p., maps.
            [Pp. 190, 363, references to the cult of Mumbo as anti-
        European nativistic reaction; see also chs. 11 and 12.]

1281   LUSWETI, B. M. W. An approach to the study of Bakusu religion.
        Journal of the Historical Association of Kenya 2 (2),
        1974, 243-249.
            [Pp. 245-248, msambwa and background to the Dini ya
        Msambwa.]

1282   McINTOSH, BRIAN G. Archival resources of the University
        College, Nairobi, relating to missionary work and inde-
        pendent churches in Kenya. Bulletin of the Society for
        African Church History (Aberdeen) 2 (4), 1968, 350-351.
            [An inventory of recorded oral testimony and documents
        on some twelve independent churches, deposited in the
        Department of History.]

1283   McVEIGH, MALCOLM J. Theological issues related to Kenyan
        religious independency, in D. B. Barrett et al. (eds.),
        item 1235, 135-143.

1284   MAINA wa KIRAGU, DAUDI. Kiria giatumira Independent igie.
        [What caused the Independent Church.] Nairobi: n.d.
        Pamphlet.
            [By the founder of the first Kikuyu independent church,
        at Gakarara, ca. 1921, ordained by Archbishop Alexander
        1937.]

1285   MAMBO, GEORGE K. The Revival Fellowship (Brethren) in Kenya,
        in D. B. Barrett et al. (eds.), item 1235, 110-117.

1286   MANYARA, JOB. The African Independent Pentecostal Church of
        Kenya Meru Branch (Occasional Research Paper 95), in
        Occasional Research Papers Religion and Philosophy
        (Makerere University Department of Religious Studies and
        Philosophy), Vol. 10, 1975, 3 p. Mimeo.

1287   MASEMBE, J. and OKUNGA, D. N. Paganism - old and new, in
        Religion and social change in modern East Africa. Kampala:
        Makerere University College n.d. [1956], 89-94. Mimeo.
            [Mau Mau and Dini ya Misambwa.]

1288   MATSON, A. T. Reflections on the growth of political con-
        sciousness in Nandi, in B. A. Ogot (ed.), Politics and
        nationalism in colonial Kenya (Hadith 4). Nairobi: East
        African Publishing House 1972, 18-45.

Eastern Africa

> [Pp. 30–32, comments on Nandi opposition to a multiplicity
> of Christian denominations, and their attitude towards
> African independent churches.]

1289 MBITI, JOHN S[AMUEL]. New Testament eschatology in an African
background. London: Oxford University Press 1971, 216 p.
[Pp. 18–19, 21–22, independents among the Akamba;
pp. 60–61, on relation to time-concepts; p. 124, confes-
sion; pp. 60–61, 186, causes; pp. 21f, 73, 77, 79, 84, 88,
114, Friends of the Holy Spirit [Church].]

1290 MIDDLETON, JOHN. Kenya: administration and changes in
African life, 1912–1945, in V. Harlow and E. M. Chilver
(eds.), item 1196, 333–392.
[Pp. 365–373, independent churches among the Kikuyu;
pp. 379–380, Western Kenya; p. 383, Elijah Masinde and the
Dini ya Masambwa [sic].]

1291 MILLER, P[AUL] M. Equipping for ministry in East Africa.
Scottdale, Pennsylvania; Dodoma: Central Tanganyika Press,
1969, 231 p.
[A study of congregations and the East African Revival
in Kenya, and the relevance of dispersed theological education and the tent-making ministry.]

1292 MORIONDO, B[ARTOLOMEO]. Comme conobbi l'Archivescove
ortodosso. Missioni Consolata (Turin) 46 (8–9), 1944,
92–94.
[On the African Orthodox Church.]

1293 MÜHLMANN, WILHELM E[MIL]. Die Mau-Mau Bewegung in Kenia.
Politische Vierteljahresschrift (Opladen) 2, 1961, 56–87.

1294 MUNRO, J. FORBES. Colonial rule and the Kamba. Social change
in the Kenya Highlands 1889–1939. Oxford: Clarendon
Press 1975, 276 p., maps, illus.
[Pp. 27–28, indigenous seers or prophets; pp. 98–122,
"Missionaries and prophets", especially pp. 110–117 on new
spirit possession cults as revitalization movement's 1896–
1913; pp. 119–121, Ndonye's millennial "cargo" movement,
1922.]

1295 MURIU, N. and NJAGA, W. Revival in Kikuyuland, in Religion
and social change in modern East Africa. Kampala:
Makerere University College n.d. [1956], 9–19. Mimeo.

1296 MURPHY, J. H. BLACKWOOD. The Kitui Akamba: further investiga-
tion on certain matters. Journal of the Royal Anthropological Institute (London) 56, 1926, 195–206.

[Pp. 200-206, Kathambi/Ngai cult - detailed descriptions of the dance from two sources; p. 206, brief reference to Kyesu (Jesus) dance.]

1297 MURRAY, JOCELYN [MARGARET]. The Kikuyu spirit churches, in Journal of Religion in Africa 5 (3), 1973, 198-234.
[Historical account, with sections on sociological and theological factors.]

1298 MURRAY, JOCELYN [MARGARET]. Varieties of Kikuyu independent churches, in D. B. Barrett et al. (eds.), item 1235, 128-134, illus.

1299 NDUNGU, JOSEPH BERNARD. Gituamba and Kikuyu independency in church and school, in Brian G. McIntosh (ed.), Ngano (Nairobi Historical Studies 1). Nairobi: East African Publishing House 1969, 131-150, illus., map.
[Gituamba village as place where a Prayer House, then the Kikuyu Independent Schools Association, were formed, and later the seminary of Archbishop Alexander; its relations to the African Independent Pentecostal Church and the African Orthodox Church.]

1300 NOTTINGHAM, J[OHN] C. Sorcery among the Akamba in Kenya. Journal of African Administration (London) 11 (1), 1959, 2-14.
[An administrative officer describes an anti-witchcraft campaign that was assisted by government in 1954-1955.]

1301 NYANGWESO [pseud.]. The cult of Mumbo in Central and South Kavirondo. Journal of the East African and Uganda Natural History Society (Nairobi) no. 38-39, May-Aug. 1930, 13-17.
[An anti-European movement among the Luo and Gusii of South-West Kenya, from 1914.]

1302 ODINGA, [AJUMA] OGINGA. Not yet uhuru: the autobiography of Oginga Odinga. London: Heinemann 1967, 323 p.
[Pp. 68-75, Nomiya Luo Church, Dini ya Roho, "Church of Joroho", African Israel Church, Dini ya Msambwa, Joshua arap Chuma's church, and Dini ya Kaggia of Bildad Kaggia.]

1303 OGOT, BETHWELL A[LAN]. British administration in the Central Nyanza District 1900-1960. Journal of African History 4 (2), 1963, 249-273.
[Pp. 256-257, John Owalo's Nomia Luo Mission, from 1907; p. 257, the cult of Mumbo; pp. 261, 263, Thuku.]

Eastern Africa

1304   OGOT, BETHWELL A[LAN]. Reverend Alfayo Odongo Mango, 1870-
       1934, in K. J. King and A. Salim (eds.), Kenya Historical
       Biographies. Nairobi: East African Publishing House 1971,
       90-111.
       [An ex-Anglican, founder of the Kager Luo Jo-Roho (Holy
       Ghost) Church; killed 1934.]

1305   OGOT, BETHWELL A[LAN] and OCHIENG', WILLIAM R. Mumboism - an
       anti-colonial movement, in B. A. Ogot (ed.), War and
       society in Africa. London: Frank Cass 1972, 150-177, map.

1306   PAINTER, LEVINUS KING. The hill of vision. The story of the
       Quaker Movement in East Africa 1902-1965. Nairobi and
       Kaimosi, Kenya: East African Yearly Meeting of Friends
       1966, 153 p., illus.
       [Pp. 100-102, "breakway churches" as a warning rather
       than as a "serious" threat; by a Quaker, not a missionary
       in East Africa.]

1307   PARKIN, DAVID J. Politics of ritual syncretism: Islam among
       the non-Muslim Giriama of Kenya. Africa (London) 40 (3),
       1970, 217-233, Fr. summary.
       [Acceptance of Islamic rituals concerning spirit posses-
       sion, divination and cure without formal or widespread
       conversion to Islam.]

1308   PICH, V[ITTORIO] MERLO. I falsi profeti al Kenya. Missioni
       Consolata (Turin) 36 (6), 1934, 84-86.
       [Early reference to the Watu wa Mungu spirit movement
       among the Kikuyu.]

1309   PICH, VITTORIO MERLO. Les aspects religieux du mouvement
       Mau Mau, in Devant les sectes non-chrétien, item 312,
       125-139.
       [Comprehensive article by a Roman Catholic missionary in
       Kenya.]

1310   RAWCLIFFE, D[ONOVAN] H[ILTON]. The struggle for Kenya.
       London: Gollancz 1954, 189 p.
       [On Mau Mau; ch. 2, the Kikuyu Central Association and
       independent churches (pp. 24-25); ch. 3, "The Dinis" -
       Dini ya Roho, Dini ya Msambwa, Watu wa Mungu (arathi),
       Dini ya Jesu Kristo, etc.]

1311   REPORTER (Nairobi). Splinter sects. Reporter July 17 1964,
       17-19, illus.; also in Millhilliana (London) 1964, 123-128.
       [Journalistic article: African Israel Church Nineveh and
       Maria Legio; a main source for Kaufmann, item 1264,

Lanternari, item 272, and Ogot and Welbourn, item 1329, appendix.]

1312 [ROLAND, HADELIN]. Strange sects of Kenya. Times Survey of the British Colonies (London) July 1950, p. 14, illus.
[As a "mass revulsion from modern progress" and intolerant Christianity; Watu wa Mungu, Watu wa Roho, Dini ya Jesu Kristo, Dini ya Msambwa and its clashes with government.]

1313 ROSBERG, CARL G., JR. and NOTTINGHAM, JOHN. The myth of "Mau Mau": nationalism in Kenya. London: Pall Mall; New York: Praeger for the Hoover Institution 1966, 427 p., illus., maps, bibl.
[Pp. 125-135 etc., independent church and schools movements; pp. 129-130 etc., African Orthodox Church; pp. 324-331, "nativistic and messianic" movements (Mumbo, Nomia Luo Mission, Dini ya Misambwa, Arathi, Dini ya Roho, etc.); et passim.]

1314 ROSENSTIEL, ANNETTE. An anthropological approach to the Mau Mau problem. Political Science Quarterly (New York) 68 (3), 1953, 419-432.
[Relates Mau Mau to nativism and cargo cults.]

1315 SANGREE, WALTER H. Contemporary religion in Tiriki (Conference Papers 64). Kampala: Makerere Institute of Social Research 1956, 7 p. Mimeo.
[The relation between traditional society and Christian missions, with briefer references to Pentecostalists, "Dini Israel", and "Dini Yawoha" and their leadership.]

1316 SANGREE, WALTER H. The dynamics of the separatist churches, in Changing Africa and the Christian dynamic (Papers of a seminar for mission board executives, Feb. 15-18 1960). Chicago: Center for the Study of the Christian World Mission, Federated Theological Faculty, University of Chicago [16 p.] Mimeo.
[Tests Sundkler's "repressed leadership" theory on the Tiriki African Israel Church.]

1317 SANGREE, WALTER H. Age, prayer and politics in Tiriki, Kenya. London: Oxford University Press for the East African Institute of Social Research 1966, xl + 312 p., maps, illus.
[Pp. xxix-xxxiii and ch. 7, "Christian church separatism in North Nyanza and Tiriki" includes p. 172-189 on Dini ya Roho; pp. 190-210 and 216-223 on African Israel Church

Eastern Africa

Nineveh and briefer references to Dini ya Msambwa and
Greek Orthodox Church.]

1318   SEITZ, RUTH.   The Odhiambos of Nairobi, Kenya: Christian
family in an African world.   Christian Living (Scottdale,
Pennsylvania) Feb. 1974, 22-25, illus.
[Report on a family belonging to the African Israel
Church, Nineveh.]

1319   SEPIA (Fort Worth, Texas).   The Dini ya Israel.   Sepia 14,
June 1965, 42-45, illus.
[Journalistic account, mainly photographs.]

1320   SLATER, MONTAGUE.   The trial of Jomo Kenyatta.   London:
Secker and Warburg 1955, 255 p.
[Pp. 192-197, Kaggia's secession from the C.M.S. in
1946, and the "Association of those who wait" or Etereri;
formation of the "Voice of World Wide Salvation and Healing Revival" in Nyanza 1955.]

1321   STONEHAM, CHARLES THURLEY.   Mau Mau.   London: Museum Press
1953, 159 p., illus.
[Pp. 102-109, Dini ya Jesu Kristo of prophet Reuben
Kihiko among the Kikuyu and Kamba; pp. 110-131, Dini ya
Mswambwa of Elijah Masinde among the Pokot (Suk).]

1322   TARGET (Nairobi).   Occasional articles on independent churches
in Kenya.   See, e.g. on the Ethiopian Orthodox Holy Spirit
Church, in Target, Aug. 1971, 19, and Dec. 1971, 15.

1323   TEMU, ARNOLD J.   British Protestant Missions.   London:
Longmans 1972, 184 p.
[Pp. 158-165, Kikuyu independent churches and schools,
and the female circumcision controversy; by a Tanzanian
African.]

1324   THUKU, HARRY.   Harry Thuku: an autobiography (with assistance
from Kenneth King).   Nairobi: Oxford University Press
1970, 100 p., maps, illus.
[Pp. 52-53, beginnings of the Kenya Independent Schools
Association; pp. 68-72, 100, the Mau Mau "Emergency";
p. 85, prayer for Thuku by Christians.]

1325   TRUST.   Magic voices of healer John.   Trust, no. 32, August
1973, [2 p.] illus.
[John Pesa, ex-Catholic founder of the (Holy Ghost)
Coptic Church of Africa.]

1326 WAKIN, E. A unique sort of church. Maryknoll 66 (1), 1972,
      38-40.
      [Brief descriptions and photographs of the Nomiya Luo
      Church.]

1327 WANYOIKE, E[RNEST] N. An African pastor: the life and work
      of the Rev. Wanyoike Kamawe 1888-1970. Nairobi: East
      African Publishing House 1974, 256 p., illus.
      [Pp. 97-105, Karing'a Independent movement; pp. 180-185,
      193-196, religious aspects of Mau Mau; pp. 151-168, East
      African Revival. By the subject's grandson.]

1328 WATHIOMO MUKINYA (Nyeri: Consolata Mission). Occasional
      articles on aspects of independent churches and movements.
      See, e.g. March 1922, September 1928, April and May 1952.
      In Kikuyu.

1329 WELBOURN, F[REDERICK] B[URKEWOOD] and OGOT, B[ETHWELL] A[LAN].
      A place to feel at home. A study of two independent
      churches in Western Kenya. London: Oxford University
      Press 1966, xiv + 154 p., illus., map.
      [The secession of the Church of Christ in Africa from
      the Anglican Church in 1957,and Zackayo Kivuli's African
      Israel Church, Nineveh, from 1942. Appendix, Maria Legio.]

1330 WERE, GIDEON S. Politics, religion and nationalism in Western
      Kenya 1942-1962: Dini ya Msambwa revisited, in B. A. Ogot
      (ed.), Politics and nationalism in colonial Kenya (Hadith
      4). Nairobi: East African Publishing House 1972, 85-104.
      [Includes discussion of Wipper, item 1335.]

1331 WHISSON, M[ICHAEL] G. The will of God and the wiles of men.
      Kampala: East African Institute of Social Research n.d.
      [1962] 34 p. Mimeo.
      [Pp. 19-26, causes of separatism among the Luo; the
      Nomiya Luo Mission church of John Owalo; pp. 26-31, the
      Revival.]

1332 WHISSON, MICHAEL [G.] Change and challenge. A study of the
      social and economic changes among the Kenya Luo. Nairobi:
      Christian Council of Kenya 1964, xiii + 255 p.
      [Pp. 153-188: independent churches - Nomiya Luo Mission,
      Roho Church, African Israel Church Nineveh, Christian
      Universal Evangelical Union, Voice of Healing, Church of
      Christ in Africa; also the Revival.]

1333 WIPPER, AUDREY. The cult of Mumbo. Kampala: East African
      Institute of Social Research 1966, 31 p. Mimeo.

Eastern Africa

> [Anti-European movement with a new god, Mumbo, among
> the Luo and Gusii of South-West Kenya from 1914 to the
> present. P. 7, Dini ya Mariam.]

1334   WIPPER, AUDREY. The Gusii rebels, in R. I. Rotberg and
        A. A. Mazrui (eds.), Protest and power in Black Africa.
        New York: Oxford University Press 1970, 377-426. Repr.
        in Rebellion in Black Africa, ed. R. I. Rotberg, London
        and New York: Oxford University Press, 1971.
          [On the cult of Mumbo.]

1335   WIPPER, AUDREY. Elijah Masinde - a folk hero, in B. A. Ogot
        (ed.), Hadith 3. Nairobi: East African Publishing House
        1971, 157-191, photo.
          [Founder-leader in the Dini ya Msambwa cult; its dis-
        illusionment with him. See also her reply to Were (item
        1330) in B. A. Ogot (ed.), Hadith 5... Nairobi: East
        African Literature Bureau 1975, xiii-xv.]

1336   YANNOULATOS, ANASTASIOS. Brief diary of a tour among the
        Orthodox of West Kenya. Porefthendes (Athens) no. 26=7
        (2), 1965, 24-28, illus.; idem, nos. 27-28=7 (3-4), 1965,
        48-52, illus.
          [Archimandrite Yannoulatos, editor of this journal of
        the Inter-Orthodox Missionary Center (30 Sina Street,
        Athens), reports a visit to the African Orthodox Church,
        and continues its history from Welbourn's account.]

See also items 97, 148, 155, 238, 272, 273, 315, 341, 354, 394, 1375,
1410.

RWANDA

1337   BUSHAYIJA, STANISLAS. Indifférence religieuse et néo-paganisme
        au Ruanda. Rhythmes du Monde (Bruges and Paris) 9 (1),
        1961, 58-67.
          [The neo-pagan attitudes and revivals that follow from
        superficial Catholicism; absence of independent churches.]

1338   LANE, ERIC. Kigeri II meets that peculiar lady, Nyurabiyoro:
        a study in prophecies. History of Religions (Chicago) 13
        (2), Nov. 1973, 129-148.

See also item 238.

SUDAN

1339   GIORGETTI, F. Brevi note sulla società segreta africana Yanda
       o Mani. Annali Lateranensi (Vatican City) 21, 1957, 9-29.
       [On Handa or Mani sect, not of Zande origin but expanded
       among them.]

1340   GIORGETTI, F. La superstizione Zande. Museum Combonianum
       18, 1966, 287-288 and 293-294.
       [Mani cult among the Zande.]

TANZANIA

1341   ABDUL KARIM BIN JAMALIDDINI. Gedicht vom Majimaji-Aufstand,
       ubersetzt und herausgegeben von A. Lorenz. Mitteilungen
       des Seminars fur Orientalische Sprachen zu Berlin 36, 1933,
       227-259; also as Utenzi wa vita vya Maji-Maji (translated
       by W. H. Whiteley, historical introduction by Margaret
       Bates). Journal of the Africa Swahili Committee (Arusha)
       June 1957.
       [A contemporary account.]

1342   BELL, R. M. The Majimaji Rebellion in the Luvale District.
       Tanganyika Notes and Records (Dar es Salaam) 28, Jan. 1950,
       38-57.
       [Especially pp. 40-42, and passim, on Ngameya and his
       holy water.]

1343   CROSSE-UPCOTT, A. R. W. The origin of the Majimaji revolt.
       Man 60, May 1960, article 98=71-73.
       [Traditional water cults behind the rising of 1905.]

1344   DOERR, LAMBERT. The relationship between the Benedictine
       Mission and the German colonial authorities. Dini na Mila
       (Kampala) 4 (1), 1969, 2-11.
       [Pp. 3-4, the Mission and Maji Maji; pp. 4-7, the after-
       math of Maji Maji.]

1345   GWASSA, G[ILBERT] C. K. and ILIFFE, JOHN (eds.). Records of
       the Maji Maji rising. Part one (Historical Association of
       Tanzania Paper No. 4). Nairobi: East African Publishing
       House n.d. [1968] 32 p., maps; also in Swahili as GWASSA,
       Gilbert C. K. (ed.), Kumbukumbu za vita vya Maji Maji 1905-
       1907 (Historical Association of Tanzania Swahili Series,
       Paper 1). Nairobi: East African Publishing House 1970.

Eastern Africa

1346   GWASSA, GILBERT C. K.   The German intervention and African
             resistance in Tanzania, in I. N. Kimambo and A. J. Temu
             (eds.), A history of Tanzania. Nairobi: East African
             Publishing House 1969, 85-122.
                  [Pp. 116-122, Maji Maji; pp. 118-119, Jujila or
             Jwiywila movement of 1904.]

1347   GWASSA, GILBERT C. K.   Kinjikitile and the ideology of Maji
             Maji, in T. O. Ranger and I. N. Kimambo (eds.), The his-
             torical study of African religion. London: Heinemann
             Education Books, and Berkeley and Los Angeles: University
             of California Press, 1972, 202-217.
                  [The role of religious and other traditional beliefs.]

1348   HASSING, PER.   German missionaries and the Maji Maji rising.
             African Historical Studies (Boston) 3 (2), 1970, 373-389.

1349   HUNTER, MONICA, [WILSON].   An African Christian morality.
             Africa 10 (3), 1937, 265-292.
                  [P. 266, passing reference to the "Ba Ngelema", an off-
             shoot of Jehovah's Witnesses in Tanzania, allowing polyg-
             amy, and the "African National Church", under African
             leadership.]

1350   HUSSEIN, EBRAHIM N.   Kinjeketile (New Drama from Africa, 4).
             Dar es Salaam: Oxford University Press 1969, 49 p.,
             illus. (in Swahili or English versions).
                  [A modern East African's view of the Maji Maji revolt,
             in the form of a play.]

1351   ILIFFE, JOHN.   The organization of the Maji Maji rebellion.
             Journal of African History 8 (3), 1967, 495-512.
                  [Especially pp. 502-510, the religious aspect expressed
             in the Kolelo cult.]

1352   ILIFFE, JOHN.   Tanganyika under German rule 1905-1912.
             Cambridge: Cambridge University Press 1969, 236 p.
                  [The Maji Maji rebellion and its effects.]

1353   JELLICOE, MARGUERITE.   Social change: traditionalism v.
             modernism? Mawazo (Kampala) 1 (2), 1967, 61-69.
                  [Pp. 63-66, religious case-history of a Muslim-reared
             boy's career through the Lutheran Church, to the Pente-
             costal Church, where as a charismatic semi-independent
             pastor he sought to relate traditional and Christian
             beliefs.]

1354   KIBIRA, JOSIAH. The church in Buhaya: crossing frontiers,
       in P. Beyerhaus and C. F. Hallencreutz (eds.), The church
       crossing frontiers.... Essays in honour of Bengt Sundkler
       (Studia Missionalia Upsaliensia XI). Lund: Gleerup 1969,
       189-205.
          [Pp. 197-199, the Revival movement.]

1355   KOOTZ-KRETSCHMER, ELISE. Safwa-Texte in Kleinen Erzahlungen
       und Briefen. Zeitschrift für Eingeborenen Sprachen
       (Hamburg) 24, 1933-34, 161-201.
          [Pp. 187-192 on new religious developments: witch-
       doctors and prophets.]

1356   MAPUNDA, O. B. and MPANGARA, G. P. The Maji Maji War in Ungoni
       (Maji Maji Research Papers, 1). Nairobi: East African
       Publishing House 1969, 30 p., map.
          [Local oral accounts from the Ngoni people of Ruvuma
       Region; pp. 15-20, the arrival of Omari Kinjala with his
       "maji" in a bottle, and its acceptance by Ngoni.]

1357   MORS, O. Soothsaying among the Bahaya. Anthropology 46 (5-6),
       1951, 825-852.
          [Includes the priestess of the Nyabingi movement.]

1358   NANKYAMAS, THEODORUS. The Orthodox Church in Tanganyika.
       Porefthendes (Athens), 5, 1963, 2-3.

1359   NGINDU MUSHETE, [ALPHONSE]. La communauté de base dans les
       églises africaines. Telema (Kinshasa-Gombe) 1 (3), 1975,
       87-92.
          [Review article on M.-F. Perrin Jassy's book, 1970
       (item 1360).]

1360   PERRIN JASSY, MARIE-FRANCE. Le communauté de base dans les
       églises africaines (Publications du Centre d'Études
       Ethnologiques, série 2, vol. 3). Bandundu [Zaïre]: Centre
       d'Études Ethnologiques 1970, 231 p., maps, bibl. Eng.
       trans., Basic community in the African churches. Maryknoll,
       N.Y.: Orbis Books 1973, 257 p.
          [A comprehensive study of independent churches in Mara
       District, N.W. Tanzania, based on doctoral dissertation
       (Sorbonne); includes Legio Maria and associated groups,
       Nomiya Luo Mission, Dini ya Roho, African Israel Church
       Nineveh, Church of Christ in Africa, Pentecostal Assemblies,
       Warrual, Fweny Mar Lam (ex S.D.A.); typology and theoret-
       ical analysis from sociological viewpoint.]

Bibliography of New Religious Movements in Primal Societies

Eastern Africa

1361   RANGER, TERENCE OSBORN. The African churches of Tanzania
       (Historical Association of Tanzania Paper No. 5).
       Nairobi: East African Publishing House n.d. [1970?], 29 p.
         [Outlines of Watch Tower (1919-), African National
       Church (1928-), Last Church of God and His Christ (1925-),
       Malekite Church (1920s) and the Revival.]

1362   RANGER, TERENCE O[SBORN]. Christian independency in Tanzania,
       in D. B. Barrett (ed.), item 1188, 122-145.

1363   [ROBERT, J.-M]. Le "Kamchape" ou la magie que se christianise.
       Petit Echo (White Fathers) no. 454=43 (oct.), 1955,
       486-490.

1364   SWANTZ, M[ARJA-LIISA]. The spirit possession cults and their
       social setting in a Zaramo coastal community (Conference
       Papers 447). Kampala: Makerere Institute of Social
       Research 1968, 15 p.

1365   TETZLAFF, RAINER. Koloniale Entwicklung und Ausbeutung.
       Wirtschafts-und Sozialgeschichte Deutsch-Ostafrikas
       1885-1914 (Schriften zur Wirtschafts-und Sozialgeschichte
       17). Berlin: Duncker und Humblot 1970, 309 p., map.
         [See Appendix on Maji Maji rebellion's impact on the
       Pangwa.]

1366   VON GOETZEN, GUSTAV ADOLF GRAF. Deutsch-Ostafrika im Aufstand
       1905-6. Berlin: O. Reimer 1909, xiii + 234 p.
         [Principal German source on the Maji Maji uprising; by
       the colony's governor.]

1367   WILLIS, R[OY] G. Kamcape: an anti-sorcery movement in South-
       West Tanzania. Africa (London) 38 (1), 1968, 1-15.
         [From 1963; a "proto-church" with an incipiently revo-
       lutionary and totalitarian doctrine of millenarian
       revivalism.]

1368   WILSON, MONICA. To whom do they pray? Listener (London),
       no. 1440=56 (1 Nov.), 1956, 692-693.
         [Includes reference to proliferation of "sects" as the
       Nyakyusa become more christianized.]

1369   WILSON, MONICA. Communal rituals of the Nyakyusa. London:
       Oxford University Press 1959, 228 p.
         [Pp. 167, 171-173, 219-220, African National Church and
       Last Church of God and His Christ; the relation of
       independency and nationalism.]

1370   ZWACK, DANIEL D.   Conversion and community.   Herder Correspon-
       dence (London) 5 (11), 1968, 346-348, also 325.
       [A Catholic mission applying the forms and methods of the
       independent churches to its own work, in Tanzania.]

See also items 341, 358.

UGANDA

1371   BAMUNOBA, Y. K.   The cult of spirits in Ankole.   Makerere
       University, M.A. thesis, 1973.
       [Includes Kashoni cults, groups of emandwa, as new
       syncretist movements by 1968.]

1372   BRAZIER, F. S[TEPHEN].   The Nyabingi cult: religion and
       political scale in Kigezi 1900-1930 (Conference Paper
       No. 494).   Kampala: Makerere Institute of Social Research
       1968, 16 p.

1373   BRAZIER, F. S[TEPHEN].   The incident at Nyakishenyi, 1917.
       Uganda Journal 32 (1), 1968, 17-27.
       [A Nyabingi-supported rebellion, and Kaigirwa, the
       priestess, in Kigezi area.]

1374   CHARSLEY, SIMON [R.].   Churches in Kigumba (Sociology Working
       Papers, 10).   Kampala: Makerere Institute of Social
       Research 1966, 10 p.   Mimeo.
       [Discusses the size of congregations, and relation of
       churches to tribe and mobility; lists five independent
       churches included in the general discussion.]

1375   CHARSLEY, S[IMON] R.   Dreams in an independent African church.
       Africa (London) 43 (3), 1973, 244-257.
       [A semi-independent branch of the African Israel Church
       Nineveh among Kenyan immigrants in Western Uganda, 1960s.]

1376   CHURCH, J[OHN] E.   William Nagenda - an appreciation.   Partners
       Together: News from Rwanda, Burundi and SW Uganda (London:
       Ruanda Mission - C.M.S.), 199, Spring 1973, 2-3, photo.
       [Leader in the Revival movement; 1912-1972.]

1377   CHURCH MISSIONARY REVIEW (London).   Notes of the month.
       C.M. Review no. 790=66 (Feb.), 1915, 122-123.
       [Mugema and Malaki in Uganda.]

Bibliography of New Religious Movements in Primal Societies

Eastern Africa

1378   CHURCH MISSIONARY SOCIETY (London). Proceedings: 1915,
      65–67; 1916, 56–57; 1917, 36.
        [The "Malaki movement or sect".]

1379   DRIBERG, J. H. Yakan. Journal of the Royal Anthropological
      Institute (London) 61, July–Dec. 1931, 413–420.
        [A secret society, also known as the Allah Water Cult,
      among the Lugbara of Uganda from 1918, and elsewhere; its
      connections with the Nebeli and other cults, and the
      earlier Mahdist movement. By a colonial administrator.]

1380   EDEL, MAY MANDELBAUM. The Chiga of Western Uganda. London:
      Oxford University Press 1957, 206 p.
        [Includes Nyabingi cult, and similar cults (pp. 138–162)
      in neighbouring areas.]

1381   KAKUNGULU, SEMEI L. Ebigambo ebiva mu Kitabo Ekitukuvu
      [Quotations from the Holy Book]. N.p.: the author, 1922,
      90 p.
        ["Quotations" from the Old and New Testaments, by the
      founder of the Bayudaya; in Luganda.]

1382   KAZINJA, LUKE. Where Africans worship in Greek. Kenya Weekly
      News no. 2124, 28 Oct. 1966, p. 21, illus.
        [Descriptive article and photograph of Reuben Spartas at
      Namungna, near Kampala.]

1383   KING, ANNE. The Yakan cult and Lugbara response to colonial
      rule. Azania 5, 1970, 1–25.
        [History and development in terms of ideology, organ-
      ization and function.]

1384   MIDDLETON, JOHN. Lugbara religion: ritual and authority among
      an East African people. London: Oxford University Press
      for the International African Institute 1960, xii + 276 p.
        [Pp. 258–269, prophets and the Yakan cult from 1883 to
      the date of research.]

1385   MIDDLETON, JOHN. The Yakan or Allah water cult among the
      Lugbara. Journal of the Royal Anthropological Institute
      (London) 93 (1), 1963, 80–108.
        [Full historical and social analysis by an
      anthropologist.]

1386   MIDDLETON, JOHN. Prophets and rainmakers. The agents of
      social change among the Lugbara, in T. O. Beidelman (ed.),
      The translation of culture. London: Tavistock 1971,
      179–201.

[The Yakan water cult from 1890; the Balokole movement,
mainly among women, seen as connected with Moral
Re-Armament.]

1387 MIDDLETON, JOHN. Spirit possession among the Lugbara, in
      J. Beattie and J. Middleton (eds.), Spirit mediumship and
      society in Africa. London: Routledge and Kegan Paul
      1969, 220-231.
      [Pp. 227-229, Rembe and his Yakan water cult;
      pp. 229-230, Balokole movement, and sundry prophets.]

1388 NANKYAMAS, THEODORUS. Orthodoxy in Uganda. African Ecclesi-
      astical Review (Masaka, Uganda) 9 (2), 1967, 124-127.
      [A brief historical outline.]

1389 NOTES ET DOCUMENTS (Rome, Centrum Informationis Patres
      Alborum). The Orthodox in Uganda. Notes et Documents
      no. 38, juin 1963, 275-278.
      [Originally published in The Tablet, March 1963.]

1390 NSHEMEREIRWE, GERSHON. The Balokole movement in Ankole. Dini
      na Mila (Kampala) 2 (5), 1967, 1-11.

1391 ODED, A[RYE]. The Bayudaya and their founder Semei Kakungulu.
      Hamizrah Hahadash (Jerusalem) 17, 1967, 92-98.

1392 ODED, ARIEH [-ARYE]. The Bayudaya. A community of African
      Jews in Uganda. Tel-Aviv: the Shiloah Center for Middle
      Eastern and African Studies, Tel-Aviv University 1973,
      52 p., map. Mimeo.
      [History of Semei Kakungulu, the founder, and of the
      community; their religious practices; contacts with world
      Jewry and renascence in 1960s. Full details of archival
      and other sources.]

1393 ODED, ARYE. The Bayudaya of Uganda. A portrait of an African
      Jewish community. Journal of Religion in Africa 6 (3),
      1974, 167-186.

1394 RIGBY, PETER. Prophets, diviners and prophetism: the recent
      history of Kiganda religion. Journal of Anthropological
      Research (Albuquerque) 31 (2), 1975, 116-148, bibl.
      [Includes a case study of Kigaanira Ssewannyana (ca.
      1934-1972) a neo-primal type of prophet; p. 138,
      John Yeboah, Ghanaian in Uganda, from 1972.]

Eastern Africa

1395   ROBINS, CATHERINE ELLEN.   Tukutendereza: a study of social
       change and sectarian withdrawal in the Balokole Revival of
       Uganda.   Columbia University, Ph.D. dissertation
       (Sociology) 1975, vi + 468 p.

1396   ROSCOE, JOHN.   The soul of central Africa.   A general account
       of the Mackie Ethnological Expedition.   London: Cassell
       and Company 1922, 336 p., illus.
           [Pp. 242-244, Semei Kakungulu's life in outline;
       pp. 262-265, his membership of Bamalaki and development of
       his own Hebraist cult; by a missionary friend who visited
       him in 1920.]

1397   SOUTHALL, AIDAN.   Spirit possession and mediumship among the
       Alur, in J. Beattie and J. Middleton (eds.), Spirit
       mediumship and society in Africa.   London: Routledge and
       Kegan Paul 1969, 232-272.
           [Pp. 258-267, spirit possession and religious change;
       pp. 262, 266, 270, Allah water cult among the Lugbara;
       p. 267, theory of incidence of "autonomous...outbreaks of
       religious expression".]

1398   STENNING, D[ERRICK] J.   Preliminary observations on the
       Balokole movement, particularly among Bahima in Ankole
       District.   Kampala: East African Institute of Social
       Research 1958, 18 p. Mimeo. (Privately circulated).

1399   STENNING, DERRICK J.   Salvation in Ankole, in M. Fortes and
       G. Dieterlen (eds.), item 203, 269-275.
           [The East African revival movement (Balokole) among the
       Ankole.]

1400   TAYLOR, JOHN V[ERNON].   The growth of the church in Buganda.
       London: Student Christian Movement Press 1958, 288 p.,
       map, illus.
           [Pp. 97-105, Church of the One Almighty God and the
       African Orthodox Church, with comments on the general
       failure of independents to grow in Buganda.]

1401   THOMAS, H. B.   Capax Imperii - the story of Semei Kakungulu.
       Uganda Journal (Kampala) 6 (3), 1939, 125-136.
           [Kakungulu's early support of Malaki, and founding of
       his own "Christian Jew" (Bayudaya) religion.]

1402   UGANDA GOVERNMENT.   Report of the commission of enquiry into
       the disturbances in Uganda, during August 1949.   Entebbe:
       Government Printer, 1950.
           [On Reuben Spartas, see paras. 165, 414, 415.]

1403   VAN DEN EYNDE [PÈRE]. L'action protestante dans les districts
        du Lac Albert et de l'Uganda. Bulletin de l'Union de
        Clergé (Brussels) 5, avril 1925, 53-61.
        [Pp. 58-59, a Roman Catholic missionary interpretation
        of the Malaki movement as due to Protestant lack of
        authority.]

1404   WELBOURN, F[REDERICK] B[URKEWOOD]. Abamalaki in Buganda,
        1914-1919. Uganda Journal (Kampala) 21 (2), 1957,
        150-161.
        [Early 20th.c. secession from the Church Missionary
        Society, the Society of the One Almighty God, now in
        decline.]

1405   WILSON, JOHN and KATARIKAWE, JAMES. The story, beliefs and
        practices of the East African Revival Movement. Fuller
        Theological Seminary, School of World Mission, M.A. thesis
        1975.
        [By two ordained ministers of the Church of Uganda
        (Anglican).]

See also items 104, 148, 155, 193, 213, 227, 238, 299.

South-East Central Africa

1406   BLOOD, A. G. B. The story of the Universities' Mission to
        Central Africa. London: U.M.C.A., Vol. II, 1957;
        Vol. III, 1962.
            [Vol. II, pp. 191, 195-197, 282, 285, on Watch Tower;
        pp. 132-134, Chilembwe; vol. III, pp. 51-52, 167, 316,
        317, Watch Tower - all as hindrances to the Mission.]

1407   CAVERHILL, AUSTIN M. Ethiopianism. Life and Work (Edinburgh)
        33, 1911, p. 383; idem 34, 1912, p. 30, and earlier, in
        briefer form, in Life and Work in Nyasaland 2, April-May
        1911, 18.
            [An article on Nyasaland and Central Africa, showing
        considerable understanding for its day.]

1408   CROSS, J. SHOLTO W. The Watch Tower Movement in Central
        Africa 1909-1945. Oxford University, D.Phil. dissertation
        (History) 1973.

1409   CUNNISON, IAN. Jehovah's Witnesses at work: expansion in
        Central Africa. Times British Colonies Review (London)
        29 (1), 1958, 13, illus.

1410   DILLON-MALONE, CLIVE. The Korsten Basketmakers: a study of
        the Masowe Apostles, an indigenous African religious
        movement. Fordham University, Ph.D. dissertation 1975,
        239 p., 179 p. appendices, illus.
            [A Shona church in Lusaka, Zambia, with background in
        Rhodesia: by a Catholic missionary.]

1411   GRAY, RICHARD. The two nations. Aspects of the development
        of race relations in the Rhodesias and Nyasaland. London:
        Oxford University Press for the Institute of Race
        Relations 1960, 373 p., maps.
            [Pp. 145-149, Ethiopianism (African Methodist Episcopal
        Church); Zionism (Last Church of God and His Christ,
        Nyasaland); Watch Tower.]

South-East Central Africa

1412   GRESCHAT, HANS-JÜRGEN. Kitawala. Ursprung, Ausbreitung und
        Religion der Watch-Tower-Bewegung in Zentral-Afrika
        (Marburger theologische Studien 4). Marburg: N. G. Elwert
        1967, 128 p., maps, bibl.
        [Includes main bibliography available on Watch Tower for
        Zaïre and South-East Central Africa.]

1413   GRESCHAT, HANS-JÜRGEN. "Witchcraft" und kirchlicher
        Separatismus in Zentral-Afrika, in E. Benz (ed.), item 137,
        90-104.

1414   HODGES, TONY. Jehovah's Witnesses in Central Africa (Minority
        Rights Group Report 29). London: Minority Rights Group
        1976, 16 p., map.
        [Pp. 9-11, Booth, Kamwana and his Watchman Healing
        Mission (= Bamulonda) from 1937; Nyirenda, Gondwe and
        other independent Watch Tower groups and their persecution
        by new African governments, especially in Malawi and
        Mozambique.]

1415   HOOKER, J[AMES] R. Witnesses and Watchtower in the Rhodesias
        and Nyasaland. Journal of African History 6 (1), 1965,
        91-106.
        [General review of the spread of Watch Tower and related
        movements; from local sources.]

1416   JAMES, C[YRIL] L[IONEL] R. A history of Negro revolt. Fact
        (London) 18, September 1938, 97 p.
        [Pp. 47-52, Chilembwe etc.; pp. 82-85, Rhodesian miners'
        revolt of 1935 and Watch Tower Society.]

1417   JEFFREYS, M. D. W. Role of the native prophet in a vanishing
        culture. Forum (Johannesburg) 5 (6), 1956, 17-18.
        [Prophetesses and their "rites of passage" - Mai Chaza
        and Alice Lenshina; nativistic movements - revivalist and
        passive types.]

1418   JOSSE, [PÈRE]. De l'hérésie à l'émeute. Les méfaits du
        Kitawala. Grands Lacs (Namur, White Fathers) n.s. 61,
        82-83-84, 1 fev. 1946, 71-76.

1419   JULES-ROSETTE, BENNETTA. African apostles. Ritual and con-
        version in the Church of John Maranke (Symbol, Myth and
        Ritual Series). Ithaca and London: Cornell University
        Press 1975, 302 p., maps, illus., tables.
        [Comprehensive study of the Apostolic Church in Zaïre,
        Zambia and Rhodesia, by an American Black sociologist who
        became a full member.]

1420 JULES-ROSETTE, BENNETTA. The conversion experience: the Apostles of John Maranke. Journal of Religion in Africa 7 (2), 1975, 132-164.
[Closely based on a part of her book, above.]

1421 KACZYŃSKI, GRZEGORZ J. Ruch Kitawala. Kultura Spoleczeństwo (Warsaw) 2, 1973, 119-137. Abstract, Le mouvement Kitawala, Africana Bulletin 19, 1974, 168-169.

1422 MEMBE, J[OHN] L[ESTER] C[OWARD]. A short history of the African Methodist Episcopal Church in Central Africa 1900-1962. Buchi (Kitwe, Zambia): the AME Church 1969, 98 p. Mimeo.
[For the author's life story, see A. Hastings, item 1543.]

1423 MOORE, N. O. and WILCOX, WAYLAND D. The report of the visit to South and Central Africa by N. O. Moore and Wayland D. Wilcox. The Sabbath Recorder (Plainfield, N.J.) 75 (22), 25 Nov. 1912, 695-735.
[The journal of the Seventh Day Baptists; basic source for the history of independent churches in Central Africa.]

1424 RAGOEN, J[OZEF]. De Watch-Towers of Getuigen van Jehova in Midden-Afrika. Nieuw Afrika (Antwerp, White Fathers) 72 (3), 1956, 111-115.

1425 RANGER, TERENCE O[SBORN] (ed.). Aspects of Central African history (Third World Histories). London: Heinemann/ Evanston: Northwestern University Press 1968, 291 p., maps.
[Reliable and convenient summaries of "independent African churches" in the context of local history, for Zaïre (Congo-Kinshasa) by John Masare, Zambia, by Andrew Roberts, Malawi, by John McCracken, and Rhodesia, by T. O. Ranger.]

1426 RANGER, T[ERENCE]\O[SBORN]. The Mwana Lesa movement of 1925, in T. O. Ranger and John Weller (eds.), Themes in the Christian History of Central Africa. London: Heinemann 1975, 45-75.

1427 RICHARDS, AUDREY I[SABEL]. A modern movement of witchfinders. Africa (London) 8 (4), 1935, 448-461. Fr. trans., Un mouvement modern pour déceler les sorcière: les Bamucapi. Bulletin des Juridictions Indigènes et du Droit Coutumier Congolais (Elisabethville [Lubumbashi]) 5 (3), 1937, 82-90.
[An anti-mission movement which swept Central Africa to the Congo ca. 1934.]

South-East Central Africa

1428   ROTBERG, ROBERT I. The rise of nationalism in Central Africa:
       the making of Malawi and Zambia 1873-1964. Cambridge,
       Massachusetts: Harvard University Press 1966, 362 p.
       [Numerous references to some eighteen groups - see index
       under "Separatist sects".]

1429   SPINDLER, MARC. Le mouvement Kitwala en Afrique Centrale. Le
       Monde Non-Chrétien n.s. 87=21, juillet-septembre 1968,
       30-41.
       [Review article on Greschat, item 1412.]

1430   WATCHTOWER PRESS. The Watchtower story. New York: Watchtower
       Press 1948.
       [The American side of the Jehovah's Witnesses Central
       African expansion.]

MALAGASY REPUBLIC

1431   ALLIER, RAOUL [SCIPION PHILIPPE]. L'enseignement primaire des
       indigènes à Madagascar. Cahiers de la Quinzaine (Paris)
       6 (4), [1904/05], 1-68.
       [Chapter 16 (pp. 113-118), "Ethiopianisme" - the
       "dissident sect" Tranozozoro considered in the context of
       Ethiopianism in Southern Africa.]

1432   ALTHABE, GÉRARD. Oppression et libération dans l'imaginaire.
       Les communautés villageoises de la côte orientale de
       Madagascar (Preface by G. Balandier). Paris: Maspéro
       1969, 359 p.
       [Chs. 3 and 5, the neo-traditional tromba possession
       cult, since 1960, which established new communities inde-
       pendent of both the existing family structures and of
       Christian congregations.]

1433   CHAPUS, G. S. and BOTHUN, F. Au souffle de l'Esprit: la vie
       consacrée du pasteur Rakotozandry et l'histoire du réveil
       de Farihimena. Tananarive: Imprimerie Luthérienne 1951,
       51 p.
       [Revival movement within the Lutheran Church from 1947.]

1434   DELORD, RAYMOND. Messianisme à Madagascar. Monde Non-
       Chrétien (Paris) n.s. 8, oct.-déc. 1948, 975-981.
       [A syncretist religion founded by a prophetic leader,
       Andrianampoinimerina.]

1435 ESTRADE, JEAN. Le Tromba. Un culte de possession à Madagascar. Paris: thèse de troisième cycle 1974, 250 p.
[A critical extension of the study by G. Althabe, suggesting tromba could be "the pentecostalism of animism" and examining the relation to Christianity.]

1436 HARDYMAN, JAMES T. Madagascar on the move. London: Livingstone Press 1950, 224 p.
[P. 152, Rainitsiandavaka's "syncretistic movement" among the Merina, 1833-34.]

1437 KING, GEORGE LANCHESTER. A self-made bishop: the story of John Tsizehena, "Bishop of the North, D.D." London: Society for the Propagation of the Gospel 1933, x + 58 p., illus.
[The "Mission Lord" or "Northern" church founded in 1885 apart from missions; joined Anglican diocese of Madagascar in 1911.]

1438 KOERNER, FRANCIS. L'échec de l'éthiopianisme dans les églises protestantes malgaches. Revue Française d'Histoire d'Outre-Mer no. 211=58 (2), 1971, 215-238, maps.
[The Église Tranozozoro, from ca. 1895, and its lessening influence with the revitalization of the "mission" churches from ca. 1911.]

1439 NAKKESTAD, GABRIEL. Fra vekkelsene på Madagaskar. Norsk Tidsskrift for Misjon (Oslo) 6 (3), 1952, 129-155.
[On revival movements.]

1440 OTTINO, P[AUL]. Le Tromba - Madagascar. L'Homme - Revue Française d'Anthropologie (Paris) janvier-mars 1965, 84-93.
[Neo-traditional possession cults.]

1441 RUSILLON, HENRY. Un culte dynastique avec évocation des morts chez les Salalaves de Madagascar: le "tromba" (Introduction par Raoul Allier). Paris: A. Picard 1912.

1442 THOMPSON, VIRGINIA and ADLOFF, RICHARD. The Malagasy Republic: Madagascar today. Stanford: Stanford University Press 1965, 504 p., maps.
[Pp. 196-197, three "syncretistic sects", including the Disciples of the Lord (among the Betsileos) which returned to the "orthodox churches", and the Église Tranozozoro (Reed Dwellers).]

South-East Central Africa

1443   THUNEM, A. Vaekkelsen på Madagaskar. Stravanger: Det Norske
       Missionsselskaps Forlag 1926, 221 p., illus.
       [On revivals.]

1444   THUNEM, A. Ny Fifohazana eto Madagaskara. Tananarive:
       Mission Norwégienne 1935, 200 p.
       [In Malagasy; sympathetic account by a Norwegian
       missionary of the Fifohazana Revival.]

See also item 103.

MALAWI

1445   CHURCH OF SCOTLAND. Reports of the Foreign Missions Committee.
       Edinburgh: Church of Scotland, annually.
       [See 1958 Report, pp. 35-37, on independency, especially
       in Nyasaland; 1960 Report, p. 13, Jehovah's Witnesses and
       influence of "Ras Tafari sect"; p. 13, brief account of
       anti-witchcraft exorcist, Chikanga, with political associ-
       ations and Christian forms, active in Nyasaland in 1960.]

1446   DUFF, HECTOR. African small chop. London: Hodder and
       Stoughton 1932, 223 p.
       [Pp. 49-52, colonialist view of Chilembwe.]

1447   DU PLESSIS, J[OHANNES]. Thrice through the dark continent:
       a record of journeyings across Africa during the years
       1913-1916. London: Longmans Green and Co. 1917,
       viii + 350 p., plates, map.
       [Pp. 347-349, Chilembwe.]

1448   FRASER, DONALD. The new Africa. London: Church Missionary
       Society 1927; New York: Missionary Education Movement of
       the United States 1928; 202 p., illus.
       [Pp. 88-90, the undisciplined nature of separatist
       movements illustrated by Chilembwe.]

1449   JONES, GRIFF[ITH BEVAN]. Britain and Nyasaland. London:
       Allen and Unwin 1964, 315 p.
       [Pp. 95-96, 215-216, etc., on Chilembwe's role in the
       development of nationalism in Nyasaland.]

1450   KAUTA, STEPHEN. Traditional religion among the Tumbuka and
       other tribes in Malawi. Ministry (Morija, Lesotho) 9 (1),
       1969, 3-11.

[P. 4, brief account of a prophet healer, Chikanga, 1957-1963, and Mcape witch-finding movement.]

1451 LACEY, A. TRAVERS. Notes on a recent anti-witchcraft movement in Nyasaland. Cambridge University, dissertation, Diploma in Anthropology 1934.
[Mcape witch-finding movement.]

1452 LANGWORTHY, EMILY BOOTH. This Africa was mine. Stirling: Stirling Tract Enterprise 1952, ix + 139 p., illus.
[Introduction by George Shepperson; written by the daughter of Joseph Booth; John Chilembwe as the Booth's "houseboy".]

1453 LINDEN, IAN with LINDEN, JANE. Catholics, peasants and Chewa resistance in Nyasaland 1889-1939. London: Heinemann 1974, 223 p., illus.
[Pp. 74-81, 90-102, 180-184, independent churches, including Watchtower, Chilembwe and minor bodies; pp. 76-77, Chewa primal prophetess Chanjiri.]

1454 LINDEN, JANE and LINDEN, IAN. John Chilembwe and the new Jerusalem. Journal of African History 12 (4), 1971, 629-651.
[Analysis of the 1915 rising in the context of millennial belief and Watchtower influence; based on primary sources.]

1455 LIVINGSTONE, W[ILLIAM] P[RINGLE]. Laws of Livingstonia: a narrative of missionary adventure and achievement. London: Hodder and Stoughton n.d. [1922], x + 385 p.
[Pp. 352-355 on Chilembwe's uprising and Law's reaction.]

1456 LIVINGSTONE, W[ILLIAM] P[RINGLE]. A prince of missionaries: the Rev. Alexander Hetherwick of Blantyre, Central Africa. London: J. Clarke n.d. [1931], 205 p.
[Pp. 85, 154-155, Chilembwe.]

1457 LIVINGSTONIA NEWS, THE (Livingstonia). Editorial comment and news reports on Ethiopianism and Watchtower, etc. in e.g.: 2 (1), 1909, 23-24 (Watchtower); 2 (4), 1909, 53 and 56-59 (Ethiopianism); 2 (5), 1909, 68, 72-74 (Ethiopianism), 74-75 (Booth); 2 (6), 1909, 81-82 (Ethiopianism), 90 (Watchtower); 3 (3), June 1910, 46-47 (Watchtower and Ethiopianism); 3 (4), 1910, 57 (Ethiopianism); 3 (5), 1910, 92-93 (Watchtower); 4 (2), 1911, 19 (Watchtower); 8 (1), 1915, 23-25 (Chilembwe "rising"); 9 (1-5), 1916, 4-10, 29 (Native Rising Commission Report of 1916).

South-East Central Africa

1458   LOHRENTZ, KENNETH P.   Joseph Booth, Charles Domingo and the
       Seventh Day Baptists in Northern Nyasaland, 1910-1912.
       Journal of African History 12 (3), 1971, 461-480, map.

1459   McCRACKEN, K. JOHN.   Livingstonia Mission and the evolution of
       Malawi 1875-1939.   Cambridge University, Ph.D. dissertation
       (History) 1967, 402 p.
          [Pp. 306-340, the earlier independent churches and the
       relations to the Mission in the northern area.]

1460   MacDONALD, RODERICK J.   A history of African education in
       Nyasaland 1875-1945.   Edinburgh University, Ph.D. disser-
       tation (History) 1969.
          [Includes the independent churches' efforts to establish
       schools, and their relation to missions and government.]

1461   MacDONALD, RODERICK J.   Religious independency as a means of
       social advancement in northern Nyasaland in the 1930s.
       Journal of Religion in Africa 3 (2), 1970, 106-129.

1462   MARWICK, M[AX] G.   Another modern anti-witch movement in East
       Central Africa.   Africa (London) 20 (2), 1950, 100-112.
          [The Bwanali-Mpulumutsi movement of 1947 in Southern
       Nyasaland among the Malawi.]

1463   MUFUKA, K. M.   Higher education: the missions' paradoxical
       contribution to empire.   Bulletin, Evangelical Fellowship
       for Missionary Studies (London) 1, March 1972, 3-11.
          [Pp. 6-11, Ethiopianism: Kamwana, Charles Domingo and
       Chilembwe as mission-educated leaders, with Robert Laws'
       attitude to them.]

1464   MWASE, GEORGE SIMEON.   Strike a blow and die: a narrative of
       race relations in colonial Africa (ed. by R. I. Rotberg).
       Cambridge, Massachusetts: Harvard University Press 1967,
       176 p.   2nd ed. with revised introduction, 1970; London:
       Heinemann (African Writers Series 160) 1975, xlvi + 135 p.,
       illus.
          [A biography of J. Chilembwe written in the 1930s by a
       fellow African.]

1465   NORMAN, L. S.   Rebellion.   Blackwood's Magazine no. 794=230
       (Dec.), 1931, 862-873.
          [First-hand account of Chilembwe rebellion.]

1466   OLIVER, ROLAND.   "Too cheaty, too thefty" - the seeds of
       nationalism in Nyasaland.   The Twentieth Century
       no. 986=165 (April), 1959, 358-365.

[A B.B.C. talk; p. 363, John Chilembwe; pp. 363-364,
influence of the radical protestantism of independent
Negro churches from U.S.A.; judging Europeans by their own
Christian standards, passim.]

1467 PACHAI, B[RIDGLAL]. The Malawi diaspora and elements (sic) of
      Clements Kadalie (Central Africa Historical Association,
      Local Series 24). Salisbury: the Association 1969, 16 p.
      Mimeo.
      [Includes accounts of Joseph Booth, Kamwana, Nyirenda,
      and Chilembwe.]

1468 RANGELEY, W. H. J. "Nyau" in Kota-Kota District. Nyasaland
      Journal (Blantyre) 2 (2), 1949, 35-49; idem 3 (2), 1950,
      19-33.
      [A Cewa secret society said to have Christian aspects.]

1469 RAWLINSON, G. C. Some lessons of the Chilembwe rebellion.
      Central Africa (London, Universities' Mission to Central
      Africa) no. 411=35 (March), 1917, p. 61.
      [An Anglican missionary's reactions to the report of the
      government commission.]

1470 ROSS, ANDREW C[HRISTIAN]. The political role of witchfinder
      in Southern Malawi during the crisis of October 1964 to
      March 1965, in Witchcraft and healing: proceedings of a
      Seminar...Centre of African Studies, University of
      Edinburgh February 1969. The Centre 1969, 55-63. Mimeo.
      [Includes references to Mcape movement and independent
      churches.]

1471 ROTBERG, ROBERT I. Psychological stress and the question of
      identity: Chilembwe's revolt reconsidered, in
      R. I. Rotberg and A. A. Mazrui (eds.), Protest and power
      in Black Africa. New York: Oxford University Press 1970,
      337-373.

1472 SHEPPERSON, GEORGE [ALCOTT]. The politics of African church
      separatist movements in British Central Africa 1892-1916,
      Africa (London) 24 (3), 1954, 233-246.
      [Excellent summary discussion of Joseph Booth, Charles
      Domingo, Elliott Kamwana and John Chilembwe and their
      relationship to early Nyasaland nationalism.]

1473 SHEPPERSON, GEORGE [ALCOTT] and PRICE, THOMAS. Independent
      African: John Chilembwe and the origins, setting, and
      significance of the Nyasaland native rising of 1915.
      Edinburgh: Edinburgh University Press 1958, 564 p.,
      bibl., illus.

South-East Central Africa

[Ethiopianism in Central Africa, the Watchtower Movement of Elliott Kamwana, and in great detail the Chilembwe rebellion from an historical point of view. See review article by P. M. Worsley, Religion and politics in Central Africa, in Past and Present 15, April 1959, 73-81.]

1474   SHEPPERSON, GEORGE [ALCOTT]. The literature of British Central Africa. Rhodes-Livingstone Journal 42=23 (June), 1958, 12-46, illus.
        [Pp. 40-43, "the role of the smaller, less orthodox missions", and independents.]

1475   SHEPPERSON, GEORGE [ALCOTT]. Nyasaland and the millennium, in Sylvia Thrupp (ed.), item 69, 144-159. Repr. in John Middleton (ed.), Black Africa: its peoples and their culture today. New York and London: Macmillan 1970, 234-247.
        [Traces the sources of millennial ideas in Central and Southern Africa, most particularly the rule of the Jehovah's Witnesses.]

1476   SHEPPERSON, G[EORGE ALCOTT]. Religion in British Central Africa, in W. M. Watt (ed.), item 410, 47-51.

1477   SHEPPERSON, GEORGE A[LCOTT]. Myth and reality in Malawi (Fourth Melville J. Herskovits Memorial Lecture). Evanston, Illinois: Northwestern University Press 1966, 27 p.
        [Includes the Chilembwe legend and its ramifications, millenarian myths and witchfinding cults.]

1478   SHEPPERSON, GEORGE A[LCOTT]. The place of John Chilembwe in Malawi historiography, in B. Pachai (ed.), The early history of Malawi. London: Longman 1971, 405-428.

1479   TANGRI, ROGER K. African reaction and resistance to the early colonial situation in Malawi 1891-1915 (Central African Historical Association, Local Series 25). Salisbury: the Association 1969, 17 p. Mimeo.
        [Pp. 8-12, Livingstonia Mission and the rise of the independent churches; pp. 12-16, the Chilembwe rising.]

1480   TANGRI, ROGER K. Some new aspects of the Nyasaland native rising of 1915. African Historical Studies (Boston) 4 (2), 1971, 305-313.
        [New hypotheses concerning Chilembwe.]

Black Africa

1481 WILSON, GEORGE HERBERT. The history of the Universities'
      Mission to Central Africa. London: Universities' Mission
      to Central Africa 1936, xvi + 228 p.
      [Pp. 164-166 on Chilembwe rising.]

1482 W[INSPEAR] F[RANK]. Mchape. Nyasaland Diocesan Chronicle,
      July 1933. Repr. in Central Africa (London: the Univer-
      sities' Mission to Central Africa) no. 611, Nov. 1933.
      [Mcape witchcraft eradication movement as seen by a
      missionary on Likoma Island.]

1483 WISHLADE, R[OBERT] L. Chiefship and politics in the Mlanje
      district of Southern Nyasaland. Africa (London) 31 (1),
      1961, 36-45.
      [Pp. 44-45, the Church of the Ancestors.]

1484 WISHLADE, R[OBERT] L. Sectarianism in Southern Nyasaland.
      London: Oxford University Press for the International
      African Institute 1965, 162 p., map, illus., bibl.
      [A comprehensive survey, including doctrine, ritual,
      officers, role in society, etc., with special reference to
      the Ethiopian Church and the Faithful Church of Christ.]

See also items 145, 149, 155, 160, 193, 260, 267, 280, 331, 347, 394.

MOZAMBIQUE

1485 DE FREITAS, AFONSO I. FERRAZ. Seitas religiosas gentilicas de
      Mocambique. Estudos Ultramarinos (Lisbon) 1, 1961, 91-122.
      [Ethiopian sects in Southern Africa sympathetically
      considered; their religious and social contributions;
      special reference to 13 principal Ethiopian sects in
      Mozambique, and the assistance given to them by American
      Protestantism.]

RHODESIA (ZIMBABWE)

1486 AFRICAN INDEPENDENT CHURCH CONFERENCE (FAMBIDZANO). Annual
      Report [No. 1] 1975. Fort Victoria: African Independent
      Church Conference 1975, 17 p., illus. Mimeo.

South-East Central Africa

1487   AFRICAN RESEARCH BULLETIN (Exeter), Zimbabwe Church of Orphans.
       African Research Bulletin 2 (9), 1965, 372-373.
          [Founded in 1962 as a religious body, but "steadily
          penetrated by elements of the banned Peoples' Caretaker
          Council".]

1488   BLAKNEY, CHARLES P.   Chipunha, a Rhodesian cult. Practical
       Anthropology (Tarrytown, N.Y.) 16 (3), 1969, 98-108.
          [Especially pp. 107-108, a possession cult as a means of
          validating change, and the way this feature enables inde-
          pendent churches to mediate modernization.]

1489   CRAWFORD, J. R. Witchcraft and sorcery in Rhodesia. London:
       Oxford University Press for the International African
       Institute 1967, 312 p., illus., tables.
          [Ch. 16, "Divination in the pentecostal churches"
          (Zionist type): Apostolic Faith churches, Maranke's
          Apostolic Church, and divination associated with baptism
          and fire-rites; all similar to traditional divining.]

1490   DANEEL, M[ARTHINUS] L[OUIS]. The God of the Matopo Hills. An
       essay on the Mwari cult in Rhodesia (Afrika-Studiecentrum,
       Leiden, Communications 1). The Hague and Paris: Mouton
       1970, 95 p., illus.
          [Pp. 64-71, the radical conflict between the cult and
          Mutende's Zion Christian Church, but not with Ethiopian-
          type churches.]

1491   DANEEL, M[ARTHINUS] L[OUIS]. Zionism and faith healing in
       Rhodesia (Afrika-Studiecentrum, Leiden, Communications 2).
       The Hague and Paris: Mouton 1970, 64 p., illus.
          [Zionist Christian Church, Zionist Apostolic Faith
          Mission, Zionist Apostolic Church, and splinter groups such
          as Zionist Reformed Churches and African Zion Church of
          Jesus, all Shona-speaking.]

1492   DANEEL, M[ARTHINUS] L[OUIS]. Het Oude Testament in nieuw
       Afrika. VU Magazine (Free University, Amsterdam) 1 (2),
       1971, 21-26, illus.
          [See also De Gaay Fortman, pp. 27-28, on Daneel's work.]

1493   DANEEL, M[ARTHINUS] L[OUIS]. Marshall W. Murphree. Christian-
       ity and the Shona..., London 1969. Bijdragen tot de Taal-
       Land-en Volken-kunde (Leiden) 127 (1), 1971, 193-207.
          [A major review article; pp. 200-207 on the Budjga
          Vapostori.]

1494   DANEEL, M[ARTHINUS] L[OUIS]. Old and new in Southern Shona
        independent churches. Vol. 1, Background and rise of the
        major movements. The Hague and Paris: Mouton 1971,
        xviii + 557 p., illus., maps, bibl. Vol. 2, Church
        growth - causative factors and recruitment techniques.
        Mouton 1974, xviii + 373 p., illus., maps. bibl.
            [A major study by a Dutch Reformed missionary who founded
        FAMBIDZANO; two further volumes are projected.]

1495   DANEEL, M[ARTHINUS] L[OUIS]. Shona independent churches and
        ancestor worship, in D. B. Barrett (ed.), item 1188,
        160-170.

1496   DANEEL, M[ARTHINUS] L[OUIS]. Project: Shona independent
        churches. Progress Report No. 1-, 1972-.
            [Occasional mimeographed paper on the formation and
        development of the African Independent Church Conference -
        FAMBIDZANO - and theological training for Shona independent
        churches. Progress Report No. 6 appeared in January 1975.]

1497   DANEEL, M[ARTHINUS] L[OUIS]. Shona independent churches in a
        rural society, in A. J. Dachs (ed.), Christianity south of
        the Zambezi. Gwelo, Rhodesia: Mambo Press 1973, 159-188.

1498   EISENBERG, LARRY. Guta ra Jehovah. African Christian Advocate
        (Cleveland, Transvaal) 23 (3), 1964, 8-9, illus.
            [Mai Chaza's "City of Jehovah".]

1499   MARANKE, JOHANNE. Humbowo hutswa we Vapostori [The new witness
        of the Apostles]. Rhodesia: the Church of the Apostles
        n.d. [ca. 1955], 22 p. Mimeo.
            [A record of Maranke's visions as dictated a few years
        before his death in 1963.]

1500   MARTIN, MARIE-LOUISE. The Mai Chaza Church in Rhodesia, in
        D. B. Barrett (ed.), item 1188, 109-121.

1501   MARY AQUINA (SISTER) [WEINRICH, A. K. H.]. Christianity in a
        Rhodesian Trust land. African Social Research 1, June
        1966, 1-40.
            [The older churches; the formation and history of Jairus'
        Ruponeso Rwakudenga [Salvation from Heaven] Church in 1964,
        at first Ethiopian, then Zionist; the Karanga people.]

1502   MARY AQUINA (SISTER) [WEINRICH, A. K. H.]. The people of the
        Spirit: an independent church in Rhodesia. Africa
        (London) 37 (2), 1967, 203-219.

South-East Central Africa

> [On one group of Johanne Maranke's Church of the Apostles (1932) in Eastern Rhodesia; a Zionist-type synthesis of Karanga religion and Christianity, with the Holy Spirit as the central divinity.]

1503   MARY AQUINA (SISTER) [WEINRICH, A. K. H.]. Zionists in Rhodesia. Africa (London) 39 (2), 1969, 113-137.
[Historical survey; economic status; organization and liturgy; comparison with Church of the Apostles; relation to Europeans.]

1504   MURPHREE, MARSHALL W[ARNE]. The Wapostori of Shonaland. African Christian Advocate (Cleveland, Transvaal) 23 (3), 1964, 10-11.

1505   MURPHREE, MARSHALL W[ARNE]. Christianity and the Shona (London School of Economics Monographs on Social Anthropology 36). London: Athlone Press 1969, 200 p.
[P. 12, Zionism; pp. 60-61, Johanne Masowe Vapostori, Kruger Vapostori, Mushakata or Independent African Church; Ch. 6, Johanne Maranke Vapostori, also ch. 7 passim; pp. 159-166, variant incidence of independency in Southern Africa; pp. 174-187, statistics.]

1506   MURPHREE, MARSHALL W[ARNE]. Religious interdependence among the Budjga Vapostori, in D. B. Barrett (ed.), item 1188, 171-180.
[Vapostori of Johanne Maranke.]

1507   MUTAMBANASHE, DENYS L. Guta ra Jehovah. Guta ra Jehova, Zimunya Reserve, Umtali, Rhodesia: the Church 1961, ca. 240 p., illus.
[Mai Chaza (d. 1958) and her movement (ca. 1952) with village Guta ra Jehova [City of God], similar to the Lumpa Church.]

1508   NDERERE, TAFADZWA JOHN. Research paper 1969: Israel Church. Spes Unica (Epworth Theological College, Salisbury) 1 (1), 1969, 1-8.

1509   PEADEN, W. R. Missionary attitudes to Shona culture 1890-1923 (Central Africa Historical Association, Local Series 27). Salisbury: the Association 1970, 41 p.
[Pp. 37-40, independent religious movements; pp. 39-40, Shiri Chena, or Original White Bird Mission.]

1510   PEADEN, W. R. Zionist churches in Southern Mashonaland 1924-33. Bulletin of the Society for African Church History 3 (1-2), 1969-70, 53-67.

1511   RANGER, T[ERENCE] O[SBORN]. State and church in Southern
        Rhodesia 1919-1939 (Central Africa Historical Association,
        Local Series 4). Salisbury: the Association n.d. [1961],
        28 p. Mimeo.
          [Pp. 3f., government opposition to American fundamen-
        talist and pentecostal missions and their African
        offshoots; pp. 26-28, the vision of an independent African
        church.]

1512   RANGER, TERENCE O[SBORN]. Traditional authorities and the
        rise of modern politics in Southern Rhodesia 1898-1930, in
        E. T. Stokes and R. Brown (eds.), The Zambesian past:
        studies in Central African history. Manchester:
        Manchester University Press 1966, 171-193.
          [Nyamanda's movement; Ethiopian influence on early
        nationalism.]

1513   RANGER, TERENCE O[SBORN]. Revolt in Southern Rhodesia
        1896-97: a study in African resistance. London:
        Heinemann 1967, 403 p., maps, illus.
          [P. 373, Ngwenya's African Mission Home Church;
        pp. 379-380, 382, M. Zwimba's Church of the White Bird;
        pp. 380-381, Watch Tower; pp. 381-382, Mai Chaza's Guta
        ra Jehova.]

1514   RANGER, TERENCE O[SBORN]. The early history of independency
        in Southern Rhodesia, in W. M. Watt (ed.), item 410,
        52-74.
          [The relation of Ethiopianism, Zionism and Watch Tower
        to politics.]

1515   RANGER, T[ERENCE] O[SBORN]. The African voice in Southern
        Rhodesia 1896-1930 (African Voice Series, 1). London:
        Heinemann/Evanston: Northwestern University Press 1970,
        180 p.
          [Spirit mediums in the Mapondera rising, and along with
        the Mwari cult in opposition to Rhodesian government;
        Shona independent churches.]

1516   [SENGWAYO, M. J.]. From the bush to the pulpit. No publi-
        cation details. 17 p. Mimeo.
          [Autobiography of Sengwayo, a semi-independent church
        evangelist, later associated with Apostolic Faith,
        Portland, Oregon, and with "55 groups...in South Africa,
        Zambia, Botswana, Malawi, Portuguese East Africa and
        Rhodesia". (Department of Religious Studies, University
        of Aberdeen, has copy).]

209

South-East Central Africa

1517   SITHOLE, NDABANINGI. Obed Mutezo: the Mudzimu Christian
       nationalist. Nairobi: Oxford University Press 1970,
       210 p.
       [The traditional and American Methodist religious
       sources of his nationalist commitment; pp. 90-94, 113-114,
       the influence of Maranke Vapostori through his wife;
       pp. 5-9, introduction by T. O. Ranger.]

1518   THOMAS, NORMAN ERNEST. Christianity, politics and the Manyika:
       a study of the influence of religious attitudes and
       loyalties of Africans in Rhodesia. Boston University,
       Ph.D. dissertation (Religion) 1968, 396 p.
       [Members of the Vapostori of Johanne Maranke, and of
       Johanne Masowe, are included in the religious groups
       sampled.]

1519   THOMAS, N[ORMAN] E[RNEST]. Functions of religious institutions
       in the adjustment of African women to life in an African
       township, in H. Watts (ed.), Focus on cities: proceedings
       of a conference. Durban: University of Natal Institute
       for Social Research 1970, 282-290.
       [Role of African independent churches dealt with.]

1520   VAN ONSELEN, CHARLES. Chibara: African mine labour in
       Southern Rhodesia, 1900-1933. London: Pluto Press 1976,
       326 p., maps.
       [Pp. 204-209, Watch Tower influence in Southern
       Rhodesian mines in 1920s.]

1521   ZION CHRISTIAN CHURCH. Zion Christian Church Rugano.
       Salisbury: the Church n.d. Mimeo.
       [A history of Mutendi's Church; in Shona.]

1522   ZVOBGO CHENGETAI, J. M. Z. The Wesleyan Methodist Missions in
       Southern Rhodesia 1891-1945. University of Edinburgh,
       Ph.D. dissertation (History) 1974, vii + 423 p.
       [Includes independency, especially Nemapare's African
       Methodist Church secession.]

See also items 341, 403, 1062, 1186.

ZAMBIA

1523   ACTUALIDAD AFRICANA (Madrid). La secta Lumpa. Actualidad
       Africana no. 151, enero 1965, 10f.

1524 AFRICA DIARY (New Delhi). Lumpa sect uprising. Africa Diary
      4 (37), 5-11 Sept. 1965 (4 p.).
      [A useful comprehensive news survey culled from five
      newspapers, some African.]

1525 AFRICA DIGEST (London). See issues: 13 (1), Jan. 1968, p. 30;
      13 (7), Oct. 1968, p. 35; 18 (6), Dec. 1971, p. 107; on
      the Lumpa church.

1526 ASSIMENG, J[OHN] M[AXWELL]. Sectarian allegiance and political
      authority: the Watch Tower Society in Zambia 1907-1935.
      Journal of Modern African Studies 8 (1), 1970, 97-112.
      [Deals with the sections independent of American control
      as well as with the official body.]

1527 CALMETTES, JEAN LOUP. Lumpa Church I: Genèse et développement.
      Institut de Science et de Theologie des Religions,
      Institut Catholique de Paris, Diploma thesis, 1969. Eng.
      trans., The Lumpa Church I: Genesis and development
      1953-1964. Chinsali, Zambia: Ilondola Mission Language
      Centre 1970, 55 p., map. Mimeo.

1528 CHARLTON, LESLIE. Spark in the stubble. Colin Morris of
      Zambia. London: Epworth Press 1969, 159 p.
      [Ch. 12 (= pp. 128-150) on Alice Lenshina and the Lumpa
      church conflict with government, with Morris' part in
      this - a good account by a journalist, including
      (pp. 129-131) document of Rev. Paul Mushindo (who baptized
      Alice) submitted to the commission of enquiry.]

1529 CHÉRY, H.-Ch. Les sectes en Rhodésie du Nord. Parole et
      Mission (Paris) 2 (7), 1959, 578-594.
      [Independent movements, from p. 584, with longer sections
      on the Lumpa Church, and the Church of the Sacred Heart.]

1530 CLAIRMONTE, PAUL. Lumpa Church based on fear. The Times
      (London) no. 56,083, 6 Aug. 1964, p. 9; see also p. 7.
      [Special article by a former administrative officer in
      Lundazi District in late 1950s. Comments on modernizing
      influence, and the attack on witchcraft raising suspicion
      against any who did not join.]

1531 CLARKE, M. A visit to Fiwila. Central Africa (London,
      Universities' Mission to Central Africa) no. 519, March
      1926.
      [Fiwila was a U.M.C.A. station in centre of Mwana Lesa
      movement.]

South-East Central Africa

1532   COLSON, ELIZABETH. Spirit possession among the Tonga of
        Zambia, in J. Beattie and J. Middleton (eds.), Spirit
        mediumship and society in Africa. London: Routledge and
        Kegan Paul 1969, 69-103.
            [Pp. 85, 92, 97, 101-102, Mangelo or angel movement from
        1959; pp. 94-95, masabe cult and European contacts; p. 102,
        woman medium with a spirit showing Christian influence.]

1533   COLSON, ELIZABETH. Social consequences of resettlement (Kariba
        Studies, 4). Manchester: Manchester University Press for
        Institute of African Studies, University of Zambia 1971,
        277 p., illus.
            [Pp. 238-244, new possession cults, including Mangelo
        (1960ff.) Cisongo, and one near Siamja, in period
        1958-1970.]

1534   CROSS, J. SHOLTO W. A prophet not without honour: Jeremiah
        Gondwa, in C. Allen and R. W. Johnson (eds.), Perspec-
        tives: papers in the history, politics and economics of
        Africa presented to Thomas Hodgkin. Cambridge: Cambridge
        University Press 1970, 171-184.
            [A Watch Tower leader in Zambia since 1923.]

1535   CUNNISON, IAN. A Watchtower Assembly in Central Africa.
        International Review of Missions no. 160=40 (Oct.), 1951,
        456-469. Fr. trans., Une assemblée de la Tour de Garde en
        Afrique Centrale. Le Monde Non-Chrétien, 20, oct.-déc.
        1951.

1536   CUNNISON, IAN. The Luapula peoples of Northern Rhodesia:
        custom and history in tribal politics. Manchester:
        Manchester University Press for the Rhodes-Livingstone
        Institute 1960, xiii + 258 p.
            [Pp. 204-208, Watchtower in Zambia.]

1537   DOBNEY, TOM. Zambezi their Jordon. Horizon (Ndola) 6 (9),
        1964, 20-26.
            [On the Vapostori of Johanne Masowe, or "Basketmakers",
        and their search for a place to settle in Zambia.]

1538   DRUM (Nairobi). Sect widows start Zambia's "Holy War". Drum
        June 1974, 12-16.
            [The Vapostori of Johanne Masowe, from the point of
        view of a secession group.]

1539   EAST AFRICA AND RHODESIA (London). Official description of
        Lumpa church, Lenshina opposition to witchcraft and

political parties. East Africa and Rhodesia no. 2080=40,
20 Aug. 1965, 941-942, 950.
[By the information department of Zambia.]

1540   FERNANDEZ, JAMES W[ILLIAM]. The Lumpa uprising: why? Africa
Report (Washington D.C.) 9 (10), 1964, 30-32, photo.
[Uprising a reaction to a situation of uncertainty in
the face of growing mission and government hostility.]

1541   GANN, L[EWIS] G. A history of Northern Rhodesia, early days to
1953. London: Chatto and Windus 1964, xvi + 478 p., map.
[Pp. 231-236, discontent in 1920s expressed in religious
and magical forms; Tomo Nyirenda (Mwana Lesa) and Watch
Tower groups' cargo cult ideas; p. 456, statistics.]

1542   GRESCHAT, HANS-JÜRGEN. Legend? Fraud? Reality? Alice
Lenshina's prophetic experience. Notes from some sources.
Africana Marburgensia 1 (1), 1968, 8-13.

1543   HASTINGS, ADRIAN. John Lester Membe, in T. O. Ranger and
J. Weller (eds.), Themes in the Christian history of
Central Africa. London: Heinemann 1975, 175-194, photo.
[Biography of an African minister of the A.M.E.C.]

1544   HEWARD, CHRISTINE [WOODS]. The rise of Alice Lenshina. New
Society (London), no. 98=4 (13 Aug), 1964, 6-8, map.
[General historical background to the Lenshina revolt of
1964, relating it to witchfinding movements.]

1545   ILLUSTRATED LONDON NEWS. For illustrated reports on the Lumpa
Church troubles in Zambia, 1964, see: Vol. 245, no. 6523,
8 Aug. 1964, p. 186; no. 6524, 15 Aug. 1964, 226-227;
no. 6525, 22 Aug. 1964, p. 256.

1546   JULES-ROSETTE, BENNETTA. Marropodi: an independent religious
community in transition. African Studies Review (Boston)
18 (2), 1975, 1-16.
[Two "Vapostori" churches, of John Masowe and of John
Maranke, in Marropodi, a suburb of Lusaka.]

1547   KALABA, ALFRED. St. Marks's College, Mapanza. Central Africa
(London, Universities Mission to Central Africa) 607,
July 1933.
[A schoolboy's essay on his experience of Mwana Lesa.]

1548   LALONDE, LEOPOLD. The Mwakalenga: African National Church.
Notes et Documents (Rome, Centrum Informationis Patres
Alborum) no. 40, sept.-oct. 1963, 385-386.
[George Nyasulo and the "Mwakalenga sect".]

South-East Central Africa

1549   LEENHARDT, MAURICE and MERCOIRET (Mme.). Prophétisme
       africaine. Le Monde Non-Chrétien 78-80, 1966, 53-62.
         [Reprint of correspondence in Propos Missionaire no. 35,
       avr. 1933, 58-61; reference to "two false prophets" in
       what is now Zambia.]

1550   LEHMANN, DOROTHEA A. Alice Lenshina. Die Lumpa Bewegung in
       Zambia. Das Wort in der Welt (Hamburg) 3, Juni 1966,
       41-47, illus., map.

1551   LONG, NORMAN [ERNEST]. Social change and the individual. A
       study...in a Zambian rural community. Manchester:
       Manchester University Press for the Institute of Social
       Research, University of Zambia 1968, 257 p., illus.
         [Ch. 8, Religion and social action, on Jehovah's Witnesses
       as distinct from the African Watch Tower movement (see
       p. 202, n. 1), but relevant to the independence movement.]

1552   MacPHERSON, FERGUS. Notes on the beginning of the (Alice
       Movement). Occasional Papers (London, International
       Missionary Council) 1, 1958, 2-5.
         [A first-hand account by the missionary most involved.]

1553   MARTIN, MARIE-LOUISE. The conflict between the Lumpa Church
       and the government in Zambia (Northern Rhodesia).
       Ministry (Morija, Lesotho) 5 (1), 1964, 46-48.
         [Based on Taylor and Lehmann, and the Mindolo Report,
       with further thoughts on messianism, religious and
       political.]

1554   MARWICK M[AX] G. Sorcery in its social setting. Manchester:
       Manchester University Press 1965, xxii + 339 p.
         [Pp. 59, 79, 93-94, 105, 257-258, the Mcape and Bwanali-
       Mpulu witchfinding movements, which differ from traditional
       sorcery beliefs in that they "rearrange and synthesize the
       old and the new".]

1555   MELLAND, FRANK H. Washing in Jordan. The African Observer
       3 (5), 1935, 36-40.
         [How the magistrate at Broken Hill deflected Watch Tower
       agitation to "wash in Jordan" as preparation for political
       freedom when company rule ended in 1924.]

1556   MURRAY, J. P. Zambia and the future. African Affairs
       (London) no. 254=64 (Jan.), 1965, 19.
         [Brief discussion of Lenshina riots as compared with
       earlier Watch Tower troubles.]

1557   MWAMBA, SIMON. Mission in a Watch Tower area. Central Africa
        (London, Universities Mission to Central Africa) no. 866=
        73, 1955, 42-44; reprinted from The Eagle, Sep. 1954.
            [An African headmaster on a special mission to counter
        Watch Tower teaching in the Luongo area.]

1558   NIGRIZIA (Verona.) Lenshina. Nigrizia 82 (9), 1964, 20-23,
        illus.
            [Popular.]

1559   NORTHERN RHODESIA, (Anglican) Bishop of, [ALLSTON JAMES WELLER
        MAY]. The Watch Tower. Central Africa (London: Univer-
        sities Mission to Central Africa) 43, June 1925, 120-122.
            [A description of the renewed appearance in 1924.]

1560   NORTHERN RHODESIA, Government of. Report of the commission to
        enquire into the disturbances on the Copper Belt, Northern
        Rhodesia. London: HMSO, Cmd. 5009, Oct. 1935.
            [Copper Belt Commission of Enquiry. Pp. 42-51, on the
        Watch Tower movement.]

1561   NORTHERN RHODESIA, Government of. Northern Rhodesia annual
        report on African affairs. Lusaka: Government Printers
        1956.
            [Pp. 23-28, et passim, the Lumpa Church.]

1562   NOTES ET DOCUMENTS (Rome, Centrum Informationis Patres Alborum).
        Lumpa Church. Notes et Documents no. 19, août-sept. 1961,
        401-410.
            [The origins, aims, doctrine and organization.]

1563   OGER, LOUIS. Lumpa Church. The Lenshina movement in Northern
        Rhodesia. Serenje, Zambia: [White Fathers Mission] 1960,
        54 p. Mimeo.
            [Pp. 1-25, first-hand report, by a White Father on the
        period 1955-60; pp. 26-54, documents of the Church: 66
        hymns, 2 animal fables, 2 prayers, etc.; in Bemba with
        English translations.]

1564   OGER, LOUIS. Le mouvement Lenshina en Rhodésie du Nord.
        Église vivante (Paris-Louvain) 14 (2), 1962, 128-138.
            [Sympathetic description of Alice Lenshina.]

1565   OGER, LOUIS. L'Église du Sacré-Coeur. Notes et Documents
        (Rome, C.I.P.A.) no. 51, nov. 1964, 421-430. Spanish
        trans., La Iglesia de Sagrado Corazón: una secta
        sincretista nacida de la Iglesia Católica. Actualidad
        Africana (Madrid) 151, enero 1965, 8ff.

South-East Central Africa

[Emilio Mulolani, and the origins and development of his secession from the Roman Catholic Church; by a White Father.]

1566   OGER, LOUIS. Mutima Church: the Catholic Church of the Sacred Heart, Emilyo Mulolani (Religious Sects in Northern Rhodesia, 2). No place [Serenje, Zambia], no publisher [White Fathers Mission?] n.d. [early 1960s?] 14 p. Mimeo. [List of sources, p. 14.]

1567   PETIT ECHO (White Fathers). Illuminisme. Petit Echo no. 450= 43 (mai), 1955, 258-265. [Pp. 260-265, Alice Lenshina.]

1568   QUICK, GRIFFITH. Some aspects of the African Watch Tower movement in Northern Rhodesia. International Review of Missions no. 114=29 (April), 1940, 216-225.

1569   RAGOEN, JOZEF. De Watch-Towers in Noord-Rhodesia. Nieuw Afrika (Antwerp, White Fathers) 72 (4), 1956, 157-161.

1570   RANDALL, MAX WARD. Profiles for victory: new proposals for Zambia. South Pasadena, California: William Carey Library 1970, 204 p., photo. [Ch. 5, the growth of independent churches. A survey, without new factual material.]

1571   RANGER, TERENCE O[SBORN]. The "Ethiopian" episode in Barotseland, 1900-1905. Rhodes-Livingston Journal 37, June 1965, 26-41. [The African Methodist Episcopal Church mission from South Africa.]

1572   REYNOLDS, BARRIE. Magic, divination and witchcraft among the Barotse of Northern Rhodesia. Berkeley and Los Angeles: University of California Press 1963, xix + 181 p., illus. [Pp. 133-138, "The Twelve Society", a healing society combining traditional elements and borrowings from the Seventh Day Adventists, and organized like a church, from 1944.]

1573   ROBERTS, ANDREW D. The Lumpa tragedy. Peace News (London), no. 1471, Sept. 4 1964, 6-7.

1574   ROBERTS, ANDREW D. The Lumpa Church of Alice Lenshina, in R. I. Rotberg and A. A. Mazrui (eds.), Protest and power in black Africa. New York: Oxford University Press 1970, 513-568. Reprinted separately: Lusaka: Oxford University Press 1972, 56 p.

1575   ROTBERG, ROBERT I.   Religious nationalism: the Lenshina move-
        ment of Northern Rhodesia. Rhodes-Livingstone Journal 29,
        June 1961, 63-78.
            [History and character of the movement, particularly its
        xenophobic character.]

1576   SMITH, EDWIN W[ILLIAMS] and DALE, ANDREW M[URRAY].   The Ila-
        speaking peoples of Northern Rhodesia. London: Macmillan
        1920, 2 vols., 423, 433 p.   2nd ed., New Hyde Park, N. Y.:
        University books, 1966.
            [Vol. 1, pp. 345-346, a local prophet. Vol. 2, pp. 136-
        152, Chilenga, Mwana Lesa, Mupumani, prophets among the
        Ila; pp. 197-212, the Mwana Lesa movement.]

1577   STONE, W. VERNON.   The "Alice" movement in 1958. Occasional
        Papers (London, International Missionary Council) 1,
        1958, 5-10.
            [A first-hand account by a Church of Scotland missionary.
        See also his later comments in Ministry (Morija, Lesotho)
        3, April 1965, p. 148.]

1578   STONE, W. VERNON.   The Livingstonia Mission and the Bemba.
        Bulletin of the Society for African Church History
        (Aberdeen) 2 (4), 1968, 311-322.
            [P. 316, the Lenshina movement, but the whole article
        is useful background.]

1579   TAYLOR, JOHN V[ERNON] and LEHMANN, DOROTHEA A.   Christians of
        the Copperbelt. The growth of the Church in Northern
        Rhodesia. London: SCM Press 1961, x + 308 p., map.
            [Part IV (pp. 216-268), by Lehmann, describes the "Alice
        movement", Jehovah's Witnesses, the African Methodist
        Episcopal Church, and the Church of the Sacred Heart.]

1580   The TIMES (London).   Malnutrition deaths among Lumpa displaced
        persons. The Times no. 56,295, 13 April 1965, p. 9.
            [An account of Kitita, a Lumpa rehabilitation centre
        with over four thousand residents; negotiations to join
        the United Church of Zambia.]

1581   VON HOFFMAN, CARL.   Jungle Gods (ed. by Eugene Lohrke).   New
        York: Holt 1929, xxiv + 286 p., illus. London: Constable
        1932.
            [Pp. 42-74, account of Mwana Lesa, based on District
        Office files; Chilembwe; Watch Tower.]

South-East Central Africa

1582   WATSON, WILLIAM. Tribal cohesion in a money economy. A study
       of the Mambwe people of Northern Rhodesia. Manchester:
       Manchester University Press for the Rhodes-Livingstone
       Institute 1958, xix + 246 p., illus., figures, tables.
          [Pp. 197-203, Anok Simpungwe's secession church, from
       Jehovah's Witnesses, 1917-1939.]

1583   WOODS, CHRISTINE M. [HEWARD]. Alice Lenshina Mulenga: a
       Bemba cult leader. University of Edinburgh, M.A. thesis
       1961.
          [Cf. her summary of her thesis, item 1544].

1584   ZAMBIA, Government of. Report of Commission of Enquiry into
       the former Lumpa Church. Lusaka: Government Printer 1965,
       36 p.
          [The causes and course of the Lumpa disturbance 1964;
       the Lumpa Church rules, marriage rules, and choir rules.]

1585   ZAMBIA, Government of. Annual report of the provincial and
       district government for the year 1964. Lusaka: Govern-
       ment Printer 1966, 11 p.
          [P. 10, Annexure A, the Lenshina disturbances.]

See also items 91, 98, 106, 182, 183, 272, 273, 294, 305, 353, 379,
416.

Southern Africa

1586 BECKEN, HANS-JÜRGEN. Das Evangelium begegnet den
vorchristlichen Religionen Südafrika. Hermannsburger
Missionsblatt (Hermannsburg) 113 (5-6), 1973, 105-108.
[Pp. 107-108, outline of Sundkler's revised views on
classification of independent movements and their relation
to primal tradition.]

1587 CHRISTIAN INSTITUTE OF SOUTHERN AFRICA. See: Annual Report
1968-9 (by Beyers Naudé). Extracts in South African Outlook no. 1180=99, 1969, 137-138; Director's report for the
period 1st August 1971-31st July 1972. Johannesburg: the
Institute 1972, 5 p.

1588 CHRISTIAN INSTITUTE OF SOUTHERN AFRICA. Newsletter
(Braamfontein, Transvaal).
[See passim for news items on independent churches:
e.g. no. 1, 1966, p. 5; no. 1-2, 1967, p. 5; no. 3, 1967,
pp. 5-6; April 1971, pp. 10-12, educational assistance.]

1589 CHRISTIAN INSTITUTE OF SOUTHERN AFRICA and the AFRICAN
INDEPENDENT CHURCHES ASSOCIATION. Occasional papers and
reports on the Institute's work among African Independent
Churches, e.g., Report on Theological Refresher Course...
24 Feb.-3 March 1969. 7 p.

1590 DUNCAN, HALL. Interview with a sect leader. African Christian
Advocate (Cleveland, Transvaal) 23 (3), 1964, 13.
[R. G. Sibande, Swazi founder of New Salem Apostolic
Church in Zion of South Africa.]

1591 EBERHARDT, JACQUELINE. Note sur l'acculturation et culte de
possession "Malombo" chez les bantous du Sud-est. Le
Monde Non-Chrétien n.s. 43-4, juillet-décembre 1957,
218-224.

1592 FRASER, ELIZABETH. Christianity in the tribal idiom: causes
and characteristics of African separatism. African World,
November 1965, 4-5, illus.
[Popular.]

Southern Africa

1593   KAMPHAUSEN, ERHARD. Anfänge der kirchlichen
        Unabhängigkeitsbewegung in Südafrika. Geschichte und
        Theologie der Äthiopischen Bewegung 1872-1912 (Studien zur
        interkulturellen Geschichte des Christentums, 6). Bern/
        Frankfurt am Main: Lang 1976, 657 p.
           [Uses new source materials to show the relationship of
        Ethiopianism with Afro-American churches and Black
        Theology.]

1594   KNOOB, WILLI J. Ethnologische Aspekte der religiösen
        Bewegungen im südlichen Afrika, in W. E. Mühlmann (ed.),
        item 57, 87-103.

1595   MARTIN, MARIE-LOUISE. Face aux mouvements prophétiques et
        messianiques en Afrique méridionale. Monde Non-Chrétien
        n.s. 64, octobre-décembre 1962, 226-255. Eng. tr., abbr.,
        The church facing prophetic and messianic movements.
        Ministry (Morija, Lesotho) 3 (2), 1963, 49-61.
           [A general survey of origins and causes; discussion of
        attitudes to be adopted by the older churches.]

1596   MARTIN, MARIE-LOUISE. The biblical concept of messianism and
        messianism in Southern Africa. Morija, Lesotho: Sesuto
        Book Depot 1964, 207 p.
           [Parts 1 and 2, biblical; part 3, pp. 89-187, on
        messianism in Africa, especially Southern Africa. A
        theological treatment which includes discussion of Xhosa
        and Tswana prophets and a typology of messianism.]

1597   NÜRNBERGER, KLAUS. Authority in Africa 2. Pro Veritate 10
        (11), 1972, 13-17.
           [Pp. 13-14, on leaders in independent churches, rather
        than African ministers in the older churches, assuming
        the authority formerly exercised by white missionaries.]

1598   PARSONS, N. Q. Independency and Ethiopianism among the Tswana
        in the late 19th and early 20th centuries, in Collected
        Seminar Papers on Southern Africa in the 19th and 20th
        centuries, Oct. 1969-April 1970. Institute of Commonwealth
        Studies, University of London. London: the Institute
        1971, 56-71.

1599   PAUW, B[ERTHOLD] A. The influence of Christianity, in W. D.
        Hammond-Tooke (ed.), The Bantu-speaking peoples of Southern
        Africa. London and Boston: Routledge and Kegan Paul,
        rev. enlarged 2nd ed., 1974, 415-440.
           [African independent churches: pp. 418-420, 424, 425,
        432, 433, 434-436.]

1600   PRETORIUS, H[ENDRIK] L.   Waarom independentisme in Afrika?
        Ned[erduitse] Geref[ormeerde] Teologiese Tydskrift
        (Capetown) 16 (3), 1975, 232-260.

1601   SCHLOSSER, KATESA.   Eingeborenenkirchen in Süd-und
        Südwestafrika. Ihre Geschichte und Sozialstruktur. Kiel:
        W. G. Mühlau 1958, 355 p., illus., bibl.
        [Chapters on Nicholas Bhengu, Cecil Hector and Indepen-
        dent Lutheran Mission Church of South Africa; South West
        African prophets; Mgijima, Lekganyane and Shembe.]

1602   SCHLOSSER, KATESA.   Die Sekten der Eingeborenen in Süd-und
        Südwestafrika als Manifestationen des Gegensatzes zwischen
        Weissen und Nichtweissen. Afrikanischer Heimatkalender
        (Windhoek) 1962, 101-107.

1603   SCHLOSSER, KATESA.   Profane Ursachen des Anschlusses an
        Separististenkirchen in Süd-und Südwestafrika, in E. Benz
        (ed.), item 137, 25-45.

1604   SUNDKLER, B[ENGT] G[USTAF] M[ALCOLM].   Chief and prophet in
        Zululand and Swaziland, in M. Fortes and G. Dieterlen
        (eds.), African systems of thought. London: Oxford
        University Press for the International African Institute
        1965, 276-290.

1605   SUNDKLER, BENGT [GUSTAF MALCOLM].   Messianisme zoulou? in:
        Centre d'Histoire de la Réforme et du Protestantisme,
        Université Paul Valéry-Montpellier, Les Missions Protes-
        tantes et l'Histoire: Actes du IIe Colloque 4-9 octobre
        1971. Paris: Société de l'Histoire du Protestantisme
        Française (Études des Colloques, 2) nd [1972] 75-82.
        Shortened version: Messies bantou? in C. J. Bleeker et
        al. (eds.), Ex Orbe religionum: studia Geo. Widengren
        (Numen, Supplementa, 21). Leiden: E. J. Brill 1972.
        246-251.
        [On the definition and kinds of messianism, and the
        movement to less messianic beliefs, with special reference
        to Isaiah Shembe and George Khambule.]

1606   SUNDKLER, BENGT [GUSTAF MALCOLM].   Zulu Zion and some Swazi
        Zionists (Studia Missionalia Upsaliensia XXIX). Lund:
        Gleerups/London: Oxford University Press 1976, 337 p.,
        map, illus.
        [Biographical studies of influential figures - both black
        and white - in the earlier stages of independent churches,
        and the history of subsequent changes in these bodies;
        based on family papers, archival sources, and extensive

Southern Africa

interviews; complementary to rather than a continuation
of Bantu prophets.]

1607   VERRYN, TREVOR D.   The role of women in traditional African
       religion.   Groenkloof, Pretoria: Ecumenical Research
       Unit 1972, 13 p.
            [P. 10, the frequency of women leaders in independent
       churches confirms the fact that women occupied important
       religious offices in traditional societies - usually as
       diviners.]

1608   WEAVER, EDWIN and WEAVER, IRENE.   Letters from Southern
       Africa.   Elkhart, Indiana: Southern Africa Taskforce
       Council of Mennonite Mission Board Secretaries 1974, 61 p.
            [Based largely on letters of E. and I. Weaver after
       visits to Swaziland, South Africa and Botswana in 1973,
       investigating independent churches; also interviews with
       D. Jacobs and J. Juhnke, and article by R. Ntoula on the
       Black Consciousness factor in the split between African
       Independent Churches Association and Christian Institute
       of Southern Africa.]

BOTSWANA

1609   GRANT, S.   Church and chief in the colonial era.   Botswana
       Notes and Records (Gaborone) 3, 1971, 59-63.
            [The Zion Christian Church of Lekganyane, from the
       1930s, in Botswana's history.]

1610   NDEBELE, JAMES.   Grassroots church in Botswana.   USPG Network
       (London) n.s. no. 40, Dec. 1975, p. 1.
            [The Anglican secretary of the Botswana Christian Council,
       interviewed in London, on Zionism's growth in Botswana.]

1611   SCHAPERA, I[SAAC] (ed.).   Ditirafalo tsa Merafe ya Batswana.
       Lovedale: Lovedale Press 1940.
            [Pp. 146-149, suppression of the Ethiopian developments
       in the BaNgwaketse Free Church in 1911.]

1612   SCHAPERA, ISAAC.   A short history of the BaNgwaketse.   African
       Studies (Johannesburg) 1 (1), 1942, 1-26, and republished
       separately.
            [Pp. 20-22, secession of the King Edward BaNgwaketse
       Free Church in 1902 from the London Missionary Society.]

BLACK AFRICA

1613   SCHAPERA, ISSAC. <u>Tribal innovators: Tswana chiefs and social</u>
        <u>change 1795-1940.</u> London: Athlone Press 1970, 278 p.,
        illus. (Originally published 1943).
        [Pp. 122-124, separatist churches discouraged by chiefs;
        pp. 237-238, "separatists": Mothowagae Motlogelwa, ex-
        L.M.S., King Edward BaNgwaketse Free Church, <u>ca</u>. 1901;
        Rev. Thomas Phiri's church, 1937, ex-D.R.C.; 1937; Zion
        African Church.]

1614   SCHAPERS, I[SAAC] (tr. and ed.). <u>The political annals of a</u>
        <u>Tswana tribe. Minutes of Ngwaketse Public Assemblies</u>
        <u>1910-1917.</u> Cape Town: the University 1947. Mimeo.
        [Pp. 23, 47, 57, 62f., "attempts to introduce new sects".]

1615   SCHIELE, M. Notes on the history of the D[utch] R[eformed]
        Mission at Mochudi. <u>Botswana Notes and Records</u> (Gaborone)
        4, 1972, 282-284.
        [P. 283, Thomas Phiri, ex-D.R.C. pastor, and the
        Bakgatla Free Church, 1937.]

See also item 1608.

LESOTHO

1616   ASHTON, [EDMUND] HUGH. <u>The Basuto</u>. London: Oxford Univer-
        sity Press for the International African Institute 1952,
        355 p., illus. 2nd. rev. ed., 1967.
        [P. 118, the Apostolic Church of Edward Motaung (also
        known as Tau, or Lion) among the Tlokoa - following at
        one time "extensive, but now exiguous".]

1617   CASALIS, A[LFRED]. Condemnation of W. Matita. <u>Leselinyana</u>
        (Morija, Lesotho Evangelical Church) 19, 1922, repeated
        in next issue, 20.
        [An official statement of the Synod of the (then) Paris
        Mission.]

1618   ELLENBERGER, VICTOR. <u>A century of mission work in Basutoland</u>
        <u>1833-1933.</u> Morija: Sesuto Book Depot 1938, 382 p. Fr.
        version, <u>Un siècle de mission au Lessouto (1833-1933)</u>.
        Paris: Société des Missions Évangéliques 1933, 447 p.
        [Pp. 322, 349, on Walter Matita's church.]

Southern Africa

1619   HALIBURTON, G[ORDON] M[acKAY]. Walter Matitta and Josiel
       Lefela: a prophet and a politician in Lesotho. Journal
       of Religion in Africa 7 (2), 1975, 111-131.
          [Ba-Nazare, "Nazarites' Association", founded by Matita
       later to develop into Kereke ea Moshoeshoe, "the Church of
       Moshoeshoe".]

1620   MOHONO, R[AYMOND] M[OLUPE]. Lengosa: Walter Matita [Walter
       Matita, (God's) Messenger]. Marija, Lesotho: Sesotho
       Book Depot 1974, 56 p.
          [Biography of Walter Matita, founder of Kereke ea
       Moshoeshoe (Church of Moshoeshoe) in the 1920s; in
       Sesotho.]

1621   PERROT, CLAUDE-HÉLÈNE. Un culte messianique chez les Sotho
       au milieu du XIXe siècle. Archives de Sociologie des
       Religions 9 (18), 1964, 147-152.
          [The influence of Molageni's [Mlanjeni's] Xhosa move-
       ment, 1850-1852.]

1622   PERROT, CLAUDE-HÉLÈNE. Les Sotho et les missionaires européens
       au XIXe siècle. Annales de l'Université d'Abidjan, série
       F, tome 2 (1), 1970, 191 p., illus., map.
          [Pp. 58, 60, 69, 70, 80, 82-88, Xhosa prophet Molageni
       [Mlanjeni]; in general on the revival of Sotho religion
       later in 19th c., hence prophetic or Ethiopian movements
       met little response in Basutoland, i.e. a "negative
       instance".]

1623   SHILLITO, E. François Coillard, a wayfaring man. London:
       Student Christian Movement 1923, 235 p.
          [P. 107, an early secession from the Paris mission,
       Basutoland, 1872; p. 228, on the return of Coillard's
       evangelists from Ethiopianism.]

1624   THOMPSON, LEONARD [M.] Survival in two worlds. Moshoeshoe of
       Lesotho 1786-1870. Oxford: Clarendon Press 1976, 389 p.,
       illus.
          [Pp. 150-153, the Xhosa prophet Molageni [Mlanjeni] and
       "revivalist movement" of 1850-51.]

See also items 103, 414, 1596.

NAMIBIA (SOUTH WEST AFRICA)

1625 BAUMANN, JULIUS. Mission und Oekumene in Südwestafrika, dargestellt am Lebenswerk von Hermann Heinrich Vedder (Oekumenische Studien 7). Leiden: E. J. Brill 1965, 168 p.
[Pp. 58-61, African Methodist Episcopal Church; pp. 23-127, Herero Church.]

1626 BERDROW, WILHELM. Afrikas Herrscher und Volkshelder. Essen: Berdrow 1908, vii + 245 p.
[Pp. 124-158, Witbooi and Stürmann.]

1627 BERICHTE DER RHEINISCHEN MISSION (Wuppertal-Barmen). Occasional articles on independent churches. See Vol. 67, 1910, 243f.; vol. 79, 1922, 189-190; vol. 80, 1923, 115-117; vol. 105, Feb. 1955, 33-35; vol. 105, Nov. 1955, 2-7; vol. 106, 1956, 148-151; vol. 106, Nov. 1956, 244-248; vol. 107, April 1957, 4-8; vol. 107, Jan. 1957, 2-8; vol. 110, 1960, 152-160; vol. 111, 1961, 143-147; vol. 112 (1), 1962, 43-48.

1628 BLEY, HELMUT. Social discord in South West Africa, 1894-1904, in P. Gifford and W. R. Louis, Britain and Germany in Africa. New Haven: Yale University Press 1967, 607-630.
[Pp. 617-620, the early relation of Moses and Hendrik Witbooi to German authorities, 1884-1894, and the first war, 1894; pp. 620-630, background to Herero and Witbooi risings of 1904-1907, especially the rinderpest epidemic of 1897, which shook the social and religious basis of the people.]

1629 BLEY, HELMUT. South-West Africa under German rule, 1894-1914. Leiden: E. J. Brill; Evanston: Northwestern University Press; London: Heinemann Educational Books; 1971, xxxi + 336 p., illus., maps.
[Based on University of Hamburg dissertation 1968. On H. Witbooi, see index, and especially pp. 27-44; Herero revolt, especially 142-152.]

1630 DE VILLIERS, W. B. The present state of the church in South West Africa. Johannesburg: Christian Institute for Southern Africa n.d. [1971?], 20 p. + map.
[A report to the Institute; pp. 17-18, the Oruuano Church among the Herero, as "the most important among the independent sects."]

Southern Africa

1631   DE VRIES, JOHANNES LUKAS. Die Religies van Suidwes-Afrika,
        by Dr. H. Vedder, en die Gevaar van die Sinkretisticse
        Bewegings. Protestant Theological Faculty of Brussels,
        thesis for Licenciate 1967, 167 p.

1632   FIRST, RUTH. South West Africa. Harmondsworth and Baltimore:
        Penguin Books 1963, 269 p., maps.
            [Pp. 32, 66, 73-75, 78, 81-82, H. Witbooi; pp. 245-246,
        conversation between German commissioner Goering and
        Witbooi, 1892, translated from Witbooi's journal; pp. 41-
        46, the Rehoboths or Bastards from late 18th c.]

1633   GROTH, SIEGFRIED. Das Ringen um die Einheit der Kirche Jesu
        Christi in Südwestafrika, in H. de Kleine and S. Groth
        (eds.), Um Einheit und Auftrag. Wuppertal: Verlag der
        Rheinischen Mission 1967, 9-38.
            [Includes separations from the Evangelical Lutheran
        Church, Nama, 1946, to African Methodist Episcopal Church;
        Herero, 1955, as Oruuano movement; Coloureds, 1958, as
        "Rhenish Bastard Congregation, Rehoboth".]

1634   GÜRICH, GEORG. Deutsch-Südwestafrika (Mitteilungen der
        Geographischen Gesellschaft in Hamburg 1891 bis 1892).
        Hamburg: Friederichsen 1895.
            [Pp. 128-137 on Witbooi.]

1635   KANDOVAZU, EHRENFRIED. Die Oruuano-Beweging. Karibib, South
        West Africa: Rynse Sending-Drukkery 1968, 40 p., illus.,
        Herero version, Oruuano rua pita vi? Same publisher 1968,
        46 p., illus.
            [An African sees missionary misunderstandings as a cause
        of the separation of the Herero Oruuano group in 1955.]

1636   KOMAMBO, KATITI. The development of African nationalism in
        South-West Africa. Présence Africaine 49 (1), 1964,
        p. 98 (Eng. edn. 21).
            [African Methodist Episcopal Church influence on
        national consciousness.]

1637   KREFT, H. H. G. The diary of Hendrik Witbooi. Journal of the
        South West Africa Scientific Society 2, 1926-27, 49-61.
            [By a director of education in S. W. Africa, setting
        forth the African view.]

1638   LEUTWEIN, THEODOR. Elf Jahre Gouverneur in Deutsch
        Südwestafrika. Berlin: Mittler & Sohn 1906, x + 589 p.
            [Pp. 298-306, 454-464, Witbooi, late 19th c., and
        Stürmann, Tswana prophet, early 20th c.]

Namibia (South West Africa)

1639   LOTH, HEINRICH. Die Ketzerbewegung in Südwestafrika, ihre
        Vorgeschichte und ihre Grenzen im Freiheitskrieg 1904 bis
        1906. Wissenschaftliche Zeitschrift der Karl-Marx-
        Universität Leipzig (Gesellschafts-und
        Sprachwissenschaftliche Reihe, 3), 9, 1959/60, 401-411.
        [Witbooi, set against background of South African
        Ethiopianism; with the text of two letters from German
        Colonial Office archives.]

1640   LOTH, HEINRICH. Die christliche Mission in Südwestafrika:
        Zur destruktiven Rolle der Rheinische Missionsgellschaft
        beim Prozess der Staatsbildung in Südwestafrika (1842-1893).
        Berlin: Akademie-Verlag 1963, 190 p.
        [A Marxist historian interprets the work of Jonkers
        Afrikaner (mid-19th c.) and Hendrik Witbooi for political
        independence in terms of alleged attempts to found inde-
        pendent churches. See review, Journal of Religion of
        Africa 1 (1), 1967, 96-98.]

1641   MENZEL, GUSTAV. Evangelische Lutherische Kirch in Südwest-
        afrika (Rheinische Missionskirche). Jahresbericht der
        Rheinischer Mission 1957. Wuppertal-Barmen: Rhenish
        Mission 1957, 28-38.
        [Racial situation in South West Africa which affects
        missions; also as one reason for the reactions leading to
        independent churches.]

1642   MENZEL, GUSTAV. Die Kirchen und die Rassen. Wuppertal-Barmen:
        Rhenish Mission 1960, 100 p.
        [Background of the rise of independent movements in
        South West Africa.]

1643   REEH, GUNTHER. The half-opened door. International Review
        of Missions no. 199=50 (July), 1961, 293-296.
        [The Herero Church in South West Africa, from 1956,
        reviving traditional customs.]

1644   SCHOLZ, HANS-GEORG. Junge Kirche und separatistische
        Bewegungen in Südwestafrika. Kirche in der Zeit
        (Dusseldorf) 16, 1961, 197-201.

1645   SCOTT, [GUTHRIE] MICHAEL. A time to speak. London: Faber
        and Faber 1968, 365 p.
        [Pp. 227-230, the Herero war; pp. 325-327, texts from
        letters of Witbooi to English magistrate, 1892, and between
        Witbooi and Governor Leutwein 1894; pp. 327-329, contem-
        porary accounts of the Herero massacre.]

1646   SUNDERMEIER, THEO. Zwei sektenkirchliche Bewegungen im alten
        Südwestafrika? Jonker Afrikaner und Hendrik Witbooi, in
        H. de Kleine (ed.), Zu einen Zeugnis über alle Volker!

Southern Africa

Jahresbericht der Rheinische Mission 1963-64. Wuppertal-Barmen: Rhenish Mission 1965, 55-94.
[A missionary scholar's response to some of the criticisms put forward by Loth (item 1640).]

1647   SUNDERMEIER, THEO. Gesetz und Gesetzlichkeit in den afrikanische Kirchen. Evangelische Theologie (Munich) 31 (2), 1971, 99-114; Eng. trans., The concept of law and the problem of legalism in the churches of Africa. Credo (Durban) 17 (1-2), 1970, 5-17.
[P. 108, the Truth Protestant Unity Church and the independent churches in general; p. 111, Kanambunga, a Herero "prophet"; an important study, with Zionist legalism discussed in context of the general problem.]

1648   SUNDERMEIER, THEO. Begegnung getrennter Bruder. Konferenz separatisticher Kirchenfuhrere in Otjimbingwe/SWA. In Die Welt-Fur Die Welt (Berichte der Vereinigten Evangelische Mission), 1972 (2), 1-3.
[Report of a conference with leaders of independent groups at Otjimbingue, July 1971.]

1649   SUNDERMEIER, THEO. Wir aber suchten Gemeinschaft: Kirchwerdung und Kirchentrennung in Südwestafrika (Erlangen Taschenbucher Band 21). Witten: Luther-Verlag 1973, 360 p., map.
[A major study with full documentation of sources; independent movements among the Nama and the Herero (Oruuano, St. John Apostolic Faith Mission, Church of Africa, the Church of the Oath of Christ, etc.), the Rehoboth Bastards; appendices of important documents.]

1650   VEDDER, HEINRICH. Das alte Südwestafrika. Berlin: Warneck 1934, xvi + 666 p. Eng. tr., South West Africa in early times... Tr. and ed. by C. G. Hall. London: Oxford University Press 1938, xv + 525 p., maps, illus.
[Includes a chapter, "Der Hendrik-Witbooi-Krieg", on Witbooi, late 19th c.]

1651   WIENECKE, W. A. Die Gemeinschaft der Ahnen und die Gemeinde Jesu Christi bei den Herero. University of Hamburg, doctoral thesis 1962.

1652   WITBOOI, HENDRIK. Die dagboek van Hendrik Witbooi, kaptein van die Witbooi-Hottentotte, 1884-1905 (Van Riebeeck Society Publications, 9). Cape Town: Van Riebeeck Society 1929, xxvii + 244 p., table, map.

South Africa

[Pp. vii-xxvi, introduction, in English, by Gustav
Voigts; diary is in a mixture of Dutch and Afrikaans as
written by Witbooi, with notes in Afrikaans.]

SOUTH AFRICA

1653   [AFRICAN INDEPENDENT CHURCHES' MOVEMENT]. Inkonzo
        Yokusindiswa Komuntu Emabandleni ka Jesu Kristu Eafrika.
        N.p., no publisher, n.d. [1973], 20 p. Mimeo.
            [In Zulu: combined Catechism and Agenda of the Movement,
        formed July 1973, under Bishop C. J. Bhengeza of V 560
        Umlazi Township, 4066 Ntokozweni, near Durban.]

1654   AFRICAN ORTHODOX CHURCH (South Africa). Its declaration of
        faith. Constitution and Canons and Episcopate with a sum-
        mary of proceedings of the First General Synod. Beacons-
        field, Cape Province: the Church n.d. [?1950], 82 p.,
        photos.

1655   AXENFELD, KARL. Die allegemeine südafrikanische
        Missionskonferenz zu Johannesburg vom 13 bis 20 Juli 1904.
        Allegemeine Missionszeitschrift (Berlin) 32, 1905, 13-29.
            [Ethiopianism, as discussed at the conference.]

1656   BACK TO GOD (East London). Magazine sponsored and published
        by N. B. H. Bhengu. Vol. 1 (2) appeared in July 1955.

1657   BANTU (Pretoria). Occasional articles, in Government publicity
        magazine, on independent churches, usually illustrated.
        See, e.g., 6, June, 1957, pp. 33-34, on N. Bhengu; 9,
        September, 1959, pp. 101-108, on legal recognition of
        independent churches; 10 (10), 1963, pp. 534-537, the
        Nazarites; 12 (3), 1965, pp. 140-142, St. John's Apostolic
        Faith Mission; 12 (6), 1965, pp. 238-241 and 244-247, Zion
        Christian Church; 13 (12), 1966, pp. 380-383, statistical
        material and a selective list of independent churches.

1658   BAUDERT, S. Äthiopische Splitterkirchen in Südafrika. Neue
        Allegemeine Missionszeitschrift 15, 1938, 97-104, 138-145.

1659   BECHLER, THEODOR. Unabhängigkeitsbewegungen der Farbigen in
        Südafrika. Evangelisches Missions-Magazin (Basel) N.F.
        47, 1903, 265-280, 324-341. Published separately (Basel
        Missions-Studien, 18), Basel: Basler Missionsbuchhandlung
        1903, 40 p.

Southern Africa

1660   BECKEN, HANS-JÜRGEN. Eine zionistische Sekte in Südafrika.
        Hermannsburger Missionsblatt (Hermannsburg) 104, 1964,
        157ff.
            [The Zion Congregational Church in Natal.]

1661   BECKEN, HANS-JÜRGEN. The constitution of the Lutheran Bapedi
        Church of 1892. Bulletin of the Society for African Church
        History (Aberdeen) 2 (2), 1966, 180-189.

1662   BECKEN, HANS-JÜRGEN. The Nazareth Baptist Church of Shembe,
        in item 1797, 10 pp.
            [History, liturgy and theology, by a Lutheran participant
        in the Church's activities, which are regarded as non-
        messianic.]

1663   BECKEN, HANS-JÜRGEN. Auf eine Missionsstation der Shembe
        Sekte. Hermannsburger Missionsblatt (Hermannsburg) 107,
        1967, 38ff.
            [The annual retreat with manual labour of the Nazareth
        Baptist Church.]

1664   BECKEN, HANS-JÜRGEN. On the Holy Mountain: a visit to the
        new year's festival of the Nazaretha Church on Mount
        Nhlangakazi, 14 January 1967. Journal of Religion in
        Africa (Leiden) 1 (2), 1967, 138-149, illus.

1665   BECKEN, HANS-JÜRGEN. Zionistischer Kirchentag auf KwaLinda.
        Hermannsburger Missionsblatt (Hermannsburg) 107, 1967,
        102ff., illus.
            [The Easter festival of the Christian Catholic Apostolic
        Church in Zion.]

1666   BECKEN, HANS-JÜRGEN. Patterns of organizational structures
        in the African independent churches movement in South
        Africa. Africana Marburgensia (Marburg) 1 (2), 1968,
        17-24.
            [Also useful on statistics and growth.]

1667   BECKEN, HANS-JÜRGEN. Liturgisches Verhalten in südafrikanischen
        Bantukirchen. Evangelische Missions-Zeitschrift
        (Stuttgart) N.F., 26 (3), 1969, 163-169.

1668   BECKEN, HANS-JÜRGEN. Die Gemeinde des Nadelöhrs. Zulu-Text
        mit Übersetzung und Anmerkungen. Afrika und Übersee
        (Hamburg) 53 (3-4), 1970, 229-240.
            [The story of Johannes Sithole and his establishment of
        a new independent church.]

BLACK AFRICA

South Africa

1669   BECKEN, H[ANS]-J[ÜRGEN]. Healing in the African independent
       churches. Credo (Rustenburg, Transvaal) 18 (2), 1971,
       14–21.
       [Includes description of a healing service in the African
       Gospel Church, Msinga, Natal.]

1670   BECKEN, HANS-JÜRGEN. The African independent churches' under-
       standing of the ministry, in D. J. Bosch (ed.),
       Ampsbediening in Afrika (Lux Mundi 5). Pretoria: N. G.
       Kerkboekhandel 1972, 134–144.
       [An examination of ministers' qualifications and their
       accounts of their divine call.]

1671   BECKEN, HANS-JÜRGEN. Bischöfe studieren. Ein Bericht aus
       Umpumulo. Hermannsburger Missionsblatt (Hermannsburg) 112
       (10), 1972, 190–193.
       [On the theological training of bishops from African
       independent churches at the Lutheran Theological College,
       Mapumulo.]

1672   BECKEN, HANS-JÜRGEN. A healing church in Zululand: "The New
       Church Step to Jesus Christ Zion in South Africa". Journal
       of Religion in Africa (Leiden) 4 (3), 1972, 213–222.
       [Founded in 1962 by A. J. Mdakanna, with a few small
       congregations in Natal.]

1673   BECKEN, HANS-JÜRGEN. Missiongemeinsam mit unabhängigen
       afrikanischen Kirchen. Hermannsburger Missionsblatt
       (Hermannsburg) 112 (5), 1972, 96–100.
       [Outlines the possibilities of co-operation with the
       Lutheran Church; includes a translation of a Bible-study
       sheet distributed by the Christian Catholic Apostolic
       Church in Zion of South Africa (Bantu).]

1674   BECKEN, HANS-JÜRGEN. Theologie der Heilung. Das Heilen in
       den Afrikanischen Unabhängigen Kirchen in Südafrika
       (Verkundigung und Verantwortung, I). Hermannsburg:
       Verlag Missionshandlung Hermannsburg 1972, 294 p.
       [Based on Heidelberg University doctoral dissertation
       1970, 2 vols, 202 + 159 pp. Mimeo.]

1675   BECKEN, HANS-JÜRGEN. Schwarze Theologie in Südafrika.
       Evangelische Missions-Zeitschrift (Korntal) N.F. 30 (2),
       1973, 75–83.
       [The Black Theology question from the independent church
       perspective, as represented by V. M. Mayatula of the Bantu
       Bethlehem Christian Apostolic Church of South Africa,
       trained at the Lutheran Theological College, Mapumulo.]

BIBLIOGRAPHY OF NEW RELIGIOUS MOVEMENTS IN PRIMAL SOCIETIES

Southern Africa

1676   BECKEN, HANS-JÜRGEN. Erneuerungsbewegungen in der
       vorchrislichen Zulu-Religion in Südafrika. Evangelische
       Missions-Zeitschrift (Korntal) N.F. 31 (4), 1974, 161-169.
       [Innovative movements in pre-Christian African religion.]

1677   BECKEN, HANS-JÜRGEN. Healing in the African independent
       churches. Lutheran Quarterly 27 (3), 1975, 234-243.
       [Amended version of his item 1669.]

1678   BERGLUND, AXEL-IVAR. Rituals of an African Zionist Church.
       Johannesburg: University of Witwatersrand African
       Studies Programme Occasional Paper 3, December 1967. 13 p.
       Mimeo.
       [A Lutheran missionary on the Zion Jerusalem Church of
       the Twelve Apostles - description and analysis of rites
       and symbols.]

1679   BERGLUND, AXEL-IVAR. The rituals of the independent church
       movement and our liturgy, in item 1797, 13 p. Shortened
       German version, Sekte oder Gottesvolk? Ein Afrikanischer
       Gottesdienst. Das Wort in der Welt (Hamburg) 47 (3), 1967,
       41-45; idem 47 (4), 1967, 57-61, illus.

1680   BERGLUND, AXEL-IVAR. Concepts of water and baptism amongst
       some African Zionist movements. Credo: Lutheran Theo-
       logical Journal for Southern Africa 16 (1), 1969, 4-11.
       [A sympathetic description and critique.]

1681   BERGLUND, AXEL-IVAR. Kring vatten och dopritual i en
       sydafrikans profetrörelse. Norsk Tidsskrift for Misjon
       24 (3), 1970, 161-175.
       [Water and baptismal ritual in the movement of Prophet
       Emmanuel Ngema, Upumulo.]

1682   BERGLUND, AXEL-IVAR. Crisis in missions - a pastoral liturgical
       challenge. Lutheran Quarterly (Kutztown, Pennsylvania) 25
       (1), 1973, 22-33.
       [A Zionist Sunday healing service described and
       discussed.]

1683   BERTHOUD, ALEX L. The missionary situation in South Africa.
       International Review of Missions no. 193=49 (Jan.), 1960,
       83-90.
       [Suggestion for an ecumenical evangelical centre open
       to "separatist churches" for training leaders.]

1684   BEYERHAUS, PETER. The African independent church movement as
       missionary challenge, in item 1797. 6 p.
       [A sympathetic survey, with theoretical implications.]

232

BLACK AFRICA

South Africa

1685 BEYERHAUS, PETER. Whither from here? in item 1797. 8 p.
Reprinted as: An approach to the African independent
church movement. Ministry (Morija, Lesotho) 9 (2), 1969,
74-80.
[A survey of the papers in item 1797, with suggested
classification into "separatist churches, Christian sects,
and nativistic (pagan) movements".]

1686 BEYERHAUS, PETER. The Christian encounter with Afro-Messianic
movements. The possessio-syncretism axis illustrated from
South Africa, in T. Yamamori and C. R. Taber (eds.),
Christopaganism or indigenous Christianity. South
Pasadena: William Carey Library 1975, 77-95.
[Based on South African movements, interpreted as pagan
syncretisms with a "black messiah"; similar outlook to that
of Oosthuizen.]

1687 BLUE BOOKS ON NATIVE AFFAIRS (Government, Cape of Good Hope).
Cited by Shepperson and Price, item 1473, as an important
source on Ethiopianism. See especially 1898, 34, 44-45;
1899, 16, 118; 1900, 4, 25, 49; 1902, 24, 54, 84; 1903,
34, 44-45; 1904, 30, 123; 1905, 22, 76; 1906, 7, 22, 32,
53-54; 1907, 17, 37; 1908, 30, 40.

1688 BOND, JOHN S. W. Pentecostalism in the Pentecostal churches.
Journal of Theology for Southern Africa no. 7, June 1974,
10-22.
[Pp. 14, 22, critical attitude to Zionists, as not truly
"pentecostal"; pp. 21-22, outline of the various pentecostal
bodies in South Africa.]

1689 BOURQUIN, W. Irrungen und Wirrungen in Silo. Missionsblatt
der Brudergemeinde (Herrnhut) 87 (4), 1913, 73-80.
[On Enoch Mgijima.]

1690 BRANDEL-SYRIER, MIA. Black woman in search of God. London:
Lutterworth 1962, 251 p., illus.
[The "Manyanos" - women's organizations within churches
of all kinds in South Africa.]

1691 BRIDGMAN, F. B. The Ethiopian movement and other independent
factors characterized by a national spirit, in Report of
Proceedings, First General Missionary Conference for South
Africa, Johannesburg, 1904. Johannesburg: Argus 1904,
162-177.
[An American missionary on the origins of independent
churches and in criticism of their activities. Pp. 177-183,
the Conference discussion and resolutions.]

233

Southern Africa

1692   BROOKES, EDGAR H[ARRY]. The colour problems of South Africa.
        Lovedale: Lovedale Press 1934, viii + 237 p.
        [Pp. 34-35, 161-162, 170, "separatist church movement";
        Appendix I: list of 323 Native separatist churches as at
        4 August 1932.]

1693   BROWN, KENNETH I[RVING]. An African experiment in Christian
        union. The Christian (Disciples of Christ) 103 (4), 1965,
        4-5; idem 103 (5), 1965, 8-9, 24.
        [A union between the Holy Catholic Apostolic Church in
        Zion, and the Conference of African Christian Churches of
        the Disciples of Christ, in South Africa, under the United
        Christian Missionary Society, 1961.]

1694   BROWN, KENNETH I[RVING]. A week-end with an African indepen-
        dent church in Natal. Ministry (Morija, Lesotho) 11 (1),
        1971, 8-16.
        [The Catholic Christian Apostolic Church in Zion.]

1695   BROWN, KENNETH I[RVING]. The independent churches of South
        Africa: a progress report. Religion in Life 41 (1),
        1972, 79-88.
        [On the African Independent Churches' Association - its
        origins, seminary, correspondence and refresher courses.]

1696   BROWNLEE, CHARLES. Reminiscences of Kaffir life and history.
        Lovedale: Lovedale Mission Press 1896, 403 p.
        [Pp. 135-170, "The cattle-killing delusion" - an eye-
        witness account of the Xhosa movement of Nonquas [Nongqause]
        and Mchlakaza [Mhlakaza] 1856-57 (contributed by
        Mrs. Brownlee).]

1697   BUCHAN, JOHN. Prester John. New York: Nelson 1910,
        vi + 376 p.
        [A widely-read novel portraying an Ethiopian-led rebel-
        lion in South Africa which was cited as a prediction of
        the Chilembwe rebellion in Nyasaland.]

1698   BUDAZA, G. S. The Native Separatist Church Movement.
        University of South Africa, M.A. thesis 1948.
        [By an African; mainly on Limba's Church of Christ.]

1699   BURCKHARDT, G. Die Tembukirche des Kaffernhaüptlings
        Dalindyebo. Die Evangelischen Missionen (Gütersloh) 2,
        1896, 235-237.
        [Nehemiah Tile's church.]

BLACK AFRICA

1700 BURKE, FRED [H.]. Missionary to mavericks. World Vision
      Magazine (Monrovia, California) 11 (7), 1967, 10-12, 28,
      illus. Also as: Ministry to Ministers, The Methodist
      (N.S.W.) 8, 1967, 4; idem 15, 1967, 7, 10. Also in
      Monthly Newsletter about Evangelism (Geneva, World Council
      of Churches) 9 (1), 1966-67, 1-5. Mimeo.
      [An interview with Burke, an American Assemblies of God
      missionary supplying biblical correspondence courses to
      ministers of independent churches.]

1701 BURROWS, N. R. (ed.). Baumannville: a study of an urban
      African community. Capetown: Oxford University Press
      1959, viii + 79 p.
      [Pp. 58-63, place of independent churches in a small
      community near Durban.]

1702 CAMERON, W[ILLIAM] M. The Ethiopian movement and the Order of
      Ethiopia. The East and the West (London, S.P.G.) 2 (8),
      1904, 375-397.
      [Relations with the Church of the Province of South
      Africa.]

1703 CHRISTOFERSEN, ARTHUR FRIDJOF. Adventuring with God. The
      story of the American Board Mission in South Africa.
      Durban: Inanda Seminary 1967, 183 p.
      [Includes sympathetic account of the separations of the
      Zulu Congregational Church and the African Congregational
      Church.]

1704 CHURCHILL, RHONA. White man's God. London: Hodder &
      Stoughton 1962, 192 p., illus.
      [Pp. 84-97, an English journalist's visits to the
      Apostles Zionist Church, and to Mrs. Nku, of the St. John's
      Apostolic Faith Mission Church.]

1705 COAN, J[OSEPHUS] R[OOSEVELT]. The expansion of missions of the
      African Methodist Church in South Africa 1896-1908.
      Hartford Seminary Foundation, Ph.D. dissertation 1961.

1706 COMAROFF, JEAN. Barolong cosmology: a study of religious
      pluralism in a Tswana town. University of London, Ph.D.
      dissertation (Social anthropology) 1974, 408 p., maps,
      tables, appendices.
      [Study made in Mafeking. Interaction of traditional and
      Christian belief systems in all churches, including
      "African independent" and "Zionist" churches; pp. 377-382,
      listing of churches of all types in the area; p. 86,
      sephiri ("secret church" - a healing "church" whose members
      are also members of white-affiliated churches.]

235

Southern Africa

1707   COPE, JACK. The fair house. London: MacGibbon and Kee 1955.
       [Fiction; "the most important treatment by a South
       African novelist of the Ethiopian scare".]

1708   CORY, GEORGE E. The rise of South Africa, Vol. vi, chapters
       one to six. Archives Yearbook for South African History
       2 (1). Capetown: Government Printer 1939. Published as
       separate volume, Pretoria: the Archives Year Book 1940;
       facsimile reprint, Capetown: Struik 1965.
       [Pp. 23-37 (26-42 in 1940 pub. and reprint), the Xhosa
       cattle-killing.]

1709   CRAFFORD, D[IONNE]. Die Heiligheidsbeweging en die Kerk van
       die Nasarener in Suid-Afrika. Ned[erduitse] Gere[formeerde]
       Teologiese Tydskrif 13 (1), 1972, 50-59.

1710   CREDO VUSA'MAZULU MUTWA. My people: the incredible writings
       of Credo Vusa'mazulu Mutwa. London: A. Blond 1969,
       257 p.
       [Ch. 16, "The national suicide of the Xhosa" - an
       account of the cattle-killing, Mhlakaza and Nongqause,
       by a Zulu traditional healer.]

1711   DAVIDSON, A[POLLON] B[ORISOVICH]. Sozdaniye Afrikanskogo
       Nationalnogo Kongressa. Narody Azii i Afriki (Moscow) 6,
       1962, 78-88.
       [Recognizes the independent Bantu churches in South
       Africa as having prepared the way for Congress, and sup-
       plied some officers.]

1712   DLEPU, B. S. Native separatist church movements, in Report,
       Sixth Missionary Conference of South Africa 1925. Cape
       Town: Nasionale Pers 1925, 110-118.

1713   DREYFUS, F. Nationalisme noir et séparatisme religieux en
       Afrique du Sud. Le Mois en Afrique (Paris) 19, juillet
       1967, 12-32.

1714   DRUM (Johannesburg). Zion Christian Church. Drum 4 (7),
       1954, 7-9, illus.
       [Edward Lekganyane's church at "Zion City Moria",
       N. Transvaal.]

1715   DRUM/POST (Johannesburg). Followers in mourning for Bishop
       Eddie. Drum/Post 1967, Nov. 5, 7, illus.
       [Leader of the Zion Christian Church.]

1716   DUBB, A[LLIE] A[BRAHAM]. Tribalism in the African church, in
       A. A. Dubb (ed.), The multitribal society. Lusaka:
       Rhodes-Livingstone Institute 1962, 111-119.
       [Pp. 115-119 on South African "separatist churches".]

1717   DUBB, ALLIE A[BRAHAM]. Community of the Saved. An African
       Revivalist Church in the East Cape. Johannesburg:
       Witwatersrand University Press for African Studies Insti-
       tute 1976, xvii + 175 p., illus., figs., tables, bibl.
       [Nicholas Bhengu's African Assembly of God in East
       London.]

1718   DUBE, JOHN L[ANGALIBALELE]. U-Shembe. Pietermaritsburg:
       Shooter and Shuter 1936, 117 p.
       [A life of Shembe, in Zulu.]

1719   DU PLESSIS, JOHANNES C. Die oorsprong van die Ethiopiese
       Kerkbeweging in Suid-Afrika. Het Zoeklicht 2, 1924,
       196-201, 232-238, 274-279.
       [The origin and growth of independent churches; the
       basic cause found in factors encouraging individualism.]

1720   DU PLESSIS, JOHANNES C. Die oorsake van Separatisme in die
       Sendingvelde van Suid-Afrika. Op die Horison
       (Stellenbosch) 1 (1), 1939, 39-42; idem 1 (2), 1939, 56-60.

1721   DU TOIT, ANTHONIE EDUARD. The Cape frontier: a study of
       native policy with special reference to the years 1847-1866.
       Archives Yearbook for South African History 17 (1). Cape
       Town: Government Printer 1954.
       [See pp. 99-104, 118-119, and index "cattle-killing" for
       this Xhosa movement.]

1722   DU TOIT, BRIAN MURRAY. Emakhahleni - a revivalistic cult.
       Communications from the African Studies Center, University
       of Florida 1 (1), 1970, 41-58.
       [A revival of traditional Zulu religion from 1937, with
       healing emphasis, communication with ancestors, and slight
       Christian influence.]

1723   DU TOIT, BRIAN MURRAY. Religious revivalism among urban Zulu,
       in E. J. de Jager (ed.), Man: anthropological essays pre-
       sented to O. F. Raum. Cape Town: C. Struik 1971, 80-103.
       [Theoretical discussion; Zulu prophet John Maphithini
       Thusi (d. 1964), his healing cult, emakhahleni, at
       Malukazi, with creed similar to Shembe's, and Shaka and
       ancestors as basic reference points.]

Southern Africa

1724   DU TOIT, H[ENDRIK] D[ANIEL] A[LPHONSO]. Die Kerstening van
        die Bantoe. Pretoria: N. G. Kerk-Boekhandel 1967, 368 p.
        [A text-book on missiology; pp. 238-248, on "separatism"
        as "obstruction against mission".]

1725   EBERHARDT, JACQUELINE [ROUMEGUÈRE]. Messianismes en Afrique du
        Sud. Archives de Sociologie des Religions 4, juillet-déc.
        1957, 31-56.
        [A survey of independent churches, all called
        "messianismes", with special attention to the Zion Christian
        Church and the Nazarite Church.]

1726   EBERHARDT, JACQUELINE [ROUMEGUÈRE]. Christianity and African
        separatist churches in South Africa. Occasional Papers
        (London: International Missionary Council) no. 4, January
        1960, 9 p. Mimeo.

1727   EISELEN, W. M. Christianity and the religious life of the
        Bantu, in I. Schapera (ed.), Western civilization and the
        Natives of South Africa. London: Routledge 1934,
        xiv + 312 p.
        [Pp. 73-76, reasons for separatist movements.]

1728   ELLIESSEN-KLIEFOTH, HELMUT. Entstehung und Gestalt der
        südafrikanischen Sekten. Kiel: Evangelical Lutheran
        Church and Kiel University thesis 1966.
        [Uses secondary material, including a number of unpub-
        lished papers.]

1729   ETHIOPIAN CATHOLIC CHURCH IN ZION. Constitutions and Canons
        of the Ethiopian Catholic Church in Zion. Bloemfontein:
        the Church 1918.
        [Founded by S. J. Brander in 1904, by secession from the
        African Methodist Episcopal Church.]

1730   ETHIOPIAN CATHOLIC CHURCH OF SOUTH AFRICA. Constitutions of
        the Ethiopian Church of South Africa. N.p.: the Church,
        n.d. [?1914].
        [With a brief historical preface.]

1731   FEDDERKE, HEINI. What shall we preach to Zionists? in item
        1797, 10 p.
        [The need for a missionary approach to this "new heathen
        religion".]

1732   FERNANDEZ, JAMES W[ILLIAM]. Zulu Zionism. Natural History
        [New York] June-July 1971, 44-51, illus.
        [A popular account; excellent colour photographs.]

1733   FERNANDEZ, JAMES W[ILLIAM]. The precincts of the prophet: a
       day with Johannes Galilee Shembe. Journal of Religion in
       Africa (Leiden) 5 (1), 1973, 32-53.

1734   FLORIN, HANS W. Lutherans in South Africa. Report on a
       survey 1964-1965. Durban: Evangelical Lutheran Church
       1965.
           [Ch. 6 deals with "The Sects - their witness and appeal".]

1735   FRANZELLI, GIUSEPPE. Lo sono il Messia. Nigrizia (Verona),
       86 (7-8), 1968, 4-9, illus.
           [Shembe's Nazarite Church.]

1736   GERDENER, G[USTAV] B[ERNHARD] A[UGUST]. Recent developments
       in the South African mission field. Pretoria:
       N. G. Kerk-Uitgewers 1958, 286 p.
           [Pp. 188-206, the trends of separatism and independence.]

1737   GREEN, E. M. Native unrest in South Africa. The Nineteenth
       Century (London) no. 273=46 (Nov.), 1899, 708-716.
           [Pp. 708-710, a prophet in Tembuland 1899; pp. 710-713,
       Ethiopianism and Dwane.]

1738   GRESCHAT, HANS-JÜRGEN. Eine "vorathiopische" süd-afrikanische
       Kirche: die Sezession der Ba-Luther im Pediland im Jahre
       1890, in G. Müller and W. Zeller (eds.), Glaube, Geist,
       Geschichte: Festschrift für Ernst Benz... Leiden: Brill
       1967, 532-541.

1739   GRUBB, KENNETH S. (ed.). The Christian handbook of South
       Africa. Lovedale: Lovedale Press for the Christian
       Council of South Africa 1938, viii + 290 p.
           [Pp. 145-158, list of "Native Separatist Churches"
       supplied by the Native Affairs Department.]

1740   HANCOCK, [WILLIAM] KEITH. Smuts: the fields of force:
       1919-1950. London: Cambridge University Press 1968,
       xiii + 590 p., illus.
           [Ch. 5, pp. 89-110, "Bulhoek and Bondelzwarts".]

1741   HASELBARTH, H. The Zion Christian Church of Edward Lekganyane,
       in item 1797, 16 p.
           [See also P. Beyerhaus (ed.), item 141.]

1742   HEWSON, LESLIE A. An introduction to South African Methodists.
       Cape Town: Standard Press n.d. [1951], 114 p.
           [Ch. 19, pp. 91-96: African disunity and Christian co-
       operation, on the relationship of Methodism to Bantu
       independents.]

Southern Africa

1743   HEWSON, L[ESLIE] A. (ed.). Cottesloe consultation.
       Johannesburg: South African Member Churches of the World
       Council of Churches n.d. [1961], 100 p.
       [The report of a consultation in 1960 at Cottesloe,
       Johannesburg; pp. 27-30, on causes of, and ways of meeting,
       the "separatist sects".]

1744   HIGGINS, EDWARD. The sociology of religion in South Africa.
       Archives de Sociologie des Religions 31=16 (janvier-juin),
       1971, 143-164.
       [Pp. 145-151, statistics and graphs concerning
       separatists' growth 1921-1960.]

1745   HILL, F. Native separatist movements and their relation to the
       problem of evangelization, in Report, Sixth General Mis-
       sionary Conference of South Africa, 1925. Cape Town:
       Nasionale Pers 1925, 110-118.
       [On the causes of these movements.]

1746   HINCHLIFF, PETER [BINGHAM]. The Anglican Church in South
       Africa. London: Darton, Longman and Todd 1963, 266 p.
       [Pp. 200-205, The Order of Ethiopia.]

1747   HINCHLIFF, PETER [BINGHAM]. The Church in South Africa
       (Church History Outlines). London: S.P.C.K. for the
       Church Historical Society 1968, 116 p.
       [Ch. 14, "Ethiopianism: Christianity and politics";
       pp. 100, 102, 104, separatist sects. An historical
       survey.]

1748   HORRELL, MURIEL (comp.). A survey of race relations in South
       Africa. Johannesburg: South African Institute of Race
       Relations, annually.
       [E.g., 1952-53, pp. 56-57, separatist church sites;
       1955-56, pp. 215-216, recognition of separatist churches;
       1957-58, pp. 39-40, prosecution; 1958-59, pp. 33-34,
       church sites; 1959-60, pp. 27, 128-129, union of separ-
       atist churches and relations with government; 1961,
       pp. 133-134, church sites; 1967, pp. 28-29, relationship
       of the Christian Institute of Southern Africa and the
       African Independent Churches Association.]

1749   HUNTER, MONICA [WILSON]. Reaction to conquest. London:
       Oxford University Press for the International African
       Institute (1936), 1961, xxiv + 582 p.
       [Pp. 349, 543, 562-565, "independent native churches",
       especially Enoch Mgijima.]

BLACK AFRICA

1750   JABAVU, D[AVIDSON] D[ON] T[ENGO]. Lessons from the Israelite
        episode. South African Outlook (Lovedale) July 1921,
        105-106.
        [On Enoch Mgijima; the origins of his "AmaSirayeli"
        church, and the reasons for his success; the Bulhoek
        tragedy.]

1751   JABAVU, D[AVIDSON] D[ON] T[ENGO]. An African indigenous
        church (a plea for its establishment in South Africa).
        Lovedale: Lovedale Press 1942, 16 p.

1752   JACOTTET, É[DOUARD]. Native churches and their organization,
        in Report of Proceedings, First General Missionary Confer-
        ence for South Africa, 1904. Johannesburg: Argus 1904,
        108-133.
        [A missionary of the Paris Mission suggests a progressive
        withdrawal of European control, in the interests of an
        indigenous church incorporating the truth in Ethiopianism.]

1753   JACOTTET, É[DOUARD]. The Ethiopian Church and the Missionary
        Conference of Johannesburg. An open letter to the...
        special conference of the African Methodist Episcopal
        Church held at Pretoria in August 1904. Morija [Lesotho]:
        Morija Printing Office 1904, 30 p. Also printed as an
        appendix to the Report of Proceedings...1904, preceding
        item.
        [The missionary attitude to independent churches.]

1754   JORDAN, A. C. Towards an African literature IX: The tale of
        Nongqawuse: "The cause of the cattle-killing of the
        Nongqawuse period". Africa South (Capetown) 3 (4), 1959,
        111-115.
        [Recording of oral tradition by an African scholar.]

1755   KELLERMAN, Abraham Gerhardus. Profetisme in Suid Afrika in
        akkulturasie perspektief. Voorborg: Zanoni 1964, 282 p.
        Offset.
        [Utrecht University doctoral dissertation with English
        summary. Based on Sundkler.]

1756   KIERNAN, J. P. The changing role of (independent) African
        churches, with particular reference to South Africa.
        University of Manchester, M.A. thesis (Social Anthropol-
        ogy) 1967.
        [A Roman Catholic priest traces the changes from
        nationalistic movements towards independent churches,
        using secondary sources.]

Southern Africa

1757   KIERNAN, J. P. Preachers, prophets and women in Zion. University of Manchester, Ph.D. thesis (Social Anthropology) 1972.

1758   KIERNAN, J. P. Where Zionists draw the line: a study of religious exclusiveness in an African township. African Studies (Johannesburg) 33 (2), 1974, 79-90.
       [Surveys the accounts of causes of Bantu independent churches; exclusiveness is not based on race, and is against fellow Africans.]

1759   KIERNAN, J. P. Old wine in new wineskins. A critical appreciation of Sundkler's leadership types in the light of further research. African Studies (Johannesburg) 34 (3), 1975, 193-201.

1760   KROPF, A. Das Völk der Xosa-Kaffern in östlichen Südafrika nach seiner Geschichte, Eigenart, Verfassung und Religion. Berlin: Berlin Evangelische Missionsgesellschaft 1899, viii + 209 p.
       [Pp. 49f., Nxele; pp. 29f., 66-71, 96, Mlandscheni [Mlanjeni]; pp. 30f., 60, 71f., 95, Mchlakaza [Mhlakaza] and Nonques [Nongqause].]

1761   KROPF, A. Ntsikana, der Erstling aus den Kaffern und ein Prophet unter seinem Völk. Neue Missionsschriften (Berlin) 2, 1891.
       [Early 19th century prophet among the Ngquika (Gaika).]

1762   KRÜGER, F. Verselbständigung der Bantukirchen in Südafrika? Neue Allgemeine Missionszeitschrift 15, 1938, 111-119.

1763   KRUGER, M[ECHIEL] A[NDRIES]. Die Zion Christian Church - n' Religieuse Bantoe-beweging in 'n tyd von Ontwrigting? University of Potchefstroom, Th.M. dissertation 1971, 199 p.
       [The church of Lekganyane.]

1764   KRUGER, M[ECHIEL] A[NDRIES]. De Zion Christian Church. Die Oes (Noordbrug, South Africa) 14 (4), 1971, 14-15; idem 15 (1), 1972, 8-9; idem 15 (2), 1973, 5-6.
       [Series of articles on the church led by Edward Lekganyane. Second article discusses their conception of the Holy Spirit and third article their conception of Jesus Christ.]

1765   KUPER, LEO. An African bourgeoisie. New Haven: Yale University Press 1965, 452 p.

[Pp. 204-206, separatist churches; pp. 311-312,
Ethiopianism; pp. 136-137, 311-316, Zionism; examples from
Durban.]

1766   LEA, ALLEN. Native separatist churches, in J. D. Taylor (ed.),
Christianity and the Natives of South Africa: a Yearbook
of South African missions. Lovedale: Lovedale Press
[c. 1928] 73-85. [Cf. item 1869.]

1767   LEA, ALLEN. The Native Separatist Church Movement in South
Africa. Cape Town & Johannesburg: Juta n.d. [1927],
84 p.
[Origin, causes, and features of the movement; the
attitude of older churches and Government.]

1768   LEE, A. W. Charles Johnson of Zululand. London: Society for
the Propagation of the Gospel 1930, 256 p.
[Pp. 108-109, why Nqutu District was not much affected
by separatist churches.]

1769   LEE, SYDNEY GILMORE M. Spirit possession among the Zulu, in
J. Beattie and J. Middleton (eds.), Spirit Mediumship and
society in Africa. London: Routledge and Kegan Paul
1969, 128-156.
[Pp. 130, 152-156, divination and possession in Zionist
churches.]

1770   LEENHARDT, MAURICE. Le mouvement éthiopien au Sud de l'Afrique
de 1896 à 1899. Cahors: printed by A. Couesland 1902,
128 p.
[A notable pioneering work; based on his B.Th. thèse,
Moutauban 1899.]

1771   LEHMANN, FRIEDRICH R[UDOLF]. Eine Form der Religionsmischung
in Südafrika. Die AmaNazaretha-Kirche in Natal, in Von
fremden Völkern und Kulturen. Beiträge zur Völkerkunde.
Düsseldorf: Droste 1955, 184-193.

1772   LENNOX, J. The relation of European and native churches, in
Report of Proceedings, Third General Missionary Conference
for South Africa, 1909. Cape Town: Townshend, Taylor and
Snashall 1909, 82-90.
[Also pp. 90-92, the ensuing discussion.]

1773   LININGTON, P. A. A summary of the reports of certain pre-
union commissions on native affairs: church separatist
movements. Pretoria: 1924.

Southern Africa

1774   LORAM, C. T. The separatist church movement. <u>International
       Review of Missions</u> no. 59=15 (July), 1926, 476–482.
       [A review of the report of the South African Government
       Commission on the 1921 disturbances.]

1775   LUTHERAN BAPEDI CHURCH. <u>The Regulations for the Lutheran
       Bapedi Church established or formed by all the leaders
       of the congregations in the Synod at Kgalatlo (By Martinus
       Sebushane) 5th May 1892</u>. Rust[enburg?]: the Church n.d.
       [1898?].
       [The oldest known printed constitution of an independent
       church in South Africa, including an account of its
       foundation.]

1776   MacDONALD, JAMES. Manners, customs, superstitions and reli-
       gions of South African tribes. <u>Journal of the Royal
       Anthropological Institute of Great Britain and Ireland</u>
       19, 1890, 264–296.
       [Pp. 280–281, Xhosa cattle-killing.]

1777   MABASO, L. Can the traditional churches learn something from
       the Bantu sects in South Africa? <u>Credo</u> (Durban) 11 (4),
       1964, 20–24.
       [An African pastor (Lutheran) gives his view on the
       independent churches, after research work with them.]

1778   MABASO, L. Ungcwatschwe Ngodumo uMakhoba. <u>Isithunywa</u>
       (Durban) 63, August 1967, 4f.
       [The life and burial of L. M. Makhoba, leader of the
       African Congregational Church.]

1779   MABOEE, A. T. Letter in reply to Beyerhaus, 1961. <u>Ministry</u>
       (Morija, Lesotho) 2 (2), 1962, 38–40.
       [An African's criticism of separatism.]

1780   MABONA, MONGAMELI A. <u>The interaction and development of
       different religions in the Eastern Cape in the late
       eighteenth and early nineteenth centuries, with special
       reference to the first two Xhosa prophets</u>. London Uni-
       versity, School of Oriental and African Studies, M.A.
       Essay 1973, 37 p., typescript.
       [Pp. 18–25, Xhosa prophets Makana and Ntsikana.]

1781   MAFEJE, ARCHIE [B. M.]. Religion, class and ideology in
       South Africa, in M. G. Whisson and M. E. West (eds.),
       <u>Religion and social change in Southern Africa</u>. Capetown:
       D. Philip/London: Rex Collings 1975, 164–184.
       [An extension of his study of Langa (1963); see item
       1898. Independent churches, <u>passim</u>.]

BLACK AFRICA

1782 MAJOLA, S. E. (comp.). Devotional hymns for use at AICA
meetings. [Johannesburg?]: n.p., n.d. [1967-68], 38 p.
[Words for 36 hymns in various South African languages,
for use by African Independent Churches Association;
foreword in English and Xhosa.]

1783 MAKHATINI, D. L. Our relationship to the Separatist Churches
of the Ethiopian type (3 p.), and Umoyo, angels (4 p.),
in item 1797.
[Sympathetic approach by a Zulu Lutheran minister.]

1784 MAREE, W. L. Ult Duisternis Geroep. Die sendingswerk van die
Gereformeerde Kerk onder die Bagatlavolk van Wes-Transvaal
en Betsjoeanaland. Pretoria: N. G. Kerk-Boekhandel 1966,
297 p.
[Pp. 214-217, history of the separation of the BakXatla
or African Free Church under Tom Piri.]

1785 MARKS, SHULA. Harriette Colenso and the Zulus, 1874-1913.
Journal of African History 4 (3), 1963, 403-411.
[P. 409, the attitude of Bishop Colenso's daughter to
the separatist movement, and her relationship to P. J.
Mzimba.]

1786 MARKS, SHULA. Christian participation in the 1906 Zulu
Rebellion. Bulletin of the Society for African Church
History 2 (1), 1965, 55-72.
[Questions the correctness of government and white
assertions that independent churches fomented the Zulu
rebellion.]

1787 MARKS, SHULA. Reluctant rebellion: the 1906-8 disturbances in
Natal. Oxford: Clarendon Press 1970, 404 p., bibl., maps.
[See index for Ethiopianism, independent churches,
millennialism.]

1788 MARTIN, MARIE-LOUISE. Wie hilfreich ist die Methode Oosthuizens?
Zum Aufsatz von Prof. Gerhard C. Oosthuizen, "Wie christlich
ist die Kirche Shembes?" (Evang. Missions-Zeitschrift,
Heft 3 1974). Zeitschrift für Mission (Basel) 1 (2), 1975,
96-101.
[A reply to G. C. Oosthuizen's article, item 1818.]

1789 MASTER, V[INCENT] M. Enoch Mgijima, in Dictionary of South
African Biography, vol. 1. Capetown: Nasionale
Boekhandel Bpk. for National Council for Social Research,
Department of Higher Education 1968, 539-540.

245

Southern Africa

1790 MASTER, VINCENT [M.] African "Israelites" in South Africa
      1896-1971. Politics and religion among Africans in South
      Africa. The Hebrew University of Jerusalem, Ph.D.
      dissertation 1976, 300 p.

1791 MAYATULA, VICTOR MASHWABADA. African independent churches'
      contribution to a relevant theology, in H.-J. Becken (ed.),
      Relevant theology for Africa (Paperbacks of the
      Missiological Institute of the Lutheran Theological
      College, Mapumulo, 1). Durban: Lutheran Publishing
      House 1973, 174-177.
      [By a minister in an African independent church.]

1792 MAYER, PHILIP. Townsmen or tribesmen: conservatism and the
      process of urbanization in a South African city (Xhosa in
      town..., vol. 2). Capetown: Oxford University Press
      1961, xvi + 306 p.; 2nd. ed., rev., 1971, x + 329 p.,
      illus.
      [Ch. 12, "Red converts to Christianity" - the impact of
      Bhengu's Church on rural pagan migrants to East London;
      sympathetic, detailed.]

1793 MEIRING, PIET G[ERHARD] J[ACOBUS]. Stemmen uit die Swart Kerk.
      Gesprekke met dertien geestelike leiers. Capetown:
      Tafelberg-Uitgewers 1975, 178 p.
      [Pp. 129-140, African independent churches' movement, a
      conversation between the author and Bishop C. J. Bengheza,
      president of the African Independent Churches' Movement.]

1794 METELERKAMP, SANNI. Namjikwa - a tale of the cattle-slaying
      of 1858. The African Monthly (Grahamstown) 3, 1908,
      479-488.

1795 METELERKAMP, SANNI. The prophetess. A tale of cattle-slaying
      1857. The African Observer (Bulawayo) 3 (2), 1935, 65-73.
      [A romantic reconstruction of prophetess Nonqua's
      [Nongqause] life.]

1796 MILLIN, SARAH GERTRUDE. The coming of the Lord. London:
      Constable 1928.
      [Fiction: the South African independents.]

1797 MISSIOLOGICAL INSTITUTE, LUTHERAN THEOLOGICAL COLLEGE. Our
      approach to the Independent Church Movement in South
      Africa. Mapumulo, Natal: the Institute 1966, 163 p.,
      mimeo.
      [Papers read at an important symposium in 1965; see
      items 1662, 1679, 1684, 1685, 1731, 1741, 1783, 1806,
      1815, 1872, 1877.]

1798   MISSION FIELD. The (London: Society for the Propagation of
       the Gospel).   Articles on J. Dwane and the Order of
       Ethiopia and its reception into the Anglican Church.   See
       no. 539=45 (Nov.), 1900, 401-405; no. 543=46 (Mar.), 1901,
       92-95; no. 574=48 (Oct.), 1903, 309-313; no. 519=49 (Mar.),
       1904, 86-89 (illus.).

1799   MOKITIMI, S[ETH] M.   African religion, in Ellen Hellman (ed.),
       Handbook on race relations in South Africa.   London:
       Oxford University Press 1949, 556-572.
       [Pp. 564-572, on "separatism", a good survey with
       statistics, by the African vice-president of the Christian
       Council of South Africa.]

1800   MOLLER, HENDRIK J[ACOBUS].   The Church, culture change and the
       meaning of the group, in David J. Bosch (ed.), Church and
       culture change in Africa (Lux Mundi 3).   Pretoria:
       N. G. Kerk-Boekhandel 1971, 66-88.
       [Paper presented at 3rd Annual Meeting of South African
       Society for Mission Studies; p. 69, classification as
       "orthodox churches with white contact", "independent
       orthodox churches", "unorthodox churches with white con-
       tact", and "independent unorthodox churches" (Zionist,
       etc.); pp. 72-73 et passim, Zionist Churches.]

1801   MOORCROFT, E. K.   Theories of millenarianism considered with
       reference to certain South African movements.   Oxford
       University, B.Litt. thesis 1966-67.   ix + 166 p.

1802   MPUMLWANA, P. M.   Indigenization of Christianity.   Ichthus
       (Stellenbosch, Students' Christian Association of South
       Africa) 14 (4), 1962, 15-18.   Also in Ministry (Morija,
       Lesotho) 4 (1), 1963, 14-18.   Reprinted by Missiological
       Institute, Mapumulo, in Relevant theology for Africa:
       preparatory papers, 1972, 28-33.
       [P. 15 (1963), historical review of the attitudes to
       Ethiopianism in the Paris, Scottish, and Anglican missions,
       by a minister in the Order of Ethiopia.]

1803   MQOTSI, L. and MKELE, N.   A separatist church: Ibandla Lika-
       Krestu.   African Studies (Johannesburg) 5 (2), 1946,
       106-125.
       [The Church of Christ, Capetown, 1910, and its later
       development under Bishop Limba; a systematic account.]

1804   MSOMI, VIVIAN V.   The healing practices of the African inde-
       pendent churches, in The report of the Umpumulo Consul-
       tation on the healing ministry of the church.   Mapumulo:

Southern Africa

> Missiological Institute, Lutheran Theological College 1967,
> 65-74. Mimeo.
> [By an African hospital chaplain; reports of interviews
> with members of eight churches; summary and evaluation.]

1805 MZIMBA, L. N. The african church, in J. D. Taylor (ed.),
Christianity and the Natives of South African. A year-
book of South African missions. Lovedale: Lovedale Press
1927, 86-95.
[The causes and aims of the separatist movement.]

1806 NAUDÉ, C[HRISTIAAN] F[REDERICK] BEYERS. Our theological
responsibility for the ministry of the African independent
churches, in item 1797, 7 p.
[Practical suggestions for help urgently needed from the
older churches.]

1807 NEAME, L. ELWIN. Ethiopianism: the danger of a black church.
Empire Review no. 57=10 (Oct.), 1905, 256-265.
[An assembly of opinions critical of Ethiopianism, with
comments on the Report of the Native Affairs Commission,
item 1855.]

1808 NICHOLLS, G[EORGE] HEATON. Bayete! Hail to the King! London:
Allen and Unwin 1923, 374 p.
[Fiction, written in 1913 by a South African senator;
an extreme expression of the "Ethiopian scare".]

1809 NORTON, G. R. The emergence of new religious organizations in
South Africa. A discussion of causes. Journal of the
Royal African Society. Part 1, no. 157=39 (Oct.), 1940,
348-353; Part 2, no. 158=40 (Jan.), 1941, 48-67.
[Based on secondary sources; cites a variety of causes
besides race.]

1810 [OLIFAN, J. W.] Exposé of the faith and practice of the
Church of Christ. N.p. [Port Elizabeth?]: the Church
n.d. [Olifan (or Oliphant) founded the Church of Christ
in 1910, and signed the major portion of this doctrine as
"moderator" before Limbe took over the leadership.]

1811 OOSTHUIZEN, GERHARDUS C[ORNELIS]. Sondebegrip by die
Separatistiese Bewegings in Afrika. Ned[erduitse]
Geref[ormeerde] Teologiese Tydskrif 5 (4), 1964, 219-225.

1812 OOSTHUIZEN, G[ERHARDUS] C[ORNELIS]. 'n Antropologies-
teologiese ondersoek van die nativisties bewegings. Suid-
Afrikaanse Akademie vir Wetenskap en Kuns
(Voortrekkerspers) 6 (2), 1966, 378-398.

1813   OOSTHUIZEN, G[ERHARDUS] C[ORNELIS]. Independent African
       churches: sects or spontaneous development? A reply to
       J. Alex van Wyk, in item 1879, 10 p.

1814   OOSTHUIZEN, G[ERHARDUS] C[ORNELIS]. Independentism in South
       Africa. South African Outlook (Lovedale) no. 1146= vol.
       96, 1966, 172-174; idem no. 1147, vol. 96, 1966, 197-200.
       Also in The Christian Minister (Rondebosch) 3 (1), 1967,
       17-22. Germ. trans., Das Wachstum unabhängiger
       einheimischer Kirchen in Südafrika. Der Ruf (Berliner
       Missionsberichte) 6, Nov.-Dez. 1968, 458-563, 466-470.
       [A survey, with classification, and summary of the
       theology.]

1815   OOSTHUIZEN, G[ERHARDUS] C[ORNELIS]. Isaiah Shembe and the
       Zulu world view, in item 1797, 26 p.; see also item 141.
       Repr. in History of Religions 8 (1), 1968, 1-30.
       [A typology and theological criticism, with full dis-
       cussion of the Zulu background of this "nativistic
       messianic (pagan) movement".]

1816   OOSTHUIZEN, GERHARDUS C[ORNELIS]. The theology of a South
       African messiah. An analysis of the hymnal of "The Church
       of the Nazarites" (Oekumenische Studien 8). Leiden:
       E. J. Brill 1967, 198 p.

1817   OOSTHUIZEN, G[ERHARDUS] C[ORNELIS]. Die "Christologie" van
       die kerk van die Nasireers (Ibandla Lamanazaretha).
       Ned[erduitse] Geref[ormeerde] Teologiese Tydskrif 14 (4),
       1973, 249-267.
       [Based on responses of members of Shembe's Church to a
       questionnaire used in interviews; tests the answers against
       the Church hymnal and concludes it is "post-Christian"
       rather than "non-Christian".]

1818   OOSTHUIZEN, GERHARDUS C[ORNELIS]. Wie christlich is die Kirche
       Shembes? Evangelische Missions-Zeitschrift (Stuttgart)
       N.F. 31 (3), 1974, 129-142.
       [Similar to previous article. See reply by M.-L. Martin,
       item 1788.]

1819   PAUW, B[ERTHOLD] A[DOLF]. Religion in a Tswana chiefdom.
       London: Oxford University Press for the International
       African Institute 1960, 258 p.
       [An important study by an anthropologist of the churches
       in a native reserve in the northern Cape Province, 1952-54;
       presents a theologically-based typology differing from
       Sundkler's. Appendix II, on St. Paul Apostolic Faith
       Morning Star Church.]

Southern Africa

1820   PAUW, B[ERTHOLD] A[DOLF]. African Christians and their
       ancestors, in V. W. Hayward (ed.), item 235, 33-46; also
       in Ned[erduits] Geref[ormeerde] Teologiese Tydskrif 4 (4),
       1963, 203-213.
           [Relationship of independents to ancestor worship, with
       special reference to South Africa.]

1821   PAUW, B[ERTHOLD] A[DOLF]. The second generation: a study of
       the family among urbanized Bantu in East London (Xhosa in
       Town, vol. 3). Capetown: Oxford University Press 1963,
       xviii + 291 p.; 2nd ed. with postscript chapter 1973.
           [Pp. 38-41, independent Bantu churches, to which 10.4%
       of his sample belonged.]

1822   PAUW, BERTHOLD A[DOLF]. Bantu, Churches among the. Standard
       Encyclopaedia of Southern Africa. Capetown: Nasou 1970,
       vol. 2, 54-56, illus.
           [A convenient survey in three classes: Ethiopian,
       Sabbatarian-Baptist, Zionist.]

1823   PAUW, B[ERTHOLD] A[DOLF]. Ancestor beliefs and rituals among
       urban Africans. African Studies (Johannesburg), 33 (2),
       1974, 99-111.
           [The survival or rejection among independent churches,
       passim.]

1824   PAYNE, ADAM. A prophet among the Zulus: Shembe. A power for
       peace and a restraining influence. Illustrated London
       News, 8 Feb. 1930, 203.

1825   PEREIRA DE QUEIROZ, MARIA ISAURA. Maurice Leenhardt et les
       "églises éthiopiennes". Monde Non-Chrétien n.s. 77,
       avr.-juin 1965, 84-101.
           [Discusses Leenhardt's methodology.]

1826   PHILLIPS, RAY E[DMUND]. The Bantu in the City. Lovedale:
       Lovedale Press n.d. [1938].
           [Pp. 254-259, 264, 274, 278, 286, the "separatist
       churches".]

1827   PRETORIUS, HENDRIK L. Kosmologie en separatisme: 'n Ondersoek
       na separatisme in Afrika as resultaat van kosmologiese
       onderskatting met seksualiteit as leedraad. University of
       Pretoria, D.D. dissertation 1973.

1828   PRINGLE, THOMAS. Narrative of a residence in South Africa.
       London: Edward Moxon 1840, 116 p.
           [Pp. 96-100, prophet Makana among the Xhosa.]

BLACK AFRICA

South Africa

1829   PRO VERITATE (Johannesburg). Articles on African independent
       churches. See e.g., 5 (5), 1966, 6-9; 5 (6), 1966, 10-13;
       7 (1), 1968, 4-5; 10 (2), 1971, 6-8; 10 (6), 1971, 18-19;
       11 (4), 1972, 14-16; 11 (9), 1973, 15-16.
       [Descriptive, historical, political aspects, and the
       role of women.]

1830   PULLER, F. W. The Ethiopian Order. The East and the West
       [London]1 (1), 1903, 75-91.
       [The Order's relation to the Anglican Church, by an
       English missionary.]

1831   RAUM, O. F. Von Stammespropheten zu Sektenführern, in E. Benz
       (ed.), item 137, 47-70.
       [Early Xhosa prophets (Makana to Nongqause); early "sect-
       leaders" (Tile to Mgijima); later founders (Limba and
       Bhengu).]

1832   RICHTER, JULIUS. Geschichte der Berliner Missionsgesellschaft
       1824-1924. Berlin: Berliner evangelische
       Missionsgesellschaft 1924, vi + 740 p.
       [Pp. 109f., Ntsikana; pp. 111f., Mlandscheni [Mlanjeni],
       Mchlakaza [Mhlakaza] and Nonqas [Nongqause]; pp. 644-647,
       Mwamafungube.]

1833   ROBERTS, E[STHER] L[INDSAY]. Shembe. The man and his work.
       University of South Africa, M.A. thesis 1936.

1834   ROUX, EDWARD. Time longer than rope. A history of the Black
       man's struggle for freedom in South Africa. London:
       Gollancz 1948, 388 p.; Madison: University of Wisconsin
       Press, 2nd. edition enlarged 1964, xviii + 469 p.
       [Ch. 2, "Makana the prophet"; ch. 8, also pp. 135, 402,
       421, "The Ethiopian movement"; pp. 135, 141, Israelite
       movement of 1909-1921.]

1835   ROUX, H. A. De Ethiopische Kerk. Bloemfontein: de Vriend
       1905, 39 p.

1836   RUTHERFORD, JAMES. Sir George Grey, K.C.B., 1812-1898. A
       study in colonial government. London: Cassell 1961,
       xvii + 707 p., illus., maps.
       [Pp. 337-370, the Xhosa cattle-killing and its after-
       math, based on government archives.]

1837   SAUBERZWEIG-SCHMIDT, P. Die kirchliche Selbständigkeitsbewegung
       unter den Eingeborenen Südafrikas. Die Reformation 3 (43),
       1904, 679-682; idem 3 (44), 1904, 698-700; idem 3 (45),
       1904, 713-717.

Southern Africa

1838   SAUNDERS, C[HRISTOPHER] C. Tile and the Thembu Church:
        Politics and independency on the Cape Eastern frontier in
        the late nineteenth century. Journal of African History
        11 (4), 1970, 553-570.

1839   SCHLOSSER, KATESA. Passahfest und Leben der "Israeliten" in
        Queenstown (13, 14 und 15 Apr. 1953). Wissenschaftliche
        Zeitschrift der Freidrich-Schiller-Universität, Jena,
        1953-1954. Math.-Nat. Series, 1954, 147-151.

1840   SCHNEIDER, THÉO. Les églises indépendentes africaines en
        Afrique du Sud. Verbum Caro (Basel) 6 (23), 1952, 116-126.
        [A summary of Sundkler, 1948, with suggestions for
        positive attitudes by older churches.]

1841   SCHNEIDER, THÉO. "Zion, ruhme Deinen Gott!" Ein "Zionisten"
        Fest im Norden Transvaals. Schweizer Mission in Südafrika
        (Zurich) 29 (162), 1953, 8-13.
        [On Edward Lekganyane's Zion Christian Church.]

1842   SCHUTTE, A[NDRIES] G[ERHARDUS]. Thapelo ya sephiri: a study
        of secret prayer groups in Soweto. African Studies
        (Johannesburg) 31 (4), 1972, 245-260.
        [Recently formed urban groups operating alongside the
        churches, claiming secret knowledge of the Bible trans-
        mitted from Christ, offering healing and salvation.]

1843   SCHUTTE, [ANDRIES] GERHARD[US]. Die politische Funktion
        religiöser Bewegungen im Südlichen Afrika. Zeitschrift
        für Evangelische Ethik (Gütersloh) 17 (1), 1973, 17-25.
        [Independent churches as a means of social action -
        whether by escapism or adventism.]

1844   SEROTE, S. E. Sect and church in the city, in The missionary
        outreach in an urban society. Mapumulo: Missiological
        Institute, Lutheran Theological College 1967, 94-103.
        [By an African Lutheran city pastor.]

1845   SETILOANE, GABRIEL M. W. The separatist movement in South
        Africa: its origins, danger to the church, and comparison
        with American Negro cults. Union Theological Seminary,
        New York, S.T.M. thesis 1955.
        [By a South African Black Theologian.]

1846   SHEMBE, J[OHN] GALILEE. Izihlabelelo za MaNazaretha. Durban:
        W. H. Shepherd for J. G. Shembe 1940.
        [222 hymns of Isaiah Shembe, edited by his son.]

1847 SHOOTER, JOSEPH. The Kafirs of Natal and the Zulu country.
London: E. Stanford 1857, 403 p.
[Pp. 167-195 on prophets or "seers"; pp. 195-212 on
Makana and other similar Bantu prophets.]

1848 SIBISI, HARRIET. The place of spirit possession in Zulu
cosmology, in M. G. Whisson and M. E. West (eds.),
Religion and social change in Southern Africa. Capetown:
D. Philips/London: Rex Collings 1975, 48-57.
[New forms of spirit possession, including that in
Zionist churches.]

1849 SMITH, E[DWIN] W[ILLIAMS]. The Ethiopian Church movement in
South Africa. Primitive Methodist Quarterly Review 23,
1905, 328-339, 504-517.

1850 SOUTH AFRICA. Report and proceedings, with appendices, of the
Government Commission on Native Law and Customs. Cape
Town: Richards & Son 1883.
[Pp. 269-270, Mhlakaza and the Xhosa cattle-killing in
the 1850s.]

1851 SOUTH AFRICA, UNION OF. Interim and final reports of the
Native Affairs Commission and telegram from Commissioner,
South African Police, relative to "Israelites" at Bulhoek
and occurrences in May 1921. Cape Town: Cape Times
Government Printers 1921.

1852 SOUTH AFRICA, UNION OF. Report of the Native Churches Commission. Cape Town: Government Printers 1925, 38 p.
[A survey of religious organizations of the Bantu, and
the origins and extent of the separatist movement.]

1853 SOUTH AFRICA, UNION OF: NATIVE REPRESENTATIVE COUNCIL.
Minutes, Native Representative Council. Pretoria: 1944,
338-349.
[An extended debate between Zulu leaders on the
fissiparous nature of separatism.]

1854 SOUTH AFRICA, UNION OF. Summary of the Report of the Commission for the Socio-Economic Development of the Bantu
areas within the Union of South Africa. Pretoria:
Government Printer 1955. 211 p.
[Pp. 20-22, the Tomlinson Report, review of Christianity
in South Africa with reference to separatist churches.]

1855 SOUTH AFRICAN NATIVE AFFAIRS COMMISSION. Report, 1903-5.
Cape Town: Government Printers 1904-5, 5 vols.

BIBLIOGRAPHY OF NEW RELIGIOUS MOVEMENTS IN PRIMAL SOCIETIES

Southern Africa

> [Cited as an important source on Ethiopianism – indexed
> under "Politics" and "Religion" in the subject index,
> vol. 5.]

1856 SOUTH AFRICAN NATIVE RACES COMMITTEE (ed.). The South African
      Natives: their progress and present condition. London:
      Murray 1908, 247 p.
      [Ch. 7, pp. 192–226, "The Ethiopian Movement – Native
      Churches".]

1857 SOUTH AFRICAN OUTLOOK. See under F. Wilson and D. Perrot.

1858 SOUTH AFRICAN OUTLOOK (Lovedale). The Israelites. South
      African Outlook, 2 Jan. 1922, 9–11.
      [On Enoch Mgijima and the legal aftermath of the Bulhoek
      incident.]

1859 SPRUNGER, A. R. The contribution of the African independent
      churches to a relevant theology for Africa, in H.-J. Becken
      (ed.), Relevant theology for Africa (Paperbacks of the
      Missiological Institute, Lutheran Theological College,
      Mapumulo, 1). Durban: Lutheran Publishing House 1973,
      163–173.
      [P. 16, report of the paper and its discussion; see also
      pp. 189–190.]

1860 STEAD, W. Y. The Order of Ethiopia and its relation to the
      Church. The African Monthly (Grahamstown) 3 (15), 1908,
      311–331.
      [A missionary criticism of the admission of the Order to
      the Anglican Church in South Africa.]

1861 STRASSBERGER, ELFRIEDE. Ecumenism in South Africa, 1936–1960
      with special reference to the mission of the church.
      University of Stellenbosch, D.D. dissertation 1971;
      Johannesburg: South African Council of Churches 1974,
      295 p.
      [Pp. 83–86, Apostolic Faith Mission; pp. 89–96, 127–129,
      African independent churches.]

1862 STRETCH, C. L. Makana and the attack on Grahamstown in 1819.
      Cape Monthly Magazine 12, 1876, 297–303.

1863 SUNDERMEIER, THEO. Ein Ersatz für den Kraal. Kooperation mit
      den "unabhängigen" Kirchen in Südafrika. Lutherische
      Monatshefte 12 (1), 1973, 14–16.

BLACK AFRICA

1864 SUNDKLER, B[ENGT] G[USTAF] M[ALCOLM]. Separatisme en die
      Sending. Op die Horison (Stellenbosch) 2 (2), 1940, 63-70.

1865 SUNDKLER, B[ENGT] G[USTAF] M[ALCOLM]. Black man's church.
      Libertas Magazine (Johannesburg) 5 (10), 1945, 18-37.

1866 SUNDKLER, BENGT G[USTAF] M[ALCOLM]. Bantu prophets in South
      Africa. London: Lutterworth Press 1948, 344 p.; 2nd ed.
      revised and enlarged, London: Oxford University Press for
      the International African Institute 1961, 381 p., map,
      illus. Ger. trans., Bantupropheten in Südafrika.
      Stuttgart: Evangelisches Verlagswerk 1964, 407 p.
      [The best-known general survey, historical, sociological
      and theological, of independent Zulu churches.]

1867 SUNDKLER, B[ENGT] G[USTAF] M[ALCOLM]. Bantu Messiah and white
      Christ. Frontier (London)3 (1), 1960, 15-23; also in
      Practical Anthropology (Tarrytown, N.Y.) 7 (4), 1960,
      170-176. Ger. trans., Bantu-Messias und Weisser Christus.
      Die Sekten südafrikas. Das Wort in der Welt (Hamburg) 41,
      1961, 26-32.

1868 SUTER, F. The Ethiopian Movement, in Report of Second General
      Missionary Conference for South Africa, Johannesburg, 1906.
      Morija [Lesotho]: Morija Printing Office 1907, 107-113.
      [Based on answers to a questionnaire on the history of
      independent churches.]

1869 TAYLOR, JAMES DEXTER. The American Board Mission in South
      Africa. A sketch of seventy-five years. Durban:
      J. Singleton & Sons 1911, 99 p.
      [Includes the formation of the Zulu Congregationalist
      Church in 1896.]

1870 TAYLOR, JAMES DEXTER (ed.). Christianity and the Natives of
      South Africa. A year-book of South African mission.
      Vol. 1. Lovedale: Lovedale Press for General Missionary
      Conference of South Africa n.d. [c. 1928].
      [Pp. 73-85, Allen Lea, item 1766; pp. 291-292, Rev. G.
      Mahon's outline of work of the Christian Catholic Church
      in South Africa, supported by Grace Missionary Society;
      p. 488, brief outline of conference dealing with
      Ethiopian movement.]

1871 THEAL, GEORGE McCALL. History of South Africa since September
      1795. 5 vols. London: Swan Sonnenschein 1908.
      [Vol. 3, pp. 190-199, the Xhosa movement of Nonquas
      [Nongqause] and Mchlakaza [Mhlakaza], 1856-57.]

Southern Africa

1872 TRACEY, HUGH. Zulus find the middle road. Natural History
      (New York) 64 (8), 1955, 400–406, illus.
          [Shembe's Nazarite Church – a popular account with many
      illustrations.]

1873 TSCHEUSCHNER, E. The biblical concept of the church related
      to the self-understanding of post-Christian churches,
      exemplified by Islamic traits, in item 1797, 6 p.
          [Biblical theology applied to both older and independent
      churches.]

1874 TURNER, VICTOR WITTER. The waters of life: some reflections
      on Zionist water symbolism, in J. Neusner (ed.), Religions
      in antiquity (Supplements to Numen, 14). Leiden: Brill
      1968, 506–520.
          [Also on symbol of whiteness.]

1875 VAN ANTWERP, C[ORNELIUS] M[ARKINUS]. Die Separatistiese
      Kerklike Beweging onder die Bantu van Suid-Afrika. Uni-
      versity of Capetown, Ph.D. dissertation 1938.

1876 VAN DEN BERG, M. R. Syncretisme als uitdaging. Amsterdam:
      Buijten and Schipperheijn 1966, 81 p.

1877 VAN ROOY, J. A. Sinkretisme in Vendaland: sinkretisme onder
      die separatistiese sektes in Vendaland. Potchefstroom
      University for Christian Higher Education, M.Th.
      dissertation 1964.

1878 VAN WYK, JOHANNES ALEXANDER. Independent African churches:
      sects or spontaneous development? in item 1797, 7 p.
          [Similar to his item 1879.]

1879 VAN WYK, J[OHANNES] ALEX[ANDER]. Independent African churches:
      sects or spontaneous development? Ministry (Morija,
      Lesotho) 4 (2), 1964, 59–63.
          [A thorough general survey from a theological viewpoint.
      See the reply of Oosthuizen, item 1813.]

1880 VAN WYK, J[OHANNES] H[ENDRIK]. Separatisme en inheemse
      kerkbeweging onder die Bantoe van die Sothogroep.
      Pretoria: Human Sciences Research Council 1973, 2 vols.,
      vii + 1005 p.

1881 VAN ZYL, DANIE. Bantu prophets or Christ's evangels. Pro
      Veritate 5 (5), 1966, 6–9; idem 5 (6), 1966, 10–13. Repr.
      in pamphlet form, no publication details [1966], 12 p.
          [Current attempts to bring independent churches together,
      especially through schemes for ministerial training.]

256

1882 VERRYN, T[REVOR] D[AVID]. A history of the Order of Ethiopia.
Pretoria: Ecumenical Research Unit 1972, 119 p., photo.
[A revised and updated version of a thesis completed in
1957, and issued in mimeo form in 1962.]

1883 VILAKAZI, ABSALOM. Isonto lama Nazaretha: the Zulu Church
of the Nazarites in South Africa. Hartford School of
Missions, M.A. dissertation 1954, 177 p.

1884 WAGNER, [HENRI MICHEL]. Les sectes en Afrique du Sud, in
Devant les Sectes..., item 312, 144-163.
[Ethiopianism, Zionism, especially Shembe's church.]

1885 WANGEMANN, HERMANN THEODOR. Geschichte der Berliner Missionsgesellschaft und ihrer Arbeiten in Südafrika. Bd. 2, 2
(Kaffer-Land). Berlin: Neu-Ruppin (printer) 1873, 390 p.
[Especially pp. 148-150, 185-192, 196-201, on prophets
and rebellions.]

1886 WELLS, JAMES. Stewart of Lovedale. The Life of James Stewart
D.D., M.D. London: Hodder & Stoughton 1908, xi + 419 p.,
maps, illus.
[Pp. 287-299, Ethiopianism.]

1887 WEMAN, HENRY. African music and the church in Africa. Uppsala:
Ab Lundequistska Bokhandeln for Svenska Institutet for
Missionsforskning 1960.
[Pp. 101-110, "The sects and folk music"; pp. 111-114,
the Nazarite hymnbook. Also firsthand description of
Shembe's January festival on the mountain, Nhlangakazi.]

1888 WEST, MARTIN [E.]. Conflict and cooperation in African
churches. This Month. Ecumenical Press Service (Geneva:
W.C.C.) Oct. 1971, 5-7.
[An historical survey of ecumenical relations among
South African independent churches, and between them and
white Christians.]

1889 WEST, MARTIN [E.]. Thérapie et changement social dans les
églises urbaines d'Afrique du Sud. Social Compass 19 (1),
1972, 49-62.
[Rapid urban development produces sickness which is
dealt with by the interpretations and power of healing
prophets.]

1890 WEST, MARTIN E. Independence and unity: problems of cooperation between African independent church leaders in Soweto.
African Studies 33 (2), 1974, 121-129.

Southern Africa

1891 WEST, MARTIN E. People of the Spirit: the Charismatic Move-
      ment among African independent churches. Journal for
      Theology in Southern Africa no. 7, June 1974, 23-29.

1892 WEST, MARTIN E. African churches in Soweto, in C. Kileff and
      W. C. Pendleton (eds.), Urban man in Southern Africa.
      Gwelo: Mambo Press 1975, 19-38.
      [A general survey of independent churches, their types,
      numbers, interrelations, leadership and functions both
      religious and secular in this group of "townships" with a
      million people.]

1893 WEST, MARTIN [E.]. Bishops and prophets in a black city.
      African independent churches in Soweto and Johannesburg.
      Capetown: David Philip/London: Rex Collings 1975, 225 p.,
      illus., map.
      [An intensive study of 13 of 900 movements in Soweto;
      fuller accounts of Bantu Bethlehem Christian Apostolic
      Church of South Africa, Apostolic Full Gospel Mission of
      South Africa, Holy United Methodist Church of South Africa,
      and African Independent Churches Association.]

1894 WEST, MARTIN [E.]. The shades come to town: ancestors and
      urban independent churches, in M. G. Whisson and M. E. West,
      item 1895, 185-206.
      [Belief in ancestors, and cults of ancestral shades,
      distinguished; relations to ancestors in independent
      churches in Soweto, Johannesburg; four case studies of
      individuals.]

1895 WHISSON, MICHAEL G. and WEST, MARTIN [E.] (eds.). Religion
      and social change in Southern Africa: anthropological
      essays in honour of Monica Wilson. Capetown: David
      Philip/London: Rex Collings 1975, 223 p.
      [See index, "churches", for individual movements; see
      also Mafeje, item 1781, Sibisi, item 1848, and West,
      item 1894.]

1896 WILLOUGHBY, WILLIAM CHARLES. Race problems in the new Africa:
      a study of the relation of Bantu and Britons in those
      parts of Bantu Africa which are under British control.
      Oxford: Clarendon Press 1923, 296 p.
      [Pp. 70-72, possession and prophets, Ethiopianism.
      Pp. 231-243, Mhlakaza and other prophets.]

1897 WILSON, FRANCIS and PERROT, DOMINIQUE. Outlook on a century:
      South Africa 1870-1970. Lovedale: Lovedale Press -
      Spro-Cas 1973, xix + 746 p., illus., maps.

[Reprint of editorials and articles from South African
Outlook (Lovedale). Introduction, p. 17, on independent
churches. Editorials: pp. 153-155, the Ethiopian Church;
pp. 158-160, the Negro Spirit; pp. 375-378, Schism.
Articles: Jacobus G. Xaba, pp. 155-156; Edouard Jacottet,
pp. 378-384; Episcopal Church of South Africa, pp. 156-158;
J. Brownlee Ross, pp. 384-389; Elijah Makiwane,
pp. 177-180.]

1898   WILSON, MONICA and MAFEJE, ARCHIE. Langa. A study of social
       groups in an African township. Capetown: Oxford Univer-
       sity Press 1963, 190 p., tables, bibl.
       [A Xhosa population on the outskirts of Capetown;
       pp. 91-103, survey of churches including independent
       bodies.]

1899   WRIGHT, BERYL. The sect that became an order. Sociological
       Yearbook of Religion in Britain. 5, 1972, 60-71.
       [The Order of Ethiopia.]

See also items 91, 110, 141, 155, 177, 182, 183, 193, 195, 198, 202,
205, 213, 227, 232, 236, 244, 247, 263, 267, 276, 315, 320, 328, 329,
331, 339, 343, 347, 353, 357, 362, 365, 368, 376, 381, 394, 397, 404,
415, 417, 1136, 1410, 1431, 1571.

SWAZILAND

1900   ARMITAGE, FIONA [LOUISE]. Social aspects of a Swazi clinic.
       Mother and Child (London) 43 (6), 1971, 13-16, 20.
             [P. 14, Zionists and marriage; p. 15, religious affilia-
       tions (33 out of 40 women were Zionists); pp. 15-16,
       Zionists encouraging saving.]

1901   ARMITAGE, FIONA LOUISE. Abakamoya: People of the Spirit. A
       study of the Zionist movement in Swaziland with special
       reference to the Swazi Christian Church in Zion of South
       Africa and the Nazarethe branch. University of Aberdeen,
       M.Litt. thesis (Religious Studies) 1976, 428 p., illus.,
       maps, appendices.
             [A social, historical and phenomenological account based
       on archives and field work.]

1902   DLAMINI, TIMOTHY L. L. The Full Gospel Church, Manzini. Uni-
       versity of Botswana, Lesotho and Swaziland, B.A. disserta-
       tion 1975, 56 p., illus. Mimeo.

Southern Africa

> [One of twelve branches of this church in Swaziland -
> its history, worship, personal testimonies in worship, and
> preaching; pp. 8-10, secessions from this white-connected
> church, including the independent Church of God of Pro-
> phecy, and the Full Gospel Bantu Church in Johannesburg.]

1903   KUPER, HILDA.   The Swazi reaction to missions. African
       Studies (Johannesburg) 5 (3), 1946, 177-189.
       [The growth of "native dissident churches".]

1904   KUPER, HILDA.   The uniform of colour. A study of white-black
       relationships in Swaziland. Johannesburg: Witwatersrand
       University Press 1947, xii + 160 p.
       [Pp. 114, 124, separatist churches among the Swazi - in
       1936, 21 sects in Swaziland, 13 of the Zionist type.]

1905   KUPER, HILDA.   The Swazi. A South African kingdom. New York:
       Holt, Rinehart and Winston 1963, 87 p.
       [Pp. 67-68, separatist churches in relation to
       nationalism.]

1906   SCUTT, JOAN.   Old tins in the homes of Swaziland. London:
       African Evangelical Fellowship, and Worthing: Henry E.
       Walter 1968, 110 p., illus.
       [By a missionary who accepts independent churches as
       partners.]

See also items 1590 and 1608.

Index of Authors and Sources

(The numbers refer to items)

Contributions to symposia etc. are indexed separately for each author; the colourless category of "Anon." has been replaced by the more informative title of the publication itself, or of the sponsoring body.

In recent years, following the policy of "authenticity", most citizens of Zaïre have changed their names. Items are given with the names under which they were published, but where a change of name is known, and where an author has published under both names, they are cross-referenced. It should be noted also that Zaïrean names, as with Arabic and Ethiopian names, are alphabetized under the first name. This is becoming the practice elsewhere, especially where a Western or "Christian" name is not used. Religious names are also alphabetized under the first, not the second, name.

Index of Authors and Sources

Akpan, N. U., 675
Alexander, D. A. R., 676
Alexandre, P. H. H. C., 100–101,
  427
All Africa Conference of
  Churches, 102
Allégret, E., 577
Allier, R. S. P., 103, 1431
Althabe, G., 1059, 1432
Aluko, T. M., 677
Alutu, J. O., 678
Ames, M. M., 2
Amon D'Aby, F.-J., 578
Amos-Djoro, E., 579–580
Anderson, J. E., 1228–1229
Anderson, W. B., 1230
Andersson, E., 916–917, 988–989,
  1060–1061
Anquandah, J. R., 492
Anson, P. F., 104
Anyenyola Welo, J.-O.,
  1062–1064
Anyiam, F. U., 679
Aoko, D., 1231–1232
Apea-Anim, P. N., 493
Apostolic Herald, 680
Appiah-Kubi, K., 105
Archives de Sociologie des
  Religions, 3
Armitage, F. L., 1900–1901
Armstrong, C. W., 494–495
Ashton, E. H., 1616
Ashton-Gwatkin, F. T. A., 1233
Assimeng, J. M., 106–108, 1526
Augé, M., 581–582
Authority, S. O. A., 681
Avery, A. W., 109
Awake, 682
Axelson, S., 918
Axenfeld, K., 1655
Ayandele, E. A., 110, 683–688
Ayorinde, J. A., 689
Azombo, S., 1065

Babalola, J. A., 690
Back to God, 1656
Baëta, C. G. K., 111–114,
  496–498
Balandier, G., 115–120, 919–923,
  990, 1011–1012
Bamunoba, Y. K., 1371

Banfield, A. W., 691
Banton, M. P., 4, 121–122,
  900–901
Bantu, 1657
Barberet, J., 1013
Barker, P., 499
Barnett, D. L., 1234
Barrett, D. B., 123–129, 1188,
  1235
Barrett, L. E., 130
Barrett, S. R., 692–694
Bartels, F. L., 500
Bastide, R., 5, 6
Batsikama Ba Mampuya Ma Ndwala, R.,
  924
Batubo, A. B., 695
Baudert, S., 1658
Baumann, J., 1625
Bazola, E., 1066
Beattie, J. H. M., 131
Beaver, R. P., 1236
Bechler, T., 1659
Becken, H.-J., 132–133, 1586,
  1660–1677
Beckmann, D. M., 7, 501
Beecher, L. J., 1237
Beetham, T. A., 134–135
Bekale, P., See under Fernandez,
  J. W.
Bell, R. M., 1342
Bena-Silu, 1067
Bender, R. T., 136
Benin, Oba of, 696
Bentley, W. H., 958
Benz, E., 137–138
Berdrow, W., 1626
Berglund, A.-I., 1678–1682
Berichte der Rheinischen Mission,
  1627
Bernard, G. M., 1238
Bernard, Guy, 1068, See also under
  Lanzas, A.
Bernus, E., 583
Berry, S. S. S., 697
Berthoud, A., 1683
Bertolino, G., 1239
Beskow, P., 8
Bessell, M. J., 1189
Bewes, T. F. C., 1240–1241
Beyerhaus, P., 9–11, 139–143,
  1684–1686

262

INDEX OF AUTHORS AND SOURCES

Lutheran Bapedi Church, 1775
Luykx, B., 285
Lynch, H. R., 286, 442, 909

Mabaso, L., 1777-1778
Maboee, A. T., 1779
Mabona, M. A., 1780
MacAulay, H., 786
McClelland, E. M., 787
McCracken, K. J., 1459
MacDonald, J., 1776
MacDonald, R. J., 1460-1461
McDonald, T. R., 788
MacGaffey, W., 944, 1129-1131,
    See also under Janzen, J. M.
McIntosh, B. G., 1282
McKenzie, P. R., 789
Mackie, S. G., 287
McLaughlin, J., See under
    Barrett, D. B.
MacLean, U., 790
Maconi, V., 288
MacPherson, F., 1552
McVeigh, M. J., 1283, See also
    under Barrett, D. B.
Mafeje, A. B. M., 1781, See also
    under Wilson, M.
Maina Wa Kiragu, D., 1284
Mair, L. P., 289-292
Majola, S. E., 1782
Makabzu, J. P., 1132
"Makengere", 1133
Makhatini, D. L., 1783
Mallo, E., 485
Mambo, G. K., 1285, See also
    under Barrett, D. B.
Manyara, J., 1286
Mapunda, O. B., 1356
Maranke, J., 1499
Maree, W. L., 1784
Margarido, A., 974-976
Margull, H. J., 293
Marin, J., 945
Marioghae, M., 791
Markowitz, M. D., 1134
Marks, S., 1785-1787
Markwell, M., 910
Martin, F., 486
Martin, J. J., 651
Martin, M.-L., 294-295, 977,
    1135-1137, 1500, 1553,
    1595-1596, 1788

Martin, S. W., 792-793
Marty, P., 617
Marwick, M. G., 1462, 1554
Mary Aquina, Sister, 1501-1503
Masembe, J., 1287
Massamba-Débat, A., 996
Massing, A., See under Korte, W.
Master, V. M., 1789-1790
Matson, A. T., 1288
Maurier, H., 296
May, A. J. W., See under Northern
    Rhodesia, [Anglican]
    Bishop of
Maxwell, J. L., 794
Mayatula, V. M., 297, 1791
Mayer, P., 1792
Mbambi, A., 997
Mbeng, J.-M., 1036
Mbiti, J. S., 298-301, 1289
Mead, M., 302
Medaiyese, J. A., 795
Meert, J., See under Tempels, P.
Meerts, H. C. G., 548
Meiring, P. G. J., 946, 1793
Melland, F. H., 1555
Mels, B., 1138-1139
Membe, J. L. C., 1422
Memel-Foté, H., 618, See also
    under Lehmann, J.-P.
Mendelsohn, J., 303
Menzel, G., 1641-1642
Mercier, E., 978
Mertens [Fr.], 549
Messenger, J. C., 796-798
Metelerkamp, S., 1794-1795
Methodist Recorder, The, 550, 619
Michel, M., 987
Middleton, J. F. M., 1290,
    1384-1387
Miller, P. M., 1291
Millin, S. G., 1796
Missiological Institute, Lutheran
    Theological College, Mapumulo,
    1797
Mission Field, The, 1798
Mitchell, H., 443
Mitchell, R. C., 304-306, 799-801
Mizan Newsletter, 307
Mkele, N., See under Mqotsi, L.
Mohono, R. M., 1620
Mokitimi, S. M., 1799

269

INDEX OF AUTHORS AND SOURCES

Index of Authors and Sources

Select Thematic Guide

Numbers refer to items

BAPTISM 152, 153, 642, 768, 1680, 1681, 1874
CATECHISMS, HYMNBOOKS, PRAYERBOOKS 426, 459, 630, 711, 715, 717, 720,
    754, 806, 807, 826, 847, 948, 1070, 1072, 1183, 1202, 1270, 1563,
    1653, 1782, 1816, 1846
EDUCATION 246, 342, 394, 532, 658, 1196, 1200, 1228, 1229, 1234, 1247,
    1269, 1299, 1460, 1496, 1589, 1671, 1700
GREEK ORTHODOXY: RELATED MOVEMENTS 104, 148, 168, 169, 233, 261, 332,
    381, 1193, 1197, 1205, 1206, 1217, 1220, 1245, 1268, 1292, 1299,
    1336, 1358, 1382, 1388, 1389, 1402, 1654
HEALING 91, 133, 141, 143, 304, 489, 490, 497, 502, 513, 528, 541,
    548, 563, 570, 589, 615, 618, 625, 630, 750, 752, 769, 773, 790,
    801, 816, 820, 869, 941, 986, 1198, 1217, 1669, 1672, 1674, 1677,
    1722, 1723, 1804, 1842, 1889
HEBRAIST MOVEMENTS 299, 331, 452, 1381, 1391-1393, 1396, 1401, 1750,
    1790, 1839, 1858
"HOLY CITIES" 522, 524, 556, 681, 692-694, 787, 808, 813, 818, 833,
    842, 862, 863, 865, 873, 1130, 1166, 1491, 1498, 1500, 1507,
    1714, 1715, 1741, 1763, 1764
HYMNBOOKS See under CATECHISMS...
HYMNS See under LITURGY...
ISLAMIC-RELATED MOVEMENTS 37, 61, 170, 177, 207, 282, 334, 340, 351,
    427, 432-434, 437, 448, 456, 654, 656, 657, 1223, 1225
LITURGY, HYMNS, PREACHING 198, 406, 413, 426, 458, 463, 506, 610,
    630, 643, 660, 704, 768, 789, 821, 845, 883, 900, 1007, 1018,
    1025, 1119, 1166, 1503, 1665, 1667, 1679, 1816, 1887
MARRIAGE and POLYGYNY 95, 236, 387, 412, 661, 724, 890
POLYGYNY See under MARRIAGE...
PRAYERBOOKS See under CATECHISMS...
PREACHING See under LITURGY...
ROMAN CATHOLICISM 150, 389, 559, 766, 1001, 1084-1087, 1097-1101,
    1104, 1108, 1115, 1138-1143, 1154, 1170-1172, 1185, 1192, 1222,
    1249-1251, 1264, 1266, 1360, 1529, 1565, 1566, 1579
TYPOLOGIES 1, 14, 15, 19, 21, 24, 30, 31, 38, 39, 41, 52, 63, 65, 73,
    76, 81, 84, 85, 89, 96, 187, 199, 219, 220, 226, 235, 241, 329,
    369, 1360, 1605, 1685, 1814, 1815, 1819, 1866
WOMEN 264, 276, 338, 656, 911, 1047, 1055, 1503, 1607, 1690, 1900
WORSHIP See under LITURGY...